FLORIDA TRAIL HIKES

UNIVERSITY PRESS OF FLORIDA

Florida A&M University, Tallahassee
Florida Atlantic University, Boca Raton
Florida Gulf Coast University, Ft. Myers
Florida International University, Miami
Florida State University, Tallahassee
New College of Florida, Sarasota
University of Central Florida, Orlando
University of Florida, Gainesville
University of North Florida, Jacksonville
University of South Florida, Tampa
University of West Florida, Pensacola

Florida National Scenic Trail sign in the Ocala National Forest

FLORIDA TRAIL *HIKES*

Top Scenic Destinations on Florida's National Scenic Trail

THIRD EDITION

Sandra Friend and John Keatley

UNIVERSITY PRESS OF FLORIDA

Gainesville/Tallahassee/Tampa/Boca Raton
Pensacola/Orlando/Miami/Jacksonville/Ft. Myers/Sarasota

Trail routes, rules, and access change over time. Please report any discrepancies to hike@floridahikes.com for the update of future editions of this guidebook.

For more information to supplement this guidebook, including interactive directions, photos, videos, additional hikes, and a mailing list to receive information on trail updates, visit floridahikes.com.

DISCLAIMER
Risk is always a factor in backcountry travel. The authors have done their best to provide the reader with accurate information and to point out potential hazards. It is the responsibility of the user of this guide to learn the necessary skills for backcountry travel in Florida's outdoors and to exercise caution in potentially hazardous situations. The authors and publisher disclaim any liability for injury or other damage caused by camping, hiking, backpacking, or performing any other activity described in this book.

Maps are presented for entertainment purposes and are not meant to represent an accurate survey of any specific location. Maps were created using GPS tracks collected by the authors and processed using CalTopo.com. Backgrounds are from open source and public sources, including USGS, USDA, and Open Street Maps.

29 28 27 26 25 24 6 5 4 3 2 1

Library of Congress Cataloging-in-Publication Data
Names: Friend, Sandra, author. | Keatley, John, 1957– author.
Title: Florida trail hikes : top scenic destinations on Florida's National Scenic Trail / Sandra Friend, John Keatley.
Description: Third edition | Gainesville : University Press of Florida, 2024. | Includes index.
Identifiers: LCCN 2023037634 | ISBN 9780813080529 (paperback)
Subjects: LCSH: Hiking—Florida. | Trails—Florida. | Sports—Florida. | Recreation—Florida. | Florida National Scenic Trail (Fla.) | BISAC: SPORTS & RECREATION / Hiking | TRAVEL / Special Interest / Hikes & Walks
Classification: LCC GV199.42.F6 F766 2024 | DDC 796.5109759—dc23/eng/20230925
LC record available at https://lccn.loc.gov/2023037634

The University Press of Florida is the scholarly publishing agency for the State University System of Florida, comprising Florida A&M University, Florida Atlantic University, Florida Gulf Coast University, Florida International University, Florida State University, New College of Florida, University of Central Florida, University of Florida, University of North Florida, University of South Florida, and University of West Florida.

University Press of Florida
2046 NE Waldo Road
Suite 2100
Gainesville, FL 32609
http://upress.ufl.edu

To Linda "eArThworm" Patton, for her decades of devotion
to the Florida Trail and to the hiking community at large.

CONTENTS

Foggy sunrise near Moore Haven,
Okeechobee West

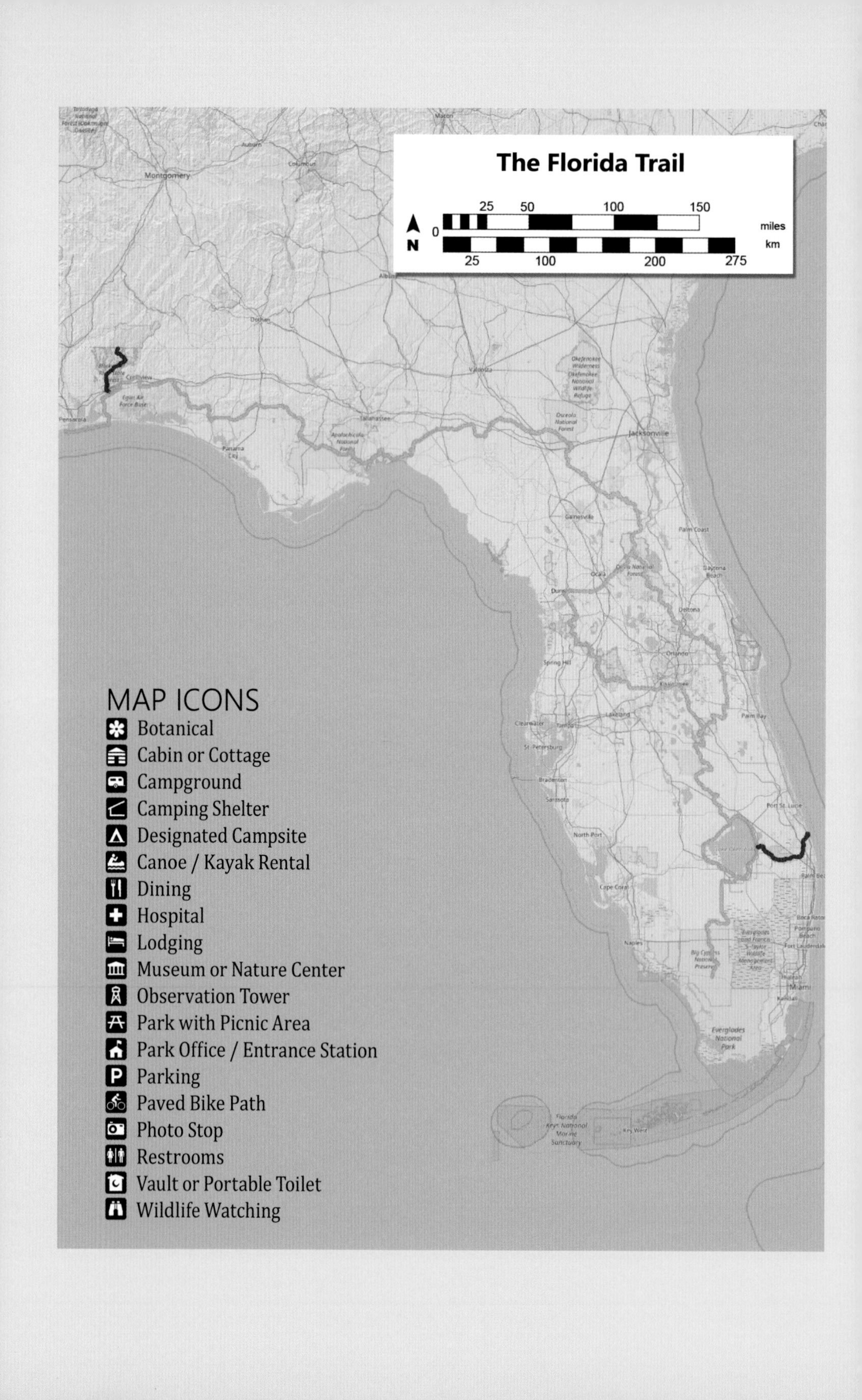

The Florida Trail
0
25
50
100
150
miles
N
25
100
200
275
km
Montgomery
Auburn
Columbus
Macon
Dothan
Valdosta
Tallahassee
Pensacola
Panama City
Jacksonville
Gainesville
Palm Coast
Ocala
Daytona Beach
Deltona
Orlando
Spring Hill
Clearwater
Tampa
Lakeland
St. Petersburg
Bradenton
Sarasota
North Port
Palm Bay
Port St. Lucie
Cape Coral
Naples
Miami
Everglades National Park
MAP ICONS
Botanical
Cabin or Cottage
Campground
Camping Shelter
Designated Campsite
Canoe / Kayak Rental
Dining
Hospital
Lodging
Museum or Nature Center
Observation Tower
Park with Picnic Area
Park Office / Entrance Station
Parking
Paved Bike Path
Photo Stop
Restrooms
Vault or Portable Toilet
Wildlife Watching

Introduction

Did you know Florida has a footpath from one end to the other? If not, welcome to your first exploration of our statewide National Scenic Trail. If you're already familiar with the Florida Trail, you'll find this book a useful guide to making the most of it.

Started in 1966 by the newly founded Florida Trail Association, with the trail's first sanctioned blazes painted across the Ocala National Forest by a group of volunteers, it has grown from a 300-mile footpath in the Florida peninsula to more than 1,500 miles of hiking from one end of our very large state to the other. Federally designated in 1983, the Florida Trail is one of eleven National Scenic Trails throughout the United States, and one of only three within a single state. The Appalachian Trail is the oldest and most well-known member of the National Trails System. The Florida Trail is its southernmost, an ideal winter hiking destination.

The Florida Trail is administered by the US Forest Service, National Forests in Florida. Florida Trail Association volunteers build and maintain the footpath. Statewide, the trail crosses more than 90 different land management units, each with their own rules and regulations.

About This Book

In this book, we highlight scenic hikes you can take along the Florida Trail. Having hiked and measured it all, we know it step by step. Parts of the trail are far more scenic and pleasant to hike than others. We selected these hikes for a variety of abilities and interests. There are short and long hikes, overnight trips, a few accessible segments, and a few that can also be biked.

While the primary focus of this book is day hikes, we include overviews of the most pleasant sections for backpacking. Since the Florida Trail is a linear trail, you won't find a lot of loops on it, but you will find most of those loops in this book. Hikes are otherwise round trips from a trailhead or linear between trailheads, requiring two vehicles and a shuttle.

We provide information about nearby towns for each section of this guide. Florida is big, so like us, you may have a long way to travel to hike in a particular area. We base camp at a cabin, campground, fish camp, motel, hotel, or B&B and spend a couple days or more hiking while enjoying local cuisine and culture. Our recommendations for base camp

Longleaf pine restoration, Nokuse

activities come from our personal travel research in Florida, mostly for the Explorer's Guide series to Florida but also for our website FloridaHikes.com.

Using This Book

Each **REGION** in this book begins with an overview of the towns you can use as **BASE CAMPS** for exploring the Florida Trail. Some are along the trail, others are near it. Campgrounds listed accept tent campers except as noted.

Regions in this guide start at the southern terminus of the Florida Trail and end at the northern terminus. Regions roughly correspond to the sections of the trail in the Florida Trail portion of FarOut Guides, an app that provides geolocated trail information for major trails around the world. As the publishers of *The Florida Trail Guide*, a logistic guide to the entire length of the trail, we update route and service changes with FarOut frequently. The app is always the most dependable source for the current trail route and mileage.

Within each region are suggested trail sections with corresponding **SECTION OVERVIEWS** as well as individual hikes described in detail. Overviews include trip planning information (including trailheads and campsites) for a specific section of the Florida Trail that makes a great backpacking trip. Each section overview calls out highlights and recommended day hikes, some of which are featured in subsequent chapters.

Each numbered **HIKE** focuses on a single hike in the region. It includes an overview and directions to the trailhead, options on how to lengthen or shorten the hike, narrative details for the hike, and a trail map. For every hike in this book, we initially collected a GPS track and waypoints for that piece of trail. For subsequent editions, our contractors as well as Florida Trail Association volunteers and staff have contributed adjustments where the trail has been relocated since our visit so we could update the **MAPS**. We use standard National Park Service icons for trail features. The red line indicates the route described. The blue lines show alternative routes. The orange line is the continuation of the Florida Trail route in either direction.

As we've written other guidebooks (*50 Hikes in Central Florida, Five Star Trails Gainesville & Ocala, Five Star Trails Orlando, and Hiker's Guide to the Sunshine State*) detailing popular segments of the Florida Trail, we've largely avoided duplicating those hikes here. Our goal with *Florida Trail Hikes* is to open a far broader look at the Florida Trail for you.

Hiking in Florida

If you're new to hiking in Florida, understanding our state is important. **OPTIMAL HIKING SEASON** is October to April, with our best backpacking from January to March. Can you hike other times of the year? Yes, but you'll have heat, humidity, thundershowers, and insects to cope with. If you hike out of season, start early in the day and keep it short. Use insect repellent, pack a rain jacket, and carry much more water than you think you should—or bring a water filter. Water availability varies by season and location. Parts of the state are much drier than others. West of the Apalachicola River, the Florida Trail crosses many reliable streams.

Florida is **BOTANICALLY DIVERSE**, with more than 80 different natural communities. One of the greatest delights of hiking the Florida Trail is experiencing its botanical beauty. Just a few inches of elevation change is all it takes to walk into a new habitat. We describe the habitats along these hikes. To understand what they are, visit floridahikes.com/florida-habitats.

With both riotous growth and botanical diversity, we have more than our fair share of **POISONOUS PLANTS**, particularly poison ivy. It comes in all sizes. One variety climbs up trees as a vine and grows huge leaves that mimic hickory leaves. Poison oak and sumac are found north of Central Florida. In South Florida, poisonwood is a concern.

Our **CLIMATE** differs significantly from the rest of the United States. It can be hot and humid on January 1, or ice cold and humid on March 24. It can both freeze and snow, although it does so rarely. Your backpacking gear must be able to handle Florida's relentless humidity and protect against hypothermia and hyperthermia. See gear suggestions at floridahikes.com/gear.

Florida has a lot of hiking through **SWAMPS**. That's because of our low elevations and how water naturally drains across landforms. Bog bridges and boardwalks span many soggy places, but there are some habitats where they can't be put. A hiking pole or two helps your balance in these wet and slippery situations. Water also collects in the trail's low spots. Expect wet feet. Heavy boots are not your friend. Wear lightweight hiking shoes that drain quickly.

There are six species of **VENOMOUS SNAKES** in Florida. We've encountered four while researching hikes for this book—diamondback rattlesnake, pygmy rattlesnake, coral snake, and water moccasin. Southern copperheads and timber rattlesnakes live here too. Avoid walking into deep brush or dense grass and be careful stepping over logs. Take the long way around any snake you don't recognize. Admire them from a respectful distance.

The same goes for Florida's top **PREDATORS**, which include alligators, Florida black bears, and the Florida panther. Panther sightings are rare. The growing population of Florida black bears means bear bagging is essential for backpackers in Florida. It's required in all our National Forests. If a Florida black bear stands its ground, look as large as you can, avoid eye contact, speak loudly, and back up slowly, leaving the bear an escape route. Fight back if it attacks. Bear-human incidents have happened over improperly stored food at campsites or a pet attacking the bear. Alligators are common anywhere there is water, even roadside ditches. Never get within twenty feet of an alligator. Like snakes, alligators normally get out of the way when they hear you coming—unless they've been hand-fed, which is illegal and makes them dangerous. If you encounter an aggressive alligator over four feet long, call 1-866-392-4286 to report it to the Florida Fish and Wildlife Conservation Commission.

Hiking the Florida Trail

The rounded triangular Florida National Scenic Trail symbol is posted at most trailheads. The trail is marked with **ORANGE BLAZES** about the size of a dollar bill. When you see two blazes, one stacked on top of the other, that means the trail is making a turn. Be alert. Blue blazes mean side trail. The entire Blackwater section is blazed blue as an official side trail of the Florida Trail. More commonly, blue blazes lead to campsites and trailheads. White or yellow blazes indicate alternate routes that usually reconnect with the Florida Trail. Some are used to bypass parts of the trail that seasonally flood. Others mark loops. Most trail junctions are clearly signposted.

DESIGNATED CAMPSITES typically have tent symbol signs. We explain when you must use them and when they are optional. In state parks and state forests, there are usually fees for campsite use. Other land managers may require a permit, either free or for a fee.

DIRECTIONS are provided northbound or southbound, since that's how they are expressed along the Florida

Dense palm hammock in the St. Johns River floodplain, Tosohatchee WMA

Trail. Its northern terminus is at Pensacola Beach. From the Suwannee River north, the trail runs due east (southbound) or west (northbound). Occasionally the trail direction will be opposite from a compass direction. In this book, we clarify the difference.

DOGS are generally welcome on the Florida Trail, although a few land managers prohibit them. Please do not take your dog into a no-dogs-allowed area. There aren't many and we mention them in the text. We also point out where you may not want to take your dog for their safety and yours. For the safety of others and of wildlife, always keep your dog leashed.

Hiker Safety

Your safety in the backcountry starts with you making smart decisions before you step out of your front door. Have you checked the **WEATHER**? If it's cold and raining, or thunderstorms are expected, perhaps today isn't a great day for a hike. Has it rained a lot lately? Research water levels along rivers in the area where you plan to hike. If you're headed into the woods alone, did you let someone know where you're headed and when you plan to return?

Are you planning a hike that fits your **ABILITY**? Some non-Floridians scoff at Florida hiking because we have no mountains. They learn the hard way that trudging through sugar sand in the heat or wading through mucky swamps in the cold can be just as exhausting as hiking at elevation. Don't tackle a 15-mile hike "because it's Florida" if your personal norm is more like 5 or 10 miles. If you're new to hiking, start with shorter mileages and work up to longer ones, easy to do on a round trip from a trailhead.

What's in your day pack? At a minimum, carry the **ESSENTIALS**: plenty of water, snacks, a trail map, sun protection (sunscreen, hat, sunglasses as needed), insect repellent, a lightweight rain jacket or poncho, and a small first aid kit personalized to your needs. Other items to consider are a GPS or compass (know how to use them), a whistle, and a small flashlight or headlamp in case you get lost and end up out after dark. Keep your cell phone on low-battery mode or airplane mode while hiking so you don't burn out the battery. For a GPS or camera, carry spare batteries.

You *must* **HYDRATE** when hiking in Florida. A lot. Dehydration coupled with long exposure to the sun can lead to heat exhaustion. It starts with nausea, chills, and dizziness, and can cause deadly heatstroke. If you feel any of these symptoms, stop hiking. Drink as much fluid as possible. Rest a while before attempting any further exertion.

INSECTS are a year-round problem in Florida unless there is a localized freeze, and then there are a couple of bliss-free months with no ticks, chiggers, or mosquitoes. During late spring, summer, and fall, yellow flies and deerflies join the parade of pesky pests. Florida ticks are known to carry Lyme disease, Rocky Mountain spotted fever, rickettsia, and ehrlichiosis. Mosquito-borne diseases include encephalitis and West Nile virus. People infected in other countries have brought limited outbreaks of chikungunya, dengue, and other tropical fevers to Florida, including malaria. Take precautions to avoid insect bites. Wear light-colored clothing, use repellent, and check for ticks frequently.

Florida's prime hiking season is also **HUNTING SEASON**. Seasons vary on every piece of public land. Wear at least 500 square inches of orange if hiking during any hunting season. Fall deer season is also known as general gun season and tends to be the busiest. The Florida Fish and Wildlife Conservation Commission provides hunting season information for all public lands that allow hunting at myfwc.com.

As hunting season ends, **PRESCRIBED BURN** season begins. Land managers burn Florida habitats to reduce the fuel load in the understory for when a wildfire happens. Habitats such as sand pine scrub and sandhills require fires to rejuvenate. While crews are supposed to post warnings at trailheads and scout the trail before burning, that doesn't always happen. Fire crews usually set the woods ablaze between nine and ten in the morning once they've decided weather conditions are favorable. We've included the phone number for every land manager in Florida so you can call ahead to find out if where you're planning to hike will be closed due to a prescribed burn. Stay alert for **WILDFIRE** warnings, too. There have been massive firestorms along portions of the Florida Trail during droughts.

At Eglin Air Force Base and Camp Blanding, stay on the trail and in designated campsites. Do not venture off the trail corridor except at access points noted on the map. Both are **ACTIVE MILITARY BASES** and Eglin is one of the largest bombing ranges in the United States. While the Florida Trail is at its edge where it borders residential communities, you will still hear aircraft, helicopters, and sometimes even bombs. If you notice any sort of ordinance—rocket, bomb, hand grenade—do not approach it. Note the location and report it. Before hiking on either base, add these numbers to your phone: 850-882-2502 for Eglin 96th Security Forces Squadron and 904-682-3125 for Camp Blanding Range Control.

Use common sense when parking your **VEHICLE** at a trailhead. Don't leave your ID or money in it, leave no items of value in sight, and lock it. If you run into problems with people, either at trailheads or in the woods, contact law enforcement and report the incident to the land manager.

Eastern coral snake seeking shelter after a prescribed burn in sandhill habitat

Permits and Fees

Some public lands require payment of a entrance fee or a permit. If they're required for a hike, we mention it. Since fees keep rising, we only state the cost if entry fees run $10 or more. Most state land day-use fees for individuals are $2–3 per person. For two or more in a vehicle, state park and federal concessionaire fees can run $4–25. Our state lands largely expect you to pay entrance fees online before arriving. Here are some ways to save money on permits and fees.

An America the Beautiful Pass—also known as a National Parks Pass or National Parks and Federal Recreational Lands Pass—takes care of entrance fees for all National Parks, National Wildlife Refuges, and National Forests, as well as other federal lands outside of Florida. The pass covers the driver and up to four adults in a vehicle. It costs $80 for an annual pass, with a few discounts available: FREE if you are active military, FREE if you have a fourth-grade student or home-school equivalent in the family, $20 for ages 62 and over (or $80 lifetime), and FREE if you volunteer at least 250 hours a year with a federal lands agency. For full details, see nps.gov/planyourvisit/passes.htm.

A Florida State Forests Annual Pass costs $45 and covers entrance fees for up to six people. The pass can be purchased at fdacs.gov.

A Florida State Parks Annual Pass costs $60 for an individual, and $120 for a family (up to eight people entering as a group). Obtain at a state park ranger station or online at floridastateparks.org.

Passes cover entrance fees. Camping costs extra. Discounts are often provided for active military, veterans, and seniors, sometimes up to 50 percent off camping.

Most state agencies use Reserve America for booking campsites. Some walk-in sites are held back daily but go quickly. When you book a campsite online, Reserve America charges a nonrefundable reservation fee on top of the campsite cost. Book at reserveamerica.com.

Support the efforts of trail maintainers by becoming a member of the nonprofit Florida Trail Association. Annual membership starts at $35. Sign up at floridatrail.org.

Hiker Support

Nineteen chapters of the **FLORIDA TRAIL ASSOCIATION** cover the state of Florida, each responsible for maintaining a portion of the Florida Trail. Most hold monthly meetings as well as guided hikes, where you can meet like-minded hikers and make new friends. Check their pages on Meetup.com for meeting places and dates as well as their upcoming activities: floridatrail.org/chapters.

Enjoy hiking the Florida Trail? Help others do so too by giving back to the hiking community. Join a volunteer trail crew or scheduled maintenance activity with any chapters or by pitching in on statewide efforts. Learn more at floridatrail.org/volunteer.

Connecting hikers and celebrating the Florida Trail hiking experience, the nonprofit Florida Trail Hikers Alliance, **FTTHRUHIKE**, coordinates resources for thru-hikers and events to bring hikers together. These include the Florida Trail Kickoff (held for long-distance

FTA volunteer Scott Lunsford leads a hike on the Ocean to Lake Hiking trail.

hikers early January to kick off thru-hiking season) and Billy Goat Day, a hiker reunion held the last Saturday in January. They also launched and oversee the Florida Trail Hikers Facebook group along with other private online discussion groups focused on the Florida Trail. Learn more at ftthruhike.org.

Cypress strand near mile 4, Big Cypress (Tami Jicha)

South Florida

The flattest part of Florida surprises hikers with panoramic views across sawgrass prairies and Lake Okeechobee, the vast freshwater sea in the heart of the southern peninsula.

BASE CAMPS

Ochopee

Home to Florida's smallest post office, Ochopee is a linear collection of services and homesteads along the Tamiami Trail, mostly along the western edge of Big Cypress National Preserve.

STAY

Everglades Swamp Cottage at Big Cypress Gallery 239-695-2428, 52388 Tamiami Tr.

Trail Lakes Campground 800-504-6554, 40904 Tamiami Tr.

EAT

Joanie's Blue Crab Cafe 239-695-2682, 39395 Tamiami Tr.

SEE AND DO

Big Cypress Swamp Tours, 239-478-4419.

Big Cypress Swamp Welcome Center 239-695-4758, 33000 Tamiami Tr.

Clyde Butcher's Big Cypress Gallery 239-695-2428, 52388 Tamiami Tr.

Everglades Adventure Tours, 800-504-6554, 40904 Tamiami Tr.

Oasis Visitor Center 239-695-2000, 52105 Tamiami Tr.

Skunk Ape Research Center 239-695-2275, 40904 Tamiami Tr.

Everglades City

Collier County's first county seat, Everglades City, was a small fishing village until the early 1920s, when workers building the Tamiami Trail were housed here. City Hall and some homes date back to that era. On an island at the end of SR 29, it is surrounded by the vast mangrove forest of the Ten Thousand Islands.

STAY

Captain's Table Resort 239-360-3937, 202 Broadway Ave E.

Chokoloskee Island Park & Marina 239-695-2414, 1150 Hamilton Ln.

Everglades City Motel 239-695-4224, 309 Collier Ave.

Everglades Adventures Hotel Suites by Ivey House 239-323-6365, 605 Buckner Ave N.

Monument Lake Campground 239-631-9988 50215 Tamiami Tr E.

EAT

City Seafood 239-695-4700, 702 Begonia St.

Everglades Rod & Gun Club 239-695-2101, 200 W Broadway.

Island Cafe 239-695-0003, 305 Collier Ave.

SEE AND DO

Everglades Area Tours 239-695-3633, 238 Mamie St, Chokoloskee.

Everglades City Airboat Tours 239-695-2400, 907 Dupont St.

Everglades National Park 239-695-4758, 815 Oyster Bar Ln.

Historic Smallwood Store 239-695-2989, 360 Mamie St, Chokoloskee.

Clewiston

Clewiston is a multicultural community with a rich history. Growing from a fishing village to a planned city designed by John Nolen in the 1920s, it retains period architecture and clues to its past as a training base for British World War II pilots and a company town for the US Sugar Corporation.

STAY

Holiday Inn Express 863-983-5100, 1024 W Sugarland Hwy.

Roland Martin's Marina Resort 800-473-6766, 920 E Del Monte Ave.

EAT

Big Eaters Cafe, 863-902-7072, 110 W Ventura Ave.

Café Tropical 863-983-0049, 307 E Sugarland Hwy.

Sunrise Restaurant 863-983-9080, 842 E Sugarland Hwy.

SEE AND DO

Ah-Tah-Thi-Ki Museum 877-902-1113, 34725 West Boundary Rd.

Big "O" Airboat Tours 863-885-1518, 920 E Del Monte Ave.

Billie Swamp Safari 863-983-6101, 30000 Gator Tail Trl.

Clewiston Museum 863-983-2870, 109 Central Ave.

Okeechobee

Once an outpost on Florida's frontier, Okeechobee remains the heart of cowboy culture in Florida. It's a major launch point for bass fishing along the lake. As the largest of the communities along Lake Okeechobee, it offers the most options for services. It also has an Amtrak station.

STAY

Best Western 863-357-7100, 3975 US 441 S.

Holiday Inn Express 863-357-3529, 3101 US 441 S.

Okeechobee KOA 863-763-0231, 4276 US 441 S.

EAT

Lightsey's Seafood Restaurant 863-763-4276, 1506 S Parrott Ave.

Pueblo Viejo IV 863-357-9641, 3415 US 441 S.

Speckled Perch Steakhouse 863-763-9983, 105 US 98.

SEE AND DO

Eagle Bay Airboat Rides 863-824-0500, 900 SR 78.

Jupiter

Home to the southern inlet of the Indian River Lagoon, where a landmark lighthouse stands, Jupiter is a bustling modern community in northern Palm Beach County. It stretches from the Seminole War battlefields of the Loxahatchee River to the Atlantic Ocean.

STAY

Best Western Intracoastal Inn 561-575-2936, 810 S US 1.

Comfort Inn 561-745-7997, 6752 W Indiantown Rd.

Fairfield Inn 561-748-5252, 6748 W Indiantown Rd.

Jupiter Beach Resort & Spa 561-746-2511, 5 N SR A1A.

EAT

Dune Dog 561-744-6667, 775 SR A1A Alt.

Food Shack 561-741-3626, 103 S US 1 Suite D3.

Old Dixie Cafe 561-747-2952, 300 N Old Dixie Hwy.

SEE AND DO

Jupiter Inlet Lighthouse 561-747-8380, 500 Captain Armours Way.

Jupiter Inlet Lighthouse ONA 561-295-5953, 600 SR 707.

Loxahatchee River Center 561-743-7123, 805 N US 1.

Hobe Sound

Named for the Indigenous Jobe peoples met along its shores by Captain Jonathan Dickinson and his shipwrecked companions in 1696, Hobe Sound was previously home to pineapple plantations and the movie industry. It now centers on a small downtown and the beauty of Jupiter Island just across the bridge.

STAY

Jonathan Dickinson State Park 772-546-2771, 16450 SE Federal Hwy.

Jupiter Waterfront Inn 772-747-9085, 18903 SE Federal Hwy.

EAT

Harry & the Natives 772-546-3061, 11910 SE Federal Hwy.

Taylor Beach House Café 772-932-7155, 9126 SE Bridge Rd.

SEE AND DO

Blowing Rocks Preserve 561-744-6668, 574 S Beach Rd.

Nathaniel P. Reed Hobe Sound National Wildlife Refuge 772-546-6141, 13640 SE Federal Hwy.

Peck Lake Park 772-221-1418, 8108 SE Gomez Ave.

Seabranch Preserve State Park 772-219-1880, 6093 SE Dixie Hwy, Stuart.

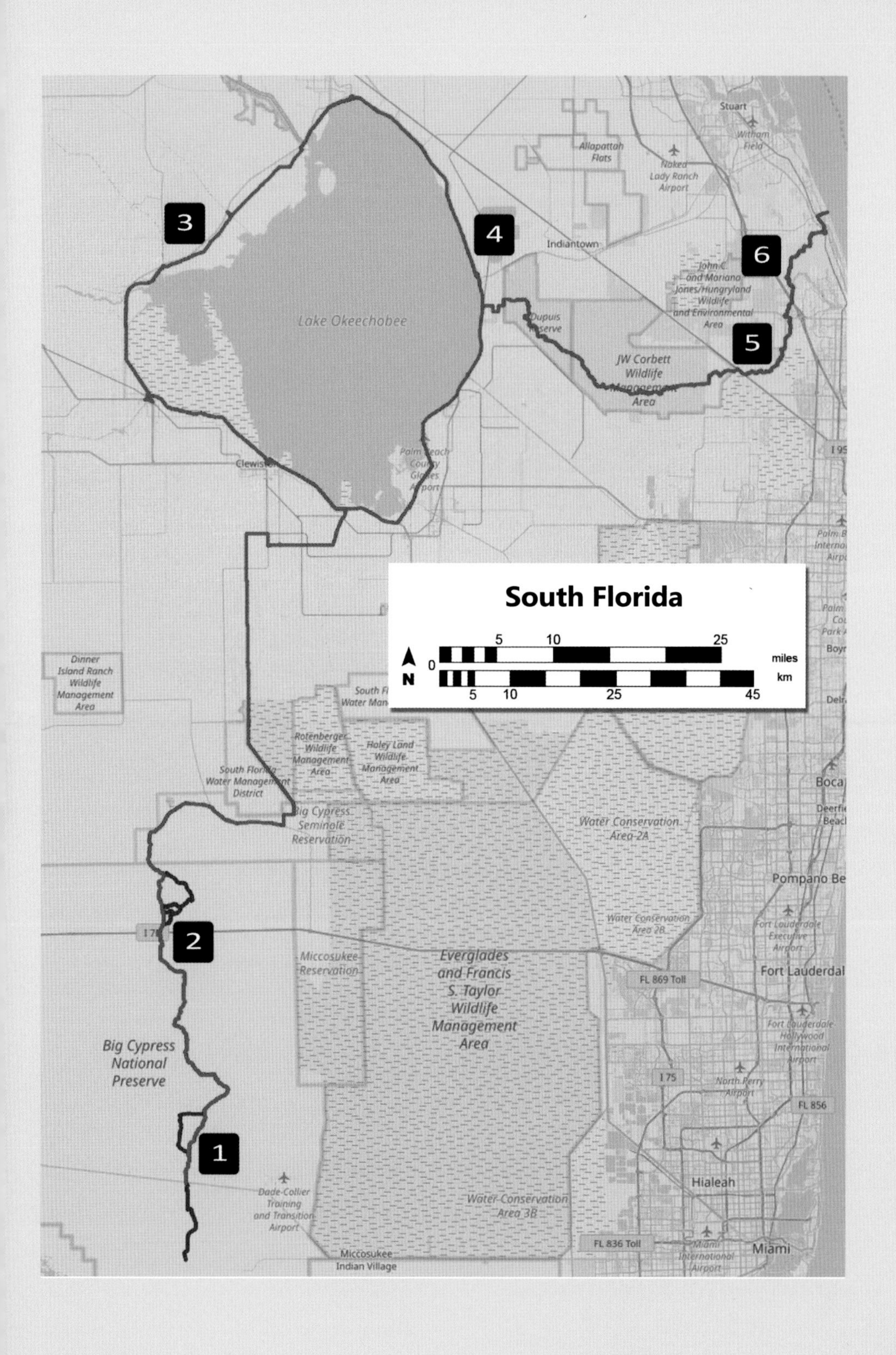
South Florida
0
5
10
25
miles
km
5
10
25
45
N
1
2
3
4
5
6
Lake Okeechobee
Stuart
Witham Field
Allapattah Flats
Naked Lady Ranch Airport
Indiantown
John C. and Mariana Jones/Hungryland Wildlife and Environmental Area
Dupuis Reserve
JW Corbett Wildlife Management Area
Clewiston
Palm Beach County Glades Airport
Dinner Island Ranch Wildlife Management Area
Rotenberger Wildlife Management Area
Holey Land Wildlife Management Area
South Florida Water Management District
Big Cypress Seminole Reservation
Water Conservation Area 2A
Water Conservation Area 2B
Miccosukee Reservation
Everglades and Francis S. Taylor Wildlife Management Area
Big Cypress National Preserve
Dade-Collier Training and Transition Airport
Water Conservation Area 3B
Miccosukee Indian Village
FL 869 Toll
Pompano Be
Fort Lauderdale Executive Airport
Fort Lauderdal
Fort Lauderdale Hollywood International Airport
I 75
North Perry Airport
FL 856
Hialeah
FL 836 Toll
Miami International Airport
Miami
Deerfi Beac
Boca
I 95

Cypress savanna south of Ivy Camp

Big Cypress

38.3 MILES | BIG CYPRESS NATIONAL PRESERVE

It has been likened to the African savanna or the Amazon, but the Big Cypress Swamp is uniquely its own. It starts with a drop of rain, a drizzle, a downpour, seeping into the earth surrounding the Okaloacoochee Slough, east of Fort Myers. As water spreads across the landscape, it inches southward toward the Gulf of Mexico, deep and clear as a raindrop.

In this rain-fed floodplain, a river stretching more than 30 miles wide and a few inches to a few feet deep, the Florida Trail starts its journey north from its southern terminus along the Tamiami Trail in Big Cypress National Preserve.

Overview

An unusual place for a day hike, Big Cypress National Preserve is even odder when backpacking the southernmost 30 miles of the Florida Trail. Between Oasis Visitor Center and Interstate 75, it is Florida's most remote wilderness hike, with no bailout points. Water, mud, and stretches of jagged rock with holes make up the footpath. Hikers rank it as one of the toughest treks in America when it's wet, which is often. It's strenuous, as you spend much of your time wading or coping with slippery mud. The footpath constantly challenges your balance, even on the drier pine islands. At mile 21, you enter a panoramic landscape of cypress savanna, diminutive cypress trees, and water to every horizon. Beneath the water's placid surface lies thick mud hiding deep solution holes. When storms arrive, there is nowhere to take shelter. There are only three pieces of dry land across the next 7 miles.

North of Interstate 75, the trail becomes an easy walk on a graded limestone road. It's flanked by swamps where massive alligators lounge in the sun along a paralleling canal. Side trails loop east to established campsites on footpaths through more characteristic swamp habitat. This section ends at a gate into Big Cypress Seminole Reservation. Only thru-hikers or section hikers who have filed a permit in advance may continue north into the reservation.

Trailheads

Access to the Florida Trail through Big Cypress is limited to two points, about an hour's drive between them. There is no vehicle access to the northern end of this section.

0.0 OASIS VISITOR CENTER
Paved parking area off US 41.

30.6 I-75 REST AREA
Complex off MM 63 of I-75.

Camping

While you can random camp in Big Cypress, there are designated campsites for a reason: they are on higher, normally dry ground but have access to water to filter. All have natural hazards, including dead trees and poisonous plants. Check your surroundings before pitching your tent. Hammock hangers have more options. South to north, designated campsites include the following.

6.9 7 MILE CAMP
Picnic table, fire ring, ample tent space.

9.5 10 MILE CAMP
Picnic table, fire ring, scattered tenting.

16.9 13 MILE CAMP
Picnic table, fire ring, limited tent space.

22.7 OAK HILL CAMP
Island with tree canopy, fit 6–8 tents.
26.8 IVY CAMP
Island with clearings for 8–10 tents.
35.7 NOBLES CAMP
Old airstrip with picnic table, fire ring.

Three designated campsites are along the 15-mile North Loop north of Interstate 75: Carpenter Camp, Panther Camp, and CCC Camp. If you've never backpacked in Big Cypress, do an overnight trip before trying the whole section. Hiking to Ivy Camp forces you to wade and deal with slippery mud, a reality of the 10 miles south of the interstate. Hiking to 7 Mile Camp from Oasis provides a good feel for the landscapes of the southernmost 20 miles. Using a bear canister is prudent, not just because of a documented bear population but also to keep smaller creatures out of your food. Options for hanging a bear bag are limited.

Trip Planning

Do not underestimate the difficulty of backpacking across Big Cypress. Rescues by emergency services are difficult and costly. Backpackers must be experienced with wayfinding, swamp walking, and field-stripping and cleaning your water filter, which will clog with the fine silt in the water. Two hiking poles are essential. Where the water is deepest, a one-mile-per-hour pace is normal. Don't expect to make time unless the swamp dries out, which adds the challenge of finding water to filter and the danger of wildfires lit by lightning strikes. Wayfinding can be difficult generally but especially in burned-over areas. We suggest using the Florida Trail section of FarOut Guides, an app showing trail routes on an interactive map. We provided them the initial route and waypoints for Big Cypress from our own hikes.

A narrow window of opportunity opens from December through February for a pleasant backpacking trip. Insects and heat make it tortuous the remainder of the year, along with the inherent danger of wildfires. Most hikers choose January. Hunters are out in force in December, and the National Park Service closes sections of the trail for prescribed burns in February. Wildfires start sparking in April.

Research hunting seasons and wear bright orange if you hike during hunting season. Fall deer hunting brings large numbers of hunters into the swamp. Established in 1974 as the first federally designated National Preserve, Big Cypress differs from how other National Parks are managed. National Preserves permit traditional uses of the land to continue, which includes hunting and the use of swamp buggies. As in a national forest, there are many hunt camp inholdings.

To hike in Big Cypress, you must have a free backcountry permit. Download the form from their website, print, and fill out four copies. Leave one on your dashboard, put one in the permit box at the trailhead, and keep two in your pack in a plastic bag. You can also obtain permits inside Oasis Visitor Center, open daily from 9:00 a.m. until 4:30 p.m., except Christmas. Check in or call ahead to ask about current trail conditions and planned prescribed burns.

Day hikers can hit the trail year-round. We've day hiked in June, July, and September to see orchids and bro-

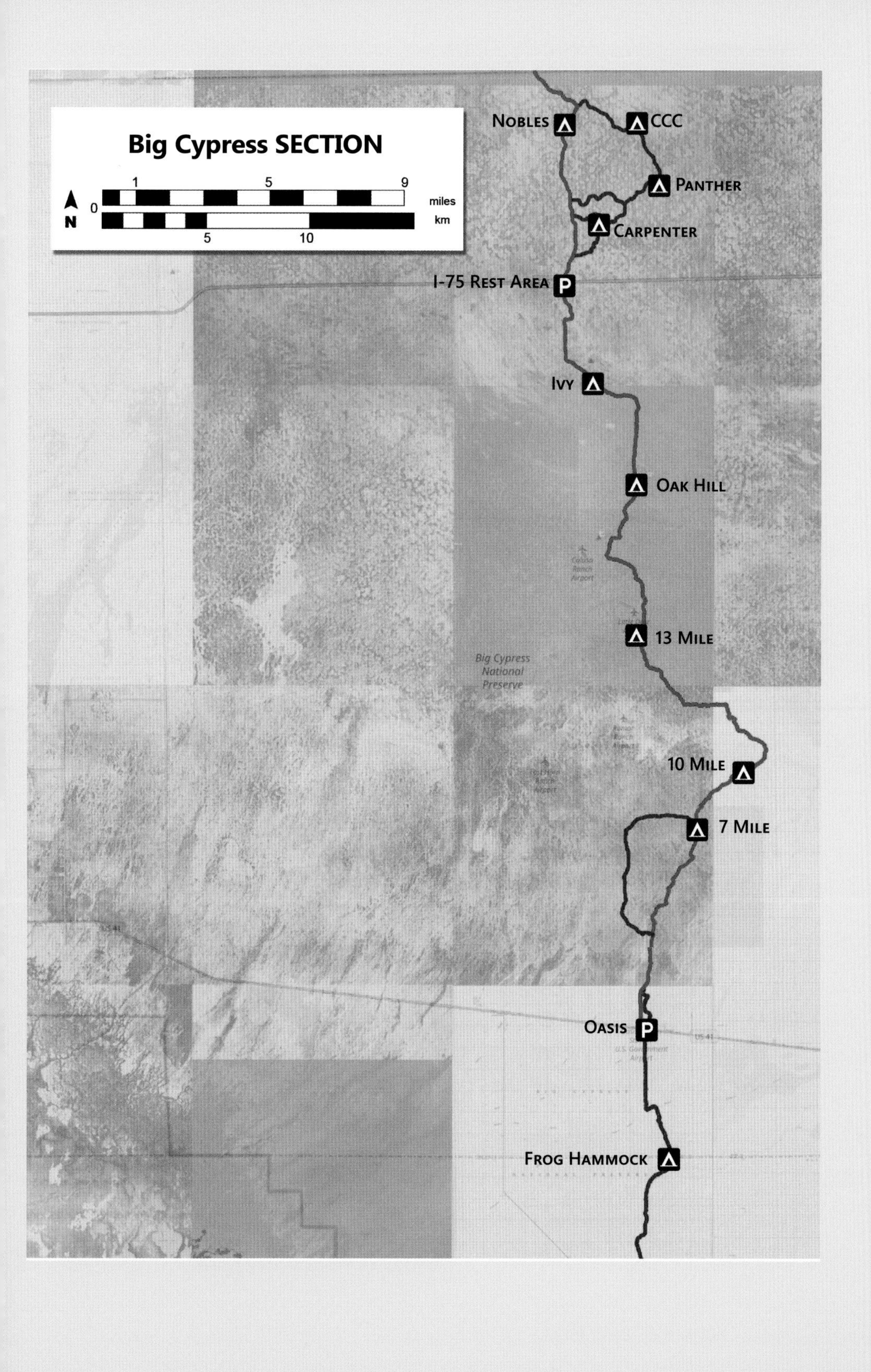
Big Cypress SECTION
1
5
9
0
miles
N
km
5
10
Nobles
CCC
Panther
Carpenter
I-75 Rest Area
Ivy
Oak Hill
13 Mile
Big Cypress National Preserve
10 Mile
7 Mile
Oasis
Frog Hammock

Pine rocklands south of 13 Mile Camp

meliads. Insect repellent, long sleeves, long pants, and even a head net are wise. It's too hot and prone to thunderstorms for backpacking. Biting flies peak in June and July, the same time as the orchid blooms. Mosquitoes and ticks are present year-round.

The preserve is home to Florida's largest predators, including the Florida panther, American alligators, and the Florida black bear. Late March through the end of May is when alligators and snakes are especially active during mating season. Wildlife roams the swamp year-round, with some of the largest Burmese pythons in Florida caught here. As John discovered while backpacking, hookworm is present: a good reason not to bring your dog along. Don't hike with open cuts or wounds you could expose to swamp water, allowing parasites to burrow in.

Brush up on identifying poisonous plants and trees found in South Florida. Avoid the copious amounts of poison ivy found along the trail and on the tree island campsites. Poisonwood trees grow in tropical hammocks: don't go near any tree with oozing black spots on its bark. Poisonwood leaves are an irritant. The tree's oils cause chemical burns, and its fruit is deadly.

Land Manager

National Park Service
52105 Tamiami Trail E, Ochopee 34141
239-695-2000
nps.gov/bicy

Highlights

Limestone Pavement, mile 0.9

For day hikers, it's worth the sometimes-sloshing trek to see a limestone pavement. Underlying this part of the Florida peninsula, the bedrock is near the surface, full of jagged holes caused by slow breakdown of rock by natural acids in the water. This is the first short stretch of it that hikers reach when walking north.

Cypress Strand, mile 4.0

Strand swamps are linear rivers of deeper water within the greater swamp. In these, the cypresses grow larger. Humidity encourages the growth of bromeliads and orchids. This is one of the showier strands that the trail passes through and is close enough to the southern terminus to make it a day-hike destination.

Pine Ridge, mile 14.9

A rocky ridge with limestone pavement (flat on top but shot through with holes and crevices you must step over) enables a pine forest to thrive between a series of rounded wet prairies that the trail also traverses.

Cypress Strand, mile 27.3

While the trees here are shorter than in the cypress strand at mile 4, this is an interesting one to slosh through as well. Large bromeliads are at face level.

Open Savanna, mile 28.2

With a feel like the plains of Africa, this broad grassland is just an inch or two out of the surrounding cypress savanna swamp that the trail trudges you through for nearly eight miles.

Ten Thousand Islands

Tropical Island, mile 28.9

A long, linear island topped with a tropical forest. The trail follows the spine of the island, using the high ground to connect the swamp traverses on either end.

Recommended Day Hikes

Mile 0.0

Oasis to Blue Loop junction, 5.8-mile round trip
Oasis to Cypress Strand, 8-mile round trip

Mile 30.3

I-75 South Gate to Ivy Camp, 7-mile round trip

Mile 30.6

North Loop and South Cross Trail, 5.2-mile loop

Side Trip

The southwesterly sheet flow of Big Cypress Swamp nourishes the mangrove forest at the tip of the Florida peninsula, the **TEN THOUSAND ISLANDS**. It's the second largest mangrove forest in the world after Sundarban Reserve Forest in Bangladesh. To explore the Ten Thousand Islands head for Everglades City, where you can rent kayaks or canoes or join a guided trip through the islands. Everglades National Park Gulf Coast Visitor Center also offers narrated boat tours through the Ten Thousand Islands. floridahikes.com/ten-thousand-islands.

Cypress dome and pines at mile 6, Big Cypress

1. Oasis to 7 Mile Camp

13.8 MILES | BIG CYPRESS

A round-trip hike to the southernmost designated campsite along the Florida Trail provides a sample of the scenic, soggy habitats of the vast Big Cypress Swamp.

Overview

Heading north from the Florida Trail's southern terminus, this hike has plenty of places where you can turn around and call it a day hike. For backpackers, it's the most pleasant overnighter in Big Cypress. It's also the oldest, the trail blazed soon after Big Cypress National Preserve opened. Experience natural beauty, physical challenges, and the nicest of the designated campsites in the preserve as your destination. While the mileage might seem suitable for a day hike, this is not a trail to hurry through. It's a swamp walk across surfaces normally wet, muddy, and slippery. Even when dry, clusters of solution holes in the limestone bedrock of the swamp require your attention to the footpath.

Trip Planning

See Big Cypress. If backpacking, let the park rangers know your vehicle will be parked in their lot overnight. Hiking poles are a must for keeping your balance. Expect wet shoes. Mud creeps into shoes and socks since it is a very fine silt. Stop and empty them out as you hike. Unless it is very chilly out, insect repellent is a must. Mosquitoes linger year-round. Sun protection is crucial: wear sunscreen and a hat. Sunglasses are helpful.

Directions

Oasis Visitor Center [25.857105, -81.032913] is along US 41 (Tamiami Trail) roughly halfway between Naples and Miami. It's 37 miles west of SR 993 (Krome Avenue) at Dade Corners, and 21 miles east of SR 29 at Everglades City and Ochopee. From Miami, follow US 41 west. From Naples, follow US 41 east. From the north, Interstate 75 to SR 29 south to US 41 east is your best route.

Options

Several landmarks are worth reaching on a day hike. The nearest is a 1.8-mile round trip to the limestone pavement, where a lone cabbage palm rises above the natural slabs of limestone. A 5.8-mile round trip to the Blue Loop junction traverses open prairies, cypress savanna, and pine islands. The showy cypress strand 1.1 miles north of the Blue Loop junction is a magical place, an 8 mile round trip that's a challenging full-day hike with sawgrass marshes, cypress domes, and a great deal of wading. Brown signs mark the Tamiami Trail Triathlon, a 2.8-mile National Park Service loop using the Florida Trail and an OHV road you meet on the first pine island. It returns to Oasis Visitor Center but it's paved with rocks the size of potatoes. Better to turn around at the junction for a 2.8-mile round trip.

On the south side of US 41 is the 8.2-mile linear blue-blazed Roberts Lake Trail, a former piece of the Florida Trail stretching to Loop Road. It immerses you in prairie and cypress strand more quickly than the hike to 7 Mile Camp, so hiking the first mile or two as a round trip from the visitor center provides an excellent introduction to the natural habitats of Big Cypress. Access it by crossing US 41 from the Oasis entrance and following the blue blazes.

Hike

Grab a photo at the southern terminus marker, drop off your backcountry permit, and sign the trail register near the boardwalk, where visitors stare at the alligators swimming below. Orange blazes lead through the picnic area to a sharp right. Head up a grassy corridor between the swamp and a fence for a half mile. The airfield behind the fence predates Big Cypress National Preserve. Prior to becoming Oasis Visitor Center, the 1960s building near the Tamiami Trail was both a gas station for travelers and a pilots' lounge. NPS now uses the airfield for firefighting and reconnaissance of the 729,000 acre preserve, and plans are in the works for a new visitor center.

North of the airfield, the fun begins. Marl mud infused with periphyton lays in a thin sheen across the landscape. When wet, it's like walking on axle grease. Take every step with care. The primary biomass of the Everglades—of which the Big Cypress Swamp is a part—periphyton adapted to the cycle of wet and dry seasons by going dormant when dry, stretching in thick webs across the mud. When slightly hydrated, its blue-green algae, bacteria, fungi, and microscopic creatures interact with the sheet flow of water, generating oxygen, decomposing into soil, and providing food for animals. Blue-green streaks appear in the mud when you slip.

Slabs of limestone across the trail mark the first stretch of limestone pavement. In this part of Florida, limestone bedrock is near the surface and shot through with jagged solution holes caused by slow erosion. Limestone pavement in Florida is similar to the barren alvar habitats of the Great Lakes. Plants take root in crevices and holes.

Gaining a little elevation beyond the slabs, enter a ridge of pine flatwoods. When you hike in Big Cypress, seeing pines ahead means there may be dry land where you can take a break. Depending on water levels, the swamp still can seep between the trees. The Tamiami Trail Triathlon loop veers right at 1.4 miles onto an OHV road to return to Oasis. Cross the road and enter a short stretch of tropical hammock. Rocks and roots invade the dry footpath; wild coffee grows in the understory. As the pines thin out, water is at its deepest in the worn tread of the trail. Enter a sparsely forested cypress dome with younger trees, solution holes lurking beneath the water. The trees thin before a prairie providing the foreground for the next horizon line of pines, which provide a brief dry spot at 2 miles. The cycle of prairies and pine ridges continues repetitively to the junction with the Blue Loop at 2.9 miles. A patch of dry land makes it a good place to take a break. The Blue Loop curves northwest to 7 Mile Camp.

Stay on the orange blazes, reaching a gate before veering northwest around the inholding. Enter a stretch of sawgrass before plunging through wet prairie and pines. Pass a second gate for the property at 3.1 miles. Snake between a cypress dome and a ridge of pines

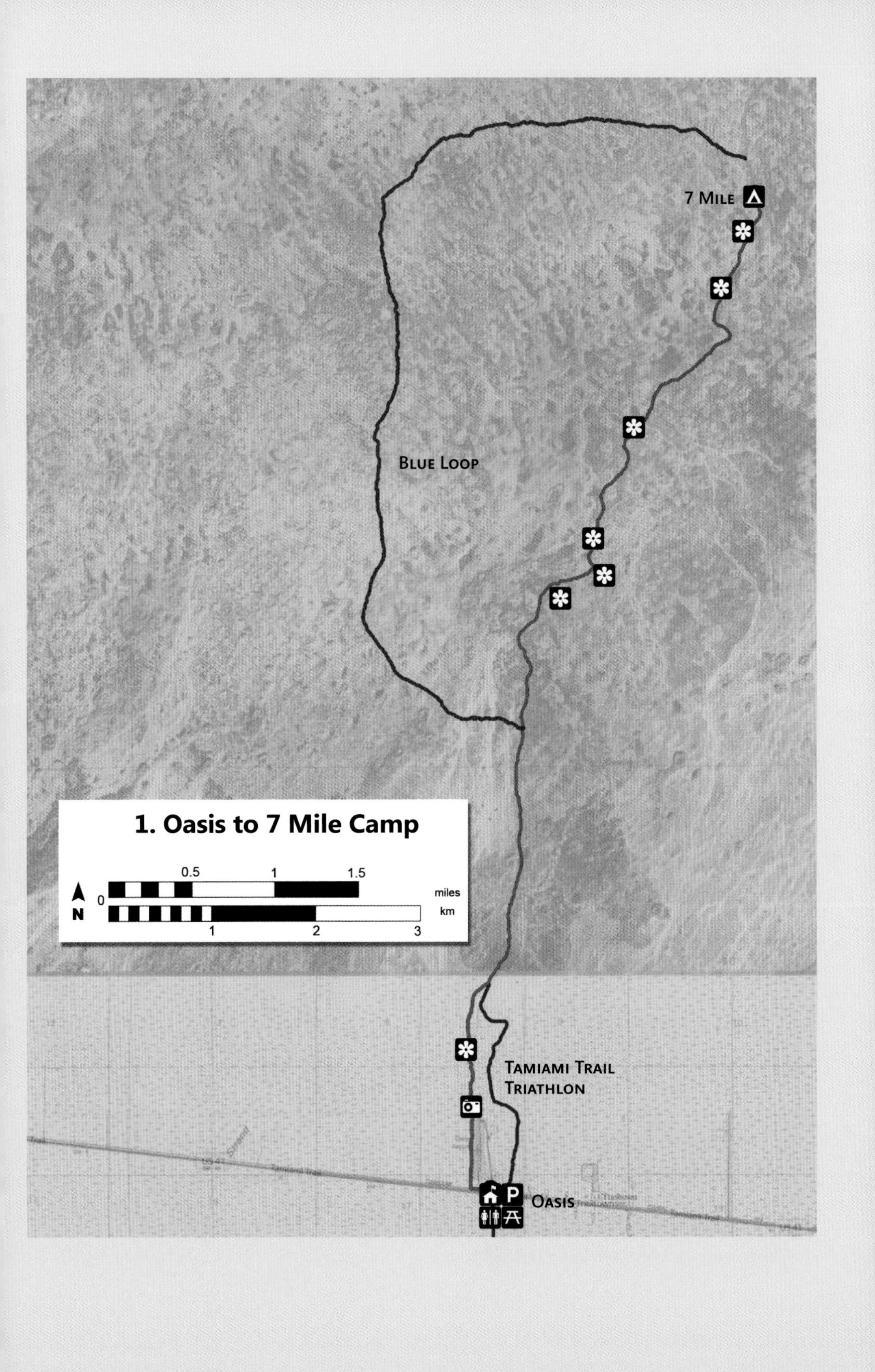

7 Mile
Blue Loop
1. Oasis to 7 Mile Camp
0.5
1
1.5
0
miles
N
km
1
2
3
Tamiami Trail
Triathlon
Oasis

Limestone pavement

in the tall sawgrass. Wayfinding skills come into play since it grows so tall it's hard to spot the next blaze. Use caution: sawgrass is sharp and can cut you. As it thins, wax myrtle, red maples, and willow signal a marsh crossing. Reaching dry land beneath tall pines is a relief.

Cross a wet prairie before reaching the next dry pine-topped ridge. At 4 miles, start the plunge into the first showy cypress strand. Water may be knee to waist deep or deeper. Where the cypresses crowd in, they are heavily laden with bromeliads. Emerging from the deep strand, enter a shallow strand with small, wizened trees for a quarter mile. After a brief stretch of dry ground, plunge into the swamp. The trail circles a cypress dome with mud-filled solution holes hiding under the water. Cross a prairie beneath spindly pines before plunging into the wet corridor to the next line of pines. Join a swamp buggy road briefly.

Walking between saw palmetto, it's a delight to have another dry spot for a moment before the next cypress savanna surrounding the Mile 5 marker. Most of these markers are a little farther than the mileage on them. The discrepancy increases as you continue north. Habitats alternate between wet cypress savanna and dry pine savanna until a curious collection of short, squat palm trees rise from holes in a broad limestone pavement, looking as if they were drawn by Dr. Seuss. Beyond this island of pine rockland—one of Florida's rarest habitats—plunge into a mixed savanna of pine and cypress. The mud is particularly slippery near the Mile 6 marker.

Briefly joining a swamp buggy road, the trail climbs toward the next pine ridge, the big island used for 7 Mile Camp. Reach the sign pointing east to the campsite with its picnic table and fire ring. The water source is at the end of a beaten path leading to a cypress dome in the opposite direction. While there are several decent places to pitch a tent near the picnic table, we found broader spaces north of the camp, not far from where the north end of the Blue Loop meets the Florida Trail at 7.2 miles. After a night under starry, quiet skies, return to the trailhead along the same route for a 13.8-mile round trip.

2. I-75 South Gate to Ivy Camp

7 MILES | BIG CYPRESS

Taking the plunge in Big Cypress is literal along this round-trip hike. It leads into a vast cypress savanna where there is no dry ground between two islands spaced two miles apart.

Overview

A taste of the wettest, wildest portion of the Florida Trail through Big Cypress National Preserve, a hike to Ivy Camp will test your mettle. Learning how to walk through a swamp without falling is key: for this hike it's necessary to keep your balance atop slippery, slimy marl mud. Wayfinding can be a challenge. The payoff is immersing in a landscape few people ever see. We recommend this hike for backpackers who are thinking of tackling the entire Oasis to Interstate 75 segment. Try this first, keeping in mind it is the gentler end of a vast cypress savanna that stretches south from Interstate 75 for over 9 miles.

Trip Planning

See Big Cypress. Leave a copy of your backcountry permit on your vehicle dashboard. Call the preserve to ensure no fires are burning across the landscape.

Insect repellent and sun protection are necessary. Don't forget a hat. Sunglasses help in the wide-open spaces. A pair of hiking poles are a must. Marl mud will creep into your shoes and socks. Remove them and shake them out occasionally to avoid hurting your toes.

Almost all of this hike is exposed to the elements. It is dangerous to be out here in a thunderstorm. Check weather forecasts before tackling this hike.

Directions

I-75 South Gate [26.167490, -81.072090] is at MM 63 Rest Area along Interstate 75 (called Alligator Alley through the Big Cypress Swamp) between Naples and Weston. The rest area complex can be accessed northbound or southbound by motorists. It is 16 miles southbound (due east) of the SR 29 exit (Everglades City and Immokalee) and 14 miles northbound (due west) of the Miccosukee Reservation exit.

Entering the complex, look for the fire station on the south side of I-75. Drive past it to the parking area in the southeast corner. Use that lot for day hiking. For an overnight trip, park your car in the northeast lot across from the north rest area, adding a mile of road-walking through the rest area complex to your hike.

Options

It's a linear hike: turn around when you feel like it. Two intermediate destinations are the tropical island and open savanna. The southern edge of the tropical island is a 2.8-mile round trip, while the southern edge of the savanna is a 4.2-mile round trip. Going to the savanna gives you a little time wading through cypress strands without hiking in muddy tracks on a swamp buggy road.

The Florida Trail continues north from the I-75 North Parking Area along a graded limestone road, Nobles Grade.

Massive alligators lounge along the paralleling canal. Florida panthers have been photographed along that section of trail, which provides access to the 15-mile North Loop and its trio of backcountry campsites.

Hike

Start at the I-75 South Gate, signing in at the trail register and filing your backcountry permit. Orange blazes lead along an old road lined with cabbage palms. Where the road splits, the left fork passes through a grassy clearing into a wall of forest to the east. Keep right. Big puddles appear as the road widens. Those thick tire tracks are the reason. Invented to traverse this rugged terrain, swamp buggies—which hunters and landowners with inholdings use—leave deep tracks in the soft marl mud of Big Cypress Swamp with their big tires. You won't run into as many of these deep ruts near Oasis, but they're a frequent sight along this stretch.

Skirting a deep puddle, reach a T intersection with a major north–south swamp buggy road. Turn left to follow this broad road south. Prairie panoramas flank both sides but the road isn't inspiring as a trail, except in a cypress strand where tiny bromeliads decorate wizened cypress trees. Keep to the edges of the big puddles to avoid the deepest mud holes.

Making a sharp right at a mile, the trail leaves the swamp buggy road. It narrows to a footpath and will stay that way for the remainder of the hike. Slip through a wet pine savanna before crossing deeper water in a cypress strand. Rising into the savanna again, the footpath can be slippery approaching a pine ridge where a small clearing has been used by campers along the north edge of the tropical island. Turn onto the ridge. Under the pines, the dense understory is a tropical forest thick with coco plum and marlberry, the footpath a pleasant walk on pine duff.

Leaving the island after 1.4 miles to splash back into the swamp, cross a swamp buggy road and a cypress strand before rising up onto the next pine ridge island. This one is circled by a pine savanna that the trail leads you through on a mostly muddy, slippery surface. Plunge into a cypress strand on the other side.

Wading begins in earnest. The corridor is well defined by use, but watch for orange blazes on the cypress. Large bromeliads cling to the trees, particularly cardinal wild pine with red and yellow spiky flowers. As the understory becomes denser, pond apple and wax myrtle creep in. Beware of cypress knees hidden in the water, easy to stub a toe on or trip over.

Crossing a swamp buggy road, reach a broad grassy savanna after 1.9 miles. Punctuated by a handful of cypress trees, it provides a view across the swamp of distant cypress domes. Wet and muddy, the footpath draws close to a tree island of tropical forest with a lone palm tree, but it doesn't lead you onto it. This open landscape affords a good look at the cloudscapes above.

Entering a thicket of cypress with scattered coco plum, exchange open savanna for a wade through a forest. It becomes a cypress strand of short cypresses with very thick bases. Because the limestone bedrock is so close to the surface, these cypress grow slowly; some

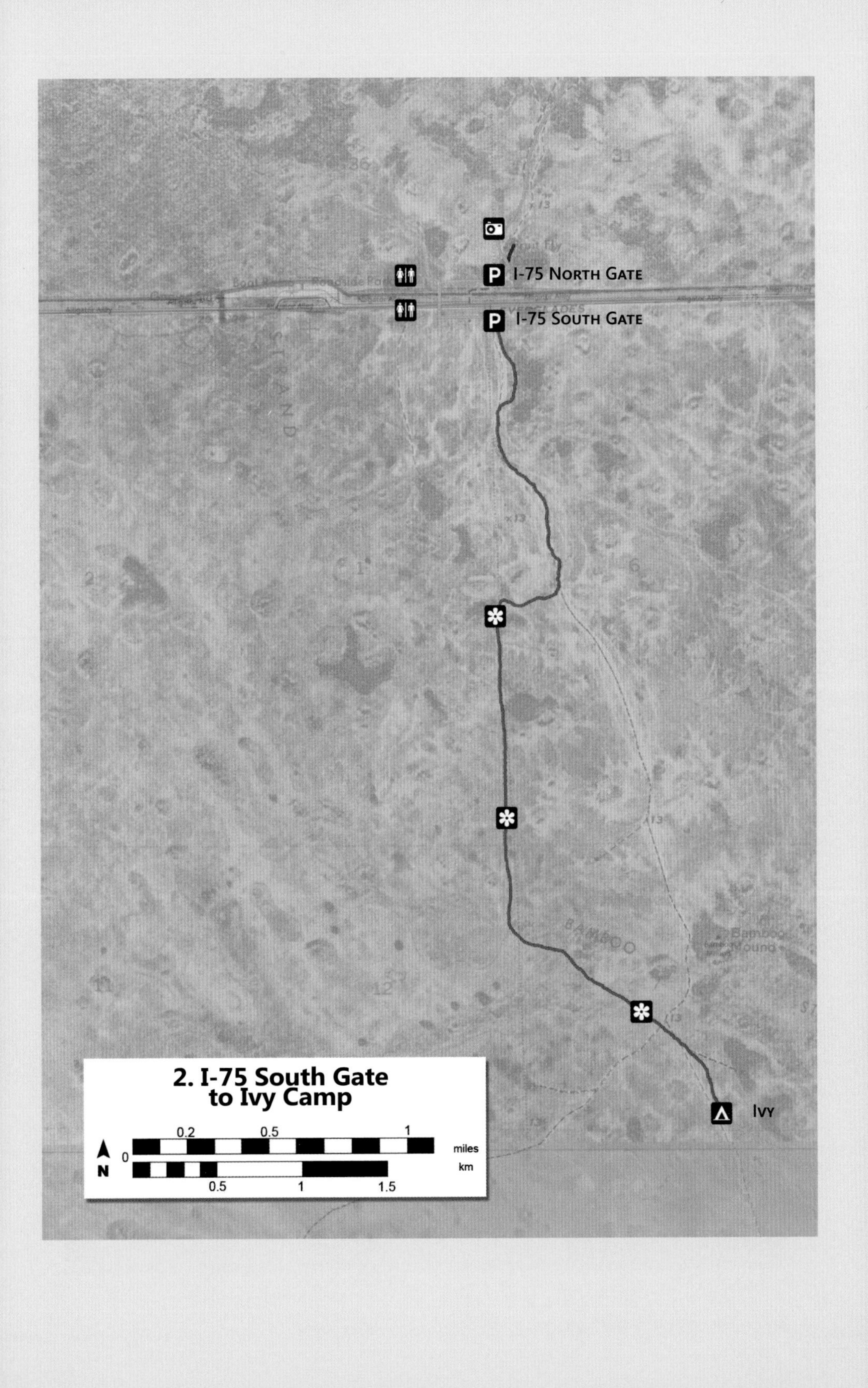
I-75 North Gate
I-75 South Gate
Ivy
2. I-75 South Gate to Ivy Camp
0.2
0.5
1
miles
0
N
km
0.5
1
1.5

may be centuries old. Delicate three-petaled yellow blooms of bladderwort and button-like white blooms of hatpins rise from their bases.

In the crystalline water, periphyton is stretched across the floor of the swamp. Expect deeper wading through this strand, which goes on for nearly a mile. It opens up into broad views before narrowing to a corridor crowded with cypress and bromeliads.

Crossing several swamp buggy roads in quick succession at 3.2 miles—including one where you can sometimes briefly step onto dry ground—the trail plunges into the type of cypress savanna that stretches southward for the next six miles. Characterized by dense grass and slimmer cypress trees, it's mucky enough that it can pull off your shoes. Tread carefully.

At 3.5 miles, reach Ivy Camp, its location acknowledged by a brown sign. A tree island, it's been mostly cleared of its tropical forest for camping, the poison ivy that gave it its name hacked out of the way by trail maintainers when they visit. A handful of tent sites are obvious. A path leads off the back of the island to deeper water suitable for filtering. Dry, cleared land is the only amenity here, and you will be thankful when you reach it. Day hikers can take a well-deserved break before heading back, while backpackers will enjoy a night under the stars. Return the same way for a 7-mile hike.

Cypress strand north of Ivy Camp

Okeechobee

112.2 MILES | LAKE OKEECHOBEE

For a sense of perspective, walk around one of America's largest lakes. Whether you cover a dozen miles on a day hike or walk the full 112 miles around Lake Okeechobee, you'll gain an understanding of a place that most residents only know of as a spot on a state map.

Overview

It is odd, this juxtaposition of big water, big sky, and agriculture in the heart of the Florida peninsula. While the shimmering lake—a virtual ocean of fresh water that stretches to the horizon—is natural, little else is. Marshes and rivers once nourished this giant shallow bowl, which tipped its waters into the grassy expanse of the Everglades. More than a century ago the dynamic changed. Agriculture transformed natural rivers into ditches and drained swamps and marshes to create farmland, prized rich black soil. After horrific hurricanes drowned thousands, the Army Corps of Engineers ringed Lake Okeechobee with a tall dike and locks, replacing the natural ebb and flow of water with water management for the sake of agriculture.

On the Okeechobee section of the Florida Trail you are 35 feet above the surrounding landscape for much of the hike, with panoramic views of open water and marsh, prairie turned to ranchland, and Everglades turned to sugar cane fields. Wildlife watching and birding are superb. Designated campsites supplement the opportunity to get to know local culture through stays at fish camps and campgrounds with cabins.

Trailheads

The Herbert Hoover Dike circles the lake, and highways circle the dike. It's easy to get to trailheads along the Okeechobee section and there are many. However, it's not a good idea to leave vehicles overnight at trailheads. If you plan to backpack around the lake, arrange to leave yours at a local business. The following are listed south to north from the bottom of this section.

0.0 JOHN STRETCH PARK
County park at the south end of the loop, with restrooms.

EAST

5.3 SOUTH BAY REC AREA
Large trailhead on lake side of dike mainly for boater access.

8.9 HATCHER ROAD
Small unpaved parking area at former barge loading area.

10.9 PAUL RARDIN PARK
Picnic grove with parking areas and restrooms.

17.1 PAHOKEE REC AREA
Large paved parking area with marina, restrooms, and campground. Formerly Pahokee State Park.

20.7 CANAL POINT REC AREA
Recreation area with parking, picnic tables on lakeshore.

26.9 NENA TRAILHEAD
Official trailhead parking off US 441 with access to two trails.

28.8 PORT MAYACA
Grassy parking area near gate on south side of Port Mayaca lock.

30.1 PORT MAYACA REC AREA
Large dirt parking area on north side of Port Mayaca lock.

37.8 CHAUNCEY BAY
Grassy lot across bridge from US 441 near J&S Fish Camp.

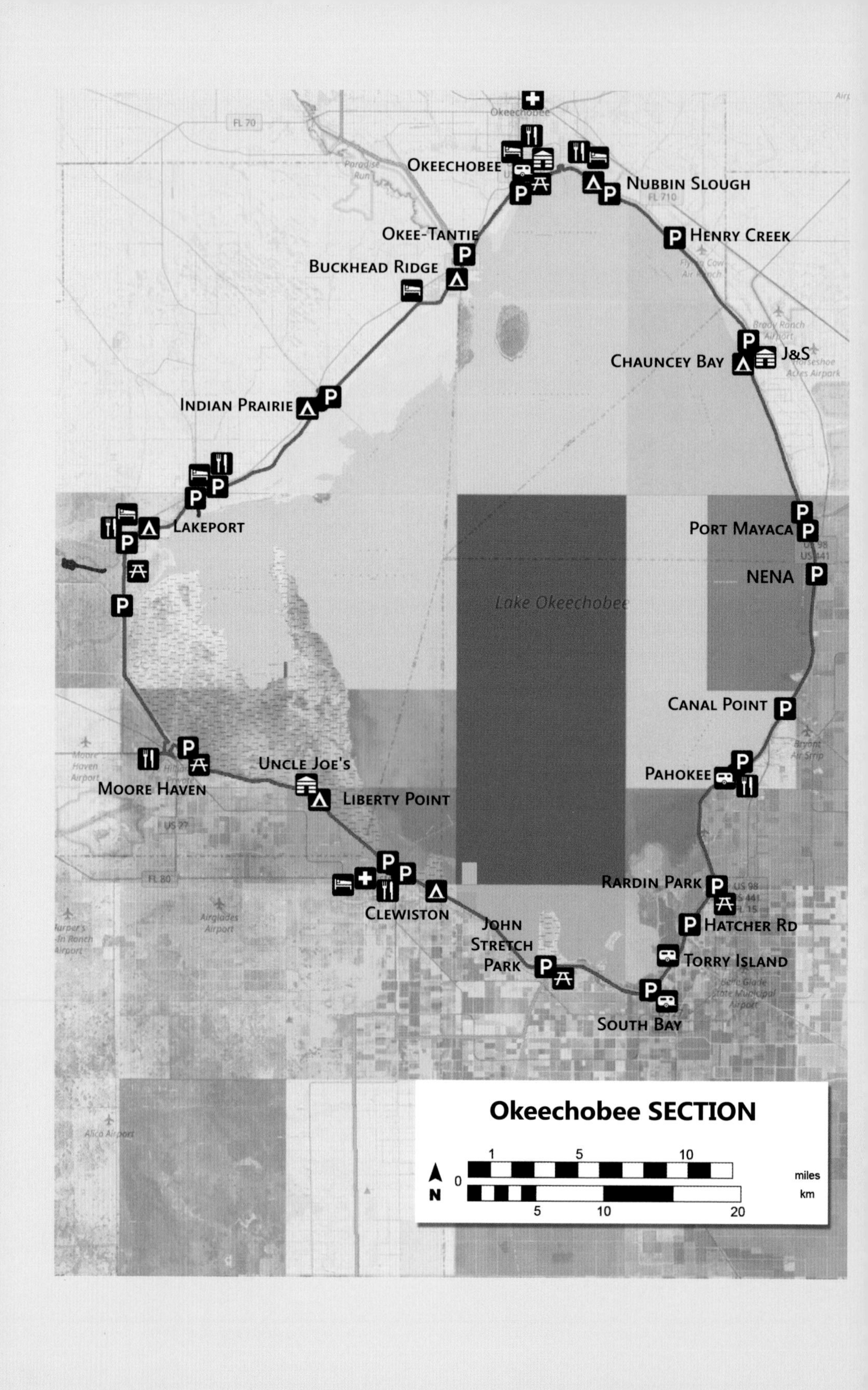
Okeechobee
Okeechobee
Nubbin Slough
Okee-Tantie
Henry Creek
Buckhead Ridge
Chauncey Bay
J&S
Indian Prairie
Lakeport
Port Mayaca
NENA
Lake Okeechobee
Canal Point
Pahokee
Moore Haven
Uncle Joe's
Liberty Point
Rardin Park
Clewiston
John Stretch Park
Hatcher Rd
Torry Island
South Bay
Okeechobee SECTION
miles
km
N

44.1 HENRY CREEK
Small dirt pull-off area adjoining Henry Creek lock.

47.8 NUBBIN SLOUGH
Large unpaved lot facing lake, adjoining S-191 lock.

52.7 CLIFF J. BETTS REC AREA
Paved lot adjoins lakefront, pier, and restrooms.

56.6 SCOTT DRIVER PARK
County park with restrooms, large paved lot along SR 78.

WEST

8.5 ARMY CORPS OF ENGINEERS
Small trailhead adjoining headquarters building in South Clewiston.

9.7 LEVEE PARK
County park along Lake Okeechobee with picnic area and restrooms.

15.0 UNCLE JOE'S FISH CAMP
Private campground, motel, and cabins. Ask permission to park.

21.4 ALVIN WARD PARK
Large county park at Moore Haven locks with picnic area and restrooms.

30.7 BOAT RAMP
Dirt parking area used by boaters, adjoins bike path and creek.

33.5 FISHEATING CREEK
Small parking area adjoining creek at Lakeport boat ramp.

37.6 MARGARET VAN DE VELDE PARK
Large county park in Lakeport with paved parking and restrooms.

38.6 BIG BARE BEACH
Paved parking area used by boaters at Dyess Ditch.

45.2 INDIAN PRAIRIE CANAL
Grassy parking area down limestone road off SR 78.

55.6 OKEE-TANTIE
Recreation area on lake side with huge paved parking lot.

Camping

Random camping is permitted. Avoid doing so near access points where vehicles can reach the dike. Designated campsites have a picnic table and a few palm trees usable for hammock hanging. On the east side of the lake from Lake Harbor to Pahokee, use county- and city-owned campgrounds at South Bay, Torry Island, and Pahokee. At Okeechobee KOA, identifying yourself as a Florida Trail hiker often helps with a discount on campsite rates.

EAST

3.9 BEAN CITY
Flat spot adjoining the C-4A pump station, view of Ritta Island.

5.1 SOUTH BAY RV PARK
County campground 0.2E of trail. Showers and laundry. Fee.

7.3 TORRY ISLAND CAMPGROUND
City campground 0.7W on island. Showers, laundry, Wi-Fi. Fee.

16.9 PAHOKEE CAMPGROUND
City campground along the lakeshore. Cabins available. Fee.

37.7 CHAUNCEY BAY
Covered picnic table and palm trees with view of lake.

48.3 NUBBIN SLOUGH
Covered picnic table and palm trees with view of lake.

WEST

4.4 CLEWISTON
Covered picnic table and adjoining trees along the lakeshore.

14.3 LIBERTY POINT
Covered picnic table and palm trees facing cane fields.

27.7 C-5A
Mowed spot with covered picnic table and palm trees at Rim Canal.

34.7 LAKEPORT
Covered picnic table and nearby palm trees on Rim Canal.

44.9 INDIAN PRAIRIE
Covered picnic table and palm trees on canal side facing ranch.

54.6 BUCKHEAD RIDGE
Covered picnic table on lakeside along edge of a prairie.

Trip Planning

While the Okeechobee section provides one of the longest loops in Florida, it's not without downsides. It's mostly paved. Great for cyclists, nice for short walks, but not ideal for backpackers. After 15 years of contractors shoring up the earthen dike, the full loop has reopened. The trail diverts to paralleling highways to cross bridges at the St. Lucie and Caloosahatchee Rivers as well as at Taylor Creek. There is also a massive garbage dump in Moore Haven, which should not have been permitted so close to the National Scenic Trail.

Clean water is also a concern. Straightening the Kissimmee River for commerce in the 1960s destroyed its ability to filter pollutants through its marshes. While that grievous mistake is still being undone, stinky mats of blue-green algae with cyanobacteria sporadically appear in Lake Okeechobee. Avoid hiking here when that happens, as it's bad to breathe. Check the Army Corps of Engineers website for alerts. Don't use the lake as your water source. Pump houses and locks along the dike have spigots with non-potable water, but it's from the lake. Marshes afford some natural filtration, but all surface water here has agricultural runoff. Better to obtain potable water whenever possible.

Because of the ease of trailhead access this section is ideal for leapfrogging vehicles when hiking with a friend. Sun protection is a must: there is no shade except where water structures and a handful of trees cast shadows. Covered benches, mainly on the northeast side of the lake, are a welcome sight. Insect repellent comes in handy when the breeze dies down. All of the trail atop the dike is fully exposed to the elements and it's the high spot in a large low-lying area. Get off the trail as quickly as possible when thunderstorms threaten.

Land Managers

South Florida Water Management District
3301 Gun Club Rd, West Palm Beach 33406
561-686-8800
sfwmd.gov

Army Corps of Engineers
525 Ridgelawn Rd, Clewiston 33440
863-983-8101
saj.usace.army.mil

Highlights

EAST

Ritta Island, mile 1.0

The first pioneer outpost along the lake, Ritta Island sits at the natural outflow of the Miami River from Lake Okeechobee. Tall royal palms mark this site on the lake side of the dike. The river once flowed across the Everglades to Miami, a pond apple swamp stretching from it to the Big Cypress Swamp. Across US 27 from John Stretch Park, the remains of the original locks built along the Miami River are in Lake Harbor across from the post office.

Pelican Bay, mile 10.9

Where the Pelican River once flowed from Lake Okeechobee into the Everglades, Pelican Bay shelters a pond apple forest in a cove visible from the dike at Paul Rardin Park. The land on the east side of the dike is sugarcane fields as far as the eye can see.

Okeechobee Ridge, mile 30.1

One of the few remaining natural landforms along Lake Okeechobee, this ridge formed the eastern shore of the lake prior to the dike being built. Topped with a tropical forest and ancient cypress trees, it's now a linear natural area that you can explore along the Raphael Sanchez Trail.

WEST

Caloosahatchee River, mile 22.8

Take in a sweeping view of the lake and river basin from the pedestrian walkway along the Caloosahatchee River Bridge. This major river empties into the Gulf of Mexico at Fort Myers but is ditched for a long stretch west of the lake. In Moore Haven, visit the Lone Cypress, the navigational marker for boats to find the river's mouth when it was still a wild waterway.

Fisheating Creek, mile 30.7

For a little more than three miles, the trail follows a paved bike path along SR 78. The reason for this is the vast Fisheating Creek floodplain, which can be seen as you cross its outflow at both ends. Fisheating Creek remains the only waterway that flows unchecked into Lake Okeechobee. The wetlands north of SR 78 bloom with swamp sunflowers in fall.

Indian Prairie, mile 38.7

Stretching along the northwest shore from Big Bare Beach toward Buckhead Ridge, Indian Prairie is a vast prairie on both sides of the dike. On the lake side, it is mostly marsh. Inland, the open prairie is punctuated by clusters of cabbage palms and populated by cows.

Recommended Day Hikes

EAST

Mile 5.3

South Bay to CR 717, 4-mile round trip

Mile 30.1

Port Mayaca to Chauncey Bay, 7.7 miles linear

Mile 52.7

Okeechobee to Taylor Creek, 4-mile round trip

Okeechobee to Okee-tantie, 7.6-mile round trip

WEST

Mile 9.7

Clewiston to Moore Haven, 11.8 miles linear

Mile 33.5

Fisheating Creek to Lakeport, 4.2 miles linear

Mile 37.6

Lakeport to Indian Prairie Canal, 7.8 miles linear

Western marshes of Lake Okeechobee

3. Lakeport to Indian Prairie Canal

7.6 MILES | LAKEPORT

Ramble alongside the marshy expanse of the western side of Lake Okeechobee on one of the last unpaved stretches of the Florida Trail around the lake.

Overview

From the western shore of Lake Okeechobee, it's hard to see open water. There is a gap in the Herbert Hoover Dike, enabling Fisheating Creek to flow into the lake, but the lake is otherwise edged by vast marshes. It wasn't always this way.

Lakeport residents remember open water and a bustling fishing industry. Before the town was founded in 1913, a commercial fishing operation ran out of Big Bare Beach. Seine nets stretched across the shallows trapped catfish, bluegill, and speck for market. Depletion of these species increased the bass population of the lake, so sport fishing became big. But then the Army Corps of Engineers drew down the level of Lake Okeechobee and kept it low for many years. Marshes took over the shallows. As one former fishing guide told us, "They did us in."

Anglers still launch at Lakeport but must travel much farther offshore to fish. This hike starts at Margaret Van de Velde Park, which bustles with boats headed out through the cut from Harney Pond Canal to the open waters of the lake in the far distance.

Trip Planning

See Okeechobee. Insect repellent and sun protection are necessary. Shade is nonexistent except at covered benches. This hike is exposed to the elements, dangerous in a thunderstorm. Check weather forecasts before heading to the trail.

Directions

All trailheads are along SR 78. From Okeechobee, follow SR 78 west for 14 miles, crossing the Kissimmee River on the way. Immediately after the bridge over Indian Prairie Canal, turn left and follow a narrow service road to the parking area [27.061016, -80.972176] at Indian Prairie Canal boat ramp. Leave a vehicle here at the ending point.

Return to SR 78 and continue west for 7 miles. There is an access point you pass at the sign for the S-129 pump station. It has no parking but can serve as an exit point 5 miles into the hike if you need to pick someone up. Entering Lakeport, cross Dyess Ditch. The road on the left leads to an alternate parking area at Big Bare Beach [27.002901, -81.052299]. Continue along SR 78 to the cluster of services at Harney Pond Canal. Turn left immediately before the bridge for the paved road to Margaret Van de Velde Park [26.995691, -81.067612]. Park near the restrooms.

Options

To shorten the hike, walk to Big Bare Beach for a 2-mile round trip or continue farther any distance you like. There aren't a lot of distinct landmarks. To the covered bench on the canal and back is 4.8 miles. Or walk in from Indian Prairie Canal to the S-129 for a

Indian Prairie campsite

5.6-mile round trip. A new pedestrian bridge over Harney Pond Canal makes for an easy 4.2-mile round trip to the "Hiker's Graveyard," an unusual collection of granite slabs that the Army Corps of Engineers drove into the dike at the S-131 lock to see if they would help stabilize it.

To lengthen this hike, start on the far side of Lakeport at the Fisheating Creek boat ramp [26.968613, -81.118622], adding 4.1 miles to the overall hike for a 11.7-mile trek. That segment is paved and includes both the Lakeport campsite and the Hikers Graveyard. An overnighter from Fisheating Creek to the Indian Prairie campsite would be 22.8 miles.

Walk or drive to the end of the peninsula at Margaret Van de Velde Park, less than a mile round trip. A paved bike path parallels the shoreline from the Florida Trail, excellent for watching wading birds and alligators, and ends at the tall Sam Griffin Observation Tower. This tower is the best place on the lake to take in a panorama of the grassy waters.

Hike

From the parking area, follow the bike path uphill to the dike. Walk around the gate to access the Florida Trail and start rambling north along a two-track road. We don't doubt that it'll be paved in the future, but for now it's a packed limestone surface. The dike has a mild slope toward Lakeport. Cabbage palms line the shore of the Rim Canal, with homes and a motel below. Toward the lake, a ribbon of blue water parallels Margaret Van de Velde Park, providing boaters access to open waters well offshore.

Approaching Big Bare Beach after the first mile, its openness is distinctive. Imagine the large sandy beach that was here before this dike was built, lake lapping at the shore. Scanning the horizon ahead, there is no lake to be seen. Turn right to look straight down Dyess Ditch, the cut beyond the boat basin, to spot it. Boaters follow that route to open water. A paved road leads left to SR 78. Near the gate, the surface underfoot becomes irregular, studded with stones. The entire Florida Trail circling Lake Okeechobee was like this until 2003. Fossils protrude from the footpath. We've found clams, scallops, and snails; a friend discovered a mastodon tooth.

Leaving Big Bare Beach behind, the character of the view changes. A screen of dense forest grows along the shoreline of the Rim Canal, which reflects the sky. Mounds of moonflower vines cover willows and cabbage palms growing along the lake side of the dike, but there is no lake, just a flat prairie as far as the eye can see. This is Indian Prairie.

As a landform, Indian Prairie extends north to meet the southern tip of the Lake Wales Ridge south of Lake Placid.

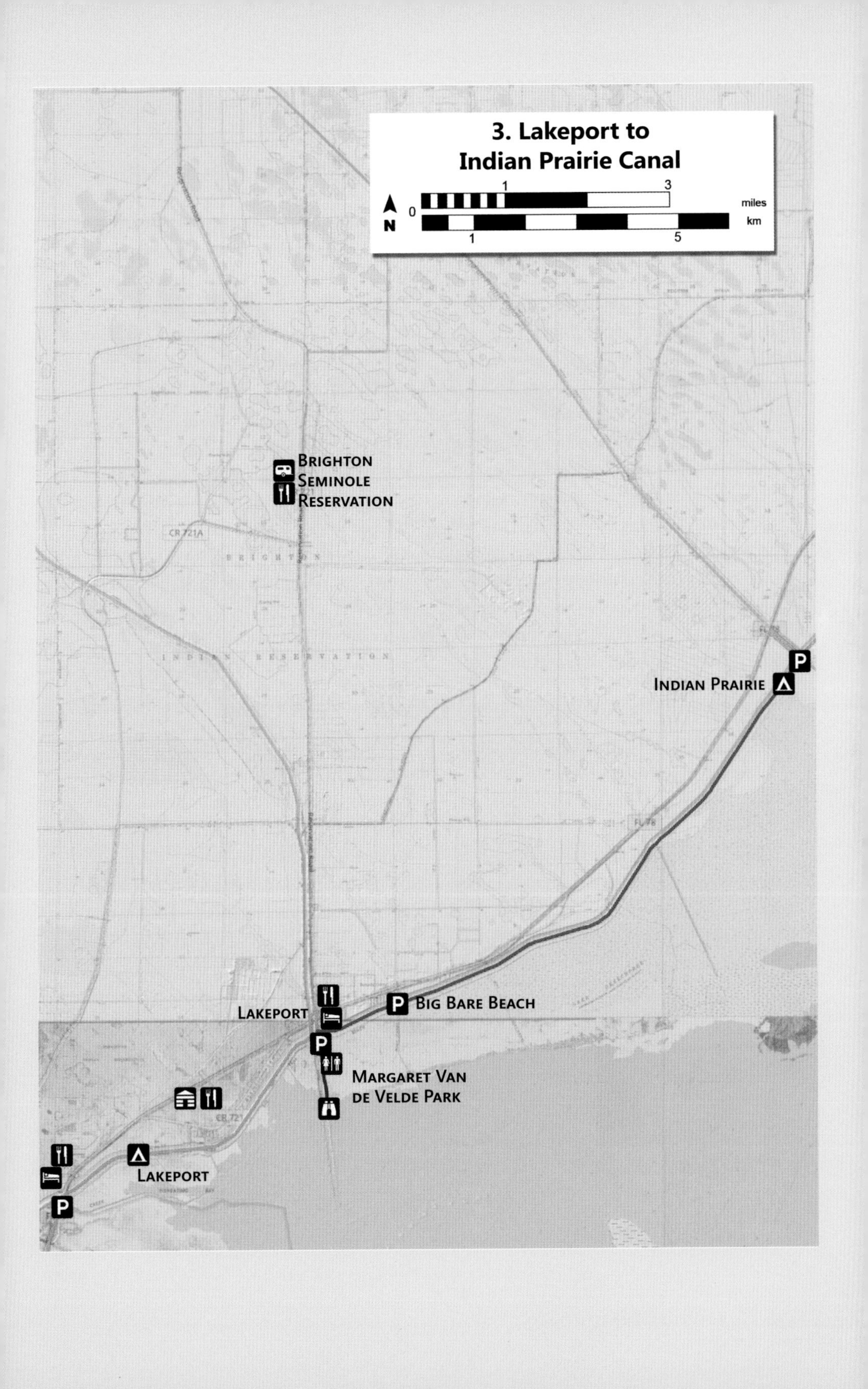
3. Lakeport to
Indian Prairie Canal
1
3
miles
0
N
km
1
5
Brighton
Seminole
Reservation
CR 721A
Indian Prairie
FL 78
Lakeport
Big Bare Beach
Margaret Van
de Velde Park
CR 721
Lakeport

Prized as ranchland, the prairie was largely drained and carved up by landowners. It has a distinctive look, seen along this hike. You're not far from the Brighton Seminole Reservation, known for its prize beef cattle, its casino, and its annual rodeo that draws participants from around the country.

A bench is at the base of the dike along the Rim Canal at 2.4 miles. Few hikers venture down there because it means climbing back up the steep slope. A mile and a half later, the dike makes a gentle curve to the right, revealing the character of Indian Prairie. Cabbage palms top the lake's original shoreline in a long line. Cattle graze closely cropped grasses. As the line of palms breaks into clumps, it's obvious where cypress trees once poked out of the marshy fringe of the lake. A row of Australian pines delineates a homestead on the Rim Canal with a dock. North of it, palm hammocks resume, surrounded by marsh yielding to the dry grassland of a ranch. A tall communications tower comes into view. Reach it at the S-129 pump station after 4.8 miles.

S-129 was among the last of the water control structures put into place by the Army Corps of Engineers along the north rim of Lake Okeechobee. While the deadly hurricane of 1926 inspired the construction of the Herbert Hoover Dike to prevent future flooding, the first segments were built along the south end of the lake with its larger population. This dike and water control structure were completed in 1962.

Indian Prairie stretches to the far horizon on the left as you leave S-129 behind, grasslands broken only by clumps of palms, fences, and the movement of vehicles along SR 78. Cattle roam across the open prairie. In autumn, the marsh on the lake side is tipped with what looks like snowfall when sea myrtle (*Baccharis halimifolia*) blooms, attracting migrating butterflies. Airboats buzz on the distant marshes, making their way toward Indian Prairie Canal.

As the dike curves left, you can see a long way down the Rim Canal. Boaters don't enter this section since there are no access points. But cattle come to it to drink, and great egrets perch along its edge. The trail gets grassy in places: great for hiking, trickier for bikes. A tree on the far side of the canal is an attention-getter since there are so few. Next to it is a ditch built to drain prairie wetlands, with a manual floodgate at the Rim Canal.

Rounding the next curve in the dike, approach a hiker oasis, Indian Prairie campsite. Shaded by a handful of cabbage palms on the flat terrace on the canal side of the dike, it has a covered picnic shelter at 7.3 miles. Up ahead, the Rim Canal seems to end. Draw closer and the reason is obvious: this dike makes a 90-degree turn, blocking it off. A pond is cradled by a tiny patch of wetlands at the end of the canal. The parking area at Indian Prairie Canal and the boat ramp appear soon after. Descend the dike to complete this 7.6-mile hike.

4. Port Mayaca to Nubbin Slough

17.6 MILES | OKEECHOBEE

One of the first pieces of the Florida Trail paved along Lake Okeechobee, this sweep along the northeast rim has unparalleled vistas of open water and extensive marshes busy with birds.

Overview

New vistas were revealed along Lake Okeechobee when the Army Corps of Engineers waged a winning war against invasive plants. When the Brazilian pepper was removed, hikers discovered panoramas in every direction, resulting in one of the best locations on the Florida Trail for birding.

Lake Okeechobee's natural shoreline is now visible east of US 441. Topped with old-growth cypresses, the rocky Okeechobee Ridge is where grassy waters lapped before the lake was girdled by levees. Native trees like strangler fig and gumbo-limbo populate the thin slice of tropical forest atop the ridge, protected as Okeechobee Ridge Natural Area. Paralleling the Florida Trail, the ridge has its own hiking trail hidden under the tree canopy.

Trip Planning

See Okeechobee. Use insect repellent. There is no shade except at covered benches, so sun protection is necessary. The hike is in high ground, exposed to the elements and dangerous in a thunderstorm. Check on the day's weather in advance of your hike.

Directions

All trailheads are along US 441 south of the city of Okeechobee. For Nubbin Slough [27.193001, -80.763824], drive south, crossing Taylor Creek. After services thin out, watch for a large open area on the right before a bridge over a canal. Parking is up and over the dike on the lakeshore side. A brown sign marks a small access point at Henry Creek [27.163174, -80.715981] three miles south of Nubbin Slough. North of the community of Upthegrove Beach, the next brown sign points to the trailhead at Chauncey Bay [27.088913, -80.662064]. A short drive leads to a large grassy trailhead adjoining the Rim Canal.

For the starting point at the Port Mayaca Recreation Area [26.986403, -80.618591], get in the turnoff lane on the right when approaching the bridge over the St. Lucie Canal. Follow the entrance road to a T intersection. Turn right and park near the kiosk.

Options

Rather than a long day hike or a couple of hours on a bike, trim this section by either hiking out and back from Port Mayaca or using one of the intermediate access points as the ending point. It's 7.6 miles to Chauncey Bay trailhead and 14 miles to Henry Creek. A designated campsite immediately north of Chauncey Bay and another a half mile north of Nubbin Slough provide potential overnight destinations. To explore the tropical hammock on the Okeechobee Ridge, hike part or all of the 5-mile linear Raphael Sanchez Trail. Its trailhead [26.986849, -80.617104] is beneath the Port Mayaca bridge in the same

Eastern shore of Lake Okeechobee

recreation area as the starting point of this hike.

Hike

After ascending the dike from the parking area, the sweep of Lake Okeechobee is at your feet. To the left, the rim of the lake curves off in the distance toward Pahokee, 12 miles south. To the right, it vanishes into haze toward Okeechobee. Straight across, there's a horizon line. The impact is that of an inland sea. Lake Okeechobee is the next largest freshwater lake in America after the Great Lakes.

Paralleling the dike on your right, the Rim Canal was the source of the muck piled up to construct the Herbert Hoover Dike. The public works project to encircle Lake Okeechobee began in the 1930s and ended in the 1960s. Before any earthen wall existed, Conner's Highway stretched from Canal Point to Okeechobee on the grassy edge of the lake. A 33-mile improved toll road, it opened July 4, 1924, eventually defining US 98. Road access led to the development of Florida's swampy interior wilderness into sugarcane fields and ranches.

The tall line of ancient cypress on the opposite side of US 441 marks the natural shoreline of the lake. As you walk this section, the line of cypress is always to the east, but not nearly as close to the lake as it is here, where the St. Lucie

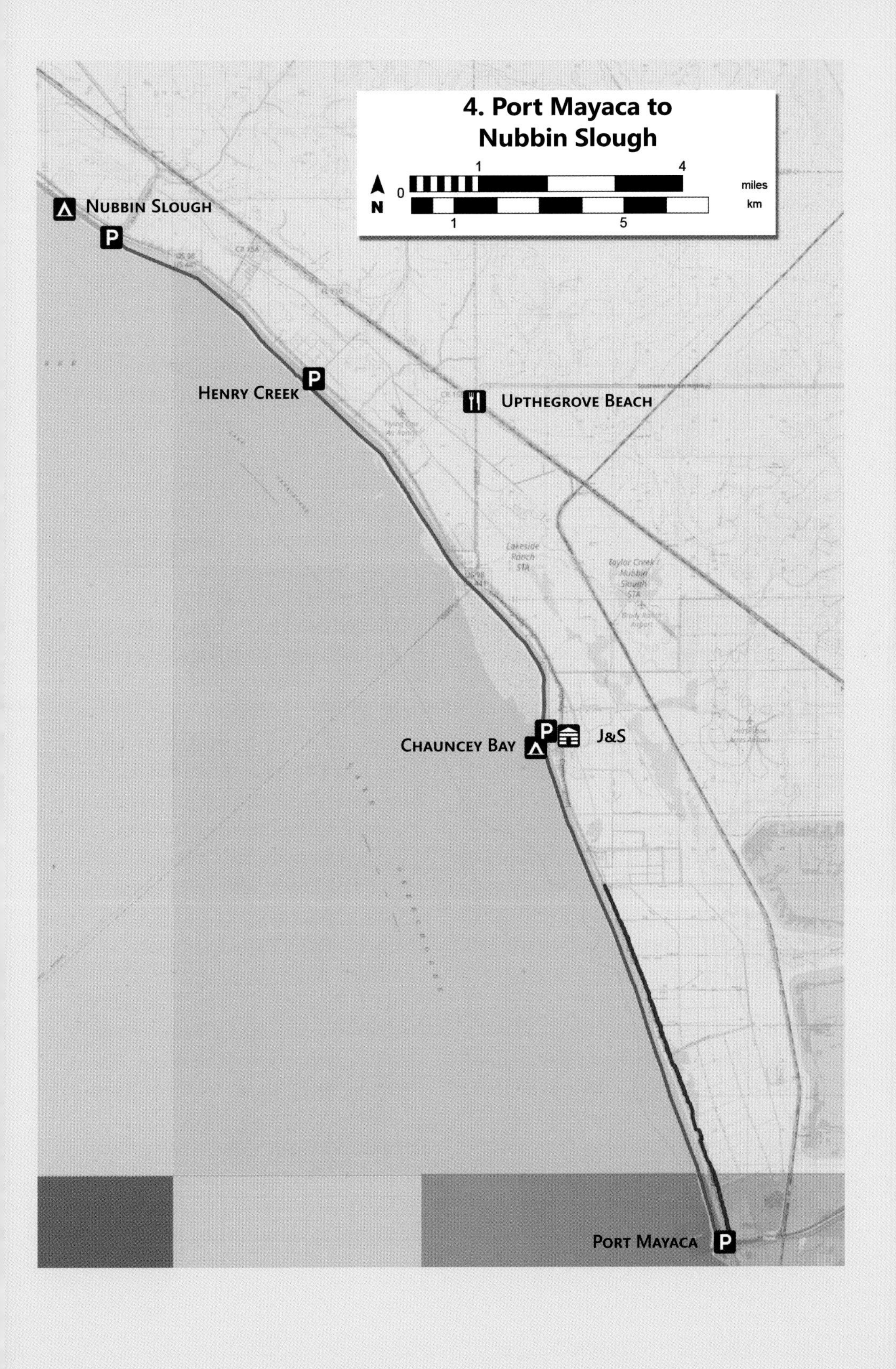
4. Port Mayaca to Nubbin Slough
1
4
0
miles
N
km
1
5
Nubbin Slough
Henry Creek
Upthegrove Beach
Chauncey Bay
J&S
Port Mayaca

River once flowed freely toward the Atlantic Ocean instead of being trapped between the walls of a canal.

Reach the first covered bench at 1.5 miles. Numbers painted on the pavement refer to mile markers set up when they started paving the dike two decades ago. Mile 0 is the Army Corps of Engineers office in Clewiston. These numbers aren't painted all the way around the lake. When you find them, they are a mile apart, so you can at least tick off the miles with them.

Just past MP 37 is another bench. Enjoy a panorama of grassy waters. Depending on the water level, individual blades of grass may jut from the expanse of blue. Swallows swoop across the dike in pursuit of low-flying insects, and queen butterflies open their wings to the warmth of the sun. At dawn, wave upon wave of cattle egrets wing low across the dike toward the lake, rising in clouds from colonies among mounds of shrubbery decorated in moonvine.

There is a transition from agricultural to residential and back again along the Rim Canal. Pass a third bench at 5.6 miles. Cormorants perch on limestone boulders defining the base of the dike. These buffer against the wave action the lake is known for when winds pick up. Large alligators cruise among grassy islands. At 7.4 miles, reach S-135 Chauncey Bay Pumping Station and its lock. Boaters sometimes wait in line below to be lifted from the lake up to the Rim Canal. Enjoy a spot of shade cast by the lock tender's building and a guardrail to sit on. Across from the lock, a canal slices toward US 441 and J&S Fish Camp, a colorful watering hole. Its campground includes historic cabins built for dike construction workers. The ramp leads to the Chauncey Bay trailhead, with J&S about a mile past it by foot. A camping sign points left for Chauncey Bay campsite, a picnic shelter and palms near the lakeshore.

As the dike curves around the breadth of the shallow marshy bay, the lake recedes into the distance. At times of higher water, passageways appear that duck hunters use to flush their quarries. Low water lets moonvine blanket the cypress standing in the shallows. Osprey and bald eagles perch on those tall trees. By 8.8 miles, the trail has a noticeable arc, the lake a thin ribbon of blue on the horizon. The Rim Canal is edged with mounds of vegetation. Behind it, white roofs peek up from RV parks and fish camps.

A cell phone tower looms ahead at 11.5 miles, with MP 48E soon thereafter. And a bench. A straight line for a while, the dike finally curves, revealing the water control structure at Henry Creek as a white blur on the horizon. Even when you first see it clearly it's two miles ahead. A palm nursery fills the space between the Rim Canal and US 441. A long line of cabbage palms ends at Henry Creek. A ramp descends to Henry Creek trailhead at 14 miles.

At the S-136 lock, a lock tender is on duty. The last tender we spoke with mentioned a bobcat as a regular visitor. Despite the dike being a human-made structure, there is a surprising amount of wildlife along it. In addition to the ubiquitous alligators and wading birds, we've spotted nutria and raccoons at the shoreline and feral hogs and otters along the Rim Canal. Shallow, narrow marshes lie in a grassy haze, blurring the

Approaching S-191

line between lake and land. Tufts of delicate lovegrass with a pinkish hue cover the slopes and chalky bluestem waves in slender sheaves. The tallest grasses grow next to the canal, where cabbage palms rise from the flat terrace.

Sweeping around a broad bay near the bench at 16.1 miles, the trail passes Upthegrove Beach. Established by Robert Upthegrove in 1912, it once was on the lakeshore. It's the only place between Canal Point and Okeechobee with a cluster of services along US 441, but you can't get there from here with the Rim Canal in between. The dike makes a curve and the water tower at Treasure Island is visible four miles ahead, marking the location of the Taylor Creek bridge. Vegetation is thick along the Rim Canal side of the dike as you draw closer to the next water structure, with lots of cabbage palms and a few cypresses birds use as a roost.

Past the MP 53 painted on the pavement, reach Nubbin Slough, the "fishingest place on the dike." Anglers cluster around the outflow and cast from the sides of the basin. Great blue herons stalk the edges. Passing through the S-191 water control structure and lock, arrive at the parking area to end this hike at 17.6 miles. If you're doing a round-trip backpack, Nubbin Slough campsite is a half mile farther north with a picnic shelter and a couple of palms lakeside. The slope of the dike is gentler there and it's quieter than this 24-hour fishing hole.

Pond crossing, Corbett WMA

Ocean to Lake Hiking Trail

61 MILES | PALM BEACH AND MARTIN COUNTIES

A microcosm of the entire Florida Trail, the Ocean to Lake Hiking Trail between Port Mayaca and Hobe Sound is an ideal proving ground for backpackers to get accustomed to the types of habitats and challenges you'll face if you want to tackle the Florida Trail end to end.

Overview

Built by the Loxahatchee Chapter of the Florida Trail Association, the Ocean to Lake Hiking Trail is a spur off the Florida Trail from Lake Okeechobee to the Atlantic Ocean. Its westernmost miles connect trail systems in DuPuis WMA and Corbett WMA built in the 1970s, when it was thought the evolving route of the statewide Florida Trail might run up the coast along the edge of population centers. The Ocean to Lake Greenway, a modern quilt of public lands championed by Palm Beach and Martin Counties, provided the remainder of the right-of-way between DuPuis and Corbett to Jonathan Dickinson State Park. This popular park protects a vast swath of land surrounding the wild and scenic Loxahatchee River and abuts Hobe Sound National Wildlife Refuge along the Indian River Lagoon. It only takes a few miles to walk from the state park's boundary through the community of Hobe Sound to the beach itself.

What's in store? A little of everything: open prairies brimming with wildflowers, dense tropical forests, stately oak hammocks, extensive pine flatwoods, marl prairies, scrub habitat on rolling sand dunes, bridges and wades across river and creek basins, marshlands, and ocean sands. Throw in a slog or two through a cypress strand, a stretch on a limestone road, levee walks, groomed trails through a public park, a short roadwalk along Old A1A, and a sidewalk beneath a canopy of ficus trees opening up to the beach. You won't get bored along this trail, but you will get wet feet.

Trailheads

Although the route is called the Ocean to Lake Hiking Trail (OTLHT), hikers generally walk from Lake Okeechobee to the Atlantic Ocean for logistic and aesthetic reasons. Access points are limited. Trailheads at Corbett WMA and Jonathan Dickinson State Park are the safest places to leave your car; there is a fee for parking.

0.0 NENA TRAILHEAD
Along US 441 with access to Okeechobee section and OTL. Paved.

5.5 GOVERNOR'S HOUSE
Unpaved lot inside DuPuis WMA at picnic area. Good place to leave a car for multiple days. Fee. 3.8W.

30.3 BALD CYPRESS BOARDWALK
In Corbett WMA near Youth Camp. Fee. Paved. Vault toilet. Day use. 0.2W.

31.3 HUNGRYLAND SLOUGH
Dirt trailhead with access to Hungryland Slough CA, 0.1E.

38.0 SANDHILL CRANE
Paved day-use parking at county natural land. 1.5E.

45.4 RIVERBEND PARK
Paved day-use parking in county park. Restrooms. Outfitter. 0.4W.

53.2 KITCHING CREEK
Paved parking in state park picnic area. Fee. Restrooms. 2.0E.

58.3 CAMP MURPHY
Small trailhead in state park for bike trails. Fee. Privy. 2.4E.

61.0 HOBE SOUND BEACH
Oceanfront park. Restrooms and showers. Free.

Camping

Hikers must use designated campsites along the length of the Ocean to Lake Hiking Trail. Reservations are necessary for all campsites east of Corbett WMA. Call in advance. Camping is no longer permitted at Everglades Youth Camp, and the facility is off-limits.

8.7 LOOP 4
Picnic table and fire ring with ample tent sites under the pines.

14.4 POWERLINE
In pines near canal. New fire ring, picnic table, benches, hammock posts.

18.6 LITTLE GOPHER
Large camping area adjoining archaeological site.

24.6 BOWMAN ISLAND
Tenting under oaks and pines on an island. Wade to get there.

29.4 BIG MARSH
Designated camping in a grassy pine savanna. No fires allowed.

40.6 SOGGY SOCKS
Small site in a tropical hammock. Reserve: 561-233-2400.

42.0 LUCKEY HAMMOCK
Tiny campsite in tropical hammock. Reserve: 561-233-2400.

50.5 CYPRESS CREEK EAST
Picnic table and fire ring in open area along small pond.

52.5 KITCHING CREEK
Large camping area with picnic table and privy. Fee. Reserve: 772-546-2771.

55.9 SCRUB JAY
Camping area with picnic table and privy. Fee. Reserve: 772-546-2771.

Trip Planning

Day hiking portions of the Ocean to Lake Hiking Trail takes little planning. Backpacking is another matter entirely. You must reserve campsites in advance and work out logistics for where to leave your vehicle and how to shuttle to your starting point. Although it's rarely obvious from the trail, public lands east of Corbett WMA are surrounded by subdivisions in Jupiter Farms, Jupiter, and Tequesta. That's why land managers require you obtain permission to camp. Dogs are not permitted on Palm Beach County public lands along the route.

DuPuis and Corbett have busy fall deer hunting seasons. During all hunting seasons, hunters use swamp buggies in Corbett and don't stick to roads, creating deep ruts across the prairies and the trail. Research hunt dates. If you wear bright orange, you're permitted to hike during hunting season, but it's more pleasant to wait until after the short seasons are done.

Jonathan Dickinson State Park requires a day-use fee for hikers as well as camping reservations and fees. Their improved backcountry sites are worth it. Corbett WMA charges a day-use fee, which doesn't apply to backpackers passing through. Day hikers have the option of setting up base camp at Jonathan Dickinson State Park, where cabins and RV sites are available. DuPuis WMA has a free family campground near Port Mayaca that simply requires online registration with South Florida Water Management District for use.

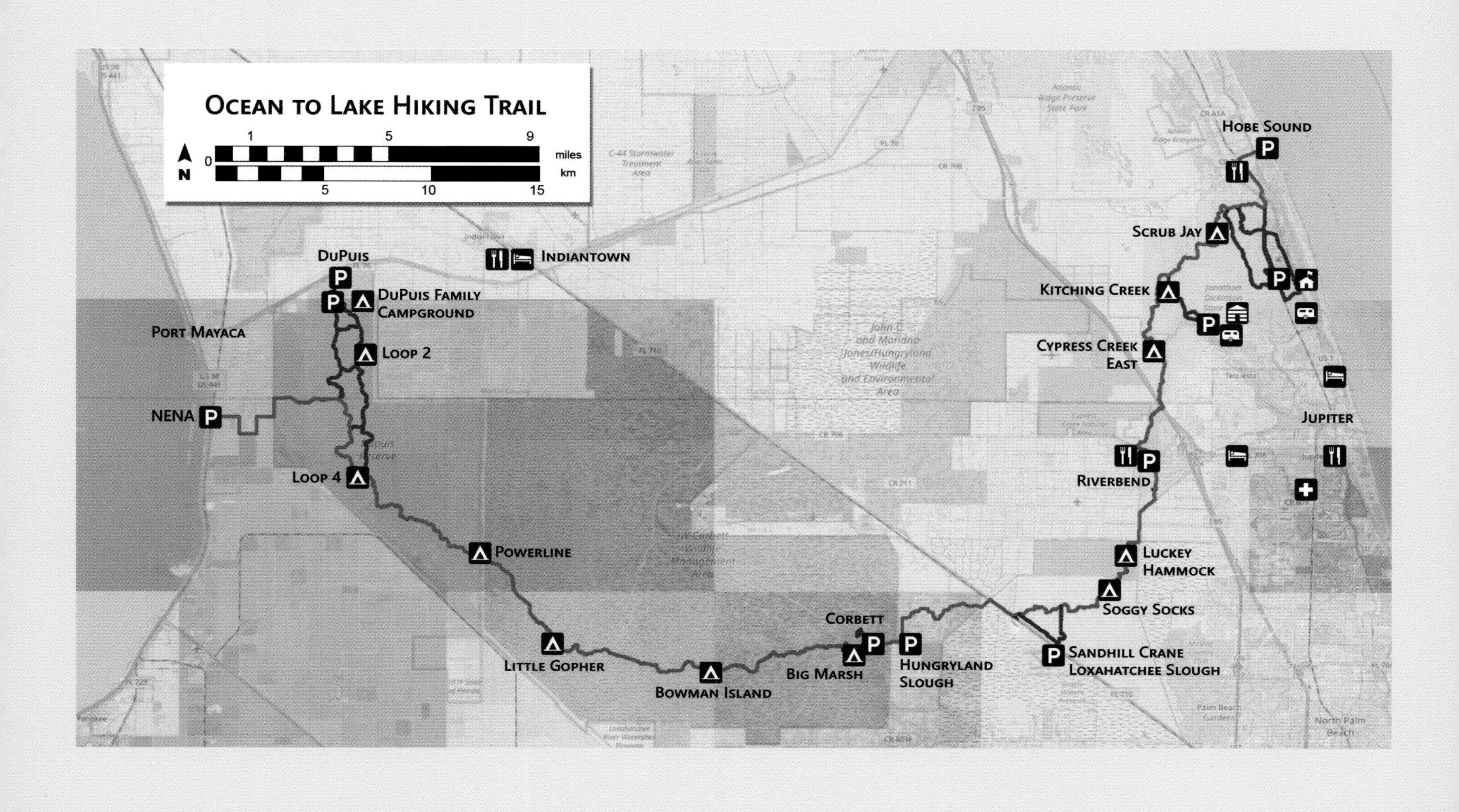
Ocean to Lake Hiking Trail
0
1
5
9
miles
N
5
10
15
km
DuPuis
DuPuis Family Campground
Indiantown
Port Mayaca
Loop 2
NENA
Loop 4
Powerline
Little Gopher
Bowman Island
Big Marsh
Corbett
Hungryland Slough
Sandhill Crane Loxahatchee Slough
Soggy Socks
Luckey Hammock
Riverbend
Cypress Creek East
Kitching Creek
Scrub Jay
Hobe Sound
Jupiter
John C. and Mariana Jones/Hungryland Wildlife and Environmental Area
JW Corbett Wildlife Management Area
Atlantic Ridge Preserve State Park
Jonathan Dickinson State Park
C-44 Stormwater Treatment Area
Palm Beach Gardens
North Palm Beach
Tequesta

Boardwalk, Loxahatchee Slough

Land Managers

Several land managers oversee the ribbon of public lands between the freshwater and saltwater coasts. The lead is **South Florida Water Management District** (561-686-8800) for DuPuis WMA and the canals the trail follows, as well as the Loxahatchee River Natural Area between Indiantown Road and Hobe Grove Canal. The **Florida Fish and Wildlife Conservation Commission** manages Corbett WMA (561-625-5122). Immediately east of Corbett, both Hungryland Slough Natural Area and Loxahatchee Slough Natural Area are managed by **Palm Beach County** (561-233-2400) as is Riverbend Park (561-966- 6617), a county park along the Loxahatchee River open during daylight hours only. **Jonathan Dickinson State Park** (772-546-2771) is a unit of Florida State Parks. **Hobe Sound Beach** (772-221-1418) is a Martin County park.

Highlights

Hatrack Cypress, mile 15.0

This cypress strand at the westernmost edge of Corbett WMA features short, squat cypresses with twisted trunks, typically caused by slow growth due to surface limestone impeding their root systems. Decorated with hanging gardens of colorful bromeliads, these cypresses can be a century or more old.

Big Gopher Mound, mile 18.6

Surrounding Little Gopher campsite, the puzzle of mounds, ponds, and narrow canals are all part of an archaeological site first excavated in the 1930s. Big Gopher Mound Complex is considered one of the most well-preserved earthworks sites in the Lake Okeechobee basin. The mounds are thought to have been bases for large communal buildings of the Jaega culture.

Hole-in-the-Wall, mile 22.6

One of the more delightful cypress strand crossings in Florida, Hole-in-the-Wall takes you through a literal wall of cypress that extends miles north and south through Corbett WMA. Densely packed and decorated with blooming bromeliads, it's a short swamp wade that's one of the more beautiful ones.

Eyeglass Ponds, mile 28.6

The Eyeglass Ponds are two similar-shaped prairie ponds between which the trail follows a very narrow spit of land that isn't always dry. It is studded with tiny yellow and purple blooms of bladderwort, a carnivorous plant that keeps the mosquito population down.

Observation Tower, mile 37.9

Immediately south of where the trail crosses Echoche Trail in the Sandhill Crane Tract of Loxahatchee Slough Natural Area, a tall observation tower provides a bird's-eye view of surrounding wet prairies.

Recommended Day Hikes

Mile 30.3

Corbett trailhead to Eyeglass Ponds, 3.4-mile round trip
South Grade to Corbett trailhead, 8.6 miles linear

Mile 38.0

Sandhill Crane Tract, Loxahatchee Slough
3-mile round trip from trailhead to tower, or 4.7-mile loop

Mile 45.6

Riverbend Park, 3.6-mile loop inside park
Riverbend Park to Kitching Creek trailhead, 10 miles linear

Side Trip

Did you know Florida has sea caves? Explore them at **BLOWING ROCKS PRESERVE** on Jupiter Island on the Atlantic Coast south of Hobe Sound Beach. Here, erosion from pounding waves has hollowed out the coastal limestone ledge to form caves visible at low tide. When the sea is rough, water spouts up through chimneys in the tops of the caves, hence the name of this preserve owned by the Nature Conservancy. floridahikes.com/blowingrocks.

Blowing Rocks

5. Sandhill Crane Loop

4.7 MILES | PALM BEACH GARDENS

Discover the wild beauty of the Sandhill Crane Tract of Loxahatchee Slough on a soggy loop hike through swamps and prairies to a tall observation tower with panoramic views.

Overview

Loxahatchee Slough was once a rough traverse on the Ocean to Lake Hiking Trail. Farming left deep furrows and mounds in wet prairies. Invasive species cloaked many views. By restoring the natural gradients and hydrology of the landscape, Palm Beach County ERM turned agriculture lands into wildlife-rich habitats on the edge of residential Palm Beach Gardens. A new trailhead opened to provide access to the Sandhill Crane Tract in 2020. With it came a collection of named trails connecting to the existing Ocean to Lake Hiking Trail. This loop is one of the best ways to experience it.

Trip Planning

See Ocean to Lake Hiking Trail. Open dawn to dusk. Trails at Loxahatchee Slough are hiking only. No cyclists, equestrians, or dogs. Shade is minimal along more than half of the loop. Use insect repellent and sun protection. Expect wet feet along the Ocean to Lake portion of the trail. Hiking sticks help in traversing the trail when it is wet.

Land Manager

Palm Beach County ERM
11855 Beeline Hwy, West Palm Beach 33412
561-804-7034
discover.pbcgov.org/erm

Directions

From Interstate 95 exit 79B in Palm Beach Gardens, follow PGA Blvd west, passing Karen Marcus Sandhill Crane Access Park at the C-18 canal after 3.9 miles. Continue 2 miles to the light at the Beeline (SR 710) and turn right. In 1.3 miles, the Sandhill Crane Tract trailhead [26.8529, -80.2152] is on the right.

Options

Some hikers will be satisfied with a 3-mile round trip to the Loxahatchee Slough observation tower, a don't-miss destination within sight of the Ocean to Lake Trail junction. A 0.6-mile round trip on the paved Nature Trail to a sheltered overlook is ADA accessible. The red-blazed Loxahatchee Loop (which includes the accessible Nature Trail) is a 1.6-mile hike around the prairies and ponds closest to the trailhead. With a look at the map on the kiosk, you can also put shorter options together on the trail system.

Hike

Start at the kiosk at the beginning of the Nature Trail. This accessible path leads through oaks and pines before emerging into an open area at a junction with a dirt road. To the left, the Loxahatchee Loop is how you'll return to this point. Cross the culverts over the canal straight ahead, keeping alert for wildlife on either side. The paved trail continues through scattered pines with a dense

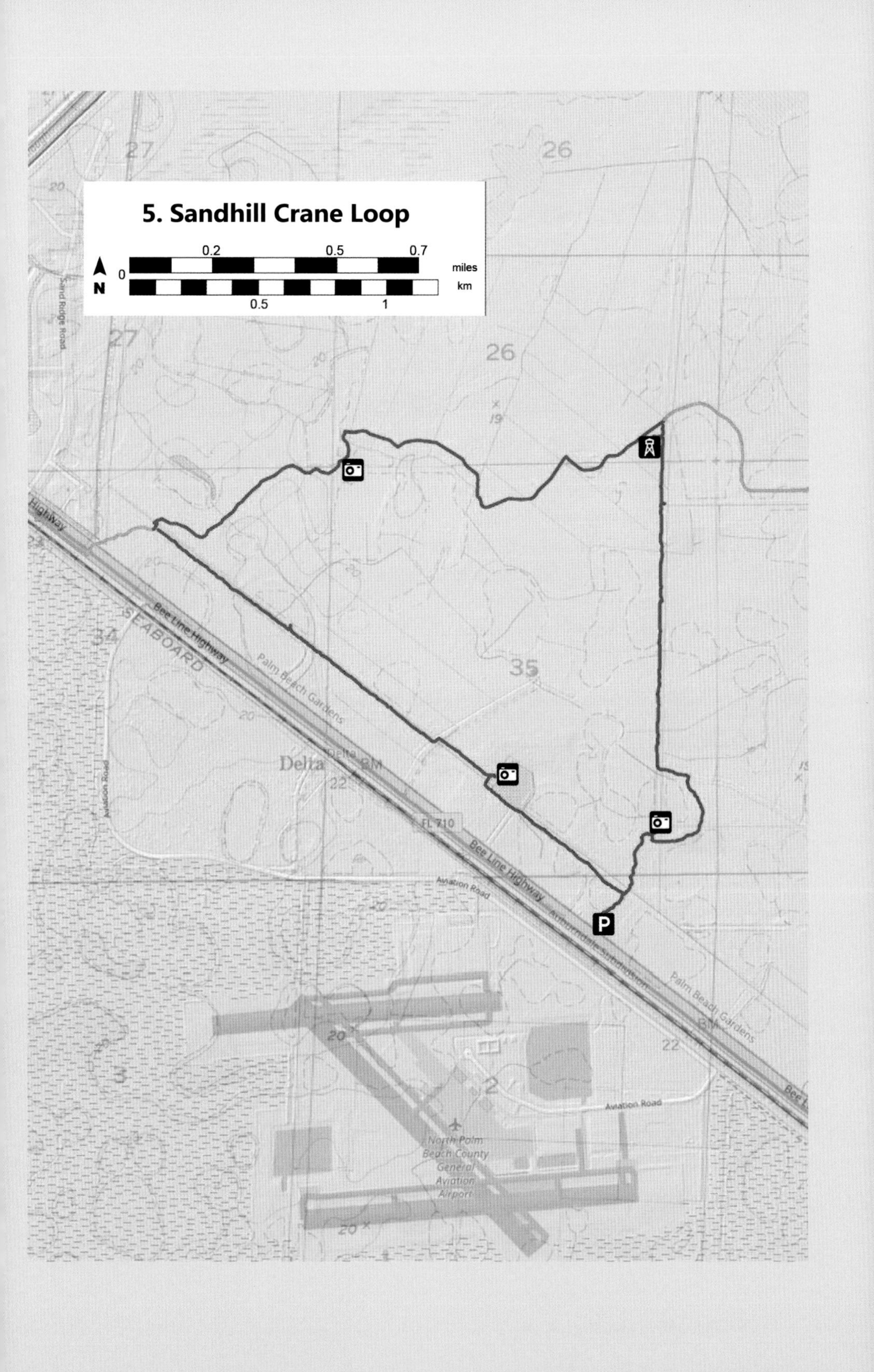

5. Sandhill Crane Loop
0
0.2
0.5
0.7
miles
0.5
1
km
N
27
26
Sand Ridge Road
Highway
Bee Line Highway
SEABOARD
34
35
Palm Beach Gardens
Delta
FL 710
Aviation Road
Bee Line Highway
Palm Beach Gardens
Aviation Road
North Palm Beach County General Aviation Airport
3
2
22
P

Observation tower, Loxahatchee Slough

understory. The skies open up as the trail approaches a large wet prairie.

At 0.3 mile, the pavement ends at a covered observation deck offering a nice panorama. Join the red-blazed Loxahatchee Loop by following the edge of the prairie east from the observation deck. The footpath can become very wet because of the outflow of the prairie. This is the first place our shoes were dunked. Emerging at a T with a maintenance road, turn left. By 0.6 miles your route reaches an intersection with the Echoche Trail, another road that heads north. Look south across the wet prairie, the observation deck now on its far shore, before turning north onto the yellow-blazed Echoche Trail.

The outstanding wetland panoramas along the Echoche Trail will draw you to the edges of their shimmering pools. Be careful around culverts since alligators are often in or near them. Moorhens and coots call from the marshes while herons and egrets pick along the edges. Largely in full sun, the trail serves as a maintenance road for management of this natural area. Spatterdock, pickerelweed, and American lotus grow thickly in the wetlands restored by the removal of roads and ditches. Looking across the ponds and marshes, it's hard to envision this as farmland. Nature heals quickly in this lush environment. A side path leads to a roosting tower and interpretive information about chimney swifts, whose numbers have declined in the region.

Reach the tall observation tower at 1.5 miles. A picnic bench is in the shade underneath it. It's quite a climb to the top. The tower soars above the surrounding pines, affording a sweeping panorama view across a restored landscape of wet prairies edged by pine flatwoods. The prairie at its base is the type where flocks of sandhill cranes may gather. Consider the tower a twist on a bird blind. Just north of it is the intersection with the Ocean to Lake Hiking Trail. A sign points that out next to a pond on the right. Turn left instead and follow orange blazes southwest.

The trail leads across the prairie that the observation tower overlooks. It was wet when we hiked it, but the footpath was well worn and discernible. On the far side of the prairie is a place we dubbed the Palm Oasis years ago. There is now a bench facing the prairie and tower. The Ocean to Lake Hiking Trail is normally a wet walk in any season. Expect flowing or standing water in the footpath for the next mile and a half, since wetlands adjoining the trail spill into it as they fill up.

At a post with a pole sticking out of it so it can be found when the surrounding grasses grow above it, turn left and head toward the pines. A dense thicket of dog fennel grows beneath them as well as scattered grasses. As sea myrtle leans in, bursting into butterfly-attracting mounds of white blooms in late fall, the footpath gets wet again. It may be a wade where the trail edges a large marsh. West of the marsh, the landscape opens into a prairie dotted with pines. But the open feel doesn't last long. Amber-colored chalky bluestem lines the trail, the tall grasses creating a tunnel effect.

Cross a boardwalk over a flowing stream between two large wet prairies at 2.6 miles. On the far side is a bench overlooking a panorama of the easternmost prairie. Curving past this sun-drenched bench, find a second one in the shade of a coco plum. This bench overlooks the larger western prairie rimmed by a canal and edged by a pond dense with alligator flag (*Thalia geniculata*).

Circle the pond into the pine flatwoods along the large prairie, where coco plum and saw palmetto edge the footpath. Enjoy one last panorama of the prairie before you enter the pines again. Tall grasses and dog fennel lean into the trail corridor as the pine flatwoods become denser. Brush past clumps of wax myrtle and sea myrtle along this often-damp footpath.

Patches of prairie create pleasant grassy open spaces beneath the pines. Between the trees is the white line of a road up ahead. Cross a culvert over a canal to reach it at 3.2 miles. This is the Wah-too-lah ("sandhill crane") Hiking Trail. Turn left to follow it. It runs in a very straight line, so you can see a long ways down it. After a stretch, the landscape opens up to the north across the canal, providing nice views. We saw herons and alligators in the canal and heard turtles splash into the water as we approached. Walking between the pines, reach a junction at 4 miles where a culvert crosses the canal for a maintenance road to the north. This is where the Loxahatchee Loop rejoins the hike route.

Keep heading east past the junction. After a short distance, reach a turnoff on the left. Take this side trail to the fishing pier. Near it are a bench and picnic table in the shade and the preserve's only restroom. The pier provides a pretty view across the lake.

Rejoin the main trail, passing a bench along the lake's edge. The red-blazed Loxahatchee Loop continues in a straight line due east from the end of the lake. Once it's past the lake, the primary point of interest is the parallel canal. Watch for alligators sunning along the far shore.

Pines line the final stretch, occasionally hiding the canal. When you emerge into the open after 4.6 miles, the junction with the paved trail marks the end of this hiking loop. Turn right to exit, following the paved path to the parking area to complete this 4.7-mile hike.

Pine-palm flatwoods, Jonathan Dickinson State Park

6. Riverbend Park to Kitching Creek Trailhead

10 MILES | JUPITER

A deep dive into the Loxahatchee River basin, this segment of the Ocean to Lake Hiking Trail has a surprising amount of wild within the orbit of Jupiter.

Overview

A federally designated Wild and Scenic River, the Loxahatchee rises from shallow wetlands fringing the edge of Jupiter, its watershed spanning 260 square miles, much of it urban. The Ocean to Lake Hiking Trail threads its way along the length of the river basin on this section of trail through the public lands that protect the river, crossing all its major tributaries.

Spanning three land management areas—Riverbend Park, Loxahatchee River Natural Area, and Jonathan Dickinson State Park—this hike treats you to the habitat diversity found in the river basin. Merely a trickle inside Riverbend Park, the Loxahatchee River expands dramatically as Cypress Creek and smaller waterways nourish it. These tributaries are fed by expansive grassy waters to the west, part of the Everglades ecosystem severed from what is now Everglades National Park by development along the Atlantic Coast.

Interrupting the middle of this hike, the trail ducks beneath two elevated highways, Florida's Turnpike and Interstate 95. It's a poignant reminder that few natural corridors in Florida remain truly wild.

Trip Planning

See Ocean to Lake Hiking Trail. Pay the entrance fee for Jonathan Dickinson State Park in advance before walking into the park. If camping at Kitching Creek, reserve your site in advance. If you leave a vehicle inside the state park, the walk-in fee is covered.

This section is a mix of deep shade and sun. Use insect repellent and sun protection. Poison ivy is prevalent in shaded areas. Expect wet feet, as one of the highlights of this hike is wading Hobe Groves Canal into Jonathan Dickinson State Park. Hiking sticks are helpful for balance.

Don't tackle this hike if the floodplain is under water. Check water.weather.gov station LXRF1 before hiking. Both the Cypress Creek and Hobe Groves Canal crossings are dangerous when their water levels are high. Never enter flowing water.

Land Managers

South Florida Water Mgt District
3301 Gun Club Rd, West Palm Beach 33406
561-686-8800
sfwmd.gov

Palm Beach County Parks and Recreation
9060 Indiantown Rd, Jupiter 33478
561-966-6617
discover.pbcgov.org

Jonathan Dickinson State Park
16450 SE Federal Hwy, Hobe Sound 33455
772-546-2771
floridastateparks.org

Directions

Jonathan Dickinson State Park is along US 1 between Hobe Sound and Tequesta, 4 miles north of Jupiter Inlet. Take the main park road to the right at the T after the ranger station. It's 3.7

miles to the Kitching Creek picnic area. Park here for the Kitching Creek trailhead [26.992649, -80.146751]. Inform park rangers if you plan to leave your vehicle overnight.

For the starting point of Riverbend Park [26.934423, -80.175095], drive south on US 1 to Indiantown Rd (SR 706) in Jupiter. Follow it west. After passing I-95 and Florida's Turnpike, continue west 1.5 miles to the entrance to Riverbend Park on the left. Cars cannot be left at Riverbend Park overnight.

Options

This linear hike provides the option of an overnight stay at Kitching Creek campsite in Jonathan Dickinson State Park. To do so, you'd need to be dropped off at Riverbend Park to start, since you can only leave a car overnight at the state park end of the hike. Both trailheads are easy to access and not far from Jupiter, so Uber or Lyft might be an option for a shuttle.

It's a pleasant and usually dry day hike from the Kitching Creek trailhead to Hobes Grove Canal, a 6.4-mile round trip. The Ocean to Lake Hiking Trail extends across the park to the east as well, connecting to the 7.4-mile White Loop and 4.8-mile East Loop.

For a round trip on the Ocean to Lake Hiking Trail from Riverbend Park, head east into the Loxahatchee River basin. Turn around at BZs Creek for 4.6 miles, Hells Ditch for 7.4 miles, Cypress Creek for 9.2 miles, or Hobes Grove Canal for a 11.2-mile round trip.

Another way to see the floodplain is a 3-mile round trip on the Italian Farms Trail just east of Indiantown Road, a 4.2-mile round trip from the Riverbend trailhead. Inside Riverbend Park, nearly 10 miles of loop trails interconnect with the Ocean to Lake Hiking Trail.

Hike

Established to protect the remaining marshes at the headwaters of the Loxahatchee River, Riverbend Park encompasses nearly 700 acres re-engineered into wetlands, streams, and ponds from former orange groves atop a significant Second Seminole War battlefield. Winding through the park are broad trails of compacted limestone a few inches above the natural flow of the wetlands.

Start at the kiosk at the end of the parking area in front of the Hal Valche Portico. Turn left on River Bend Trail and left onto East Slough Trail, which meets the Ocean to Lake Hiking Trail at a signposted junction at 0.4 miles. Turn left. An underpass leads beneath Indiantown Rd. Italian Farms Trail starts at a sign for Loxahatchee River-Cypress Creek Management Area. Following orange blazes, bear left before the sign, over a stile and into a ribbon of forest. Cross two forest roads before emerging at a field. Keep left to stay on the worn track closest to the highway.

After a mile, exit a gate to cross the Loxahatchee River on the pedestrian part of the highway bridge. A strip mall and gas station sit on the opposite side of the highway. Leaving Indiantown Road, the trail zigzags between the cabbage palms of a tropical hammock. Pass a little cabin built in 1893 by George Lainhart, one of the earliest settlers. Follow a farm fence to reach dense oak hammocks on the bluff above the Loxahatchee River.

The footpath descends into cypress

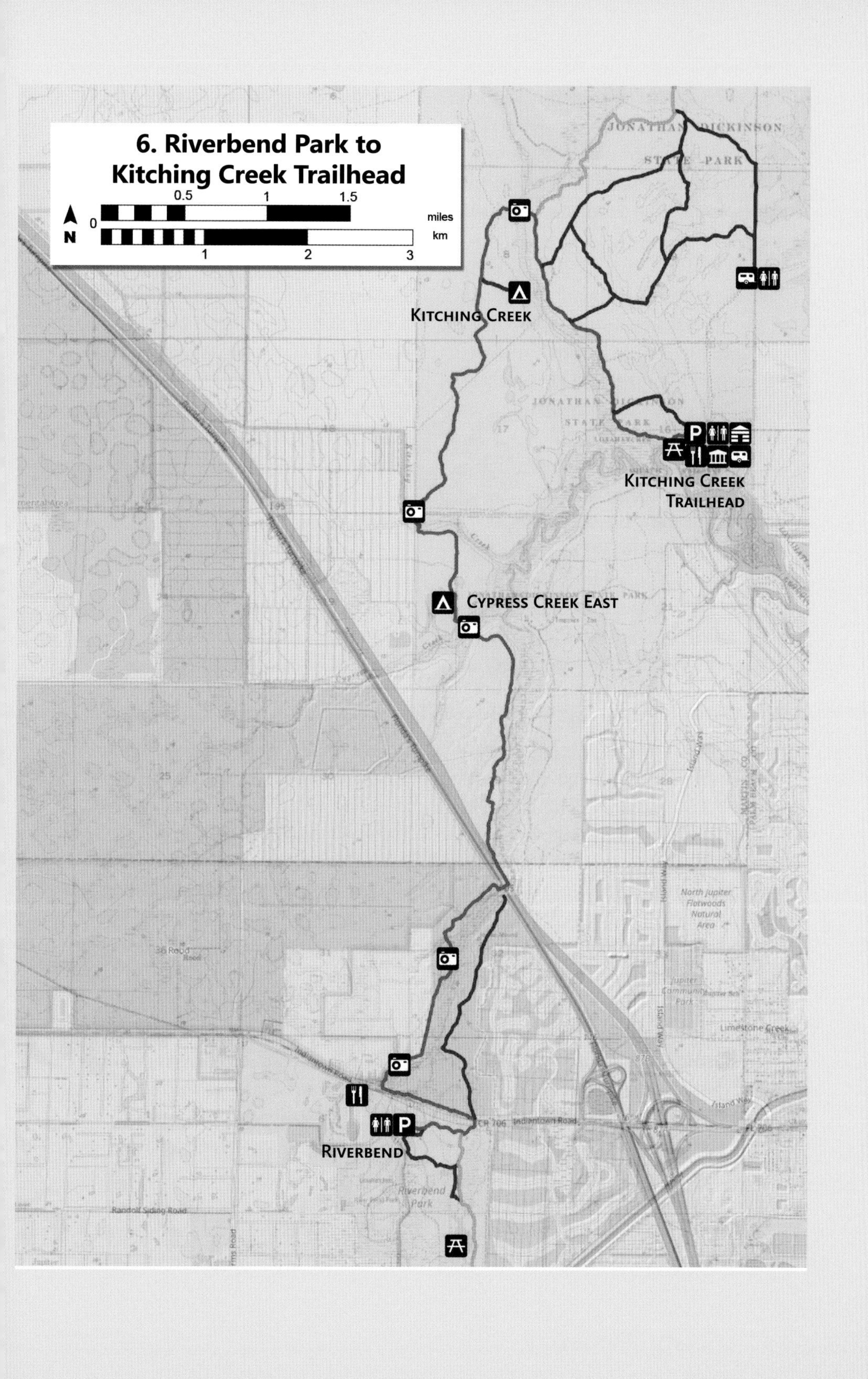
6. Riverbend Park to Kitching Creek Trailhead
0
0.5
1
1.5
miles
km
1
2
3
N
Kitching Creek
Kitching Creek Trailhead
Cypress Creek East
Riverbend
Jonathan Dickinson State Park
North Jupiter Flatwoods Natural Area
Jupiter Community Park
Limestone Creek
Island Way
Indiantown Road
CR 706
Riverbend Park
Randolf Siding Road
36 Road

bottomland in the river floodplain at 2 miles and may be wet or mucky for the next mile and a half. Crossing BZs Creek, ascend into scrubby flatwoods with a dense understory of saw palmetto and gallberry. Dip through a creek before rising into a scrub forest with diminutive trees. Cypress trees mark the edge of the river floodplain. At a fence at 2.8 miles, blazes lead to a sign guiding you under twin highway underpasses, a passage shared with the Loxahatchee River. At a sharp left, ascend into scrubby flatwoods while following a wall along Interstate 95. Leaving the highway's edge, the footpath enters stark, shadeless scrubby flatwoods.

Dropping into Hells Ditch at 3.7 miles, the trail climbs into scrub, leaving Interstate 95 for tree line. At a three-way intersection, continue straight ahead. Approaching Cypress Creek, one of the larger tributaries of the Loxahatchee River, a line of cabbage palms offers the first real shade since Hells Creek. At 4.6 miles, Cypress Creek is a beautiful spot, its long bridge a place to relax in the sun. East of the creek, meander through a tropical hammock on boardwalks before emerging into higher, drier pine flatwoods. The Cypress Creek East campsite is along a lake at the end of a blue blaze to the west. Following an old forest road, continue through the pines to the edge of former Hobe Groves.

Turning away from the citrus grove, follow the footpath through a steep dip to cross Moonshine Creek. At the top of the next bluff, look down on Hobe Groves Canal at 5.7 miles. The sides are steep and the water may be deep. For a hike from Riverbend Park, this is a turnaround point. Wading Hobes Grove Canal takes effort if the water is higher than shin deep. Most hikers remove their shoes and socks. The bottom has been bolstered with rocks and mats. It's quite a scramble up the other side before you can stop to put socks and shoes back on, so expect sand-coated feet.

East of the canal, enter Jonathan Dickinson State Park at a kiosk. This corner of the 10,500-acre park is primarily pine flatwoods. In 1942, this was Camp Murphy, a top secret army base for training soldiers how to use radar to track and target planes overhead. Little remains in this part of the woods to offer clues to the former base, but historic buildings and foundations are close to the park entrance off US 1.

At 7.3 miles, reach the white-blazed side trail to Kitching Creek campsite, a favorite destination for backpackers. Nicely situated under the pines, it offers many possible places to pitch a tent. Picnic tables, a fire ring with benches, a vault toilet, and a pitcher pump for water round out the facilities. Past the campsite turnoff, wind through pine flatwoods with a gentle haze on the forest floor from its grassy understory.

Dropping into a very different habitat along the floodplain of Kitching Creek, you're swallowed up by verdant vegetation. Climbing into pine flatwoods after crossing the bridge over the creek, meet a junction with a forest road and a set of benches at 8 miles. Turn right, leaving the orange blazes of the Florida Trail for a red-blazed forest road following Kitching Creek downstream. This is part of Eagles View Trail, open to equestrians and cyclists. Passing the Yellow Trail coming in from the left, continue another half mile to where the red blazes

Backpacking Loxahatchee River Natural Area

turn left. Continue straight, edging the floodplain. Cabbage palm flatwoods sweep into the distance.

By 9.4 miles, reach the upper tip of the Kitching Creek Nature Trail. An observation deck provides a view of the broadened waterway, a sluggish brackish creek. Continue along the Kitching Creek Nature Trail, staying close to the floodplain. Cross a small bridge over Wilson Creek. After 10 miles, your hike ends at the picnic grove and trailhead for the Kitching Creek Nature Trail, with nearby restrooms and a camp store by the Loxahatchee River.

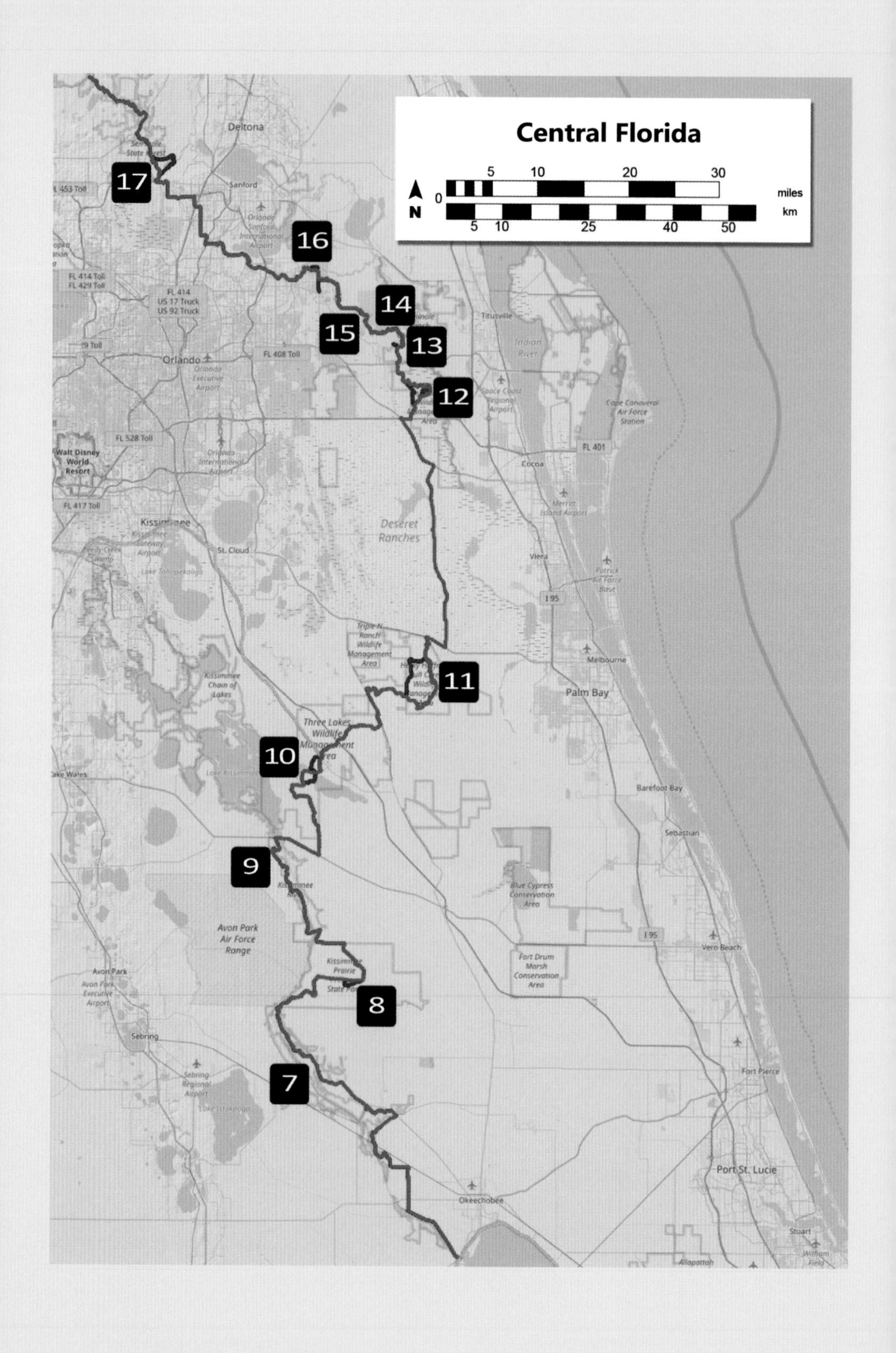

Central Florida
miles
km
N
17
16
15
14
13
12
11
10
9
8
7
Deltona
Sanford
Orlando
Titusville
Cocoa
Kissimmee
St. Cloud
Deseret Ranches
Viera
Melbourne
Palm Bay
Barefoot Bay
Sebastian
Vero Beach
Fort Pierce
Port St. Lucie
Stuart
Okeechobee
Sebring
Avon Park
Avon Park Air Force Range
Three Lakes Wildlife Management Area
Kissimmee Chain of Lakes
Walt Disney World Resort
Cape Canaveral Air Force Station
Blue Cypress Conservation Area
Fort Drum Marsh Conservation Area

Central Florida

Following the floodplains of the Kissimmee and St. Johns Rivers, the Florida Trail provides extreme contrasts between prairies under starry skies and the city lights of the Orlando metro.

Little Big Econ State Forest

BASE CAMPS

Kenansville

A crossroads that once served Henry Flagler's railroad, this speck of a village in the ranchland of Osceola County is named for the railroad magnate's in-laws.

STAY

Lake Marian Paradise 407-436-1464, 901 Arnold Rd.

Middleton's Too (Overstreet Landing) 407-436-1966, 4500 Joe Overstreet Rd.

EAT

Griffis Cafe 407-436-0110, 955 S Kenansville Rd.

Kenansville Country Store 407-436-1995, 50 S Kenansville Rd.

SEE AND DO

Wild Florida Airboats & Gator Park 407-957-3135, 3301 Lake Cypress Rd.

Christmas and Titusville

The Florida Trail crosses SR 50 in a rural community dating back to the Second Seminole War around a fort built Christmas 1837. On the opposite side of the vast St. Johns River floodplain is Titusville, home to Kennedy Space Center.

STAY

Christmas RV Park 407-568-5207, 25525 E Colonial Dr. No tents.

Courtyard by Marriott Titusville KSC 321-966-9200, 6245 Riverfront Center Blvd.

TownePlace Suites 321-603-0811, 4815 Helen Hauser Blvd, Titusville.

EAT

Durangos Steakhouse 321-264-2499, 4825 Helen Hauser Blvd.

El Leoncito 321-267-1159, 4280 S Washington Ave, Titusville.

Indian Sizzler 321-603-2016, 3520 S Washington Ave, Titusville.

Third Culture Kitchen 321-225-4103, 1000 Cheney Hwy.

SEE AND DO

Airboat Rides at Midway 407-568-6790, 28501 E Colonial Dr.

American Space Museum 321-264-0434, 308 Pine St, Titusville.

Canaveral National Seashore 386-428-3384, end of SR 402 [28.644433, -80.684619].

Fort Christmas Historical Park 407-254-9312, 1300 N Fort Christmas Rd, Christmas.

Jungle Adventures 407-568-2885, 26205 E Colonial Dr., Christmas.

Kennedy Space Center 1-855-433-4210, Space Commerce Way, Merritt Island.

Merritt Island National Wildlife Refuge 321-861-0669, 1987 Scrub Jay Way, Titusville.

Sanford

Along the St. Johns River at what was the upper extent of steamboat travel when it was incorporated as a planned city in 1877, Sanford has a historic downtown and a beautiful riverfront with a riverwalk.

STAY

Park Place Inn & Cottages 407-549-9131, 1301 S Park Ave.

SpringHill Suites by Marriott 407-995-1000, 201 N Towne Rd.

EAT

Colonial Room Restaurant 407-323-2999, 105 E 1st St.

Hollerbach's Willow Tree Cafe 407-321-2204, 205 E 1st St.

Zorbas Greek Food 407-915-6082, 115 E 1st St.

SEE AND DO

Gallery on First 407-323-2774, 211 E 1st St.

Central Florida Zoo & Gardens 407-323-4450, 3755 W Seminole Blvd.

Maya Books & Music 407-321-6504, 204 E 1st St.

Sanford Museum 407-688-5198, 520 E 1st St.

St. Johns Rivership 321-441-3030, 433 N Palmetto Ave.

DeLand

A historic city with a vibrant walkable downtown, DeLand is the closest place to stay to where the Florida Trail crosses Seminole State Forest to the Ocala National Forest.

STAY

Artisan Downtown 386-873-4675, 215 S Woodland Blvd.

Courtyard by Marriott Downtown 386-943-9500, 308 N Woodland Blvd.

St. John's Marina & Resort 386-736-6601, 2997 SR 44 W.

The DeLand Hotel 386-624-6710, 442 E New York Ave.

Highland Park Fish Camp 386-734-2334, 2640 W Highland Park Rd.

EAT

BakeChop 386-873-6524, 110 Artisan Alley.

Brian's Bar-B-Que 386-736-8851, 795 N Spring Garden Ave.

St. John's River Grille 386-855-2427, 2999 SR 44 W.

SEE AND DO

Blue Springs State Park 386-775-3663, 2100 W French Ave.

Gillespie Museum of Minerals 386-822-7330, 234 E Michigan Ave.

Hontoon Island State Park 386-736-5309, 2309 River Ridge Rd.

Museum of Art-DeLand 386-734-4371, 600 N Woodland Blvd.

De Leon Springs State Park 386-985-4212, 601 Ponce De Leon Blvd.

Palm hammock along the Kissimmee River

7. Micco Bluff

11.6 MILES | KISSIMMEE PUBLIC USE AREA, BASINGER

Melding picturesque panoramas of the vast floodplain of the Kissimmee River with walks in the woods along the river's historic shoreline, this linear hike is a destination for scenic beauty.

Overview

In 2013, the long-standing route of the Florida Trail shifted from the west side of the Kissimmee River to the east. Moving nearly 50 miles of footpath was a major undertaking for local FTA volunteers, but a necessary one. In the 1960s, the Army Corps of Engineers turned the 103-mile Kissimmee River into an arrow-straight 56-mile canal, the C-38. Removing the river's sinuous curves destroyed the ecosystems along it and damaged Lake Okeechobee.

In 1999, the Corps of Engineers began to restore the natural flow of the river. Existing pieces of the Florida Trail permanently flooded. The state government stepped in by buying former ranchlands to protect the changing floodplain. The new eastern shore route was envisioned by longtime section leader Jack Hailman. Along with his wife, Liz, and other tireless volunteers, he kept moving the trail. Replacing a roadwalk with river views, the Micco Bluff Trail honors Jack's vision with its blend of immersion in shady hammocks mixed with views of wide-open spaces.

Trip Planning

Hiking sticks help to steady yourself in water and mud along this section. Although dogs are permitted, don't take them along unless you're only planning a round trip. Past the three-mile mark, it'll be tough going for them and risky along the floodplain.

Because of its lock and dam system, the Kissimmee River can rise quickly. Check river levels before hiking, either on the South Florida Water Management District website or by phone. If you encounter flowing water on the trail, turn around.

Kissimmee Public Use Area (PUA) is a popular destination for hunters during fall deer season and spring turkey season. Research hunting seasons in advance. If you hike during hunting season, wear bright orange.

Backpackers can utilize either of two campsites (Micco Landing or Oak Creek) by obtaining a free permit from South Florida Water Management District online. The campsites are nearly at each end of this section, so they aren't a help in planning an overnight trip unless you hike in and out from one end or the other for an overnight stay. Each has picnic tables and a fire ring but no water source. Water is available from the river and ditches, but be wary of alligators frequently seen near access points.

Land Manager

South Florida Water Management District
3301 Gun Club Rd, West Palm Beach 33406
561-686-8800
sfwmd.gov

Directions

The end point at Oak Creek trailhead [27.447531, -81.128059] is along Micco Bluff Rd. Drive north from Okeechobee along US 98 to the small town of Basinger, just past Chandler Slough. At the

Alton B. Chandler Community Center, turn right on Micco Bluff Rd. It makes a quick left. Follow it through farms and ranches for 7.6 miles to the trailhead on the left. Micco Landing trailhead [27.3832, -81.0417] is along US 98 another half mile past the community center (the water source for Micco Landing campsite) at a prominent entrance on the right.

Options

This is a linear hike with no intermediate access. If your time or ability to cover this distance is limited, take a round trip from Micco Landing trailhead. The southernmost three miles are the most scenic part of the hike, with a ranch access road your turnaround point for a 6-mile hike. To hike to Micco Bluff itself, drive to the Oak Creek South campsite [27.4440, -81.1428] to skip walking along the entrance road. It's a 1.8-mile round trip from the campsite to the bluff. A hike in and out to Chandler Ranch Rd is an 8-mile round trip from Oak Creek South.

Across US 98 from the Micco Landing trailhead, Chandler Slough West extends 3.5 miles along another scenic piece of the river basin. It's a pleasant 7-mile round trip hike through a string of oak hammocks and a cypress strand.

Hike

Adjacent to the trailhead kiosk, a pedestrian gate provides access to the footpath. Curving around the edge of a prairie, it enters an oak hammock with large live oaks. Blue blazes lead to Micco Landing campsite, which has a picnic table and fire ring. The orange-blazed Florida Trail veers toward the edge of the Kissimmee River floodplain within the first quarter mile. Atop a low levee, the next quarter mile offers a scenic panorama of the river basin. Reach a trail junction of white and orange blazes. The white-blazed high-water route stays atop the levee straight ahead for another 0.7 miles for better views of the river and better birding.

The main route, which can be very wet and muddy at times, leaves the levee to the right on the orange blazes, edging a marsh before curving into the shade of an oak hammock dense with cabbage palms. After a sharp left, burrow into a palm hammock, a dense wonderland of green in a sea of face-level fronds.

After a mile, cross a two-track road on a levee. Shaded by an oak hammock, skirt a circular prairie to its east. Soon after the scenic white-blazed high-water route rejoins the trail at 1.4 miles, citrus dangles from wild orange and grapefruit trees naturalized in the hammock. The footpath ascends a narrow tramway and follows it for nearly a quarter mile. A divot in this dike lets water flow from the swamps on one side to the other. Emerging into a clearing, you can see water shimmering in a grassy open space: Heart Pond, its shape obvious from a satellite view. Sweeping around the oak hammock along its shoreline, reach a small pond and wetland at 2.1 miles. Wild irises grow in profusion in the often-damp ground.

Reaching the shade of the oaks on the other side of this clearing, orange blazes tack between open prairie and oak hammocks. Cross another small wetland with wild iris emerging from the footpath. A ranch fence is visible to the east, and then the rancher's home.

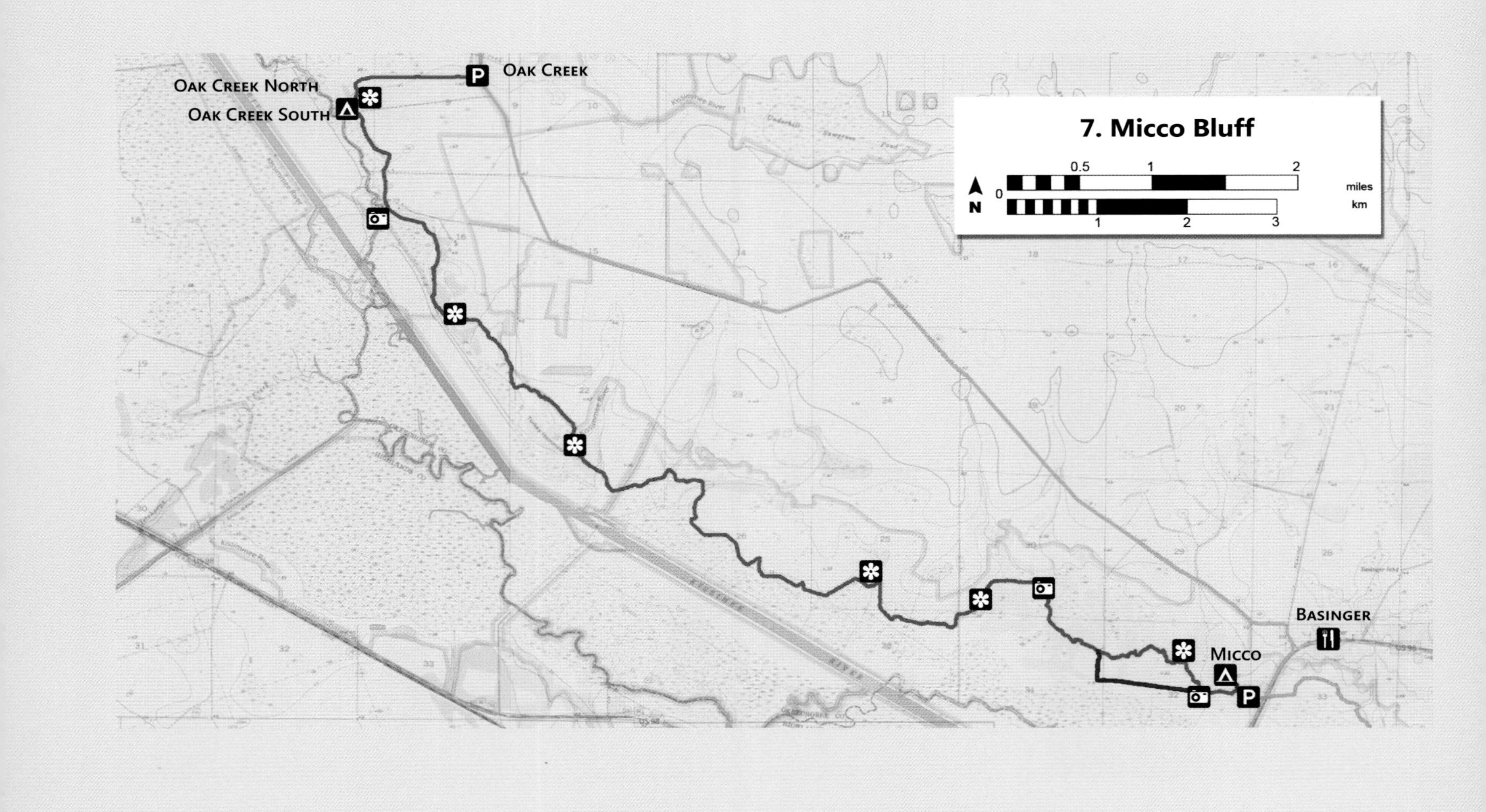
7. Micco Bluff
0
0.5
1
2
miles
km
1
2
3
N
Oak Creek
Oak Creek North
Oak Creek South
Basinger
Micco

Levee through Kissimmee River marshes

Turn to enter a very lush live oak hammock. Resurrection ferns and bromeliads swaddle thick branches overhead. A dense stand of towering cabbage palms yields to ancient live oaks. At 3 miles, cross a two-track road in the hammock, a good turnaround point for a day hike from Micco Landing trailhead.

Beyond this point, you learn about the balance between public land and private land along the Kissimmee River. Since the 1840s, ranchers have had enormous spreads along the river basin. It was one of the earliest places that settlers came to after Florida was declared a US Territory. Free-range grazing with cowboys rounding up herds was a way of life. Fencing off land didn't come until much later.

The state of Florida lays claim to what are called submerged lands. The state will often buy additional lands adjoining the submerged lands to help protect the watersheds. To do so, they must find willing sellers. As you will experience over the next seven miles of trail, the footpath is often squeezed against ranch fences because the public land *is* the river basin. While being along the floodplain makes this a scenic hike, there are long stretches along fence lines. Boardwalks mitigate some muddy spots, but floodplain grasses don't make for easy walking.

Follow blazes out of the oak hammock along a fence. Dog fennel rises from the floodplain near a palm hammock at 3.4 miles. Beyond it, the trail turns a corner along a fence line, revealing the open water of the Kissimmee River. Views continue until the next oak hammock. Rejoin the fence at a small paddock. The trail passes a line of large live oaks behind the fence. Expect to see cattle, especially Brahma bulls, in the near pasture. The river is still visible from the higher points and turns along the fence. There may be mucky spots. Don't be surprised to see thousands of birds in the shallows of the floodplain.

Passing a ranch gate at 5.2 miles, follow the fence into an oak hammock. It's the first shade in more than a mile. Turning left, continue under the live oaks before leaving the fence to follow a grassy two-track between the cabbage palms. Skirt around or slosh through a slough at 5.8 miles, the dark water reflecting the surrounding palm fronds. Clumps of saw palmetto grow beneath the mature live oaks. Work your way around the next slough to a lush palm hammock on the other side. Return to an open area lined with mounds of blackberry bushes trailside.

Walk through an oak hammock and emerge at a soft sand road at 6.5 miles. Now a private road, Chandler Ranch Rd once provided access to a lock that was removed along the river. The oak hammock continues for a little ways before the trail turns to mud along the edge of a slough. A long green tunnel stretches to the next oak hammock, which has many mature trees and a nicely knit canopy of intertwined branches overhead. Cabbage palms crowd a portion of the understory, soon succeeded by saw palmetto. Draperies of vines hang low. Meeting a fence again, follow the edge of a scrub habitat before reaching a marshy slough at 7.3 miles caused by drainage off the ranch. Enjoy beautiful views of the floodplain.

In the shade of the next hammock, turn away from the fence into an area dense with ferns along the edge of a swamp. Cabbage palms tower overhead. Reaching drier ground, the footpath snakes its way between the oaks and palms. A small pond sits below a swale before the next oak hammock, which has some of the biggest trees along this hike. Thistles and blackberries adjoin the trail, which curves away from the fence into the cabbage palms. Cross another marshy area before returning to the fence. At 8.3 miles, a plank bridges a clear waterway in an oak hammock. Return to the fence, passing through a tunnel of vegetation before the oaks take over.

Lone palm trees rising from a marsh provide a clue that something is about to change. The trail gains a little elevation before crossing the marsh on a boardwalk. Paralleling the fence, reach Micco Bluff, the destination that this section is named for. At 9.6 miles, it is a true bluff with a bench, a nice overlook where the Kissimmee River swirls around a bend. Alligators often sun on the near and far shores. Views of the river continue as you walk north, the limbs of large live oaks stretching over the trail, providing shade.

At a sharp turn past a fence topped with metal sheeting, star rush blooms in the footpath. The "Safety Zone" sign indicates the edge of Oak Creek South campsite. Of the two campsites at Oak Creek, this one at 10.5 miles is best for backpackers since it is along the trail. Large live oaks shade a pair of picnic tables. River access is a hundred yards from the campsite. Alligators sometimes make it impossible to get to the water.

Campers are permitted to drive to the campsites of Oak Creek, so you may encounter vehicles along this last blazed stretch of the Micco Bluff section. Follow the forest road as it winds between big oak trees in a park-like setting. At the next intersection of roads, signs point out Oak Creek North campsite as well as the one you just walked through. Follow the orange blazes up the road along the ranch fence. This final stretch is in full sun for three-quarters of a mile, as is the Oak Creek trailhead. Arrive there after 11.6 miles.

Palmetto prairie

8. Kissimmee Prairie Loop

5.5 MILES | KISSIMMEE PRAIRIE PRESERVE STATE PARK, OKEECHOBEE

On a day hike into one of our state's largest prairies, sample Florida's own "big sky" at the state's first International Dark Sky Park, with horizon-to-horizon views.

Overview

Home to some of Florida's most wide-open spaces, Kissimmee Prairie Preserve State Park is well off the beaten path. Long known as an astronomer's destination, it has a special campground for those who want to train telescopes to the skies. Volunteers run evening programs explaining the stars above. Sunrises and sunsets stretch out over time and space.

The preserve's primary purpose is to protect endangered species, most notably the Florida grasshopper sparrow, found only in dry prairie ecosystems along the Kissimmee River. They've also hosted a breeding colony of whooping cranes. Along with more common species, birders may see white-tailed kites and find burrowing owls in open spots in the dry prairie.

Reclaimed from former cattle ranches in the Kissimmee River floodplain, the preserve has two distinct faces: wet and dry. Uplands are dominated by palmetto prairie, horizon to horizon for miles. Occasional oak and palm hammocks break up this extensive flatness. Before the Kissimmee River was ditched by the Army Corps of Engineers, it meandered across broad wetlands. Sloughs and marshes within the park are part of the river floodplain.

The trail network is made up of former ranch roads cutting across vast open landscapes. As a side trail off the primary orange-blazed Florida Trail near the park office and campgrounds, the Prairie Loop offers a more intimate look at this vast preserve's habitat diversity.

Trip Planning

Entrance and camping fees apply. Leashed dogs are permitted, but park staff tell us enormous alligators live in the ditches along Military Trail. Most of the trail is in the open, dangerous in a thunderstorm. Check the weather forecast before you hike.

For a night of stargazing, backpack to the primitive Prairie Loop Camp, set in a gorgeous oak hammock. Reserve a site in advance: P3 offers the best view of the prairie. Use a red-light headlamp to let your eyes focus on the stars. This is an excellent destination for beginning backpackers and families with small children.

Land Manager

Kissimmee Prairie Preserve State Park
33104 NW 192nd Ave, Okeechobee 34972
863-462-5360
floridastateparks.org

Directions

From Florida's Turnpike at Yeehaw Junction, follow SR 60 west briefly. Turn south on US 441 at the traffic light and drive 17.7 miles to NW 240th St. The first sign for the park points right. Drive 13.2 miles through farms and ranches

Sunset on Kissimmee Prairie

before a sharp right on NW 192nd Ave. After a few miles, this road enters the park gate. Continue 5 miles on unpaved roads in a gorgeous prairie setting to reach the trailhead [27.584209, -81.045357] in front of the park office. From Okeechobee or Sebring, take US 98 to Basinger and follow NW 176 Ave north; follow the signs.

Options

The Florida Trail crosses the entire preserve. From the park office, make a round trip in either direction or use cross trails to make longer loops. In both directions, expansive landscapes look the same for miles. Military Trail is relatively flat and dry. Hiking north requires wading unless the sloughs have dried up. The interpretive mile-long Kilpatrick Hammock Trail loops the shady oak hammock behind the park office. Trails are multiuse, open to equestrians and cyclists. On weekends from late fall to early spring, the park offers guided tours on swamp buggies.

Hike

In front of the rocking chairs at the park office, a large sculpture commemorates the final sighting of flocks of Carolina parakeets across this prairie before they were driven to extinction by hunters in 1918. Follow the orange blazes west from here along Military Trail, a dirt road that stretches to the horizon, passing both the turnoff to the Florida Trail headed north through the astronomer's camping area and along the edge of the equestrian campground shaded by the rim of Kilpatrick Hammock. Slip through a gap in the fence to avoid the

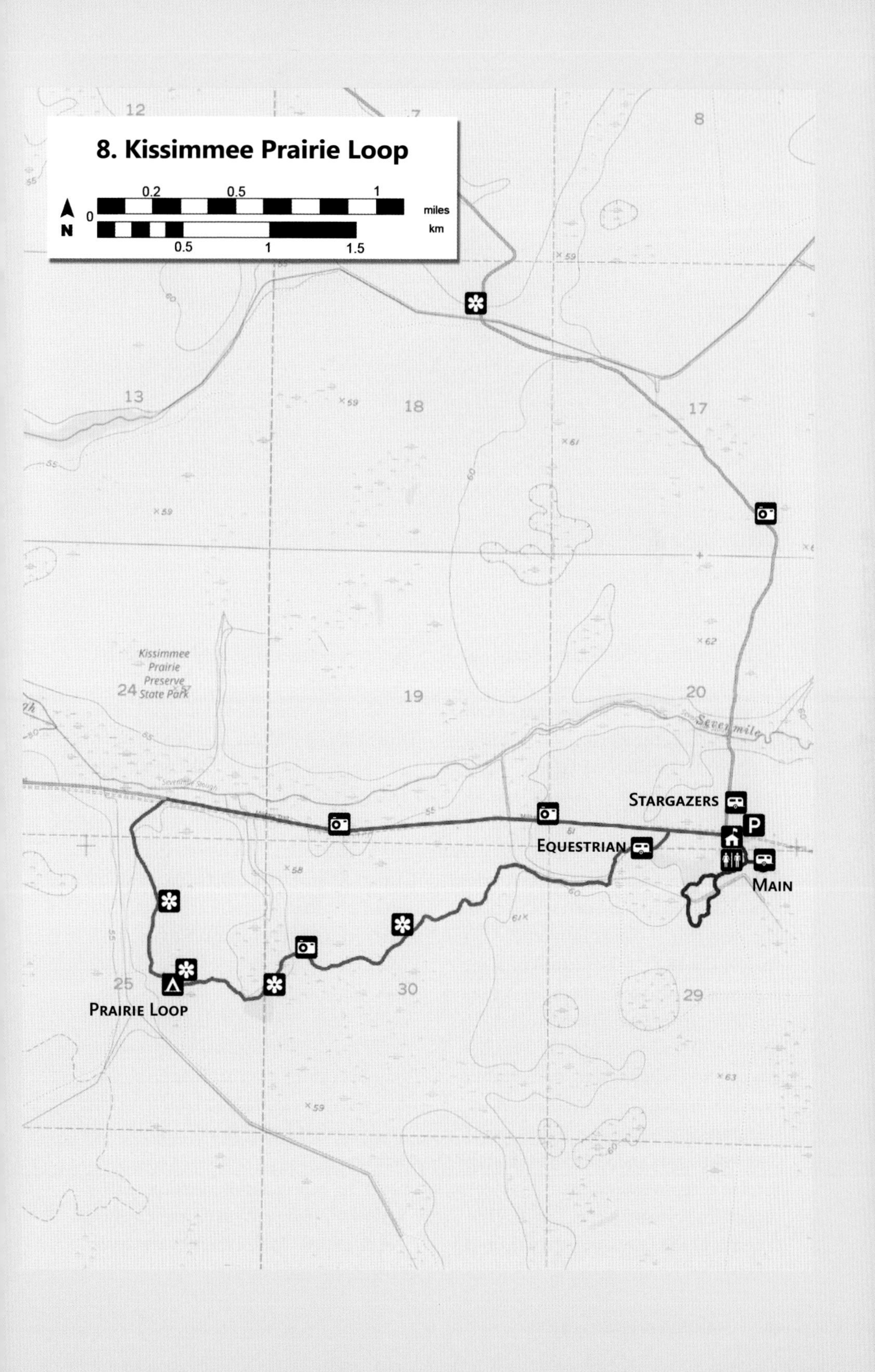
8. Kissimmee Prairie Loop
0.2
0.5
1
0
miles
N
km
0.5
1
1.5
Kissimmee
Prairie
Preserve
State Park
Stargazers
Equestrian
Main
Prairie Loop

Following an old ranch road

chain-blocking vehicles from driving down Military Trail. The flat palmetto prairie goes on to a distant line of cabbage palms to the north. The tree line in this habitat signals a waterway.

Concentric rings of grasses surround a circular marsh near the line of palms at 0.7 miles. Cross a culvert over a slough. The road becomes grassy underfoot. Walk past a lone oak with a blaze. The next line of palms is up ahead. Constructed in 1842, this portion of Military Trail was indeed a footpath for soldiers marching from Fort Drum to Fort Kissimmee. Telltale wax myrtle, wetlands grasses, and alligator flag point out the marshes that edge the trail, as well as warning signs about the alligators. A lone palm casts shade before the alligator flag creeps close to the trail. Meet a ragged line of palms at 1.2 miles. The textures of the landscape vary from jagged saw palmetto to a willow marsh with cattails.

Military Trail heads for a gap in the next tree line. Cross another set of culverts after a half mile, passing an orange blaze on a cabbage palm. While it seems closer, reach the turnoff onto the Prairie Loop at 2 miles, just before the tree line. Turn left and follow blue blazes along another broad, open ranch road, this one rising gently toward a dry prairie. Wind along the prairie's edge in a pretty oak hammock, a sliver of forest with a willow marsh along it. Leaving the oaks, walk amid prairie grasses with cabbage palms dotting an otherwise level plain. The footpath is grassy, making for easy walking as it leads toward another oak hammock.

At 2.7 miles, a trail junction with a yellow-tipped post meets the Grasshopper Sparrow Trail, a lengthy traverse southwest toward Long Hammock and the Cowboy Crossing campsite along the Florida Trail. Stay with the blue blazes to the left to enter the oak hammock. Grandfather live oaks shelter the campsites of Prairie Loop Camp. P1, with a picnic table and fire ring, looks out to the northeast. P2 is deeply shaded, orchids and bromeliads creating a textured ceiling above a broad grassy area with a covered picnic pavilion. It has a lot of space to pitch tents and looks like it is used by groups. P3 is in a niche looking over the prairie.

Meet a trail junction just beyond the edge of the oak hammock at 2.9 miles and turn left. Follow blue blazes along a narrow path toward open prairie, the landscape swiftly engulfing the trail as it tacks between clusters of trees. Reach a palm hammock making a sweeping arc along an extensive wetland at 3.2 miles. The shade of the cabbage palms provides a vantage point for views across shallows busy with herons and egrets. Ascend a small sandy ridge where St. Peter's Wort blooms in winter. Plunge through a shady hammock into open prairie.

This prairie is a mixture of dry and wet grasslands with wax myrtles, reaching a vast plain of saw palmetto at 3.5 miles. Enjoy panoramic views for a quarter mile. Enter a stretch of wetlands to cross a mild, sometimes mucky swale in the otherwise flat prairie, rising into the saw palmetto again. By 4.2 miles, enter a hammock of younger oaks and cabbage palms. Winding through a narrow shaded space adjoining a wetland, you're on high ground, tacking toward the next hammock northeast. Marsh ferns and sawgrass grow at the base of the cabbage palms in the next shady spot, signals that the footpath can flood.

After 4.5 miles, climb a small rise and follow what appears to be a dry streambed on the left. With the hydrology of this park tied to rainfall across Central Florida, the stream may fill quickly after a rain. Pickerelweed sports brilliant purple blossoms in spring and summer. Leaving the shade but still paralleling the waterway, emerge into a broad open prairie. A cell tower is in the distance. An oak hammock along the waterway casts shade.

Curving away from the prairie, cross the waterway. Reach a T intersection at 4.9 miles and turn right to stay on the blue blazes. They lead into Kilpatrick Hammock. At a Y intersection, stay left to walk along the edge of the prairie. Emerge onto the Equestrian Campground loop. Follow this campground road past the camp host and vault toilet to Military Trail and turn right. Return to the park office after 5.5 miles.

Long Hammock

9. Long Hammock Loop

2.9 MILES | KICCO WILDLIFE MANAGEMENT AREA

In uplands along the Upper Kissimmee River, this easy loop hike makes use of the Florida Trail and a none-too-busy forest road through Long Hammock, a shady old-growth live oak hammock, along a route used regularly for cattle drives during Florida's pioneer days.

Overview

Long before Florida had roads, trails and waterways were how people moved across the landscape. Flowing from the Kissimmee Chain of Lakes to Lake Okeechobee, the Kissimmee River was the highway of Florida's frontier days, connecting cattlemen in Kissimmee and St. Cloud with a lucrative trade with Cuba via Punta Rassa, a former port in what is now Fort Myers. To transport cattle to the port, cowmen working for the Kissimmee River Cattle Company (KICCO) rode their horses to drive herd to market south along a well-worn track on the west side of the Kissimmee River, passing by homesteads and small riverside villages.

At KICCO WMA, the Florida Trail follows a portion of the actual route the KICCO drovers used. To reach the trailhead you'll drive through River Ranch, a dude ranch entertainment complex themed around Florida's frontier past. It, too, is shaded by Long Hammock. While River Ranch features faux covered wagons and teepees as upscale lodging options, neither were ever used along this route. At nearby Lake Kissimmee State Park, a living history Cow Camp illustrates how the cowmen lived and worked along this trail, setting up camp in canvas tents.

Trip Planning

Leashed pets are permitted. Ruts from feral hogs rooting up the forest floor may make footing difficult. Long Hammock campsite is along the trail and two drive-in primitive campgrounds aren't far from the trail. All are free but require a permit obtained online in advance from South Florida Water Management District. There is no potable water, so haul it in. Determine hunting seasons for KICCO WMA in advance. If you hike during hunting season, wear bright orange. A camp host lives adjacent to the trailhead during hunting seasons.

Land Manager

South Florida Water Management District
3301 Gun Club Rd, West Palm Beach 33406
561-686-8800
sfwmd.gov

Directions

From Florida's Turnpike at Yeehaw Junction, follow SR 60 west and cross US 441 at a traffic light. Continue 19.5 miles west through vast ranches. A mile past the bridge over the Kissimmee River, turn left onto River Ranch Blvd and follow it 3 miles to an entrance gate. Tell the guard you are headed for KICCO trailhead. The signposted turnoff for KICCO is at the corner with the giant teepees. The unpaved KICCO Grade leads 0.8 miles between fenced-off pastures and forests within River Ranch to the trailhead [27.76037, -81.19136] outside the gate.

Options

Since the Florida Trail northbound from the KICCO trailhead is a roadwalk through River Ranch to KICCO North, focus your attention south. To extend this hike, cross KICCO Grade instead of returning along it and continue another 0.6 miles through oak hammocks and scrub to where the trail emerges on the road to cross Ice Cream Slough. Either backtrack on the FT or follow KICCO Grade north to the trailhead.

With a free vehicle permit from South Florida Water Management District, you can drive the length of KICCO Grade and park at spots where the trail crosses, using the road as your return loop. One of the most scenic hikes is 2.7 miles linear between Rattlesnake Hammock trailhead [27.691999, -81.150497] and Tick Island Cypress #7 gate, largely under the shade of oak hammocks. Along that route, the Florida Trail passes through the camping area at the ghost town of KICCO [27.669121, -81.144310], with views of the Kissimmee River from what was once a bustling community at a steamboat stop.

Hike

A walk-through stile provides access to the Florida Trail. Turn left at the FNST sign adjoining KICCO Grade and walk past the camp host down a grassy corridor lined by oaks. In an open area at a four-way junction, continue straight.

Trailside slough

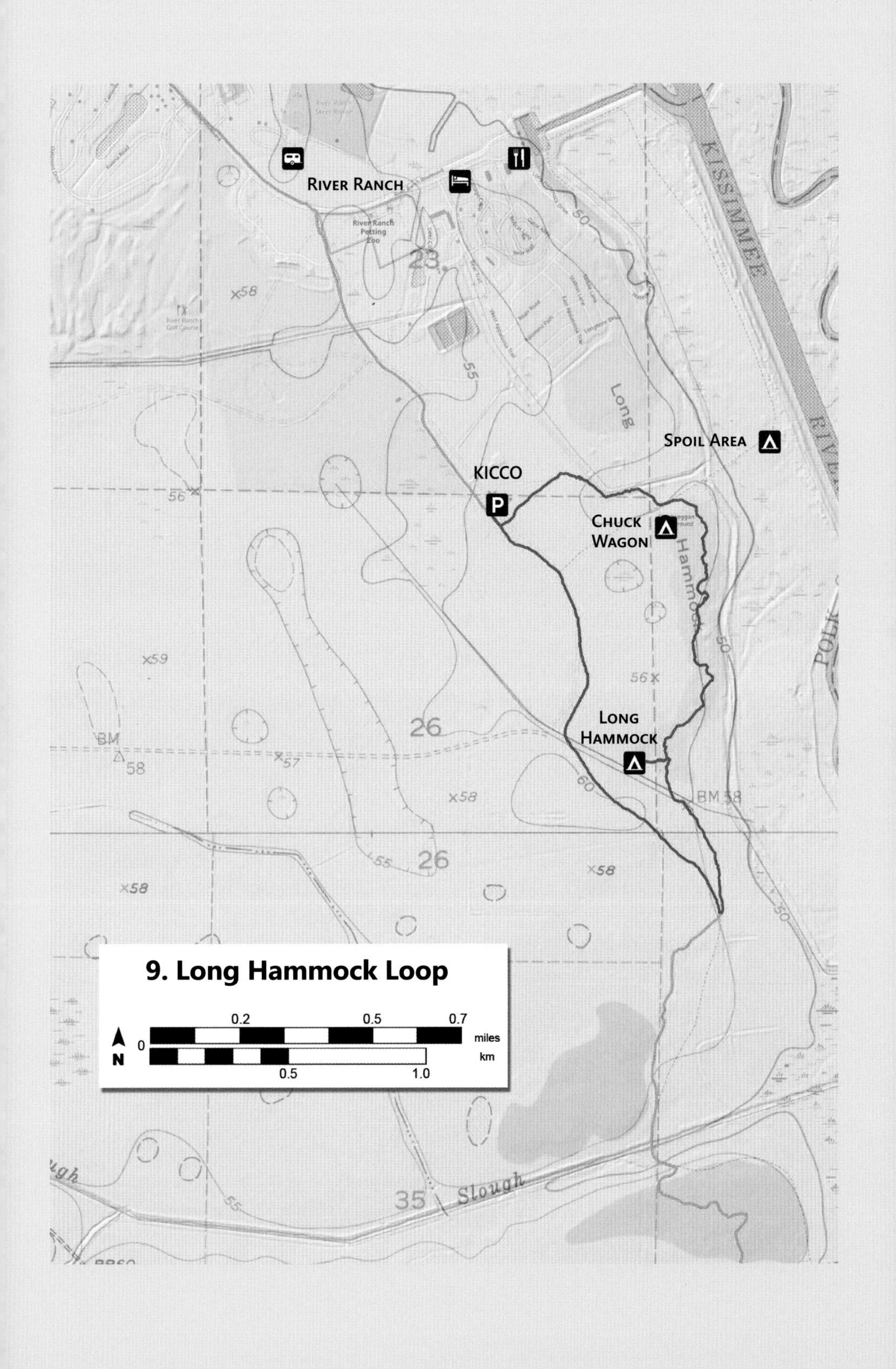
River Ranch
KICCO
Spoil Area
Chuck Wagon
Long Hammock
Kissimmee River
Long Hammock
Slough
9. Long Hammock Loop
0
0.2
0.5
0.7
miles
km
0.5
1.0
N

Under the ancient live oaks of Long Hammock

A blaze post set among tall bluestem grasses confirms your choice as the trail curves past a clump of saw palmetto, heading into ranchland with relict patches of prairie broken up by oak hammocks.

At 0.3 mile, reach a slough and join the footpath paralleling it atop a low levee. Tall dog fennel obscures the route in places. Cross a two-track road at a half mile, staying to the right of a depression marsh. The trail curves away from it and quickly reaches a broad graded road.

There are two primitive campgrounds along this road. Shaded Chuck Wagon Campground [27.75998, -81.18518] is a tenth of a mile west and Spoil Area Campground [27.76244, -81.18132] a quarter mile east, an equestrian-friendly camping area in full sun set next to a levee along the Kissimmee River. Defining the eastern boundary of KICCO WMA, this part of the Kissimmee River was channelized by the Army Corps of Engineers in the 1960s. Over the past two decades, the Corps of Engineers has been undoing that hydrological mistake. In segments north and south of KICCO, they've removed dams and levees, enabling the river to meander through its floodplain once more. Filtering heavy nutrient loads through its marshes, the Kissimmee flows into Lake Okeechobee.

Unless you are taking a side trip to a campsite or to the river via the graded road, look for signage and orange blazes guiding you into Long Hammock on the other side of this road. Passing several massive live oaks, enter a deeply shaded hardwood hammock, its understory a thicket of lush vegetation. Marked by double blazes, the trail twists and winds past cabbage palms. Cascades of shoelace fern dangle from moss-covered trunks.

In a large clearing under the oaks at 1.2 miles, a low wooden sign indicates a safety zone from hunting and the location of Long Hammock campsite down a short blue blaze. Nicely shaded, Long Hammock has two picnic tables, a fire ring, and a large expanse of leaf-strewn forest floor, perfect for groups to camp. From the campsite junction, follow the orange blazes into a glorious corridor where fern-covered live oak limbs form the canopy and clusters of saw palmetto edge the leafy footpath. The landscape becomes more park-like, with grassy spots between the trees and a depression marsh visible to the right in a large clearing the trail briefly crosses. The footpath continues into a stretch of oak hammock with limbs knit tightly overhead.

It's almost a surprise to step out of the woods onto KICCO Grade after 1.8 miles. The Florida Trail crosses it, but this hike loops back here. Turn right and walk north along KICCO Grade, a hard-packed limerock road that reflects the sun. Long Hammock is on the right, and patches of prairie and scrubby flatwoods on the left. Bald eagles and caracara may soar above, and sandhill cranes often browse the prairies. It's a quicker walk along this road than the hike through the hammock, and there is little to no traffic.

At 2.7 miles, bear left at the Y intersection. To the right is the road leading to the primitive campgrounds. An oak hammock shades KICCO Grade in the distance. When you reach it, the surroundings are familiar. Seal this loop at the FNST sign by the camp host's building and exit via the walk-through stile, completing a 2.9-mile hike.

Palmetto prairie and cypress dome

10. Prairie Lakes Loop

11.4 MILES | THREE LAKES WMA PRAIRIE LAKES UNIT, KENANSVILLE

Alternating between the lush shade of moss-draped oak hammocks and panoramic views on wide-open prairies, this hike between two major lakes of the Kissimmee River basin is a beauty.

Overview

Preserving the upper Kissimmee Prairie, Three Lakes Wildlife Management Area covers more than 98 square miles east of the Kissimmee River between Yeehaw Junction and Kenansville. Unlike Kissimmee Prairie Preserve State Park to its south, it is more upland than lowland, with vast swaths of dry prairie. Inside Three Lakes is the Prairie Lakes Unit, formerly a Florida State Park in the 1970s. Designed and built by Florida Trail Association volunteers as a backpacking destination for the park, the Prairie Lakes Loop makes a figure-eight centered on an isthmus between Lake Jackson and Lake Marion.

Trip Planning

Leashed dogs are welcome. A day-use fee applies. Pay online or at the iron ranger at Prairie Lakes trailhead and display the receipt on your dashboard. Three Lakes WMA is managed by the Florida Fish and Wildlife Conservation Commission and is busy during deer hunting season, as evidenced by many permanent deer stands along the trail. Research hunting seasons for Prairie Lakes in advance. If you hike during hunting season, wear bright orange.

Three campsites—Parker Hammock, Lake Jackson, and Dry Pond—offer backpackers choices. Lake Jackson has a vault toilet, is accessible by vehicles, and is close to where you'll hear airboats at night. The other two campsites are primitive, with picnic tables and pitcher pumps that work sporadically. Unless you're thru-hiking the Florida Trail, it's necessary to obtain a free permit for camping. Call FWC for a permit. Prairie Lakes Group Camp has picnic benches, amphitheater-style seating, a large fire ring, and a vault toilet. It's a good base camp for Scouting groups to put in miles along the Florida Trail. It connects to the eastern side of the North Loop via a half-mile blue blaze to Road 19. Call FWC to reserve.

Land Managers

Florida Fish and Wildlife Conservation Commission
1239 SW 10th St, Ocala 34471
352-732-1225
myfwc.com

St. Johns River Water Mgt District
525 Community College Pky SE, Palm Bay 32909
321-984-4940
sjrwmd.com

Directions

From US 192 in St. Cloud, follow Canoe Creek Rd—east of Neptune Rd and west of Michigan Ave—due south for 25.4 miles. The Prairie Lakes entrance is well marked. Turn right on Prairie Lakes Rd. Prairie Lakes trailhead [27.927691, -81.124893] is on the right.

Options

Day hike or overnight the full loop or tackle each one at a time. Use Prairie Lakes trailhead for the 5.4-mile North Loop, and the parking area at Lake Jackson [27.909201, -81.150009] for the 6-mile South Loop. A parking area at the west end of Road 16 [27.891466, -81.173683] provides access to a 1-mile round trip to Lake Jackson Tower for the views. A 1.6-mile round trip from Prairie Lakes trailhead to the end of the Pole Cypress Ponds boardwalk is also pleasant.

Three Lakes WMA extends north and south of Prairie Lakes. The Florida Trail crosses it diagonally 26.6 miles across Osceola County. Hike north from Three Lakes South trailhead [27.807198, -81.129059] (off SR 60 west of Yeehaw Junction) 15.5 miles to Prairie Lakes trailhead. The southern seven miles are mainly open prairie. Beautiful Godwin Hammock and bird-rich Fodderstack Slough are highlights, and Godwin Hammock campsite is a pleasant overnight stay with no permit required. There is no trailhead at the north end of Three Lakes WMA. Hikers emerge onto US 441 and roadwalk to the next segment of the Florida Trail inside Crescent J Ranch. It's 12.9 miles from Prairie Lakes trailhead to the US 441 wayside [28.020243, -81.033272]. Don't leave vehicles at the wayside overnight.

Hike

Look for the Florida National Scenic Trail sign on the opposite side of the entrance road from Prairie Lakes trailhead. Follow the mowed footpath into the pine-dotted prairie within view of Canoe Creek Rd, a broad, open landscape. Watch for sandhill cranes settling into open patches between the palmettos. Hiking along the edge of Pole Cypress Ponds, a large cypress strand, enter it at 0.7 miles on a boardwalk with benches along it. After the boardwalk ends, ramble through pine flatwoods with a palmetto understory and a fire tower up ahead. Pass under a power line at 1.5 miles. The fire tower is now to your right. Cross a sand road and leave the pine flatwoods panorama for the deep shade of an oak hammock, the first of many along this loop.

Emerging from the oaks to the edge of North Canal—connecting Lake Jackson and Lake Marian—cross Road 16, the primary access road within Prairie Lakes. Benches overlook the waterway. At a trail junction along the canal, face the white blazes of the return side of the North Loop. Turn left and cross the footbridge at 2.4 miles. The junction for the South Loop is on the south side of the footbridge, offering the same choices: white or orange blazes. Make a right to stay with the orange blazes, paralleling the canal briefly before crossing a bridge over a culvert. Zigzag from blazed tree to blazed tree through a dense hammock of live oaks and cabbage palms. Leaving the hammock, walk a corridor adjoining a fern-lined waterway.

Cross Boat Ramp Road at 3.3 miles, which leads to Lake Jackson. Parallel the road before diving into Kettle Hammock. Its live oaks are lush with large bromeliads dangling from their limbs, especially giant air plants, uncommonly abundant at Prairie Lakes. Walk into Campsite 3 at the Lake Jackson Campground. It's the best of the sites, farthest

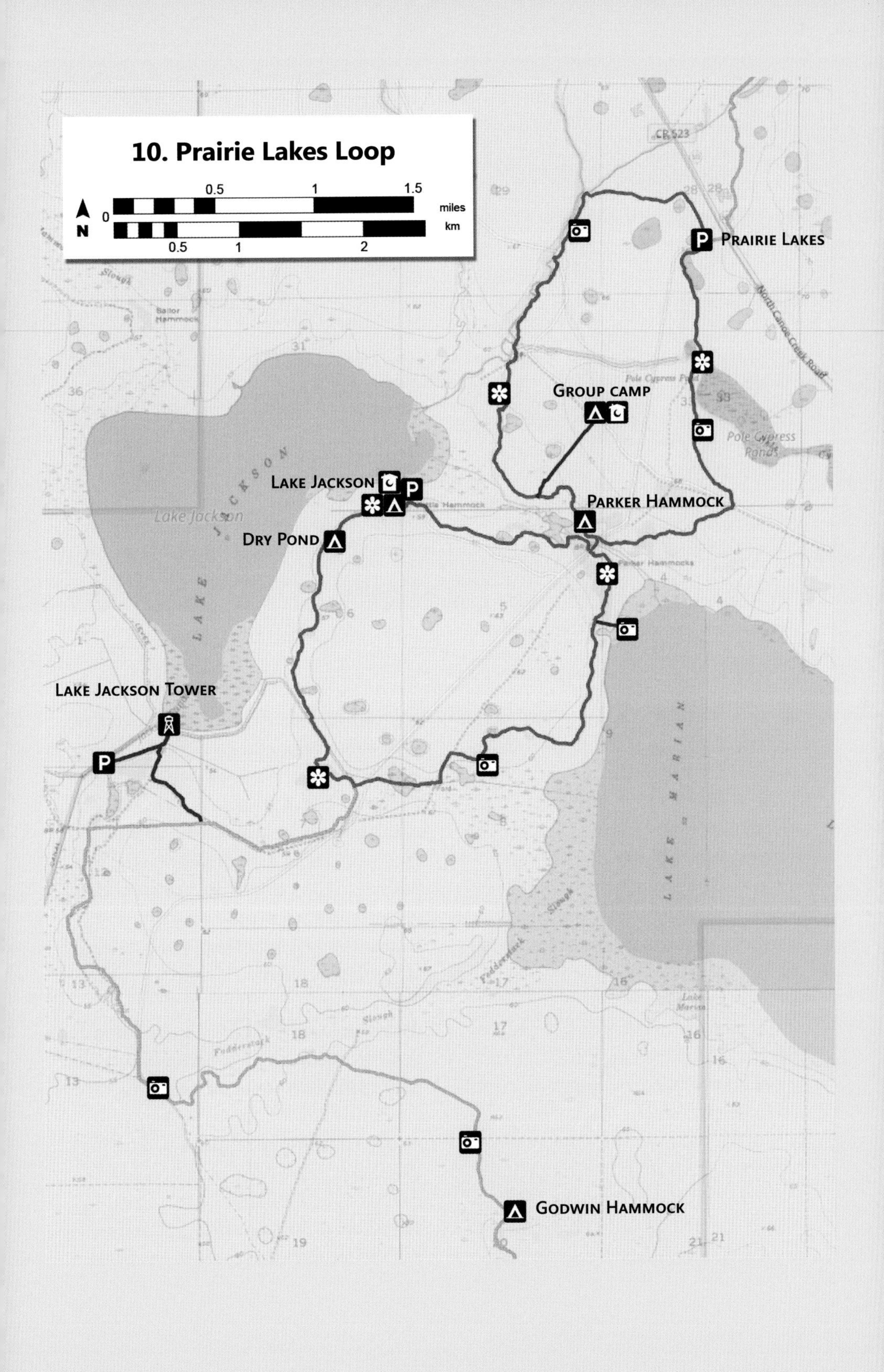

10. Prairie Lakes Loop
0
0.5
1
1.5
miles
0.5
1
2
km
N
Prairie Lakes
Group camp
Lake Jackson
Parker Hammock
Dry Pond
Lake Jackson Tower
Godwin Hammock
Lake Jackson
Pole Cypress Ponds
North Canoe Creek Road
CR 523
Lake Marian

Wet prairie in the middle of the isthmus

from the boat ramp and parking area. A two-track road leads to the vault toilet and parking area at the lake.

The sign at 3.9 miles indicates a side trail to Dry Pond campsite. Set along the edge of Kettle Hammock under grandfather oaks, it provides a vista of open prairie. Listen for eagles, which nest in a large pine visible to drivers along Road 16. Like the pond itself, the pitcher pump at Dry Pond is usually dry. South of the campsite, enter the open prairie. The trail aims for a single oak tree in a sea of orange-hued pinewood dropseed, a tall, slender, waving grass. On the far side of the prairie, tackle a mazy route blaze by blaze through a series of lush live oak and palm hammocks, the footpath ill-defined. Spanish moss hangs in thick draperies. When it falls during a windstorm, it creates fuzzy gray puddles on the forest floor.

A bridge over a narrow canal leads to a small bench set atop a berm. The canals and ditches date to the former ranch on this land, built to drain the wet prairies in the isthmus. Berms are the piles of dirt tossed aside while digging. Follow this one under dappled sunlight streaming through the Spanish moss on the oaks overhead. At the next bench, reach the south end of the South Loop at 5.4 miles. The orange blazes of the Florida Trail continue south. Stay on the Prairie Lakes Loop by switching to white blazes for the return trip, crossing a bridge over the canal. At a break in the oak hammock, continue across Road 16. The footpath sticks close to South Canal, the second human-made waterway between Lake Jackson and Lake Marian. Blazes occasionally jog around a tributary flowing into the canal.

After 6 miles, cross South Canal on a narrow footbridge at a former cattle ford and climb over an earthen mound. The footpath may be wet approaching the rim of the vast prairie that makes up the center of Prairie Lakes. Making a sharp turn away from a panorama of prairie, weave through a series of oak hammocks forming the high ground between the wetlands along the rim of Lake Marian and the prairie in the middle of the isthmus. Panoramas open where the trail skirts between the oak hammocks, the big prairie a backdrop for wetlands in the foreground.

Reaching the shade of the next oak hammock, be mindful of where the blazes lead. Cross a plank bridge over an ephemeral waterway, drawing closer to the wetlands of Lake Marian. The trail burrows deep into the next oak hammock, its narrow corridor flanked by cabbage palms yielding to an open understory beneath gnarled live oaks.

The landscape opens up to reveal a wet prairie. Reach a forest road on a berm at 7.4 miles at the back side of a sign. The Spanish moss-draped levee to the right leads to an observation deck on Lake Marian. Take this 0.4-mile round trip. Nearly 5,800 acres of fresh water stretches in front of you at the deck, Lake Marian sparkling under broad skies. One of the smaller lakes in the Kissimmee Chain of Lakes, Lake Marian is a favorite for anglers looking for black crappie.

Return to the South Loop and turn right to enter a series of live oak ham-

Lake Marian, one of the three lakes of Three Lakes WMA

mocks, their canopies a wonderland of ferns and bromeliads. As the last oak hammock thins, the North Canal and its control gates are visible ahead. Cross Road 16. The footpath roughly parallels the road inside the shade of the oak hammock. Giant air plants dangle overhead. At 8.3 miles, complete the South Loop at the trail junction on the south side of the North Canal.

Now it's time to finish the North Loop. Cross the footbridge and turn right. White blazes lead left almost immediately into the deep shade of Parker Hammock. Reach a blue-tipped post with a picnic table and pitcher pump beyond it. This marks the edge of Parker Hammock campsite. Flat spots for tents and a second picnic bench are in the oak hammock past the sign in the distance that says "Parker Hammocks."

Leaving Parker Hammock, emerge into sunny scrubby flatwoods. Open patches of bright-white sand intermingle with the scrubby understory in the pine flatwoods, the trail corridor often defined by dense saw palmetto. At 8.8 miles, a sign marks the half-mile blue-blazed connector northeast to Prairie Lakes Group Camp, which has a vault toilet. Return to the edge of oak hammocks along Parker Slough. One opening provides a prairie view with a lone loblolly bay in a little grassy cove. Past a thicket of saw palmetto, emerge onto a forest road. Keep left at the Y intersection.

By 9.5 miles, meet the corner of a fence line and follow it briefly before veering right toward the more pleasant environs of a line of trees along the edge of the prairie. Crossing the end of a forest road, join the bluffs along Parker Slough, a natural waterway flowing sluggishly toward Lake Jackson. Beautiful and narrow, it winds beneath a canopy of cypresses and oaks as you follow it upstream. A bridge spans the outflow of Pole Cypress Ponds into Parker Slough. Extremely tall cypress knees rise from the bottom of the deeply eroded basin. For a short stretch, the trail dives into the slough floodplain. Short cypress knees jut from the footpath.

At a Y with a forest road at 10.2 miles, stay left, veering back to the bluff. A picnic bench in a scenic clearing may have served as a campsite in the past. Just north of the bench, cross Road 19. The white blazes veer from the edge of the floodplain toward the open pine-dotted prairie. Crossing one final forest road a half mile later, break away from Parker Slough for the last time into open palmetto prairie as the trail starts an eastward turn. In the late afternoon, sunlight makes the cypress dome in the distance glow.

Drawing within sight of traffic on Canoe Creek Road, make a sharp right and parallel the highway through the pines, with a sweeping expanse of prairie to your right. At 11.4 miles, finish the hike at Prairie Lakes trailhead.

11. Bull Creek Loop

17.3 MILES | HERKY HUFFMAN BULL CREEK WMA, HOLOPAW

Crossing the floodplain of Bull Creek on historic tramways, this large loop west of the St. Johns River treats hikers to extensive panoramas of pine savannas and flatwoods.

Overview

When the Indian River Chapter of the Florida Trail Association began routing this trail in 1983, one of the puzzles was how to cross the cypress swamps. The land manager suggested using the historic tramways. Narrow elevated berms supported narrow-gauge railroads for the Union Cypress Company as they cut the ancient cypress growing along the tributaries of the St. Johns River. After fifty years of abandonment, the trestles weren't viable, so footbridges replaced them. The tramways created the foundation for the east side of the loop. It was typical for volunteers to build destination backpacking loops at that time, so the west side of the loop was routed through mostly high, dry landscapes of palmetto prairie and pine savanna.

Trip Planning

Leashed dogs are welcome. Bull Creek WMA draws many deer hunters in the fall. Research hunting seasons in advance. If you hike during hunting season, wear bright orange. A camp host is resident during hunting season with car and small trailer camping available at the hunt camp. Check river levels in the St. Johns floodplain before hiking: water.weather.gov station MELF1. The east side of the loop will be largely underwater when Bull Creek floods. Never enter flowing water.

Land Managers

Florida Fish and Wildlife Conservation Commission
1239 SW 10th St, Ocala 34471
352-732-1225
myfwc.com

St. Johns River Water Mgt District
525 Community College Pky SE, Palm Bay 32909
321-984-4940
sjrwmd.com

Directions

Access Bull Creek WMA via Crabgrass Creek Rd along US 192, 4.1 miles east of the US 441 traffic light at Holopaw and 19.2 miles west of Interstate 95 at Melbourne. Turn south on the unpaved road, which is sometimes rough to traverse. Follow it 6 miles to the hunt check station. Hunt Camp trailhead [28.082708, -80.962234] is between the campground entrance and the gate. The US 192 trailhead [28.116550, -80.932610] is 4.9 miles east of Crabgrass Creek Rd along the south side of US 192. Parking is limited; don't block the gate. Unlike Hunt Camp, this trailhead does not provide direct access to the loop.

Options

You can tackle the loop in either direction. We describe it clockwise. Within the WMA, Loop Road touches the loop at two points, enabling hikers to spot a second vehicle for day hikes between Hunt Camp and Yoke Branch on the east side, or Hunt Camp and Billie Lake on the west side. Using two vehicles,

Historic tramway on east side of loop (Chris Stevens)

hike between US 192 and Hunt Camp. This piece of the trail includes a showy and often wet traverse of the Crabgrass Creek floodplain. It's 5 miles between trailheads, or a 7.8-mile round trip from Hunt Camp trailhead to Jane Green campsite, which lies 0.9 miles south of the US 192 trailhead. As part of a 34.2-mile trip between this trailhead and Prairie Lakes trailhead (see the previous chapter) and US 192, Crescent J Ranch allows backpackers to cross their property south of Bull Creek and camp at Tracey Branch Camp. Call 321-258-8633 or 407-288-9648 in advance of your hike and pack out everything you pack in.

Hike

Follow the road past the camp host from Hunt Camp trailhead. After a half mile, the white blazes leave the road to cut a diagonal northeast from a road junction into open pine flatwoods. Cross a small drainage a quarter mile later, continuing through palmetto prairie and pines with open views and distinctive wildflowers. At 1.4 miles, dip through a tributary feeding Crabgrass Creek to the north. Turn south on a forest road before jogging east again, passing a bench and a small pitcher plant bog. White blazes meet orange at 2 miles, where prominent signage indicates you've reached the Florida Trail. Turn right to continue southbound.

After a half mile of palmetto prairie, emerge between a set of benches at a junction with Loop Road. Straight ahead is a blue-blazed bypass to avoid the swampiest part of this hike, which traverses the confluence of Crabgrass Creek with Bull Creek. Turn left to follow the forest road briefly. Make a right at 2.9 miles, joining the historic Union Cypress Company tramway. For the next six miles, the trail largely remains on this tramway.

A series of three narrow bridges connect broken pieces of the tramway in quick succession. Cabbage palms and tupelo crowd the footpath. Relics of the old railroad, including railroad ties, are scattered on the forest floor. A bridge spans deep, dark water. The next one may be dry underneath. Curve west to parallel Yoke Branch, meeting the blue-blazed bypass coming in from the right. Turn left to join Loop Road to cross Yolk Branch on the road bridge at 4 miles. Veer left onto the orange blazes to follow the tramway southeast for the next half mile before leaving it for drier ground under oaks and pines. Cross a low area, returning to the tramway. It

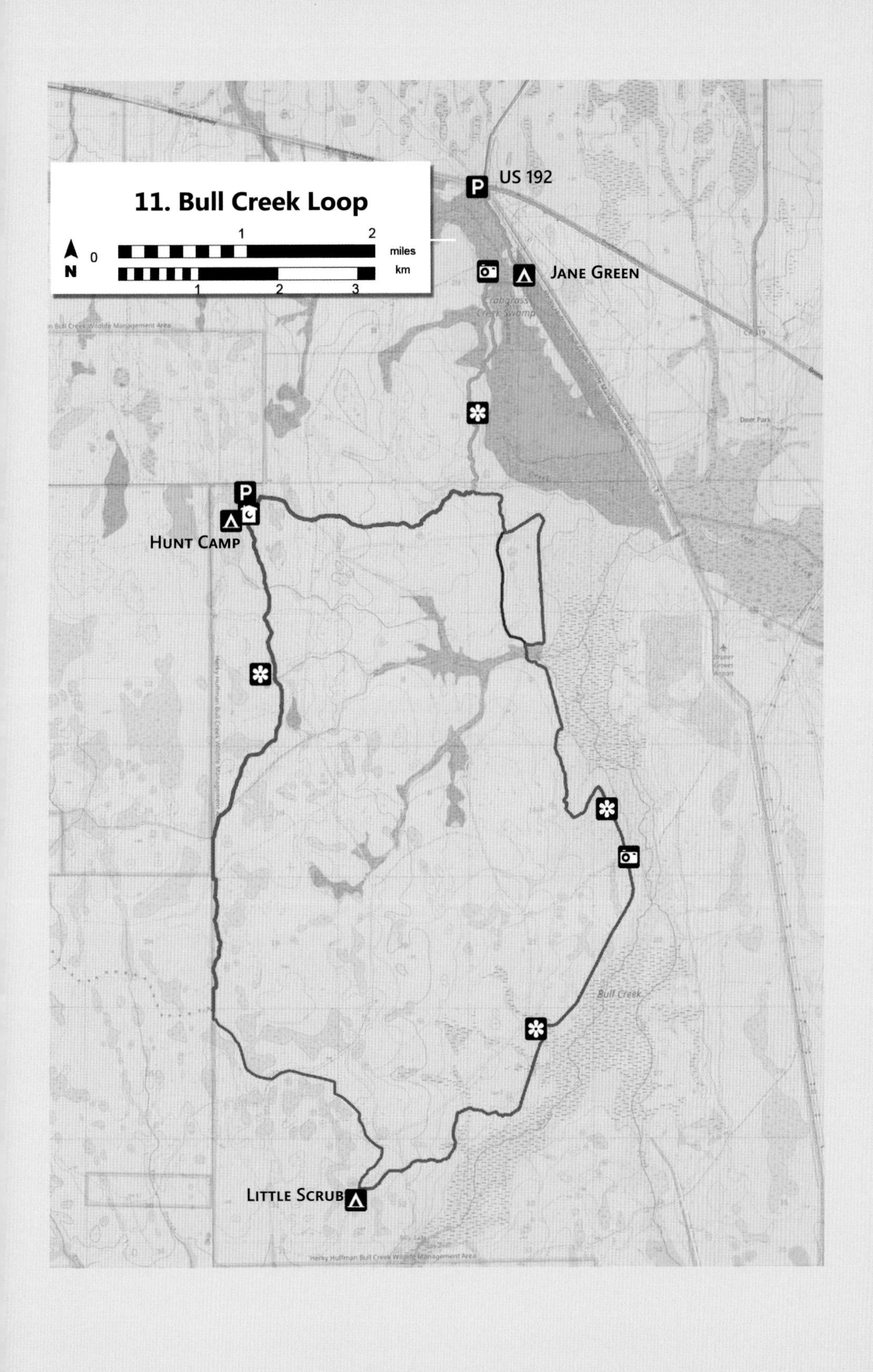
11. Bull Creek Loop
0
1
2
miles
km
1
2
3
N
US 192
Jane Green
Hunt Camp
Little Scrub
Bull Creek
Crabgrass Creek Swamp

Pine flatwoods along west side of loop

now draws close to Bull Creek, entering the floodplain. Walk through a showy cypress strand at 6 miles. Splash across a stream a quarter mile later, with cypress knees at shin level. A brief detour east on a forest road provides a scenic view across Bull Creek and a place to filter water.

Within three-quarters of a mile are a series of bridges connecting broken pieces of the tramway. Marshes edge the trail and cabbage palms flank the footpath. After a bridge over a narrow but deep channel that empties into the Bull Creek basin at 8 miles, circle a pine savanna where carnivorous plants peek from the tall grasses. The next footbridge crosses an ephemeral stream that drains the pine flatwoods after a heavy rain.

A bridge adjoins a cluster of cabbage palms just before the narrow footpath leaves the Union Cypress Company tramway for the final time at 8.7 miles. A sign marks the spot. Turning into the flatwoods, immerse in a grassy haze of pine savanna in a well-defined corridor of saw palmetto. Cross an access road connecting Loop Road with the Bull Creek floodplain. Continue through pine flatwoods, descending to a creek crossed on a bridge with benches at either end.

Dropping through a small drainage, begin a turn away from Bull Creek into the pine savanna. On the other side of Billie Lake Rd—a vehicle access point from Loop Rd to a lake in Bull Creek—ascend into scrub habitat, its bright-white sand a sharp counterpoint to the swamps and forests along the hike so far. Reach Little Scrub Campsite at 10.4 miles, the southernmost point along this loop and an excellent location for stargazing on clear nights. Set in the dry scrub with a picnic table and bench, it also has a pitcher pump that's known to fail.

The orange blazes lead north into the scrub. Turning at Billie Lake Rd, head northwest into a corridor of saw palmetto. Reach a gravel road before turning onto a grassy forest road into scrubby flatwoods, the trail weaving between cypress domes. Come to the boundary fence with adjacent Crescent J Ranch at 12.8 miles. The Florida Trail crosses the stile to continue south across this private preserve. You do not.

Stay on this side of the fence, following white blazes for the remainder of the hike. Walk due north along the fence, rounding a marshy pond. Small bogs host carnivorous plants among tall prairie grasses. The footpath narrows as it leaves the fence, snaking through a thicket of gallberry and cabbage palms close to a cypress strand. White bands painted around pines indicate endangered red-cockaded woodpecker nesting sites.

Past a clearing at 13.9 miles, continue along an improved forest road studded with nubby limestone rocks whenever it hits low spots. Flip some over and you may find beautiful orange calcite crystals growing inside fossilized clams. At a Y in the road, stay left. The road becomes grassy, its surroundings a fine example of a longleaf pine forest. At 14.6 miles, cross an east–west tramway that was part of the Union Cypress Railroad. A murky swale holds water.

Beyond several white-banded pines the trail narrows, leading deeper into the pine flatwoods. Hazy spots breaking up the saw palmetto thicket are small wet prairies. At a T intersection, swing east and join a wide forest road. Leave it at a Y to veer east, passing a large cypress dome. A double-blaze turn leads to a narrower forest road. This branch of the road makes a beeline for a small slough, where a cabbage palm stands above a soggy crossing at 15.8 miles.

The footpath resumes beyond the slough through a grassy prairie damp and dotted with hooded pitcher plants and butterworts. At a forest road, enter a cluster of pines with a deer stand. Passing several small ponds, weave through the pine flatwoods. Saw palmetto stretch toward tree line. White blazes guide you north into a tall stand of loblolly pine at 16.5 miles. A slough crossing the trail drains a cypress strand. Parallel its wall of cypress for some time.

Broadening into a forest road, the trail enters denser pine flatwoods with taller saw palmetto. If the hunt camp is occupied, you'll see the trailers in the distance. Partly hidden by saw palmetto, a low wall marks the former location of an observatory. Cross a forest road and walk into the campground. Follow the white blazes across it past two vault toilets. Exit the campground to Hunt Camp trailhead at 17.3 miles.

Pine-palm flatwoods along the White Trail

12. Beehead Ranch Loop

7.7 MILES | TOSOHATCHEE WMA, CHRISTMAS

Following part of the original Tosohatchee backpacking loop, this well-shaded hike through the botanical diversity of the St. Johns River basin also illuminates its cultural history.

Overview

Built in the early 1900s for the foreman of the Tosohatchee Ranch, the ranch house at Beehead Ranch was close enough to the St. Johns River for water access but above the floodplain in an oak hammock. Palm logs held up the porch and cut-glass doorknobs added a touch of class. When the ranch folded, the house became a hunting lodge for a private sportsmen's club. Tosohatchee Game Preserve sold their land to the state in 1977, which reopened it as Tosohatchee State Reserve, a Florida State Park. The Florida Trail Association was invited to build trails in the park.

The original Florida Trail loop had a 17-mile perimeter trail with several interior loops. A 1991 map shows a parking area for the trail system adjoining Beehead Ranch. To protect the home from vandalism, it was moved to nearby Fort Christmas Historical Park in 1993 and can be visited there today. The transfer of the park to FWC in 2006 turned Tosohatchee back into a hunter's destination. Parts of the trail system had to be abandoned due to changes in the floodplain. But the Beehead Ranch Loop persists at the heart of the preserve. It hits the don't-miss highlights of Tosohatchee, including its virgin cypress forest along Jim Creek and ancient live oak hammocks. Using portions of the Florida Trail, the White Loop, and several cross trails, it's a fascinating day hike accessible from several trailheads off Fish Hole Rd.

Trip Planning

Pay the day-use fee in advance online. Leashed dogs are welcome. Roads are unpaved but generally well-graded. Parking areas have limited space. Rampant throughout the forest, poison ivy swarms into the footpath and up tree trunks. Deep shade means insect repellent is a must.

Research hunting seasons in advance. For your safety, avoid hiking in Tosohatchee WMA during deer season and during hunting season where dogs are used to track wildlife. If you hike during hunting season, wear bright orange. Camping is not permitted during hunting season unless you are a thru-hiker.

Check river levels before hiking: water.weather.gov station COCF1. When the St. Johns River is in its flood stage, you should not attempt this hike.

Land Manager

Florida Fish and Wildlife Conservation Commission
1239 SW 10th St, Ocala 34471
352-732-1225
myfwc.com

Directions

Exiting Interstate 95 at SR 50 in Titusville, drive 10 miles west into Christmas. Turn left on Taylor Creek Rd and continue south 2.9 miles to the preserve entrance on the left just after a broad bridge. A pull-off just inside the preserve has a kiosk with maps and a vault toilet. Continue along Beehead Rd, which used to lead directly to the ranch. It now makes a sharp left and meets Powerline Rd. Turn right and continue east on Powerline Rd to Fish Hole Rd. Turn right and drive south along Fish Hole Rd to Parking Area 33 [28.4916, -80.9501] on the left.

Options

Using the Florida Trail, the Yellow Loop, the White Loop, and forest roads, you can put together a variety of loop hikes inside Tosohatchee. The White Loop—which has the Florida Trail as its north and east sides—is the longest at 12 miles. The Yellow Loop, which you meet 0.6 miles east of this trailhead, is 3.3 miles, or a 5-mile loop starting at Parking Area 33.

The linear Florida Trail across the preserve is 11 miles. There are no trailheads at either end. The best access points are on Powerline Road [28.5039, -80.9501, and 28.5039, -80.9408] as well as Parking Area 32 [28.4834, -80.9499] on Fish Hole Rd and Parking Area 6 [28.5115, -80.9797] north of Youth Camp. Backpackers can camp at Tiger Branch Camp along this loop or Hoot Owl Camp north of Tootosohatchee Creek. Tiger Branch has tent platforms and a pitcher pump. Permits and a small fee are required for camping. Call FWC to arrange a stay.

Hike

From Parking Area 33, follow yellow blazes east into a lush stand of palms providing a low canopy under tall pines, the fronds filling the understory. Tosohatchee is a vibrant place where something is always growing. Marsh ferns rise from swales that capture rainfall. Soft hues of green blanket the forest floor. After 0.6 miles, reach a T junction with yellow blazes. This is the original Yellow Loop, evidenced by an antique metal sign with trail features and mileages from the state park days. Turn left to proceed north toward the old homestead.

Under a canopy of pines and palms, reach a wall of oak hammock, its understory jam-packed with saw palmetto. Every limb of every oak is swaddled in bromeliads, ball moss catching sunlight through its slender tips. It feels jungle-like where the trail curves into a palm hammock beneath these decorated trees. Young cabbage palms and bluestem palms compete with ferns to obscure the forest floor. Fungi swarms over rotting logs. Vines droop low, and poison ivy creeps into the footpath.

Gaining a little elevation, leave the hammock, edging a low area where sweetgum and red maple dominate. Passing beneath towering pines and large oaks, round a bed of ferns to end up among the trunks of tall cabbage palms. A narrow wooden bridge leads to Parking Area 35 [28.4994, -80.9410] on Ranch Rd, another potential access point at 1.4 miles. Cross the road and a boardwalk through a wetland where blue flag iris bloom in spring. Enter a palm hammock. Towering overhead, these cabbage palms have curved trunks. Emerge into a large grassy clearing. This is a portion of a larger clearing, visible on satellite maps, where the Beehead Ranch house once stood. Slipping back into a forest of pines and palms,

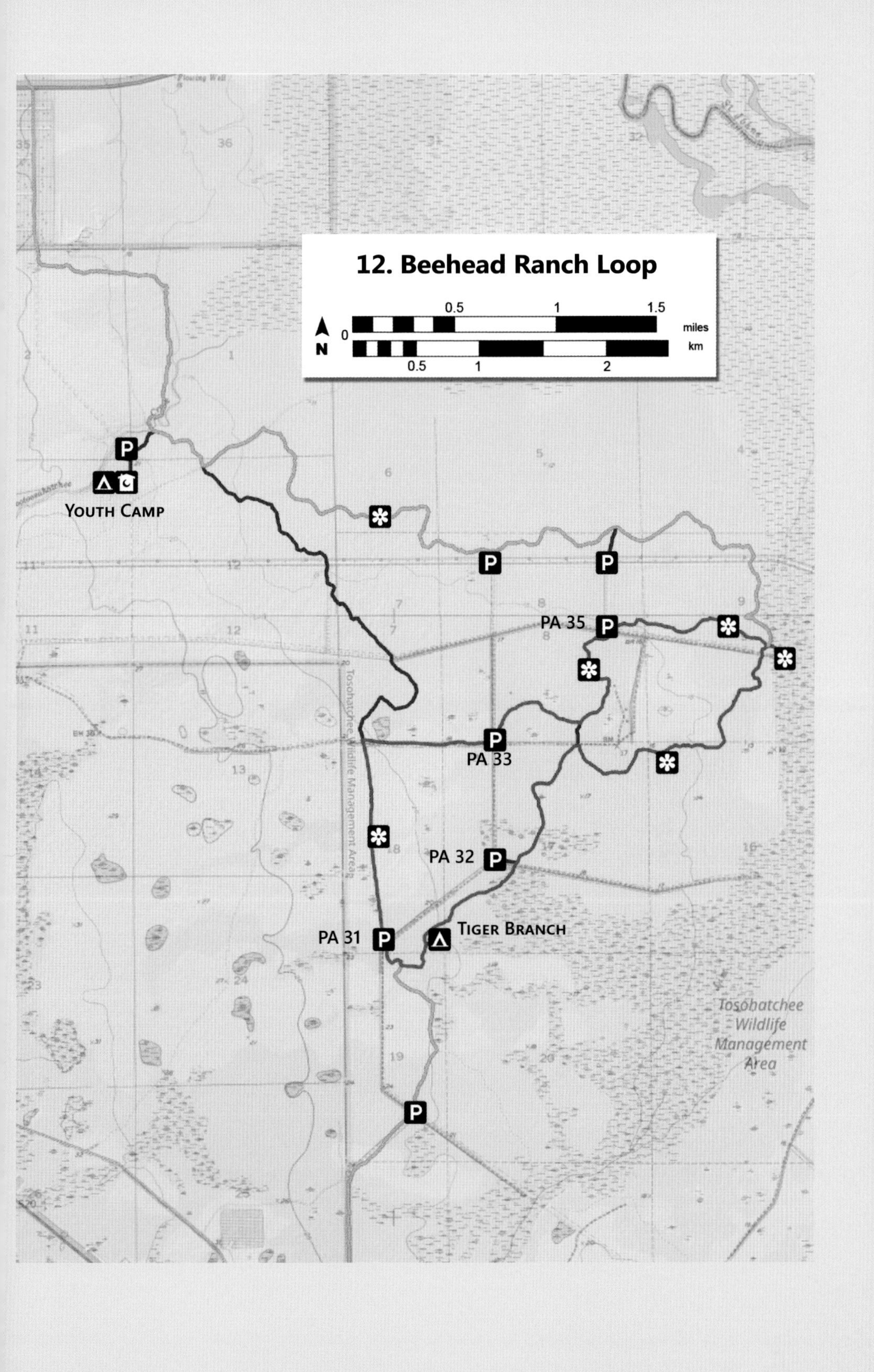

12. Beehead Ranch Loop
0
0.5
1
1.5
miles
km
0.5
1
2
N
Youth Camp
PA 35
PA 33
PA 32
PA 31
Tiger Branch
Tosohatchee Wildlife Management Area
Tosohatchee
Wildlife
Management
Area

Lush palm hammock near Jim Creek

zigzag through a maze of trunks on a distinct footpath.

At 2.4 miles, the Yellow Loop meets the orange-blazed Florida Trail at a signposted junction. Across it is the Swamp Spur, a short blue blaze leading to Jim Creek Swamp. Continue straight ahead for this scenic side trip but mind where you put your feet: the forest floor is a puzzle of cypress knees. Most of the giant cypress were logged long ago, but a handful of ancient trees remain. This spur ends at the "Trail End" sign within sight of sluggish Jim Creek.

Return to the trail junction and make a left to follow the Florida Trail south into the next wonderland of an old-growth palm hammock. Cross Ranch Rd (it connects by foot to Parking Area 35 to the west) and rejoin the palm hammock, interspersed with Southern red cedars with peeling bark. Sunlight glints across marshes beyond the forest's rim.

Scramble through a ditch, climbing past giant leather ferns and royal ferns to a forest road crossing. The trail turns west, tunneling into a dense palm hammock. After a short stretch of pine-palm flatwoods, enter an ancient forest at 3.8 miles. It's moist and cool, bromeliads and lichens flourishing. Sunlight scarcely penetrates the canopy formed by cedars and live oaks. Cross a forest road in the pine-palm flatwoods and meet the second junction with the Yellow Loop at 4.3 miles. To shorten your hike to 5 miles, take the yellow blazes north to the junction with the antique sign and turn left to reach your vehicle.

Follow the orange blazes south toward Tiger Branch to stay on the Beehead Ranch Loop, noting the profusion of showy wildflowers in the pine-palm flatwoods. Tiny white bog buttons rise in clusters on slender stems. Blue flag iris sports purple blossoms in a soggy spot. Crossing a forest road at 5.1 miles, look right to see the white limestone surface of Fish Hole Rd. This is another access point (or exit) for the loop at Parking Area 32.

Cross a ditch next to the remains of a 1970s footbridge. The forest becomes denser and damper as sweetgum and red maple fill in the canopy. Marsh ferns jut from the footpath. As the trail gains elevation, the forest thins to tall slash pines above cabbage palms. Grasses fill the open spaces. A sign points to Tiger Branch campsite at 5.7 miles. Since it has seating in both sun and shade, this backpacker campsite with tent platforms, picnic bench, and a pitcher pump is a nice place to take a break. Beyond the next forest road, the habitat transitions from wet to dry, the forest opening up. Reach the junction with the White Loop a quarter mile later.

Choose the direction that doesn't have a sign that says "Thru Trail" and follow the white blazes. At 6.1 miles, cross Fish Hole Rd next to Parking Area 31 [28.4776, -80.9589] and the bridge over the ditch beyond it. Tall, skinny slash pines rise over an understory of saw palmetto and cabbage palms. Turning north onto an often narrow, slightly elevated corridor between the pines, the trail feels like it's on a tramway. A piece of railroad rail bolsters the theory. Enjoy an immersive walk through healthy wet pine flatwoods. Amid a sea of saw palmetto, one ancient cluster stands high above the rest. As younger pines surround the trail, the saw palmetto understory thins.

Reach a forest road at 7.1 miles. A sign points in the direction you've come to note the distance to the campsite. Turn right, leaving white blazes for yellow. Beneath pines, palms, and oaks, walk due east along the forest road. Past a small slough crowded with wild iris in bloom each March, the white ribbon of Fish Hole Rd is visible ahead. Return to Parking Area 33 after 7.7 miles.

Blue flag iris

Columns of palms at Seminole Ranch

13. Seminole Ranch Loop

5.6 MILES | SEMINOLE RANCH CONSERVATION AREA, CHRISTMAS

Featuring an immersion in palm hammocks along the St. Johns River floodplain, this scenic loop through Seminole Ranch pairs the Florida Trail with a portion of its former route through a forested corner of Orlando Wetlands—and a long boardwalk for wildlife watching.

Overview

If you've been to Orlando Wetlands, you may have wondered how, in a maze of levees and marked roads that visitors walk or bike to watch the birds, two trails through the woods came to be. Both the South Woods Branch Trail and the North Woods Branch Trail were built as part of the Florida Trail. Both had primitive campsites along them too.

Two decades ago, the first time we walked the Florida Trail through Central Florida, Bronson State Forest did not exist. To get to Christmas from Little Big Econ State Forest meant following an old railroad grade through Chuluota and walking on roads, past the Hitching Post Bar and Lake Mills Park to Fort Christmas Rd, and along that road to Orlando Wetlands. Inside the park, the Florida Trail followed the fence line until it reached the northeast corner. That's where these two footpaths led hikers toward the front gate, providing cool shade and a place to camp. After Bronson State Forest opened in 2011, the Florida Trail was moved out of Orlando Wetlands, but the old routes remain. This hike utilizes both. In between them, a new boardwalk opened in 2023. Crossing the purpose-built wetlands, it provides up-close viewing of roosting roseate spoonbills, foraging purple gallinules, and the inevitable alligators.

Trip Planning

Pets are not permitted in Orlando Wetlands for their safety and yours. Expect to be in full sun for a small portion of the loop; the remainder is in deep shade. Protection from mosquitoes is wise. Potable water and restrooms are available at Orlando Wetlands .

Hunting is not permitted in Orlando Wetlands, but it is at Seminole Ranch WMA. Research hunting seasons in advance. If you hike during hunting season, wear bright orange. Seminole Ranch has free-range cattle roaming through some of its woods.

Check river levels before hiking: water.weather.gov station COCF1. When the St. Johns River is in flood stage, do not attempt the Seminole Ranch portion of this hike. Orlando Wetlands will be unaffected.

Land Managers

Orlando Wetlands
25155 Wheeler Rd, Christmas 32709
407-568-1706
orlando.gov

St. Johns River Water Management District
525 Community College Parkway SE, Palm Bay 32909
321-984-4940
sjrwmd.com

Directions

Exiting Interstate 95 at SR 50 in Titusville, drive west for 10.3 miles through the town of Christmas to Fort Christmas Rd. Turn right. Continue 2.3 miles, passing Fort Christmas. Turn right onto Wheeler Rd as Fort Christmas Rd makes a sharp left curve. Continue 1.5 miles down Wheeler Rd to the large trailhead [28.569200, -81.013183] on the right. You can also park at Orlando Wetlands across from it, but their gates close at 5 p.m.

Options

One of our favorite hikes in Seminole Ranch is a 4.4-mile round trip from the parking area off SR 50 [28.540464, -80.988113] north to the Wheeler Rd connector junction. It's very easy to get to the starting point, and the whole hike is beautiful. There are no restrictions on hiking with dogs and no fees to worry about. A linear hike from this trailhead via the Wheeler Rd connector to Wheeler Rd trailhead is 3.1 miles, or 6.2 miles round trip. Northbound from Wheeler Rd trailhead to Joshua Creek trailhead [28.591867, -81.042351] is 8.6 miles and has a couple miles of rugged, swampy terrain with deep mud holes. Joshua Creek trailhead is off Fort Christmas Rd at the end of Phillips Rd in Bronson State Forest. A fee is charged to park there.

There are also many miles of trails to roam inside Orlando Wetlands. With the exception of the woodlands trails, the Perimeter Trail, and the boardwalk this route follows, all are roads atop dikes with scenic views of the marshes and some of the best birding in Florida.

Hike

Cross the road from the Wheeler Road trailhead to enter Orlando Wetlands. After a stop at the interpretive pavilion for a map and to sign in, top off your water bottles and head downhill past the picnic pavilion. Crossing a service road, look for the sign for the South Woods Branch Trail, which can get wet and muddy after a heavy rain. Walk into a stand of tall cabbage palms, thick with lichen swarming up their bases, and follow the meanders of the footpath.

A quarter mile in, reach the "Seminole Campsite" sign and turn left. The forest opens to a clearing with a chickee at the site of a former camping area. Follow a beaten path that emerges onto a levee at the Cypress Boardwalk, a popular addition to the park. The boardwalk sits low to the water, the better to watch the bustle of bird life on the surface and the alligators looking up at you. Passing a large cypress dome where the flash of pink wings mean roseate spoonbills are roosting, the boardwalk has a Y intersection. Veer right. The long straightaway parallels tall cypresses where great blue herons nest in spring, reaching the far shoreline at 0.9 miles.

Continue straight ahead to the topmost levee and turn right at the Vulture View signpost to follow the hard-packed limestone road. Views extend across Lake Searcy, named for the ranching family who once owned this land. This human-made lake is the deepest water in the park, although it has a natural slope and a marshy shoreline where moorhens cluster.

At 1.4 miles, a clearing opens up in the woods on the left. Walk down the grassy slope to a thatched-roof chickee marking the start of the North Woods Branch Trail. This is the second piece of the old Florida Trail in the park. Fol-

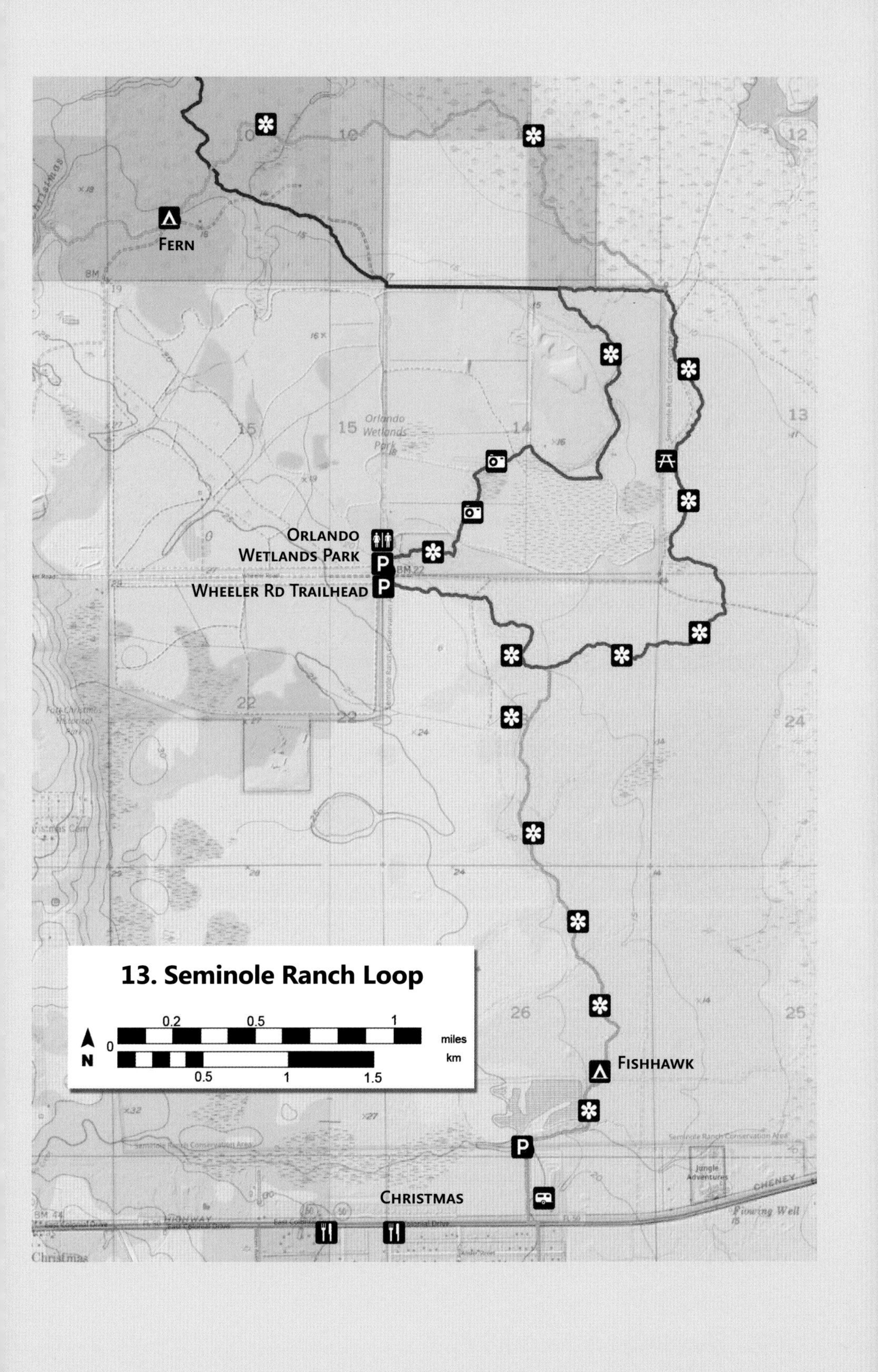

Fern
Orlando Wetlands Park
Wheeler Rd Trailhead
Fishhawk
Christmas
13. Seminole Ranch Loop
0
0.2
0.5
1
miles
km
0.5
1
1.5
N

Orlando Wetlands

low the white blazes. The trail starts out soggy, with a series of bog bridges to carry you over the marshy spots. A little rise in elevation makes for a spot covered in puffs of deer moss. The footpath curves around a marsh area with wax myrtle and red maples. It can get muddy at certain times of year. Following a forest road under the oak canopy, make a quick left to cross a wooden bridge over a waterway that often dries up. Enter a showy palm hammock with ancient live oaks. Dwarf palmetto crowd the understory. Look up, as resurrection ferns, bromeliads, and greenfly orchids decorate the limbs of the live oaks. Cross a grassy forest road at the "Orange Mound" sign—the location of another former campsite—into a beautiful stretch of palm hammock.

Emerge into a clearing at 2.2 miles. At the brown sign that tells you the Florida Trail lies straight ahead, cross the bridge to meet the Perimeter Trail at the back fence of the park. Signs point out connections to the Florida Trail. A left leads to a connector trail into Bronson State Forest, a useful shortcut for the optional hike to the Joshua Creek trailhead. Make a right.

Blazed blue, the Perimeter Trail tunnels through the forest along the fence line, providing peeks at the waterway flowing out of the wetlands. Past a side gate into Bronson State Forest, palm fronds from young cabbage palms and bluestem palm lean into the footpath. A black gate with a blue blaze provides an exit from Orlando Wetlands at 2.6 miles. A few paces past it, greet the orange blazes of the Florida Trail at a T intersection in Seminole Ranch Conservation Area. Turn right to cross the culvert under which the creek flows toward the St. Johns River.

Shaded by cedar trees, the trail provides peeks into the floodplain to the left before crossing a forest road where you can more clearly see open landscape stretching toward river marshes. Once prairie, it was converted to pasture by ditching the land to drain the water. Turn right to follow the road briefly before the blazes lead into a tightly clustered stand of cedar trees and cabbage palms. Marsh ferns cast dappled shadows across the forest floor. Gain a little elevation to find ancient oaks interspersed through the woods. Palm fronds take over the understory.

At 3.3 miles, a picnic bench is down a short side path to the right, a nice stop for a break. The forest is not as dense to its south, primarily cabbage palms and oaks in an upland area with pines and grapevines adding to the mix. It's easy walking through a very pretty habitat, especially when the cabbage palm trunks draw close together in a woodland maze. Look up to spot the many giant air plants like pineapple tops perched in the trees. As the palms thin, the understory thickens in a transition to oak hammock. Tree limbs create a low canopy. Cross a plank boardwalk over a ditch where blue flag iris blooms in spring. Nearby signs at 4 miles say "Parking Area 5" and "Garden Spot Trail." During hunting seasons, hunters are permitted to drive into the preserve and park here.

Continue along the orange blazes into an array of massive oaks and tightly clustered cabbage palm groves. A saw palmetto with silvery-blue fronds flags an unusual oak behind it, an enormous double-trunked tree that splits at the forest floor. Climb over a fence at 4.4 miles in a palm hammock, where the forest floor gets soggy seasonally. Thoughtful trail maintainers covered the barbed wire under the stile with garden hose. Side trails created by cattle can be distracting, but the footpath is well worn and well blazed through the dense palm hammocks.

At 4.7 miles, meet the prominent intersection with the trail to the Wheeler Rd trailhead. Turn right to follow the blue-blazed connector through the palm hammock. Crossing a narrow bridge over an ephemeral waterway, exit the palm hammock into a tunnel of scrub forest where rusty lyonia bends crooked limbs overhead. It's a different woodland than any thus far on this hike, deeply shaded and fascinating in its play of natural textures. The trail loses a little elevation entering the next palm hammock. The dark, rich earth can be damp here. Winding between natural columns of cabbage palm trunks, walk beneath an ancient oak tree leaning over the trail. Once lyonia appears again, the palms thin out.

Reach a forest road with a water symbol sign pointing toward the hunt check station for Seminole Ranch at 5.2 miles. Cross the road and another stile. Remember the warning about cattle? In this final part of the loop, ranchers are still permitted to run a herd in Seminole Ranch. Mind the cow patties in the footpath. Tacking between large live oaks, the trail passes through a gateway formed by thick oak trunks before it emerges into open pasture. Follow the worn path across the grass to the wooden fence marking the parking corral at the Wheeler Rd trailhead. Open the gate to exit to the trailhead at 5.6 miles.

Historic Christmas Creek

14. Bronson State Forest

5.4 MILES | BRONSON STATE FOREST, CHRISTMAS

Another easy-to-reach hike near Orlando, this linear arc along the St. Johns River floodplain connects wildlife-rich wetlands with palm hammocks and pine flatwoods, with historic Christmas Creek a central feature between the two trailheads.

Overview

Spanning more than 11,000 acres of former ranchland and forests along the St. Johns River, Charles H. Bronson State Forest offers significant mileage for hikers to explore. Yet it remains lightly used because it's hidden behind other public lands. Little Big Econ State Forest, Chuluota Wilderness, Orlando Wetlands, and Seminole Ranch Conservation Area all front Bronson State Forest, which only has two trailheads. Both are at dead ends of back roads with no signage to lead you there. Only 4.9 miles of the orange-blazed Florida Trail traverses Bronson State Forest. But the connectors to be able to hike it add up and offer alternatives for longer loop hikes. Using this particular approach to Bronson through Orlando Wetlands provides an impressive overview of its human-made wetlands and the wildlife that thrives within before trading chattering birds for the quiet of a ribbon of forest along the St. Johns River floodplain.

Trip Planning

Pets are not permitted in Orlando Wetlands. If you hike any options that don't include the wetlands, leashed dogs are welcome. The park has potable water and restrooms at its trailhead. If you leave a vehicle at Bronson State Forest, pay the day-use fee in advance online and sign the trail register.

Expect to be in full sun traversing the wetlands. The rest of the hike is largely in deep shade. Protection from mosquitoes would be wise. Check river levels before hiking: water.weather.gov station COCF1. When the St. Johns River is in flood stage, do not attempt this hike. At least two miles of the trail in Bronson will be underwater.

Both Bronson State Forest and Seminole Ranch have designated hunting seasons. If you hike during hunting season, wear bright orange and expect to encounter hunters. Both properties also have free-range cattle roaming through the woods. Backpacker campsites in Bronson State Forest require a paid permit in advance, obtained online.

Land Managers

Orlando Wetlands
25155 Wheeler Road, Christmas 32709
407-568-1706
orlando.gov

St. Johns River Water Mgt District
525 Community College Pky SE, Palm Bay 32909
321-984-4940
sjrwmd.com

Charles H. Bronson State Forest
1350 Snow Hill Rd, Geneva 32732
407-971-3500
fdacs.gov

Directions

Exiting Interstate 95 at SR 50 in Titusville, drive west for 10.3 miles through the town of Christmas to Fort Christmas Rd. Turn right. Continue 2.3 miles, passing Fort Christmas. The sharp curve in the road marks the point between the two trailheads. To leave a vehicle at the end of the hike, continue a half mile. Turn right on Philips Rd. Follow it 1.5 miles, taking the track at the sign for Bronson State Forest to Joshua Creek trailhead [28.591867, -81.042351].

To return to the start of the hike, return to Fort Christmas Rd and turn left. At the curve, turn left onto Wheeler Rd and follow it 1.5 miles into Orlando Wetlands. Wheeler Rd trailhead [28.569200, -81.013183] is on the right when the road ends at a gate. You can also park at Orlando Wetlands, but their gates close at 5 p.m.

Options

Both the prior chapter and the next chapter offer hikes interconnecting with this one. There are also many miles to roam in Orlando Wetlands itself. We use a direct 1.3 miles across the wetlands to minimize your time in full sun. Another 0.9 miles on the River Trail brings you to the orange blazes of the Florida Trail at the boundary fence with Bronson State Forest.

At this junction are two alternative options to the hike described in this chapter. The first is to use the River Trail to make a balloon hike. Cross the stile and turn right to follow the white blazes, which lead deeper into the palm hammocks along the St. Johns River. After 2.8 miles, take the County Line Trail, a 0.8-mile connector to the Florida Trail. Go south on the Florida Trail, passing Joshua Creek campsite and the connector to Joshua Creek trailhead. Close the loop by continuing southbound to the boundary fence. Cross the stile and return on the white blazes to Orlando Wetlands for a 12.6-mile round trip and loop.

The other option is to turn right and hike south on the Florida Trail. It's a scenic, swampy, wet jungle-like stretch of trail through palm hammocks close to the river floodplain with some deep mud holes. After 2.5 miles, reach a gate into Orlando Wetlands. Enter it to follow the Perimeter Trail along the fence for a mile to close the loop. Return to the trailhead through the wetlands the same way you reached the boundary fence for a 7-mile hike. For other tweaks to this loop, you can use the Seminole Woods route (first bridge over the canal inside Orlando Wetlands) to return to the trailhead as described in the opposite direction in the previous chapter or use the Seminole Ranch Loop from the back gate of Orlando Wetlands to Wheeler Rd trailhead, hikes of 7.4 and 7.7 miles respectively.

Hike

Cross the road into Orlando Wetlands. Join the road on the berm on the left, which passes the restrooms and picnic pavilion. Established more than twenty-five years ago, Orlando Wetlands was the first wetlands park built in Florida, and many more have been modeled after it. Its broad roads and open landscape are a serious contrast to the rest of the hike. The road splits in two in front of a large environmental education center. Take the left fork.

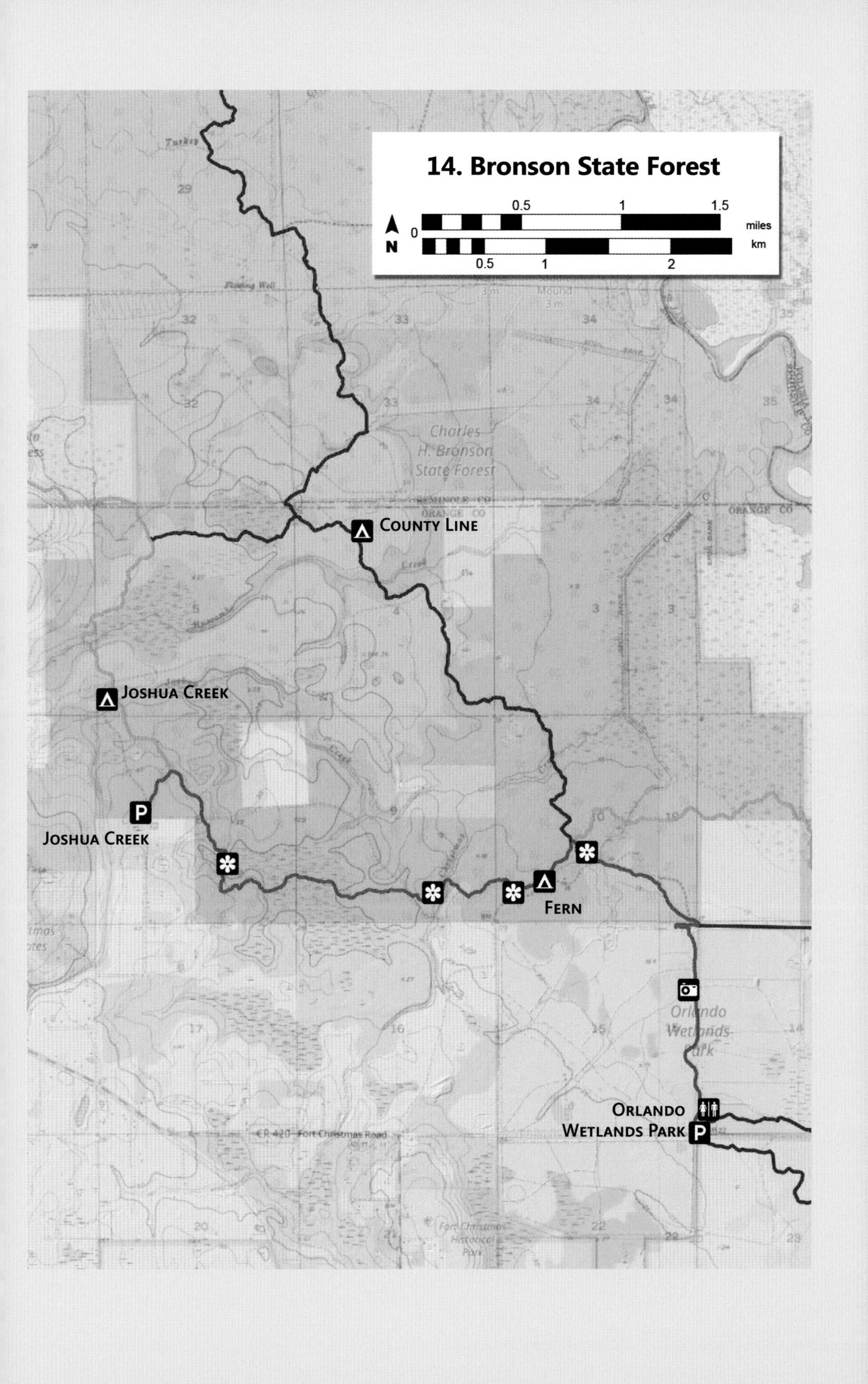
14. Bronson State Forest
0
0.5
1
1.5
miles
km
0.5
1
2
N
County Line
Joshua Creek
Joshua Creek
Fern
Orlando Wetlands Park
Charles H. Bronson State Forest
Orlando Wetlands Park
CR 420 Fort Christmas Road
Fort Christmas Historical Park

While the path is wide and obvious, don't let your guard down. Dozens of huge alligators live in this park, and we've met one striding toward us on this very path. Keep at least twenty feet away from any alligators you see. Built and managed by the city of Orlando, the park is a giant filtration system, the final step of purifying municipal wastewater. Reclaimed water enters through an inflow structure. Gravity moves it slowly through a series of wetland cells where aquatic plants like pickerelweed, duck potato, and giant bulrush pull phosphorus and nitrogen from the water. The process can take a month or more before the water is discharged into the St. Johns River floodplain.

The levees break the park into cells. Most have trails atop them and there are signposts at all junctions. Stay on the due north Wetlands Blvd as you reach each one. Water levels differ in each cell. The wetlands attract an amazing array of birds and other swamp-dwelling wildlife such as alligators and otters. North of Bobcat Trail are expansive views on both sides. Flocks of moorhens and coots gather in the reeds; herons nest in

Alligator on the move, Orlando Wetlands

cypress trees. Past Limpkin Lane, a canal parallels on the right as you pass Alligator Alley on the left. At 1.2 miles, reach a T intersection with a picnic shelter at Bald Eagle Blvd. Turn left. Walk up to a small white building and look for a bridge on the right. Take it across the perimeter canal to the Perimeter Trail. Turn right at the fence. In less than a quarter mile, approach a staircase stile over the back fence of Orlando Wetlands. A Florida National Scenic Trail sign is on the other side. This is the start of the River Trail inside Seminole Ranch Conservation Area.

Take the stile over the fence and start following white blazes beneath the live oaks. This is a nicely shaded stretch of trail with both mature oaks and younger pine trees along it. Past a jog through a cluster of cabbage palms, resurrection ferns make the oak limbs overhead look downright furry. Saw palmetto fills the spaces under the oaks. One showy ribbon of bluish-tinged palms sits beneath the oaks near an opening with a grassy wetland on the left. Emerging from a dense oak hammock into younger pines, the white blazes are visible ahead for some distance. Cross an old ranch road before entering a bromeliad-laden oak hammock. Past another old track, walk between the trunks of sand live oaks into a palm hammock.

The junction with the orange-blazed Florida Trail is at 2.3 miles, with another stepladder stile straight ahead. Cross it to enter Bronson State Forest. Turn left to follow the orange blazes north. Graze the fence briefly before turning away from it into a dense hammock of cabbage palms and live oaks. The open space beyond them is the floodplain

Pond pine flatwoods near Joshua Creek

of the St. Johns River, a vast expanse stretching toward Titusville. Less than a quarter mile past the stile, reach Fern Camp. It has a picnic table and fire ring. Walk beneath an oak-shaded expanse before entering a dense hammock where cabbage palms rise like columns amid underbrush creating a jungle-like feel. The forest floor is earthy and often damp.

When the trail leaves the hammock, the transition to pine savanna is almost jarring. Tall grasses and dense underbrush fill the spaces between the pines. As saw palmetto takes over the understory, cross a forest road. Just past it is Christmas Creek, a tannic waterway sluicing toward the St. Johns River. A long bench above the creek has poison ivy sprouting around it. Take the bridge over the creek at 3.1 miles.

The trail climbs to higher ground with a forest of mature saw palmetto edging the footpath. Cypress knees rise from the leafy forest floor. After a brief jog through a palm hammock, ascend into pine savanna. Well-hidden clusters of hooded pitcher plants grow in low damp spots. Palmetto prairie takes over near a forest road where an equestrian trail crosses. Watch for the FNST marker as the trail veers left into an open landscape dense with short saw palmetto. Under the deep shade of a mature oak hammock, wind between oaks and palms. A sand road is in the middle of this hammock. Emerging from a saw palmetto corridor, circle a bayhead before rising into pine flatwoods.

A steady descent leads to the bridged trickle of South Slough through a fern-filled basin at 4.6 miles. Climbing past massive southern magnolias, enter pine flatwoods, their understory a solid wall of saw palmetto. The habitat transitions to sandhills beyond a ranch road beneath a power line at 5 miles. Pine needles carpet the footpath, but many cattle trails cross the Florida Trail at distracting angles. Keep an eye on the orange blazes to stay on course. A quarter mile past the power line, reach the signposted junction to the Joshua Creek trailhead. Turn left to follow blue blazes through the sandhills to the trailhead, wrapping this hike after 5.5 miles.

To extend this hike, continue north on the Florida Trail at the Joshua Creek trailhead junction for a traverse of pond pine flatwoods into the lush Joshua Creek basin. A series of narrow boardwalks end near the Joshua Creek campsite at 5.8 miles. Backtrack to the trailhead junction and exit the forest for a 6.5-mile hike.

Rosemary scrub

15. Chuluota Wilderness Loop

1.6 MILES | CHULUOTA WILDERNESS AREA, CHULUOTA

In a scrub forest above the St. Johns River floodplain, this loop hike through a county wilderness park offers an immersion in rare patches of Florida rosemary scrub within a sand pine scrub.

Overview

Florida rosemary is a curious shrub. When mature, it has a very rounded appearance, almost as big around as it is tall. Hardly anything else grows near it, because it releases a chemical into the ground that prevents other plants from growing. You don't see them all that often, because they need a certain type of well-drained sand to thrive. They mainly grow on ancient sand dune ridges well inland. On this hike you'll walk through an entire forest of these odd plants, the trees in the sand pine scrub surrounding them covered in lichens and mosses.

Backing up to Bronson State Forest, Chuluota Wilderness offers its own double loop connected to the Florida Trail. Meandering deep into floodplain forests, the 2-mile East Loop Trail is popular with equestrians. The 2.2-mile West Loop Trail sticks to higher, drier habitats along the southwest boundary of the preserve. Our loop hike uses the Florida Trail and the inner leg of the West Loop to visit the high points of this preserve.

Trip Planning

Leashed pets are permitted. The hike is primarily in high, dry habitats and can be sunny in places. If you take the suggested side trip to the boundary pavilion, expect insects in the swamps that the boardwalks traverse. Hiking poles are a help on those boardwalks as they can be slippery. Safety markers are at major trail intersections. They include a location code starting with CW and a USNG locator to share with 911 for emergency assistance. Hunting is not permitted in Chuluota Wilderness, but it is permitted in adjoining Bronson State Forest.

Land Manager

Seminole County Natural Lands
100 E 1st St, Sanford 32771
407-665-2211
seminolecountyfl.gov

Directions

Exiting Interstate 95 at SR 50 in Titusville, drive west for 10.3 miles on SR 50 to Fort Christmas Rd. Turn right. Continue 2.3 miles, passing Fort Christmas. Follow the road around the curve, passing turnoffs for the trailheads for the hikes in chapters 13 and 14. After 6.3 miles and a couple of sharp turns, Fort Christmas Rd ends at a T with Lake Mills Rd. Turn right. Continue 1 mile to a right turn onto Curryville Rd where Lake Mills Rd makes a sweeping left curve. Follow Curryville Rd for 2.5 miles. Chuluota Wilderness trailhead [28.62322, -81.063278] is on the right just before the road ends.

Options

When you reach the three-way trail junction at 0.7 miles, you have several options in addition to the hike described here. Add 2.6 miles to the hike by staying on the orange blazes for a scenic round trip to the boundary with Bronson State Forest, turning around at a covered bench. Crossing numerous boardwalks, it's a botanically interesting hike. Or add 2 miles by taking the East Loop Trail. Optimized for equestrians, it's primarily a broad forest road and may be muddy or underwater in low spots. Or use the outer side of the West Loop Trail to add 0.3 miles. Since it stays close to the preserve's boundary fence, we prefer the route described below. A linear hike from Chuluota Wilderness trailhead south to Joshua Creek trailhead [28.591867, -81.042351] is 4.1 miles, usually a wade for a stretch past the boundary fence. Using the County Line and River Trails in Bronson, make a 9.1-mile loop. For trip planning in Bronson, see the previous chapter.

Hike

Enter the woods at the Florida Trail sign to the left of the trailhead kiosk. The footpath winds through sand pine scrub, quickly crossing a forest road that is part of the equestrian loop for the preserve. Meander between the crooked limbs of rusty lyonia and sand live oaks. Seafoam-colored bubbles of deer moss rise from the forest floor.

Within the first quarter mile is the first Florida rosemary, a large dark-green shrub shaped like a tumbleweed. There are dozens in this rosemary scrub, the trail a sandy path through a mossy forest floor. Chapman and myrtle oaks with spiky branches create thickets. The towering sand pines are too tall and skinny to cast much shade in this desert-like habitat with its diminutive trees. Slim fingers of green emerge from the bright-white sand, the spikes of sandspike moss. Look for scrub holly and scrub olive trees in this landscape in miniature.

Cross a firebreak before entering a denser rosemary scrub. Rusty lyonia provides a low canopy here, the trail corridor tightly defined by Florida rosemary bushes. Twisting and winding as it loses elevation, the footpath leads toward a distant line of pines.

Individual rosemary bushes stand out under the sand pines. Duck under a branch with a prominent orange blaze, not far from a gopher tortoise burrow. Transition from scrub into a hardwood hammock with saw palmetto, a hallway of green opening up suddenly into the three-way junction with the East and West Loop Trails at 0.7 miles.

Leave the orange blazes here and turn right. As soon as the forest road rises out of the hammock, it reaches an intersection at Marker CW 4, the bottom of the West Loop Trail. Continue straight. Palmetto prairie spreads to distant pines on the left, while sand pine scrub edges close on the right. Watch for deer's tongue and tarflower along the road's edge.

By a mile, draw within sight of a large depression with a prairie pond in the middle. Sandhill cranes often gather in this vicinity. A bird blind perches on the rim of the bluff above the pond. A beaten path leads to this observation point, a perfect perch for birders. Return to the main path, the trail curving along

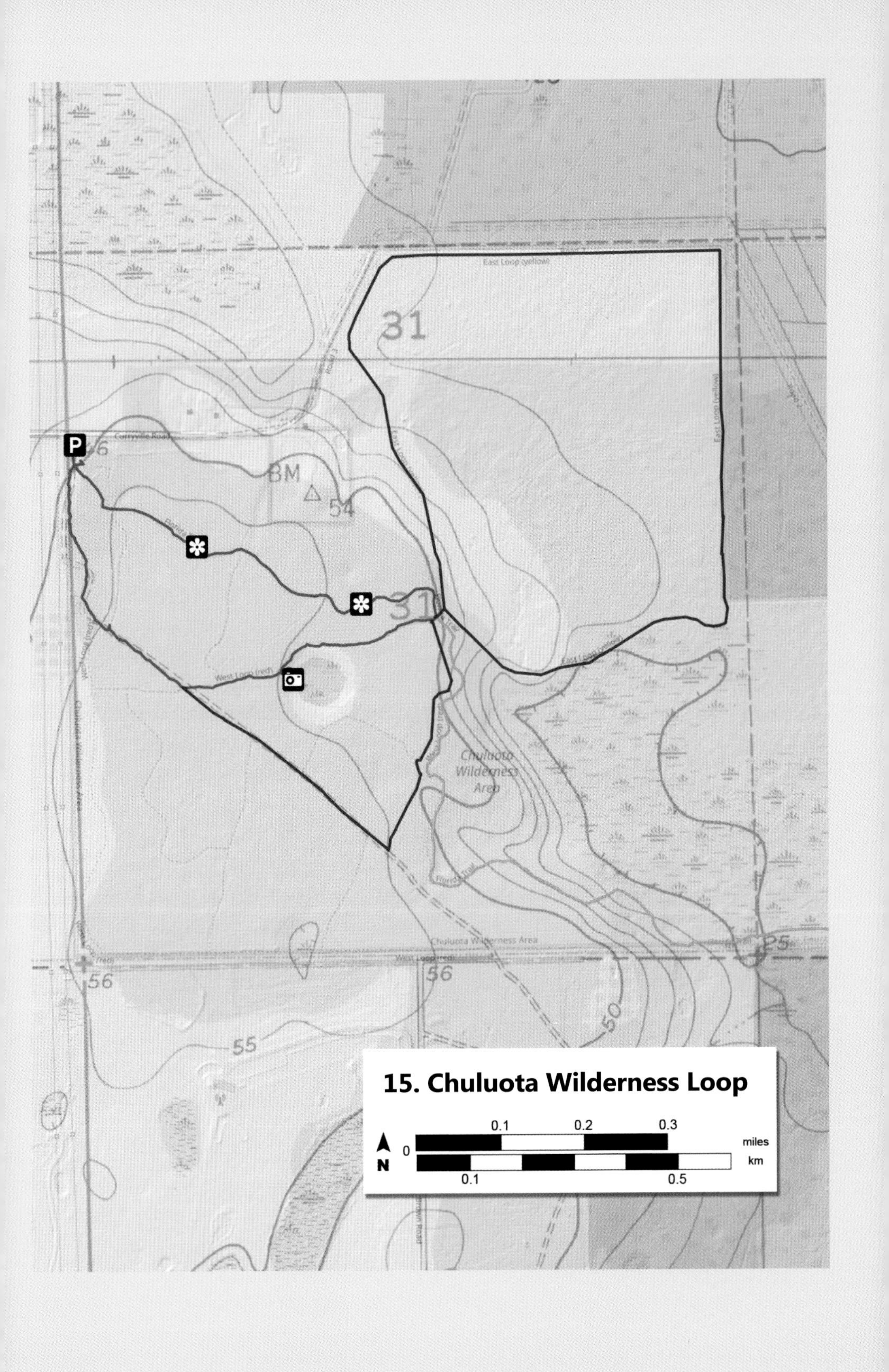
15. Chuluota Wilderness Loop
0.1
0.2
0.3
0
miles
km
0.1
0.5
N
P
31
BM
54
56
55
50
25
East Loop (yellow)
Curryville Road
West Loop (red)
Chuluota Wilderness Area
Florida Trail

West Loop

the sand pine scrub as it provides a delineation between habitats. As it leaves the palmetto prairie, pines become more prevalent. Pass a trace of a sand road on the left, where an arrow with a horse symbol points forward.

After a straightaway along the scrub, meet a junction with a forest road as it enters an oak hammock. Another arrow points forward. Soon after, reach the top of the West Loop Trail at 1.2 miles. The sign points in the direction from which you came and to the left. Continue straight.

The forest road aims northwest toward a large open pasture on adjacent ranchland. Beneath the live oaks, the trail reaches the fence line and turns to follow it, paralleling a high-tension power line. Watch for gopher tortoise burrows beneath the barbed wire fence along this linear stretch. Emerging at the trailhead kiosk after 1.6 miles, complete the loop.

16. Kolokee Loop

5.5 MILES | LITTLE BIG ECON STATE FOREST, OVIEDO

Branching off one of the most popular segments of the Florida Trail, this easily accessed scenic loop shows off a lush riverside forest and bluffs above the Econlockhatchee River.

Overview

There's a reason the Barr Street trailhead for Little Big Econ State Forest is huge. Thanks to its proximity to Orlando and name recognition, this section of the Florida Trail is heavily hiked. A series of well-appointed primitive campsites are close enough to the trailhead for family getaways. The Florida Trail in both directions is simply beautiful. Kolokee was the name of a turn-of-the-century railroad town along the Florida East Coast Railway. While most reminders of its existence are long gone, a walk on this loop includes part of the old rail line, where sturdy posts once supporting a trestle over the river still stand.

Trip Planning

Leashed pets are welcome. There is a parking fee at Barr Street, payable online in advance. The primitive campsites at West Camp must be reserved online. The portion of the hike along the old railroad line is on the Flagler Trail, shared with off-road cyclists and equestrians.

Check river levels before hiking: water.weather.gov station LECF1. Since the trail dips through floodplains along the river, never enter flowing water. Prominent "LE" signs, each numbered, provide a distinct location for emergency responders should you have an injury or medical issue while hiking this loop.

Land Manager

Little Big Econ State Forest
1350 Snow Hill Rd, Geneva 32732
407-971-3500
fdacs.gov

Directions

From the intersection of CR 426 and SR 46 in Geneva (7.3 miles east of SR 415 in Sanford and 16.3 miles west of Interstate 95 at Mims) follow CR 426 (Geneva Dr.) west toward Oviedo for 4.5 miles. The Barr Street trailhead [28.687403, -81.159278] is on the left past a small bridge over Salt Creek.

Options

Stretching more than ten miles along the river basin and the uplands around it, the Little Big Econ segment of the Florida Trail is a beautiful hike. Junctions are clearly signposted. A linear hike northbound to Lockwood Blvd trailhead [28.667009, -81.176689] along the bluffs and river tributaries is 2.8 miles, passing a small cascade called Boonie Falls. Or skip the Kolokee Trail and continue along the river bluffs to the bridge shared with the Flagler Trail. Cross the river and stay in the Flagler Trail's tunnel of trees past the Florida Trail turnoff to reach Snow Hill Rd trailhead [28.649584, -81.129799] in Chuluota after 4.8 linear miles. Another scenic route is a 4.1-mile linear hike between Barr Street and the White Trail trailhead [28.683637, -81.11767] at forest headquarters off Snow Hill Rd. At mile 2.5 of this hike, make the left onto white blazes to follow them through

Econlockhatchee River

Kolokee Trail

lush palm hammocks above the river floodplain, ending at a picnic pavilion a short walk from the river bluffs.

Hike

A deeply shaded blue-blazed trail leads from Barr Street trailhead to a signposted intersection with the Florida Trail. Turn left and cross Salt Creek on a footbridge at a quarter mile. Make a sharp right as the orange blazes parallel a forest road and the creek's flow toward the Econlockhatchee River. Reach the river at benches on a bluff. Follow the narrow footpath downriver, with river views between screens of vegetation; a memorial bench occupies a scenic perch. Turning toward the forest road, the trail joins it briefly to cross a tributary before returning to the bluffs.

The numbered campsites of West Camp are in the pines along this road, each in its own little clearing with a picnic bench. Pass the final campsite at 0.6 miles. Leaving the pines, enter a lush humid hardwood forest. After edging around a tributary to cross it on one of the many footbridges on this section, the footpath turns sandy beneath oaks and hickories. Reach the signposted trail junction with the Kolokee Trail at 1 mile at the LE-32 sign. Turn left.

White blazed, the Kolokee Trail quickly diverges from the Florida Trail. Cedars and oaks dominate the canopy, with the softly draped fronds of bluestem palm in the understory. Low spots cradle tannic waters. During fall and winter, sweetgum and red maple sport autumn colors through the sparse forest canopy to the left, revealing floodplain swamps where cabbage palms thrive. A quarter mile along the white blazes, cross a bridge over a deep but narrow waterway. The humidity created by floodplain swamps covers the tree limbs above in a soft fur of bromeliads and resurrection ferns. The trail narrows to a tunnel between palm fronds where dark waters creep close to a low bridge over a cypress slough. A two-plank boardwalk arcs around a floodplain forest. Reach

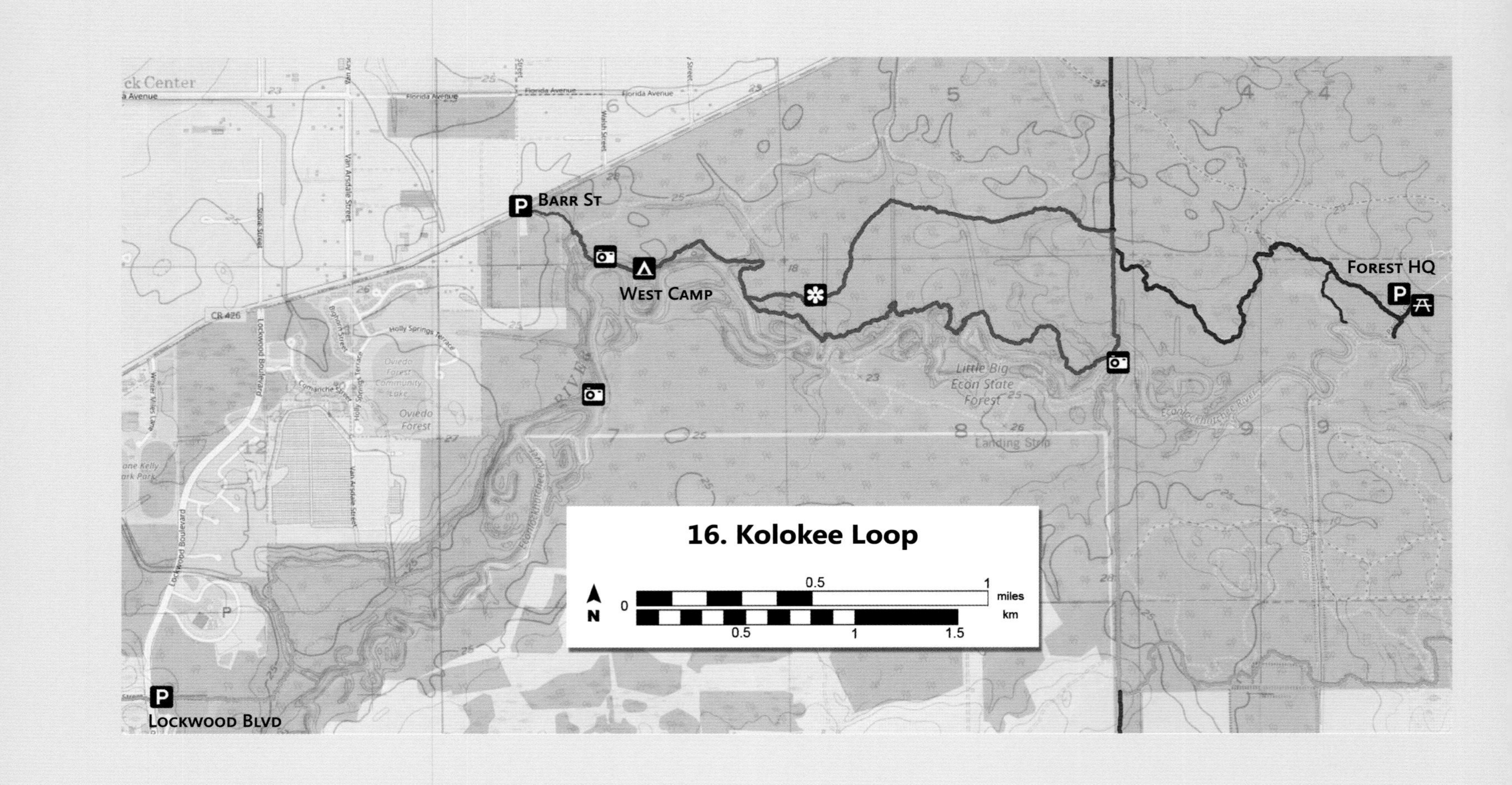
16. Kolokee Loop
Barr St
West Camp
Forest HQ
Lockwood Blvd
Little Big Econ State Forest
Landing Strip
Oviedo Forest
Florida Avenue
Walsh Street
Van Arsdale Street
Lockwood Boulevard
CR 426
Holly Springs Terrace
0
0.5
1
miles
km
1.5
N

higher ground in pine flatwoods above the swamps.

Pass the LE-34 sign before crossing a bridge at 1.9 miles into a palm hammock. Palms yield to pines and oaks with low-hanging limbs. A paralleling equestrian trail is to the left. Watch for mucky spots in the footpath up to the next bridge. Rise into sandhill habitat beyond it, emerging at a prominent intersection at 2.4 miles. Two shaded benches flank the corners. Turn right at the Mile 6.5 marker to join the Flagler Trail.

This multiuse segment of trail follows the railbed through what was once Kolokee, a town along a spur of the Florida East Coast Railway built in 1910 to help develop land owned by Henry Flagler in what is now Chuluota. Timber and turpentine industries supported Kolokee, which had a school and a post office as well as a railroad station. Once there were no more old-growth cypress or pines to harvest, the town faded into obscurity. The railbed offers enough height above the floodplain to keep your feet dry. Pass a white-blazed trail on the left (it goes to a trailhead on Snow Hill Rd). The deeply shaded straightaway quickly reaches a bowl of swamp, the footpath leaving the railbed to cross a natural spillway. Continue over a sturdy bridge and follow blazes between the vine-tangled wooden piers of the former railroad trestle. Rejoining the railbed, face the broad bridge over the Econlockhatchee River at 2.9 miles. Walk onto the span to take in the downstream view.

Rejoin the Florida Trail's orange blazes northbound where you stepped onto the bridge. Passing a bench, follow the river bluffs upriver. Oaks tower above this vibrant humid hardwood forest. Round a swamp covered in duckweed before meandering into a palm hammock. The girth of one of the loblolly pines made us stop and stare at its crown. Edge to the bluffs, glimpsing the river through palm fronds and pine needles. Cross a bridge at the LE-41 sign at 3.6 miles and swing toward the bluffs again for more river panoramas. Below are beaches where massive alligators soak up the sun. We spotted them along several curves in the river and on sandbars. Curve around a massive bowl of swamp where alligators lounge on sunny spots on the far shore.

Magnolias and oaks sport a dense array of bromeliads in the forest beyond the big swamp. After another peek at the river, follow a tributary upstream crossed on a long, high bridge. Circling the next swamp basin, the trail is crowded by bluestem palms before it works its way toward the river bluffs again. Cross a short bridge at 4.2 miles. A sandy path leads to a view of a peninsula between the side channel and the river. Lush forest crowds the footpath again, with loblolly pines towering over the canopy. Cedars form a screen behind which a bowl of swamp sits. Reach the intersection with the Kolokee Trail to close the loop after 4.5 miles.

Continue straight ahead on the orange blazes, backtracking through familiar territory past West Camp and along the river bluffs. Cross Salt Creek on the footbridge and turn right on the blue blaze to the Barr Street trailhead, completing a 5.5-mile hike at the kiosk.

Scrubby flatwoods

17. Seminole Scrub Loop

5.3 MILES | SEMINOLE STATE FOREST, SANFORD

Connecting the Florida Trail with the Lower Wekiva Loop in the southern end of Seminole State Forest, the Scrub Loop showcases scrub habitat not far from the Wekiva River.

Overview

Protecting nearly 28,000 acres, Seminole State Forest is an integral part of a wildlife corridor between the Wekiva River basin and the Ocala National Forest. It's one of the more likely places along the Florida Trail to see a bear. Wildlife is always present along this section of the trail, with sandhill cranes around Boggy Creek Lake and herds of white-tailed deer in the flatwoods.

Florida scrub-jays call the southern portion of the scrub forest home. Found only in Florida, these jays prefer scrub of a certain height. They forage on the ground, bury acorns, nest low in scrub oaks, and live in family groups where mature siblings help parents take care of the next brood. One member of the family acts as a sentinel, perching high to warn the others of any potential threat walking up on them. Large and bright blue, they are obvious against the greens of the forest.

This loop circles a healthy sand pine scrub forest in the south part of Seminole State Forest, close to suburbia. It doesn't have an official name, so we call it the Scrub Loop.

Trip Planning

Leashed dogs are welcome. Bicycles are not permitted. A day-use fee is charged at the Sand Pond and Cassia trailheads, payable online in advance. Use sun protection as much of the hike is in full sun. Insect repellent helps for the shady parts of the hike.

Backpackers can camp at a trail shelter along this loop. Three additional primitive campsites are off the Florida Trail and the Lower Wekiva Loop. Reserve online or at the trailhead kiosk; there is a fee. Bear bagging or a bear canister is a must.

Check hunting seasons before hiking at Seminole State Forest. There aren't many, so it's best to leave the forest to hunters during those dates. If you hike during hunting season, wear bright orange.

Land Manager

Seminole State Forest
28500 SR 44, Eustis 32736
352-589-1762
fdacs.gov

Directions

From Interstate 4 exit 101C (Sanford), follow SR 46 west. The Wekiva Parkway (SR 429) swoops in and divides SR 46 in two at Orange Ave. Stay on SR 46 westbound, which dips under the toll road and goes through traffic circles. Crossing the Wekiva River on its own bridge parallel to the Wekiva Parkway, SR 46 reaches Wekiva River Rd at 4.4 miles. Turn right to go under the overpass into Seminole State Forest. A mile later, reach Bear Pond trailhead [28.8196, -81.4287], a large lot adjoining the pond. This recreation area has a

Scrub forest

picnic shelter, fishing pier, nature trail, and vault toilet. A large kiosk adjoins the Florida Trail entrance across the lot from the pond.

Options

This loop ties together the Florida Trail with the Lower Wekiva Loop by using a forest road between them as a connector. Add mileage by following this route past the turnoff on East Spur Road to the second turnoff for the Lower Wekiva Loop at 3.7 miles. Follow the Lower Wekiva Loop back to Shelter Camp and return to Bear Pond for a 10.6-mile hike. Or use the blue-blazed Blueberry Cross Trail to shorten that trek to 9.9 miles, a route that hits the high points of the floodplain between Black Water Creek and the Wekiva River.

The Florida Trail runs south to north through Seminole State Forest. It's 7.5 miles between Bear Pond and the Cassia trailhead on SR 44 via a blue-blazed connector. Beyond East Spur Road, memorable turnaround points on a round trip solely on the orange blazes are the picnic table at Black Water Creek for an 8-mile round trip and Shark Tooth Spring for a 10.4-mile round trip. An easy 0.7-mile nature trail also loops Bear Pond at Bear Pond trailhead.

Hike

Enter the Florida Trail through a gap in the fence next to the kiosk. Leading you along the edge of an oak hammock, the footpath makes a gentle curve bounded by saw palmetto. After a half mile, it descends slightly into a lush forest of

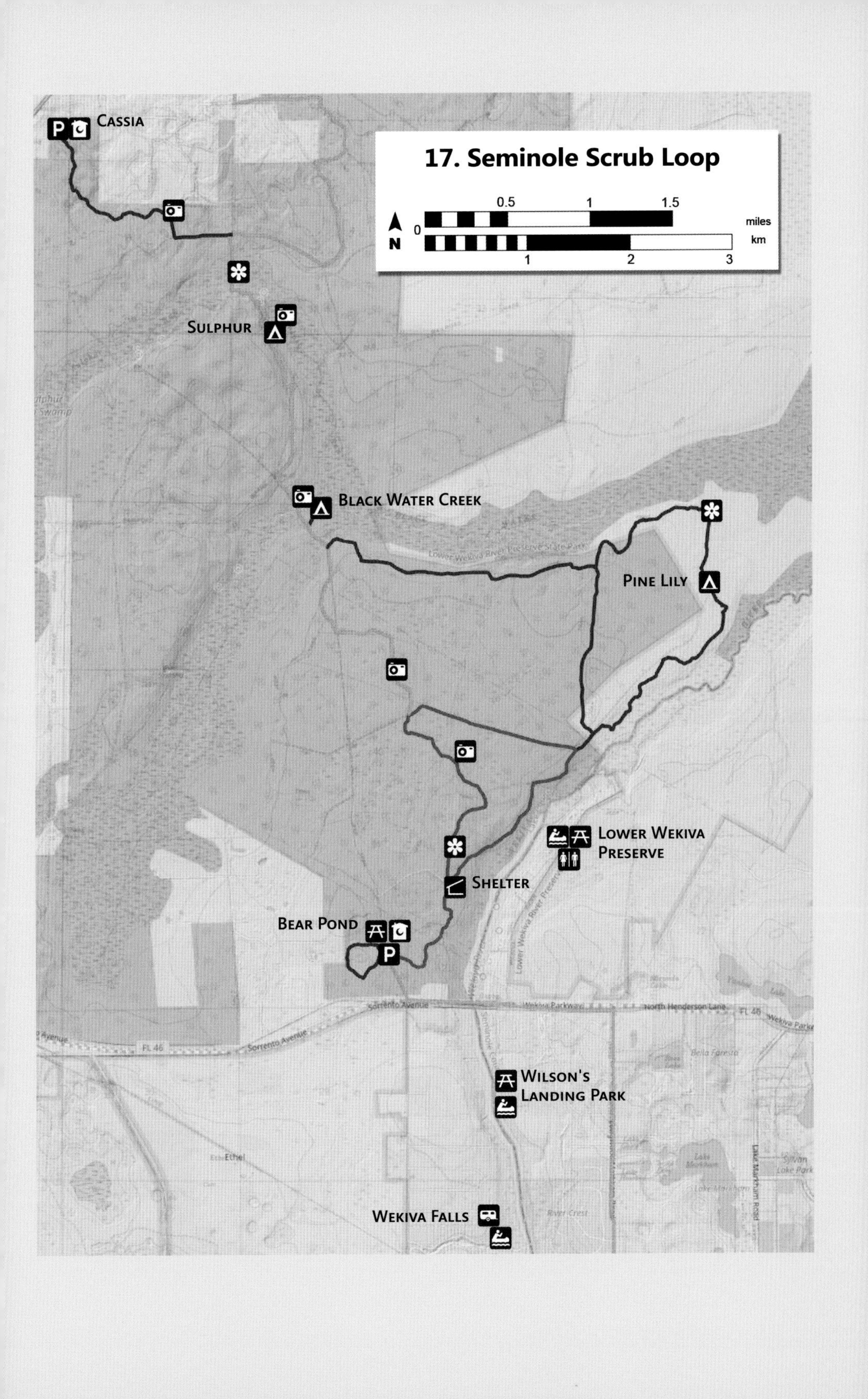

17. Seminole Scrub Loop
0.5
1
1.5
0
miles
km
N
1
2
3
Cassia
Sulphur
Black Water Creek
Pine Lily
Lower Wekiva Preserve
Shelter
Bear Pond
Wilson's Landing Park
Wekiva Falls
Lower Wekiva River Preserve State Park
Sorrento Avenue
Wekiva Parkway
North Henderson Lane
FL 46

Shelter Camp

palms and pines surrounding a creek that flows to the Wekiva River. Climb out of the creek basin into scrubby flatwoods along the well-worn trail.

Past a line of cabbage palms, step into the clearing at Shelter Camp, a camping area surrounding a rarity on the Florida Trail, an Appalachian Trail–style shelter. Built in 1992, it's been updated since. Just past it is the trail junction with the Lower Wekiva Loop at 0.8 miles. Sign the trail register and keep left at the junction to enter the enormity of the scrub. Surrounded by trees that scarcely reach shoulder height, it's a walk through Florida's own desert amid a collection of plants that thrive on the loose well-drained sands of ancient sand dunes. The pines, both short and tall, are sand pines. Adapted to a dry habitat, they don't release their pine cones until triggered by a forest fire. Scrub is fire-dependent, rejuvenating after a burn.

The thicket of understory is mainly made up of short scrub oaks, myrtle oaks, and Chapman oaks, all adapted to live in dry conditions. They provide the food source Florida scrub-jays need. Myrtle oaks have rounded leaves, while scrub oaks have leaves folded in on themselves like little canoes. Blazing is minimal but the trail is obvious. The white sand underfoot is very reflective in the sunshine. A few Florida rosemary—big, rounded shrubs—grow in the footpath. Thanks to the height of the trees, this part of the scrub is the most likely place to spot Florida scrub-jays. Once one wings by in a flash of blue, you usually see more.

After tunneling through the oaks, cross a sand road at 1.5 miles. Continue straight into the dense understory of oaks, a view of a grassy prairie opening up behind a line of saw palmetto. Longleaf pine stands atop a distant ridge and the views sweep across its top. Longleaf pines rise from the edge of the scrub, creating a short stretch of scrubby flatwoods.

At 2.3 miles, reach East Spur Road. Hunters can drive it during hunting seasons and cyclists can use it any time. For this hike, it's your connector to the Lower Wekiva Loop. A sign explains the young longleaf pine you just walked through, a reforestation project. Longleaf pine forests were once the dominant habitat in the Southeast. Unrestricted logging and clearing for agriculture and homes decimated these slow-growing forests. Less than 3 percent of the original longleaf forests of the United States remain.

Turn right and walk down East Spur Road. It starts as a graded two-track with a grassy center and shoulders, surrounded by scrubby flatwoods. After a half mile it becomes a service road, open only to forest personnel and recreational use. It becomes sandy underfoot past a yellow-blazed equestrian trail heading north. Walk beneath slash pines before reaching a turn where a wooden sign says "No Horses No Bikes" straight ahead. Leave the road to walk around the sign, joining a footpath through a scrub forest that crowds the trail.

At 3.3 miles, reach the Lower Wekiva Loop at a T intersection. Turn right. If you're hiking this loop backward, it's easy to miss this connector. (If you end up at the Blueberry Cross Trail, turn left onto it and left onto the jeep track and that will lead you to East Spur Rd.)

Following white blazes, hike south. The richly textured hardwood forest to the left is along the floodplain of the Wekiva River. Although you never see the river from any of the trails in Seminole State Forest because of its swampy shoreline, it defines the eastern side of this forest. It is a favorite of paddlers, a nationally designated Wild and Scenic River emptying into the St. Johns River. River access is on the opposite shore at Lower Wekiva River Preserve State Park and at Wilson's Landing Park, where an outfitter has rentals and offers tours.

While the upper part of the Lower Wekiva Loop grazes the river floodplain, this southbound portion stays in uplands. Transition from scrubby flatwoods into an oak hammock, passing mature saw palmetto with trunks that rise up off the forest floor. The low canopy of oaks provides minor shade allowing bracken fern to thrive. Exiting the oaks near a faint track leading west, it's back to the scrubby flatwoods along a long, straight stretch. Across the pine savanna is a distant line of pond pines, which the trail reaches and passes by.

A walk across the white sugar sand with scrub oaks perfect for scrub-jay activity briefly yields to an incursion of the hardwood forest. The young sand pines with their fluffy needles make the last half mile through the scrub a delight. Feel a mild uphill as the trail continues deeper into the scrub forest. It's almost a surprise to seal the loop after 4.5 miles at the junction with the Florida Trail at the mailbox with the trail register.

Turn left and walk into Shelter Camp, a nice stop for a break. Follow the narrow footpath along the orange blazes through a final ribbon of scrub before descending through the ferns to the bridge over the creek, the water source for Shelter Camp. Walking through the archway of oaks once more, keep left at the next fork. Emerge at Bear Pond trailhead after 5.3 miles.

Turkey oaks, Green Swamp

Central Florida West

Half of a large circle that the Florida Trail makes around Central Florida, the Western Corridor ties together long-standing segments of trail in Withlacoochee State Forest with a more recent unbroken ribbon of footpath on the Cross Florida Greenway.

BASE CAMPS

Dade City

The county seat of Pasco County, Dade City has a vibrant historic downtown just a few miles west of the Withlacoochee River and the Green Swamp.

STAY

Hampton Inn 352-567-5277, 13215 US 301 S.

Withlacoochee River Park Campground 352-567-0264, 12449 Withlacoochee Blvd.

EAT

ABC Pizza 352-567-1414, 37941 Heather Pl.

Florida Cracker Lunch on Limoges 352-567-5685, 14139 7th St.

Kafe Kokopelli 352-523-0055, 37940 Live Oak Ave.

SEE AND DO

Colt Creek State Park 863-815-6761, 16000 SR 471, Lakeland.

Pioneer Florida Museum 352-567-0262, 15602 Pioneer Museum Rd.

Withlacoochee River Park 352-567-0264, 12449 Withlacoochee Blvd.

Brooksville

Along the Fort King Road, an 1825 military route, Brooksville became a town before the Civil War, drawing settlers who established plantations, farms, and ranches.

STAY

Dolan House B&B 352-631-8822, 701 Museum Ct.

Hampton Inn 352-796-1000, 30301 Cortez Blvd.

Holiday Inn Express 352-796-0455, 30455 Cortez Blvd.

Silver Lake Campground 352-797-4140, 31475 Silver Lake Rd.

EAT

Coney Island Drive Inn 352-796-9141, 1112 E Jefferson St.

Deep South BBQ 352-799-5060, 7247 Cedar Ln.

Florida Cracker Kitchen 352-754-8787, 966 E Jefferson St.

Papa Joes Italian Restaurant 352-799-3904, 6244 Spring Lake Hwy.

SEE AND DO

Boyett's Grove 352-796-2289, 4355 Spring Lake Hwy.

Chinsegut Hill Historic Site 352-770-2188, 22495 Chinsegut Hill Rd.

1885 Railroad Depot Museum 352-799-4766, 70 Russell St.

Weeki Wachee Springs State Park 352-592-5656, 6131 Commercial Way.

Inverness

Named for the blue waters of Tsala Apopka Lake, this historic phosphate mining and railroad community is the county seat of Citrus County. The Florida Trail goes through town through Whispering Pines Park and the Withlacoochee State Trail.

STAY

Central Motel 352-726-4515, 721 US 41 S.

Holiday Inn Express 352-341-3515, 903 E Gulf to Lake.

Holder Mine Campground 352-797-4140, 4399 Trail 10.

Mutual Mine Campground 352-797-4140, 4771 Trail 16.

EAT

Cinnamon Sticks 352-419-7914, 727 US 41.

Stumpknockers 352-726-2212, 110 W Main St.

SEE AND DO

Fort Cooper State Park 352-726-0315, 3100 Old Floral City Rd.

Whispering Pines Park 352-726-3913, 1700 Forest Dr.

Withlacoochee State Trail 352-726-0315, 3100 Old Floral City Rd.

Dunnellon

Founded in the 1890s during Florida's phosphate-mining boom, Dunnellon sits at the confluence of the Rainbow and Withlacoochee Rivers.

STAY

Comfort Suites 352-533-5234, 20052 Brooks St.

Dinner Bell Motel 352-489-2550, 12094 S Williams St.

Gator Den Motel 352-489-2397, 12189 S Williams St.

Ross Prairie Campground 352-732-2606, 10660 SW SR 200.

EAT

Blue Gator 352-465-1635, 12189 S Williams St.

Go For Donuts 352-465-2551, 20372 E Pennsylvania Ave.

Front Porch 352-489-4708, 12039 N Florida Ave.

Swampy's 352-547-4777, 19773 E Pennsylvania Ave.

SEE AND DO

Rainbow River Canoe & Kayak 352-489-7854, 12121 River View.

Rainbow Springs State Park 352-465-8555, 19158 SW 81st Pl Rd.

Belleview

Established around Nine Mile Pond along an old military trail, Belleview is one of the older communities in Marion County and a Florida Trail Gateway Community. Services are along US 27/301/441 and at Interstate 75.

STAY

Hampton Inn 352-347-1600, 2075 SW CR 484.

Santos Campground 352-369-2693, 3080 SE 80th St.

Shangri-La Campground 352-347-1163, 12788 SW 69th Ct.

Sleep Inn 352-347-8383, 13600 SW 17th Ct.

EAT

B. D. Beans 352-245-3077, 5148 SE Abshier Blvd.

Chicken Time 352-307-0555, 10819 SE US 441.

Pasta Faire 352-347-3100, 10401 SE US 441.

SEE AND DO

Don Garlits Museums 1-877-271-3278, 13700 SW 16th Ave.

Paradise Springs Diving 352-368-5746, 4040 SE 84th Ln Rd.

Santos Bike Trails 352-236-7143, 3080 SE 80th St.

Silver Springs

Since the 1880s, the massive first-magnitude spring at Silver Springs, one of the world's largest, has attracted visitors from all over to marvel at its deep-blue depths and to cruise across it in glass-bottomed boats.

STAY

Holiday Inn Express 352-304-6111, 5360 E Silver Springs Blvd.

Silver Springs State Park Campground 800-326-3521, 1425 NE 58th Ave.

Sun Plaza 352-236-2343, 5461 E Silver Springs Blvd.

EAT

Mojo Grill 352-291-6656, 4620 E Silver Springs Blvd.

Silver Springs Diner 352-355-2850, 5300 E Silver Springs Blvd.

SEE AND DO

Appleton Museum of Art 352-291-4455, 4333 E Silver Springs Blvd.

Fort King National Historic Site 352-629-2489, 3925 E Fort King St, Ocala.

Silver Springs State Park 352-236-7148, 1425 NE 58th Ave.

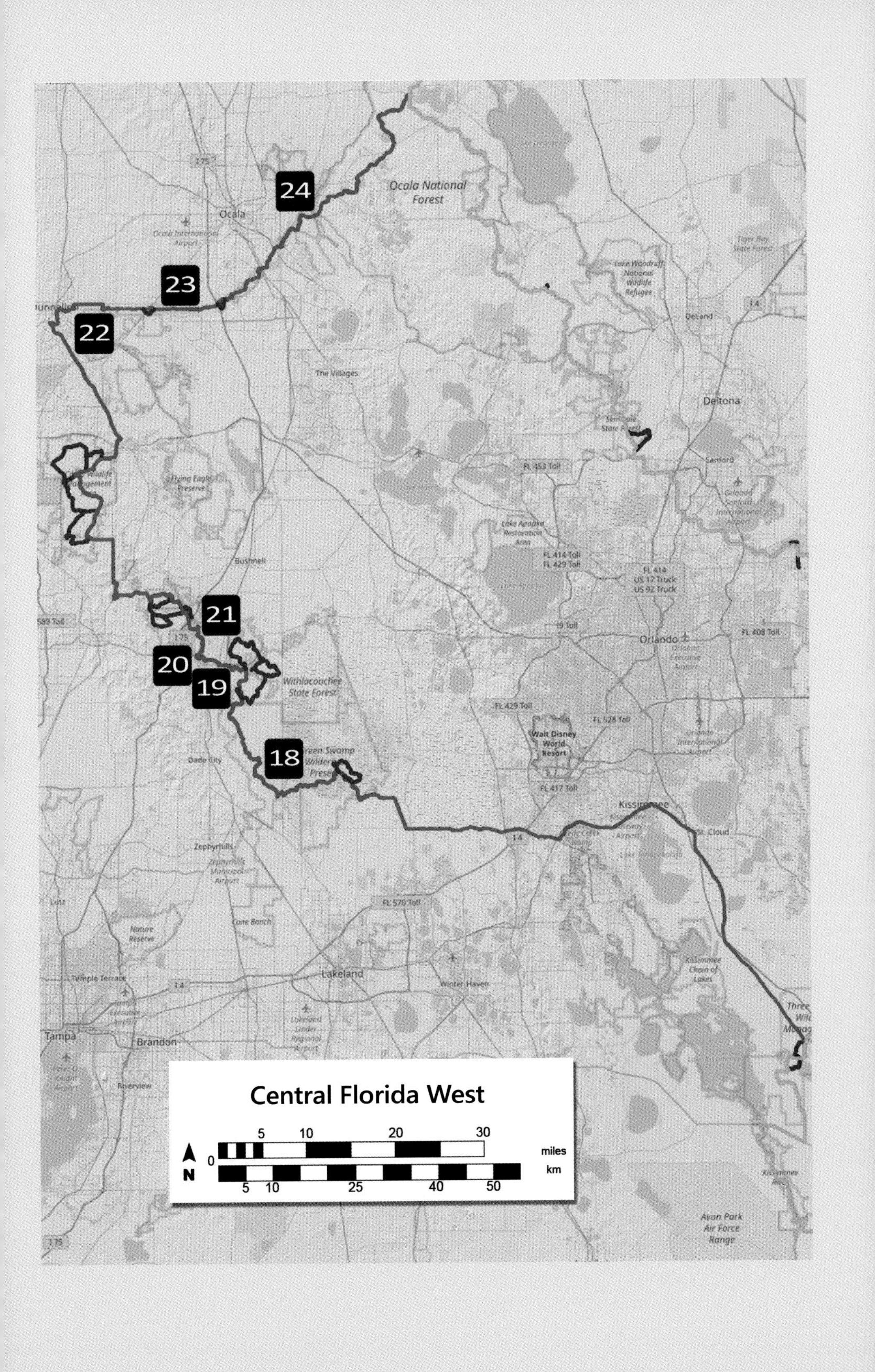
Central Florida West
miles
km
0
5
10
20
30
5
10
25
40
50
N
24
23
22
21
20
19
18
Ocala National Forest
Ocala
Ocala International Airport
Lake George
Tiger Bay State Forest
Lake Woodruff National Wildlife Refuge
DeLand
Deltona
The Villages
Flying Eagle Preserve
Sanford
Orlando Sanford International Airport
Lake Apopka Restoration Area
Lake Apopka
Bushnell
Orlando
Orlando Executive Airport
Withlacoochee State Forest
Walt Disney World Resort
Orlando International Airport
Dade City
Kissimmee
St. Cloud
Zephyrhills
Zephyrhills Municipal Airport
Lake Tohopekaliga
Lutz
Nature Reserve
Cone Ranch
Lakeland
Winter Haven
Kissimmee Chain of Lakes
Temple Terrace
Tampa Executive Airport
Lakeland Linder Regional Airport
Tampa
Brandon
Peter O Knight Airport
Riverview
Lake Kissimmee
Avon Park Air Force Range
FL 453 Toll
FL 414 Toll
FL 429 Toll
FL 414
US 17 Truck
US 92 Truck
FL 408 Toll
FL 528 Toll
FL 417 Toll
FL 570 Toll
589 Toll
I 75
I 4

Gator Hole

18. Green Swamp West

7.2 MILES | GREEN SWAMP WILDERNESS PRESERVE, DADE CITY

When is a swamp not a swamp? When it's a mosaic of wet and dry habitats slowly releasing rainfall into a river basin—or in this case, four river basins. On this hike between two trailheads in the Green Swamp, you'll be surprised at how dry the landscape is.

Overview

As the Withlacoochee River rises from the Green Swamp, it flows north in a gentle arc past Dade City. Inside this curve is the West Tract of Green Swamp Wilderness Preserve, more than 37,000 acres of pine flatwoods. Public lands protect over 170 square miles of the Green Swamp watershed, which extends across this part of Central Florida for 875 square miles. Following a route established several decades ago, the Florida Trail across Green Swamp West intertwines with interconnecting loop trails inside Bigfoot Wilderness Camp.

Trip Planning

Leashed dogs are permitted except during scheduled hunting season. The trail traverses a mix of shade and sun. Use insect repellent. Obtain free permits in advance online if you wish to use the campsites. Seasonal hunting is busiest during the fall deer season. Research hunting dates for Green Swamp West in advance. If you hike during hunting season, wear bright orange. Flooding along the Withlacoochee River can be a problem at the north end of this hike. Check the river level beforehand at water.weather.gov station TRBF1 and ensure it is below 7 feet.

Land Manager

Southwest Florida Water Management District
2379 Broad Street, Brooksville 34604
352-796-7211
swfwmd.state.fl.us

Directions

From Interstate 4 exit 32 (Lakeland/Dade City), take US 98 north 13 miles to CR 471. Turn right and continue 4.6 miles, passing Colt Creek State Park. McNeil West Tract trailhead [28.314831, -82.055977] is on the left after the river bridge. For Lanier trailhead [28.352977, -82.1248285] at the north end, stay on US 98 for 6.9 miles past CR 471 to CR 35A (Old Lakeland Hwy). Follow north 2.4 miles to Enterprise Rd and turn right. Continue 2 miles to Auton Rd and turn left. Just past the entrance gate to Withlacoochee River Park, turn right onto Ranch Rd. Cross the Withlacoochee River. Lanier trailhead is on the left.

Options

A satisfying short hike from McNeil West Tract trailhead is a 3.4-mile round trip to Gator Hole, a landmark just past the campsite of the same name. Use the blue-blazed connector trails within Bigfoot Wilderness Camp (BWC)—established long ago by the Boy Scouts and still maintained by FTA volunteers—to make any number of loops, the longest 9.9 miles if you follow the perimeter of all three of the loops and return along the Florida Trail. Since they are closer to the river, they may not stay as dry as the Florida Trail. Nearby Colt Creek State Park has the 10-mile Flatwoods Trail open to hiking and biking; their 0.9-mile Mac Lake Nature Trail traverses a more natural cross section of Green Swamp habitats.

Hike

Sign in at the trail register at the kiosk for Green Swamp Wilderness Preserve. A map on the kiosk shows hiking, off-road biking, and equestrian trails crisscrossing this vast preserve, many following existing forest roads. Follow the orange blazes of the Florida Trail on a broad corridor into the pine flatwoods with dense clumps of saw palmetto throughout the understory. The footpath narrows as the understory closes in, then weaves between full sun and dappled shade in an oak hammock. Cross a forest road at 0.7 miles with a line of cypress to the east. Round a wet prairie dense with marsh fern and St. John's wort; other small prairies are in the distance in this vast sweep of pine flatwoods. The deep shade of an oak hammock provides a counterpoint, sand live oak limbs speckled with red blanket lichen overhead. Islands of sand live oaks like this are common among the pine flatwoods and sandhills of the Green Swamp.

Meet a trail junction at a mile with a blue-blazed trail leading left. It's the easternmost loop of the BWC trail system. Stay with the orange blazes. Ascending from the oak hammock into sandhills, the footpath becomes white sand. Small turkey oaks rise from open grassy areas between the pines. Enter another sand live oak hammock and emerge on a bluff overlooking a lily-dotted pond in a colorfully textured prairie basin. Circle the pond along a forest road on a sand ridge into the shade of a moss-draped oak hammock. Views of the prairie continue.

The landscape drops into planted pines on the right, where a ditch roughly parallels the trail. At the "Main Trail" sign at 1.4 miles, reach Gator Hole campsite. Like a natural room in the forest, it's in a clearing under the sand live oak canopy with plenty of flat space for tents. Two picnic tables flank a bench and fire ring. Beyond the campsite, a worn path drops through the ditch to the other side, an approach for backpackers to filter water from Gator Hole. Partly shaded by a large live oak, this deep pond is a beauty spot cradled below a bluff.

Walk past Gator Hole through the oak hammock, reaching Thrasher Ridge Prairie a quarter mile later. The shaded bluff provides a sweeping panorama across a wet prairie colorful with purple pickerelweed in late spring, its namesake ridge in the distance. The junction with 8 Mile Pond Trail is at 1.8 miles. Its campsite is just a tenth of a mile west.

Crossing a forest road, continue through a stand of red maple. Ascending to sandhills, the footpath alternately snakes through sandy scrub and open prairies of gold-hued grasses. These shifts in habitat are typical of the Green Swamp, which is less swamp than forest. It has many dry habitats absorbing rainfall like a sponge. The sand ridges shape the directions of its watersheds. Four of Florida's major rivers rise in the Green Swamp, each flowing in a different com-

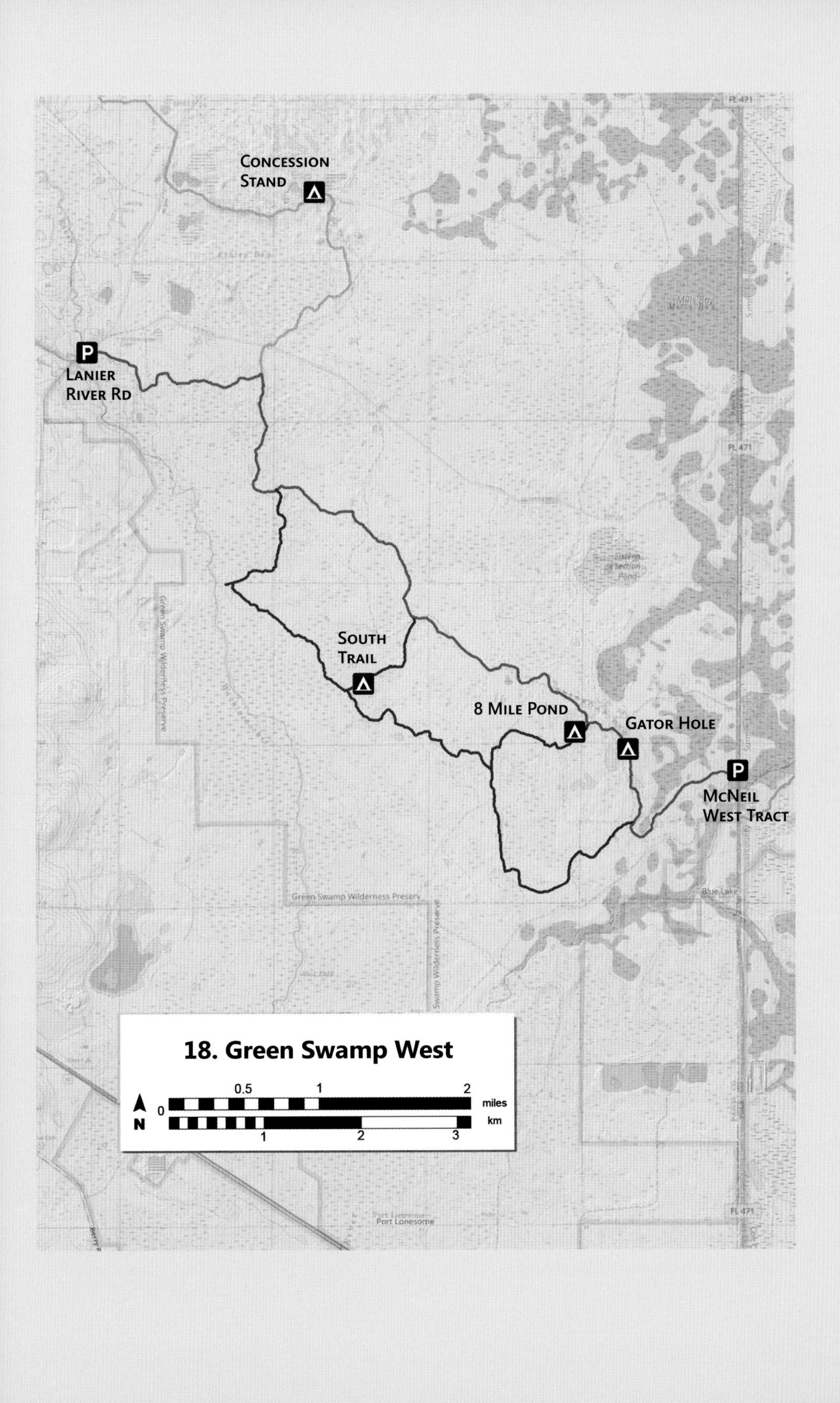

Concession Stand
Lanier River Rd
South Trail
8 Mile Pond
Gator Hole
McNeil West Tract
Mills Bay
FL 471
Green Swamp Wilderness Preserve
Blue Lake
Port Lonesome
18. Green Swamp West
0.5
1
2
miles
0
N
km
1
2
3

Thrasher Ridge Prairie

pass direction: southwest for the Hillsborough, south for the Peace, northeast for the Ocklawaha, and northwest for the Withlacoochee.

The trail enters pine flatwoods with scattered pines and a sea of saw palmetto and gallberry in the understory. Distant cypress domes rise on the horizon as you navigate this expanse. A quarter mile past a cypress dome is the junction with South Trail at 3.4 miles. The footpath slices through thick green brush before crossing an old ditch on a small wooden bridge, the outflow of a cypress dome. Cross Pistol Grade Rd, a limerock road, by 4 miles.

Habitats become progressively damper on the approach to the swampy floodplain of the Withlacoochee River. Sumac rises between tall grasses, sporting leaves that turn bright crimson in fall. Shinyberries cluster alongside the trail next to vibrant purple hairy chaffhead stalks. The final junction with the BWC loops is with North Trail at 4.8 miles.

The Florida Trail turns compass north soon after, with short detours onto forest roads to avoid some of the wetter areas. Vegetation and shade increase as the pathway winds between cypress stands. At one swampy crossing, an old bridge covered in vines assists hikers across standing water. By 5.7 miles, reach a signpost for the blue-blazed connector to Lanier trailhead. Turn left.

A shaded corridor through oak hammocks for most of its length, the connector trail pops into an open area at its halfway mark, with a view of old pastureland and Cumpressco Grade in the distance. Walking beneath the oaks, reach the trailhead kiosk at 7.2 miles.

19. Richloam River Loop

2.6 MILES | WITHLACOOCHEE STATE FOREST RICHLOAM TRACT, LACOOCHEE

For an up-close look at the Withlacoochee River, follow the Florida Trail on a loop combining an ancient cypress swamp along the river floodplain with uplands in Withlacoochee State Forest.

Overview

The southernmost portion of Withlacoochee State Forest is also its wettest. Bounded by the Withlacoochee River, the Little Withlacoochee River, and the Green Swamp, rare is the time when the Richloam Tract is not damp. The enormous cypress thriving under these wet conditions caught the attention of Cummer & Sons, a timber company that had already tapped out stands of old-growth forest in Michigan. In 1922, they built a modern electric-powered sawmill and a box factory less than three miles west of the river, spawning a company town, Lacoochee. Cummer & Sons Cypress Company then stripped the Withlacoochee River floodplain of its bounty, turning virgin cypress into shipping crates. By 1959, leaving this forest mostly bare, they closed their doors. This short hike shows off the most impressive trees left behind. Not every cypress was felled. Any with flaws—misshapen trunks, knotholes, or strangely thick limbs—could damage the expensive equipment in the sawmill. This hike also provides perspectives of a rocky natural shoreline along the upper Withlacoochee River.

Trip Planning

Leashed dogs welcome. Most of the hike is deeply shaded and the River Trail leads through a swamp, so insect repellent is a must. Check the river level beforehand at water.weather.gov station TRBF1 to ensure it is below 7 feet. You can't hike here when it floods: the watermarks were over our heads. The trail can be wet and mucky between the ancient cypress even when the river is low. Poison ivy is common, both along the footpath and in the trees. Seasonal hunting occurs throughout Withlacoochee State Forest and is busiest during fall deer hunting season. Determine dates in advance. If you hike during hunting season, wear bright orange.

Land Manager

Withlacoochee State Forest
15003 Broad St, Brooksville 34601
352-797-4140
fdacs.gov

Directions

From Interstate 75 exit 301, Brooksville, follow SR 50 east to its intersection with US 301. Continue east 1.5 miles. Immediately after the railroad tracks, turn right on CR 575 (Burwell Rd) and follow it south for 2.1 miles to Lacoochee Clay Sink Road. Turn left and drive 1.4 miles to the trail crossing [28.472433, -81.134270]. There is space for several vehicles to park.

Options

Richloam has a 25.6-mile loop trail with connector trails breaking it into three

Ancient cypress

loops. The southwestern loop uses part of this hiking route as a corner of its loop. The 12.3-mile loop south of SR 50 circles Yankee Swamp, passing through an unusual grove of eucalyptus trees and following an old railroad tramway for a portion of the hike. Hiking in Richloam beyond the orange blazes usually leads to very wet feet. An exception is to start this hike at the Richloam Fire Tower [28.500238, -82.112740]—the main trailhead in the forest and the only place to leave your car overnight for backpacking—and hike the 0.7-mile connector to the Florida Trail, then south along the orange blazes 3 miles to the north end of this loop. While it crosses some creek basins, the habitats are mainly pine flatwoods and oak hammocks. Extending your hike by starting at the fire tower makes it a 10-mile hike.

A linear backpacking trip from the Richloam Fire Tower south into Green Swamp West (previous chapter) is 18.3 miles to the Lanier trailhead or 22.7 miles to the McNeil trailhead. It's largely high and dry and has several campsites along the route. One barrier should not be taken lightly: Devils Creek. Hydrological changes from development to the north of the Green Swamp have changed what was once a trickle of a tributary to knee deep with a strong current or worse. Backpackers have been swept off their feet. There are future plans for a bridge, but for now it's a ford. If it's flowing fast or deep, don't try to cross. Devils Creek is 0.8 miles south of the Richloam Loop, so it's easy to turn around and do all or part of the loop instead.

Hike

Head south from Lacoochee Clay Sink Rd and enter a hardwood forest, quickly reaching the trail junction sign "Scenic Low Water River Trail." Turn right to follow the blue blazes. Beneath a sparse canopy of skinny slash pines, the understory of the pine flatwoods crowds up against the River Trail, yielding to a corridor lined with saw palmetto. Walk beneath impressive live oaks stretching high to the sky, their limbs covered in resurrection fern. Nearing the Withlacoochee River, the trail becomes a grassy footpath edged by a dense thicket of young trees. After a quarter mile, it emerges on a bluff above the river. Walk to the edge to see cypresses and oaks reflected in the placid water downriver.

With sloped sides, the river looks like a ditch, not unusual with floodplain rivers. Like the Suwannee and Econlockhatchee, the Withlacoochee rises swiftly after heavy rains, scouring its own channel clean before spilling into the surrounding floodplain. That's why there are water marks up the banks and the tree trunks on both sides. Flowing north to the Gulf of Mexico, the Withlacoochee River rises from the Green Swamp roughly 25 miles southeast.

At the base of the bluff are "deadheads," sunken cypress logs, sticking out of the water. They slipped under during the logging days. The state claims ownership to them but issues permits to individuals who learn how to remove them from the rivers. More valuable than freshly cut wood because of their tight grain, they are used to make fine furniture, flooring, and paneling.

Follow the blue blazes upriver along a grassy, shaded corridor under the oaks.

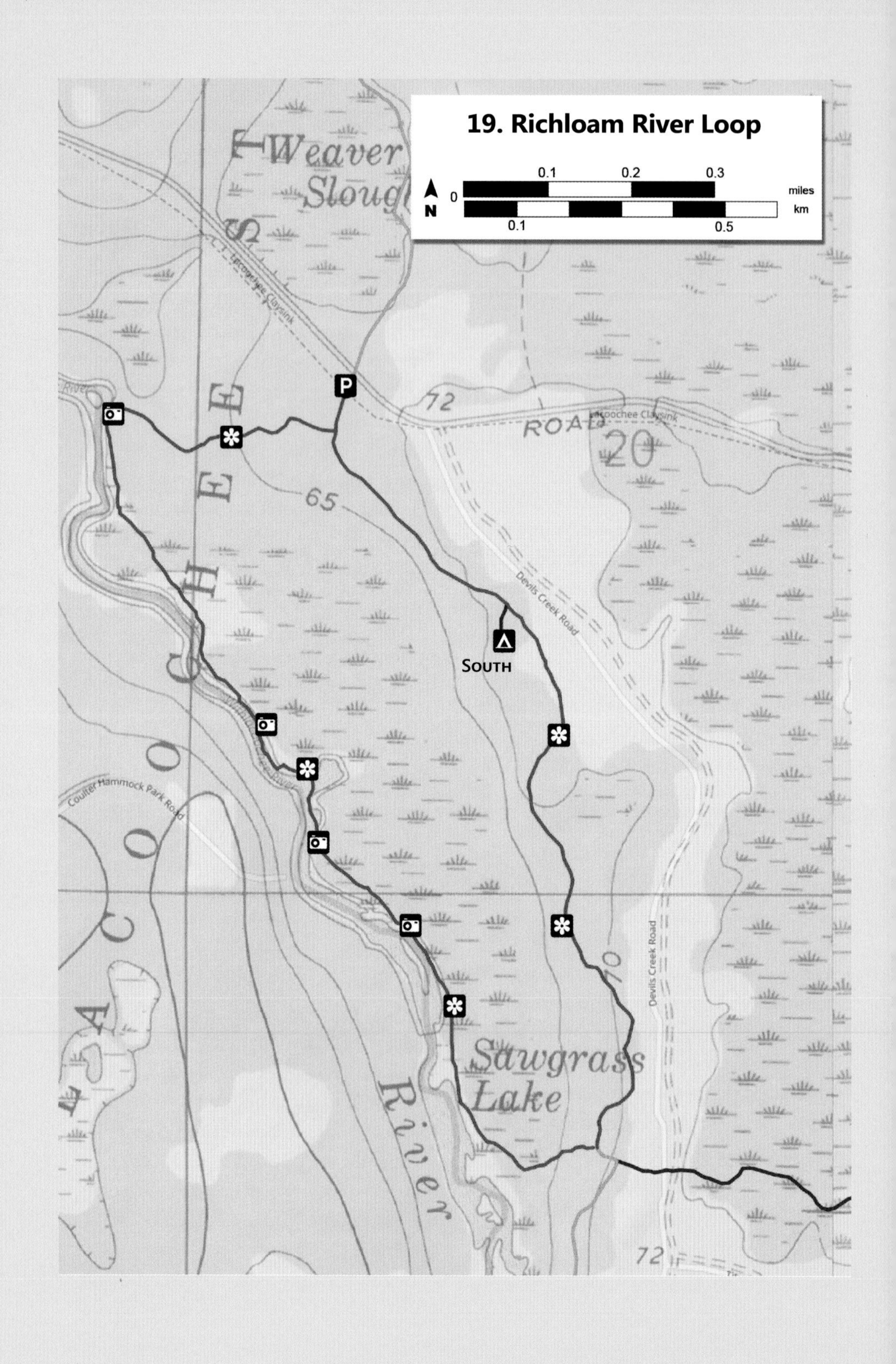
19. Richloam River Loop
0.1
0.2
0.3
0
miles
N
km
0.1
0.5
Weaver
Slough
P
72
ROAD
20
65
Devils Creek Road
South
Coulter Hammock Park Road
Sawgrass
Lake
River
70
72

Shoals on the Withlacoochee River

Along a curve in the river, enjoy the views from a bluff. The footpath narrows to a slender trace past this point, entering a younger forest where cypress knees poke out of the ground, creating a tripping hazard. Past a small clearing busy with star rush, follow the ecotone between hardwood hammock and a cypress swamp with shallow pools of water on the bluff.

An oddity of hiking along the Withlacoochee, flood shadows surround you, a line of darkness that stretches up the tree trunks to the watermarks from the last major flood. Drawing closer to the river, you are surrounded by cypresses. The oldest ones have deeply fluted bases. Some have very bizarre shapes, including multiple trunks. That's what saved them from the sawmill.

At 0.6 miles, cross a bridge in the cypress swamp. Walk to the river's edge at the next bluff to see the line of cypress knees growing along the far shore, and imagine how, under the old-growth cypress, this entire river was once canopied by the grand trees. Some of the ancients still rise on the far shore. Other

Among the cypress

than the "damaged goods" left alone by the lumberjacks, most of the cypress here now are less than a century old.

A set of rocky shoals adjoins the trail. Large boulders jut out of the river, moderating its flow around a bend. The trail keeps close to the bluff as it passes the shoals, providing a place to walk down to a beach busy with cypress knees. Cross a bridge over a side channel and wind into the forest. Blue blazes can be tough to spot when trees are leafy green.

Returning to the bluffs, pass an old cypress that looks like a woman in a hoop skirt reaching for the sky. Young cypresses cluster along the far shore, a ribbon of cypress knees at their feet. The flood shadow is a strong presence as the trail leaves the bluff to thread through a stand of tall cypress trees at 1.2 miles, a breathtaking place to stop and take in their beauty. Some are so large it would take four or more people to hold hands to circle their bases. This is the most immersive and interesting stand of big cypresses along the Florida Trail.

Turning from the river as it leaves the cypresses behind, the trail gains elevation as it enters the hardwood hammock, passing under a large live oak. Reach the end of the blue-blazed River Trail at its junction with the Florida Trail at 1.5 miles. Turn left to follow the orange blazes northbound on a comfortable, shaded corridor between the saw palmettos. The forest understory becomes denser, the footpath nicely cushioned by leaves and pine needles. One low spot with needle palms grazing its edge can be soft underfoot. Sweetgum and pignut hickory trees tower overhead. Pass an oak with an oddly split trunk, and a stand of ancient saw palmetto with fronds sprouting from tall trunks.

At 2.2 miles, a side trail leads to South campsite, the southernmost of the designated camping areas in Richloam. Ramble down the blue-blazed path to a clearing under a grand canopy of oaks with a picnic table in the shade. Flat spaces for tents are scattered around a low grassy swale. There is no water here, so you must haul it in with you.

Back on the orange blazes, keep walking north. The forest transitions to pine flatwoods, the trail corridor edged with saw palmetto, bluestem palm, and grapevines. Like the cypress, the ancient pines were stripped from these woods by the loggers. Slash pines and loblolly now dominate. When you reach the trail junction sign for the River Trail, you've finished the loop. Walk up to the road to complete this 2.6-mile hike.

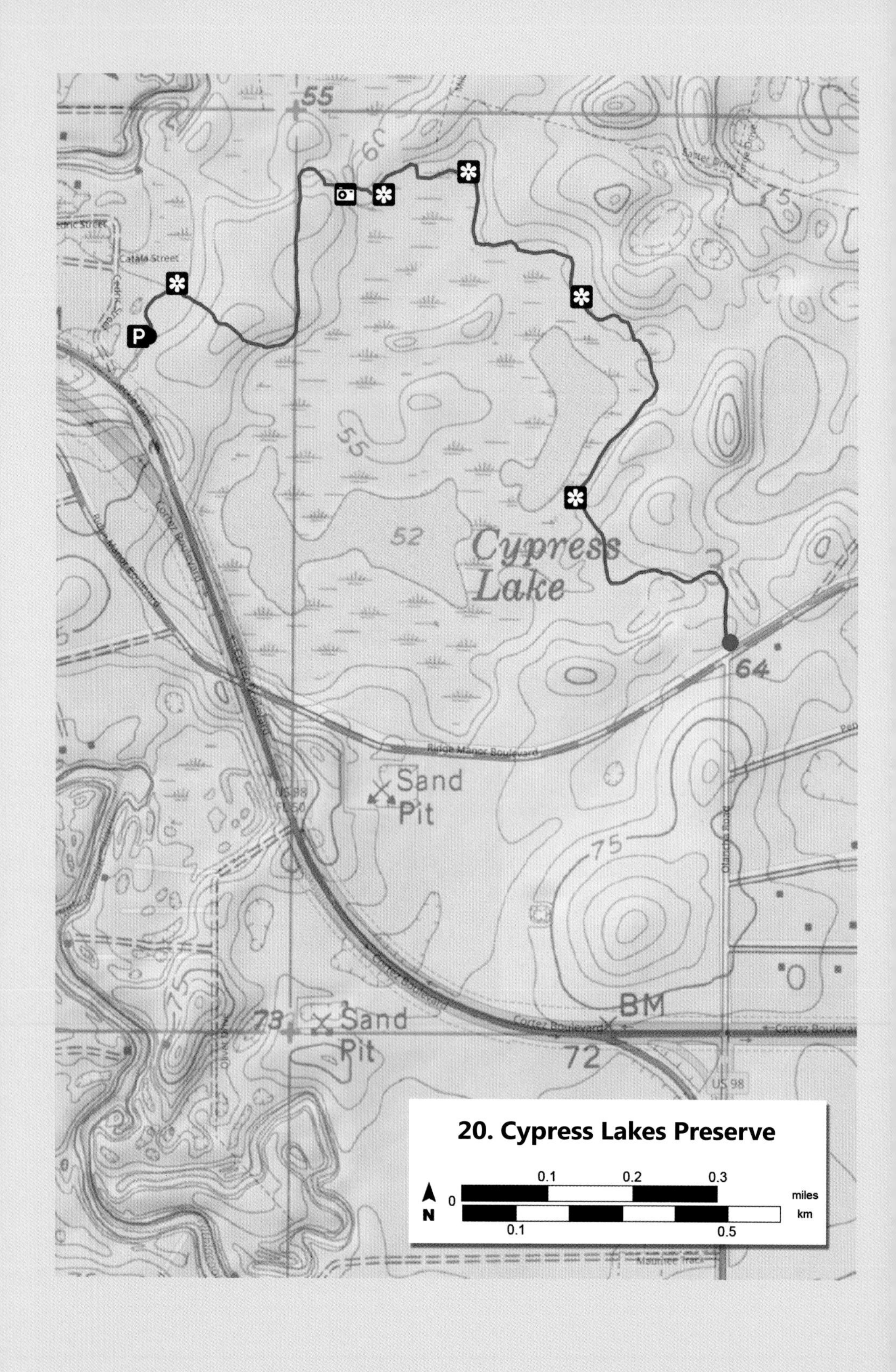

Cypress Lake
Sand Pit
Sand Pit
Ridge Manor Boulevard
Cortez Boulevard
Catala Street
BM
20. Cypress Lakes Preserve
0.1
0.2
0.3
0
miles
km
0.1
0.5
N

20. Cypress Lakes Preserve

3.2 MILES | RIDGE MANOR

Rounding cypress-lined lakes in the Withlacoochee River floodplain east of Brooksville, this short segment of the Florida Trail is a botanical delight.

Overview

If you've ever looked up at a tree and realized you could fit into a hole in its trunk, you were probably among the redwoods in California. Well, here's a secret: Florida once had cypress that towered that tall, but most became lumber more than a century ago. We only know they existed thanks to historic photos that show single cypress logs filling flatcars on a train. Few remain. At Cypress Lakes Preserve there are many cypresses, but one of them is one of Florida's ancients. Established in 1998 under the Hernando County Environmentally Sensitive Lands Program, Cypress Lakes Preserve is home to both big cypresses and uncommon wildflowers. On its brief traverse of the preserve, the Florida Trail provides an easy, interesting walk.

Trip Planning

Pets are not permitted. Most of the hike is deeply shaded and surrounds a swamp. Insect repellent is a must. Check river levels beforehand at water.weather.gov station TRBF1. Don't hike here if the river isn't below 7 feet. If the river is even a little high, the trail can be wet and mucky.

Land Manager

Hernando County Environmentally Sensitive Lands
16161 Flight Path Dr., Brooksville 34604
352-754-4031
hernandocounty.us

Directions

From Interstate 75 exit 301, Brooksville, follow SR 50 east for 2 miles, passing under the long bridge that carries the Withlacoochee State Trail overhead. Get in the left lane. After crossing the Withlacoochee River, make the first left onto Paul Steckle Ln (Old SR 50). Drive past the fire station. There is a dirt road leading into the preserve at a sign on the right, leading to a very small unpaved parking area [28.51976, -82.206528].

Options

You can be dropped off at the other end of the preserve at the junction of Ridge Manor Blvd and Olancha Rd to walk 1.6 miles across it, but the hike is short and interesting enough that a round trip is worthwhile. Consider the Keyhole Cypress and the last of the cypress lakes as intermediate turnaround points for a 1.4-mile round trip and a 2.6-mile round trip, respectively.

Hike

From the trailhead, follow the dirt road deeper into the forest to a locked gate and pedestrian stile in the fence. Orange blazes lead into an oak hammock. Sweetgum and red maples intermingle in the forest, signaling the edge of a floodplain. From a crook in one gigantic oak tree, a bluestem palm waves its fronds while resurrection fern swarms across the oak's thick limbs. Notice the dark line across the forest that indicates just how high the Withlacoochee River can flood. While you can't see the river from here, you are in its floodplain.

Some cypress trees have knees three and four feet tall. These distinctive parts of the roots protrude above the soil and the usual water level around the tree, helping to stabilize it. Rounding a curve, pull away from the floodplain, tunneling downhill into oak hammock. Walk under a showy archway of oaks, each decked in a bounty of resurrection ferns, before reaching an open flat area along a very dense cypress swamp. Passing beneath more grand oaks, slip along a passageway crowded with plants in every hue of green. The tunnel effect continues for nearly a half mile before things change.

The forest opens up, with bluestem palm lining the footpath. Walking through a bed of pine needles, emerge at a small clearing with sandhill wildflowers. The green tunnel starts again. Keep alert to blazed turns to avoid side paths. After 0.6 miles, a boardwalk bridges the waterway between the Cypress Lakes and the Withlacoochee River. To the left is a water-filled sinkhole with a marsh in it. To the right, not clearly visible, is the first of the lakes.

Walk past a bench after the boardwalk ends and the trail slopes to lake level. This end of the lake is dark, almost spooky. Royal ferns grow in the deep shade of the cypresses, with open water obvious beyond the trees. Watch for alligators and weirdly shaped cypress knees. One looks like a giant bongo drum stuck between two trees. Follow the edge of the lake. The cypresses get larger and odder. Some have bases like giant wooden hoop skirts. When logging was in its heyday, the loggers skipped over misshapen cypress since they could damage the sawmill. Flaws

West end of Cypress Lakes

saved these old-growth cypress so our generation could enjoy them.

Ascend away from the cypress into sandhills briefly, passing a perimeter fence before descending to the next stretch of cypress swamp. The edge of this lake has enormous cypress not far from its shoreline. We named the largest of them the Keyhole Cypress. It looks like two enormous cypresses fused together at several places where their limbs met, leaving gaps like keyholes. The middle keyhole is five or six feet high. The base of the tree is folded like a collapsing pyramid tent.

Keyhole Cypress

Climbing away from this lake, enter another deeply shaded oak hammock before reaching the next lake. This one has cypresses with massive bases and knees that rise nearly five feet tall right along its edge. While it's tempting to try and walk out to them for a closer look, the solid-looking soil of the swamp gives way easily under your weight.

Sweeping uphill, the trail makes a sharp right at a forest road, entering sandhill habitat at a mile. This forest floor invites close inspection, as a large patch of sand squares crowds both sides of the footpath. These odd wildflowers have square sets of blooms and are joined by foxglove and roseling blooming in the summer months. Walk along the rim of an oak hammock within sight of open sandhills before passing a massive live oak with a blaze on it.

The footpath drops to the edge of a lake, cypresses crowding the shoreline. Some of the trees have gaps in their trunks large enough for animal dens. All are surrounded by knees and swampy ground. Since bald cypresses are usually found along flowing water, these lakes were likely once part of the Withlacoochee River, which changed its course and left them stranded.

Leave the last of the lakes at 1.3 miles. Orange blazes lead uphill into a sandhill restoration area, tacking between forest roads under the oaks for its final quarter mile. Reaching the gate at Ridge Manor Rd and Olancha Rd, complete the 1.6-mile traverse of Cypress Lakes Preserve. Turn around and retrace your route for a 3.2-mile hike.

Cove on the Withlacoochee River

21. Croom River Trail

6.3 MILES | WITHLACOOCHEE STATE FOREST CROOM TRACT, RIDGE MANOR

Following the western bluffs of the Withlacoochee River, this ribbon of footpath leads you past old-growth trees and to scenic overlooks above the river's northward flow.

Overview

A ferryboat crossing along the Withlacoochee River north of Brooksville grew into a short-lived industrial powerhouse during the birth of Florida's first railroad system. In 1885, the Florida Southern Railway completed their line to Pemberton Ferry and Brooksville, replacing the ferry with an iron bridge. The following year, the South Florida Railroad extended their line north from Lakeland to meet it. By 1890, the town changed its name to Croom, home to the Buttgenbach mine. This early phosphate-mining operation employed many.

Today there isn't much to Croom except place names and a few relics of the former community. These lands acquired by the US Department of Agriculture became Withlacoochee State Forest in 1958. The Croom Tract encompasses more than 20,000 acres on both sides of the river. The piers of the iron bridge still stand at a recreation area of that name. What remains of the open pit mine is now the Croom Motorcycle Area. The right of ways for the long-vanished railroads are now paved bike paths, the Good Neighbor Trail—a 10-mile paved bike path from the depot in Brooksville—meeting the Withlacoochee State Trail where the railroads once met at Croom. Connecting Ridge Manor to Brooksville, they are part of the 250-mile paved Florida Coast-to-Coast Trail.

In the 1970s, Florida Trail Association volunteers started building trails across the Croom Tract, including a series of stacked loops for backpackers. The Croom River Trail is a more recent addition, created after the Florida Trail through the region moved from the east side of the river to its western shore. With easy-to-find trailheads and a beautiful campground along its route, it provides many options for hiking.

Trip Planning

Leashed pets are permitted. Check river levels beforehand at water.weather.gov station CRMF1. Although the footpath is generally dry, you can't hike this trail when it floods. We've seen watermarks on the trees over our heads. Insect repellent is a must. Seasonal hunting at Withlacoochee State Forest is busiest during the fall deer hunting season. Research hunt dates in advance. If you hike during hunting seasons, wear bright-orange clothing.

Land Manager

Withlacoochee State Forest
15003 Broad St, Brooksville 34601
352-797-4140
fdacs.gov

Directions

From Interstate 75 exit 301, Brooksville, follow SR 50 east a mile to Croom-Rital Rd, the traffic light immediately before the Withlacoochee State Trail bridge over the highway. Turn left and follow the road a quarter mile to a prominent trailhead on the right. Ridge Manor trailhead [28.526758, -82.218781] serves as the main access point for cyclists on this section of the bike path as well as hiker access to the Croom River Trail. Leave a vehicle here. Continue north along Croom-Rital Rd for 2.7 miles to the Croom trailhead [28.563416, -82.222015]. It is a small grassy parking area on the right, adjoined by a Croom WMA sign. If it's full, shorten this hike with a drive to the trailhead at Crooked River Campground. Continue north another 0.7 mile to Silver Lake Rd and turn right. In a quarter mile, turn right and follow the forest road past Cypress Glen Campground to Crooked River Campground. Crooked River trailhead [28.56576, -82.20764] is on the right. From here, it's a 5.2-mile hike to Ridge Manor trailhead.

Options

Day hikers have multiple routes to choose from. This can be made into a loop hike: it's a linear 2.6 miles between the Croom and Ridge Manor trailheads along the paved Withlacoochee State Trail to make an 8.9-mile loop. From Crooked River Campground, hike south and use the Blue Trail loop to return for a scenic 9-mile hike. Or hike north from Crooked River to Silver Lake via the Florida Trail and the Cypress Glen Trail, which passes through Silver Lake Campground and continues under Interstate 75 along the lake. Keep left at the trail junction to meet the Florida Trail again. Turn left and head back to Crooked River for a 5.8-mile hike. Or keep right at the junction and follow the blue blazes along the Withlacoochee River back to the Florida Trail, heading south to Crooked River for an 8.5-mile hike. For a short hike from Ridge Manor trailhead, pair the Blue Trail and the Florida Trail for a 3.9-mile loop.

The Croom Loops are north of this hike, good for a backpacking trip. Leave your car at Crooked River Campground. Northbound, the Florida Trail reaches the middle of the stacked loops at 3.6 miles. Follow the perimeter of the loop system along B and C loops, stopping at Tucker Hill Recreation Area for water. It's the only reliable water source along the loops. Camp at the A Loop Camping Zone 0.4 miles north. Reaching the orange blazes the next morning, turn right and hike south to Crooked River, reaching it in 11.4 miles for a 21.6-mile overnighter.

Hike

Leaving Croom trailhead on a wide mowed swath tunneling through a hardwood forest, the Florida Trail opens into sandhill habitat before a junction with the Cypress Glen Trail at a quarter mile. That blue-blazed trail leads to Silver Lake. Turn right, where the signpost says "River Trail" with an orange blaze. Walk past saw palmetto on the edge of a prairie before entering a forest. The blue-blazed Cypress Glen Trail turns off at a half mile toward that campground. Pass by it and beneath a large live oak. Circling a large depression pond beneath the oaks, follow the footpath through a haze of little bluestem grass before joining a well-defined corridor under the oaks and pines.

At 1.1 miles, reach the River Trail trailhead at Crooked River Campground. Continue straight ahead along a broad corridor paralleling a power

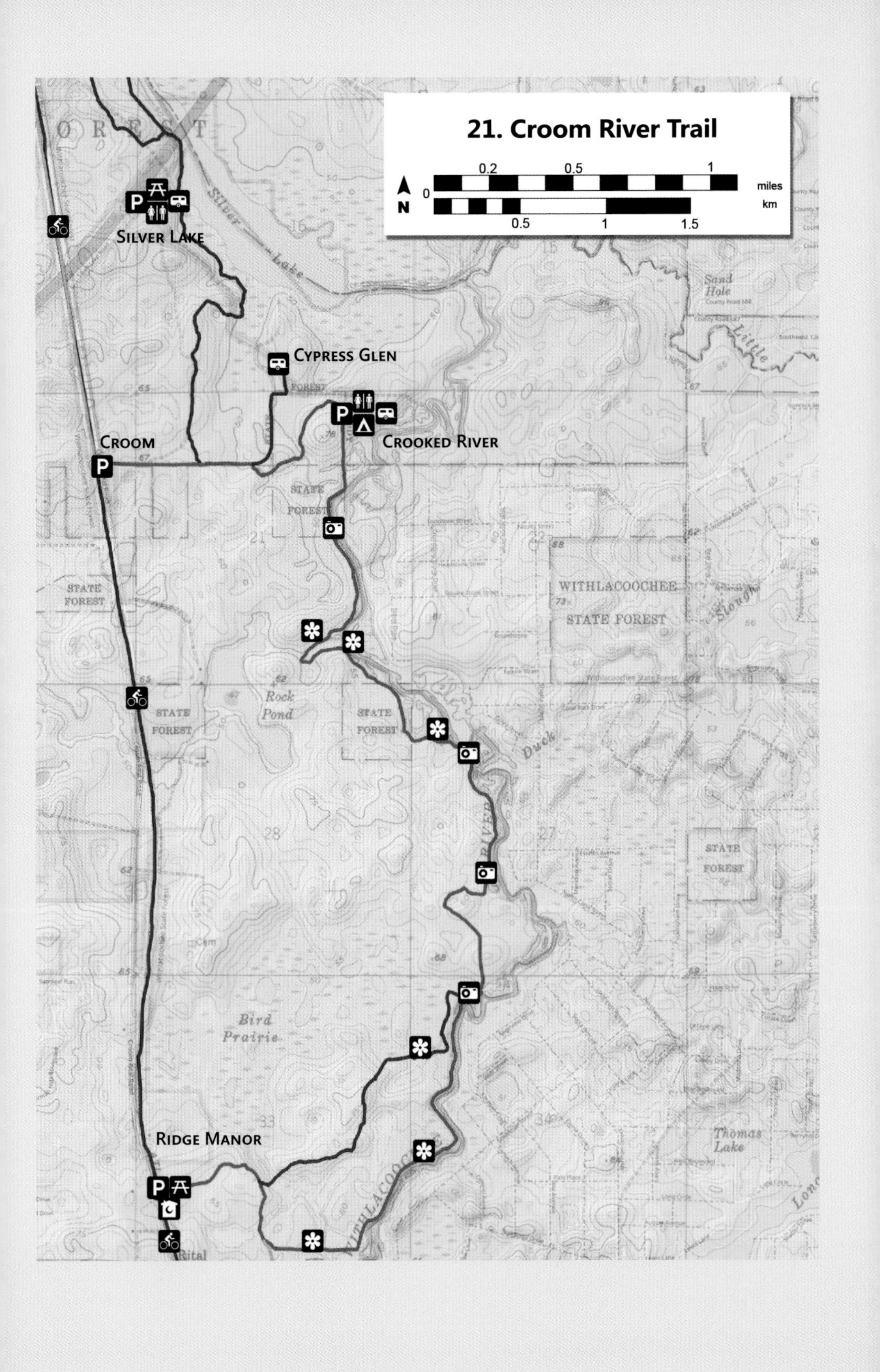

21. Croom River Trail
0
0.2
0.5
1
miles
N
0.5
1
1.5
km
Silver Lake
Cypress Glen
Croom
Crooked River
Rock Pond
Withlacoochee State Forest
Bird Prairie
Ridge Manor
Thomas Lake
Sand Hole

Tunnel of oaks

line. An old barbed wire fence adjoins the trail as it reaches the river bluffs at 1.4 miles. The Withlacoochee River sparkles below. Make a sharp right to parallel the river under the dappled shade of sand live oaks. The old fence is supported by vintage railroad ties. Upriver, a large bald cypress leans into the north-flowing current. Other cypresses tower along the far shore. At the base of the bluff, the river is very tannic, tea-colored in the shallows.

Pass an overlook with a bench at 1.6 miles. The trail turns but keeps close to the river, shaded by a tunnel of sand live oak and water oak draped in Spanish moss. Gaining elevation, it enters an oak scrub. A side road is signposted "Not for Public Use." Forestry staff use it as a connector to Rock Lake. Bright sand reaches the bluff's edge, where the fence persists. Across the river are homes half-hidden by the trees surrounding them. The footpath edges very close to the bluff.

Enter a grove of large sand live oaks at 2 miles. They show off odd shapes caused by pruning during hurricanes, spreading out instead of up. Hanging gardens cover their limbs, with orchids among the ferns. A thick crust of lichens coats the tree bark. The younger oaks sport crooked upper limbs. A small bridge crosses the iffy outflow of Rock Lake before you make a sharp curve past a bench through this impressive grove of oaks.

A cypress swamp at 2.3 miles is characterized by massive trees. At the bluff near the river, ease off the footpath and look back for a better view. Curving south, parallel the river along a series of oxbow pond swamps. In one of these is the curiosity of cypress knees growing inside a cypress tree, clearly visible in a gap in the trunk at water level. Strewn with oak leaves, the footpath follows the floodplain, passing a showy stand of sand live oaks. Forming a tunnel around the trail, the oak canopy provides shade before you emerge at a river view where willows grow in the shallows below the bluff. A bench offers a perch at a scenic spot.

At 3 miles, the trail leaves the river for the next half mile. Passing another "Not for Public Use" junction, meet a forest road through a longleaf pine restoration area. The footpath curves along a prairie before another stretch of young forest takes over. To the east, the river is briefly visible. Don't get lulled into following the forest road. The orange blazes jump off it at 3.5 miles, turning left under an oak with low-hanging limbs to round a sinkhole. Past another "Not for Public Use" sign in a longleaf pine restoration area, the footpath resumes. Southern magnolias grow beneath tall oaks. Round a cypress swamp and follow a causeway through it, crossing a bridge to a scenic spot. A bench provides a river bend view at 4.1 miles, adjoining the outflow of the swamp.

Just past this stop is the first junction with the Blue Trail. It takes a more direct route to the Ridge Manor trailhead than the Florida Trail, 1.7 miles versus 2.2 on the main trail. While the Blue Trail traverses cypress swamps in the floodplain, the Florida Trail provides a more scenic route. Continue along the orange blazes to reach a panorama at a broad spot in the river with its own bench on the bluff. From this bluff you can look straight down into the water rushing around the bases of large cypress trees. Mature saw palmetto, a century old or more, rise up on their long trunks instead of lying down as they usually do. Leaves dapple the river view, but it is a near-constant companion for some time. Tall cypresses rise from a crescent-shaped oxbow pond at 4.9 miles. The south end of the pond broadens and the cypresses are larger. So are their knees, rising up to five feet tall.

Past the next bench, the trail broadens and is shaded by oaks. At 5.3 miles, it makes a sharp turn away from the river, that final view somewhat obscured by the trees. Facing straight down the corridor it looks like a long tunnel, and that's exactly how it feels as you hike through it. When you emerge from the shade into a sunny prairie, it's quite a contrast. Pay attention to the trail junction. It's been signposted and blazed differently on each of our visits. Do *not* follow the orange blazes to the left, which lead south to SR 50. Follow the blazes curving to the right along the pines, whatever color they happen to be. This is the route to the Ridge Manor trailhead. Following an old road through the sandhills, it meets the second junction with the Blue Trail at a sign at 5.8 miles. Continue straight ahead.

After a final "Not for Public Use" sign, make a sharp left into a longleaf pine restoration area. At the end of this forested corridor is a fence with a gap where a kiosk stands beneath a massive live oak. Walk through the gap and look back at it to see the big "River Trail" sign on the fence. Continue through the picnic area past the pavilion and the restroom along the paved Withlacoochee State Trail. At 6.3 miles, your hike ends at the Ridge Manor trailhead.

Ancient oak near Land Bridge trailhead

Cross Florida Greenway

39.2 MILES | OCALA

An environmental nightmare reborn as a corridor of green space between the St. Johns River and the Gulf of Mexico, the Marjorie Harris Carr Cross Florida Greenway offers hikers surprisingly hilly day hikes near Ocala and a place to backpack undisturbed by hunting seasons.

Overview

While it's tough to understand why prior generations wanted to slice the Florida peninsula in two with a canal, the plan was on the table for nearly a century. It started before the Civil War, with the military looking for a quicker way to get ships to the Gulf of Mexico, and ramped up as a make-work project for the unemployed as part of the Works Progress Administration (WPA) during the Great Depression. With hand tools and mule carts to haul away dirt, men dug deep trenches southwest of Ocala. Abandoned when World War II broke out, the canal dream roared to life again in the 1960s. Literally. A massive tractor called the "crusher crawler" mowed down floodplain forests along the Ocklawaha River near St. Johns River so the Army Corps of Engineers could turn it into a ditch for commerce. Local politicians were all for it. Dams were built at Rodman, Eureka, and Inglis. But the intended route would have a terrible impact on the Floridan Aquifer. A group of scientists concerned about the devastating potential to our fresh water supply formed a group called Florida Defenders of the Environment. After a change of leadership in Tallahassee, they caught the attention of both the governor and the Secretary of the Interior. Work on the canal came to a halt in 1969 so its impact could be properly studied. In 1971, President Richard Nixon ended the project to "prevent a past mistake from causing permanent damage."

In the 1990s, the federal government transferred the canal right-of-way to the state of Florida. This corridor was designated Florida's first greenway in 1998, named for the woman who led the fight against the canal, Marjorie Harris Carr. By 1999, local Florida Trail Association volunteers, Sandra included, scrambled to build a new section of the Florida Trail along the Greenway between the Ocklawaha and Withlacoochee River basins. Belleview resident and longtime Florida Trail Association leader Kenneth Smith became known as "Mr. Greenway" for championing and coordinating the effort. On National Trails Day 2000, Kenneth, Sandra, and FTA vice president of trails Joan Hobson represented the hiking community by cutting the ribbon for this new trail at the dedication of the Land Bridge over Interstate 75.

Trailheads

From south to north (compass west to compass east), these are the trailheads along the Cross Florida Greenway:

0.0 CR 39
Paved parking at the south end of the Dunnellon Trail.

1.4 BLUE RUN PARK
Small paved parking area 0.3W along paved trail leading to Dunnellon.

2.3 BRIDGES ROAD
Large dirt parking area off a bumpy dirt road off CR 484. Portable toilet.

7.3 PRUITT
Large parking area off a graded access road, picnic benches.

12.2 ROSS PRAIRIE
Paved parking off SR 200, 0.7E via blue blazes. Campground, restrooms.

16.1 SHANGRI-LA
Campground and parking area with restrooms, 0.7E via blue blaze.

19.0 SW 49TH AVE.
Unpaved parking 0.2E off SW 49th Ave. Portable toilet, picnic area.

22.4 LAND BRIDGE
Paved parking off CR 475A. Restrooms, picnic, equestrian area.

27.4 VORTEX
Small dirt parking area for adjoining mountain bike trails complex.

29.1 SANTOS
Paved trailhead 0.1W adjoining campground. Restrooms.

34.0 BASELINE
Large paved trailhead with restrooms, picnic area, and playground.

36.1 SE 64TH AVE.
Along paved bike path 0.2E to small trailhead with portable toilet.

39.1 MARSHALL SWAMP
Unpaved parking off Sharpes Ferry Rd with restrooms.

Camping

Use only designated camping areas. Florida Trail Association members do not need a permit for primitive campsites but should have a membership card along in case you are questioned about being there. Others should call the land manager to inform them of your planned route. Between Dunnellon and the western edge of Marshall Swamp, there is no surface water. Obtain potable water at trailheads with restrooms, or filter it out of horse troughs at Pruitt, SW 49th Ave, and the west side of the Land Bridge. South to north, designated camping areas include:

12.2 ROSS PRAIRIE CAMPGROUND
0.7E via blue blaze. Bathhouse and showers. Fee.

13.6 ROSS PRAIRIE
Campsite atop hill east of SR 200 crossing. Bench and fire ring.

14.1 SPRING PARK
Equestrian camp with picnic table, spaces under pines.

16.1 SHANGRI-LA CAMPGROUND
0.7E via blue blaze. Nicely shaded. Bathhouse. Fee.

19.1 SW 49TH AVE
Atop steep hill east of SW 49th Ave trailhead. Bench and fire ring.

22.2 LAND BRIDGE
Small clearing 0.1E of trail in oak hammock with picnic bench.

29.1 SANTOS CAMPGROUND
Large, open campground adjoining US 441. Bathhouse and showers. Fee.

If backpacking end to end, ask to leave your car behind the office gates at Marshall Swamp or at one of the campgrounds. Bear bagging or a bear canister would be prudent—not just to keep your food from raccoons; bears have been seen along this section of trail.

Trip Planning

Leashed dogs are welcome. Because the central portion of the Greenway is high and dry, it's an excellent choice for hiking with a dog, particularly between Pruitt and Santos trailheads. Other parts of the trail are busier and may have alligators present. Equestrians and cyclists have their own separate parallel trail systems that frequently cross the Florida Trail along the Greenway. Except at underpasses, bridges, paved sections, trail-

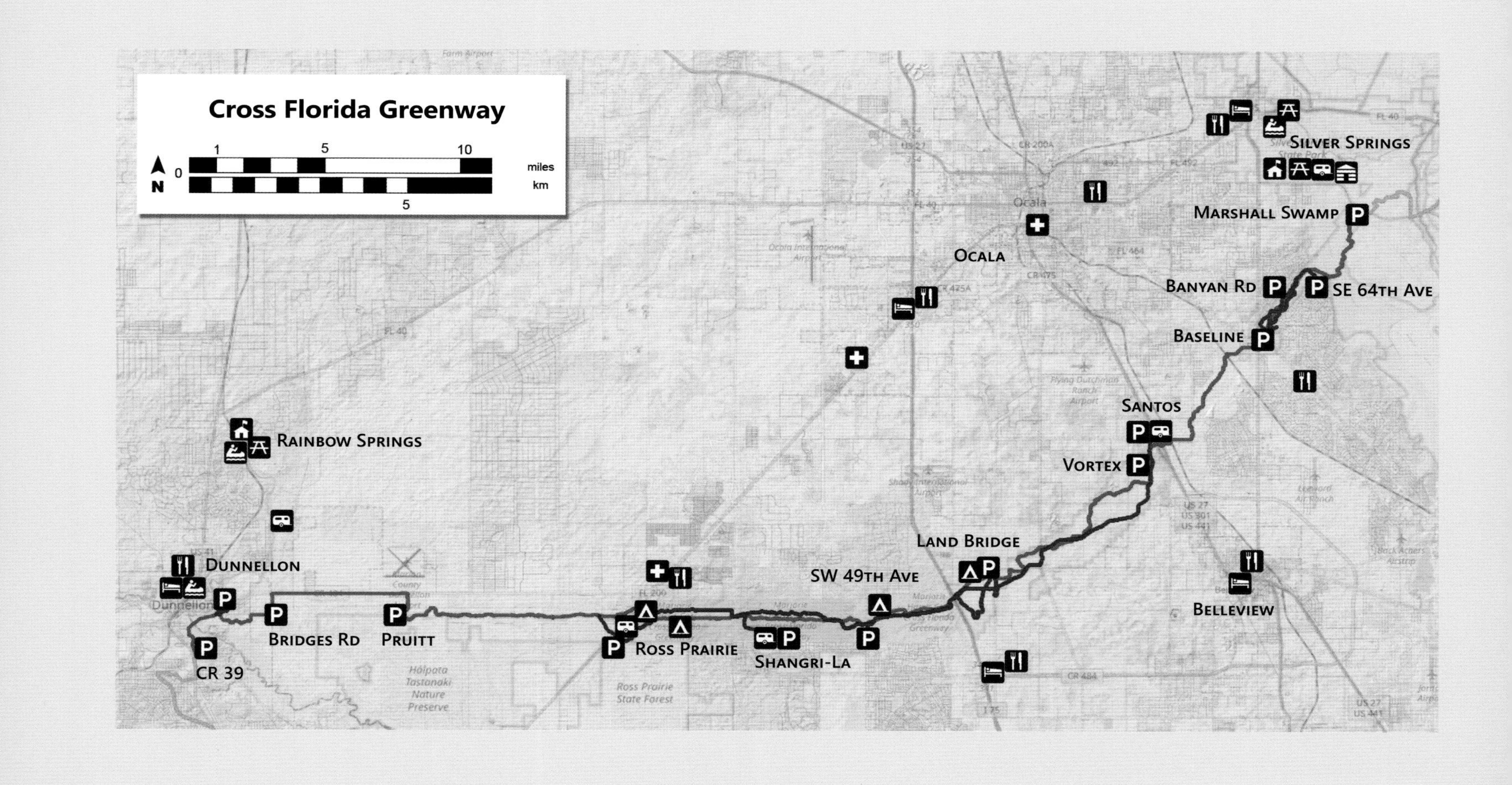
Cross Florida Greenway
0
1
5
10
miles
5
km
N
Silver Springs
Marshall Swamp
Ocala
Banyan Rd
SE 64th Ave
Baseline
Santos
Vortex
Rainbow Springs
Land Bridge
SW 49th Ave
Dunnellon
Belleview
Bridges Rd
Pruitt
Ross Prairie
Shangri-La
CR 39
Hólpata Tastanaki Nature Preserve
Ross Prairie State Forest

Hiking north into Marshall Swamp

head access points, and across Marshall Swamp, the Florida Trail is hiking only.

Land Manager

Marjorie Harris Carr Cross Florida Greenway
8282 SE CR 314, Ocala 34470
352-236-7143
floridastateparks.org

Highlights

Withlacoochee River, mile 0.8

A big bridge built to replace the former railroad trestle over the river, this perch above the Withlacoochee shows off the cypress-lined waterway upriver and downriver.

Stonehenge, mile 7.9

A circle of stones memorializing the son of the family whose land was purchased and preserved for this portion of the Greenway, Stonehenge sits in a natural cathedral of ancient live oak trees.

Canal View, mile 11.1

The first place where you can see the outline of the ditches dug by WPA workers, this low bench on the edge of what was to be a canal affords a panorama across the open space that would have been filled by water.

Canal Diggings, mile 21.0

After the WPA workers hit a sand ridge in a sand pine scrub forest and dug right through it, subsequent erosion over more than 70 years created a giant sand dune. A side trail leads from a bench along the Florida Trail to the showiest part. Walk to the top for the best view.

Land Bridge, mile 21.2

When it opened in 2000, this structure over Interstate 75 was the first land bridge in the nation. A giant planter filled with dirt, trees, and a watering system, the bridge made it possible for wildlife to cross the highway while recreational users shared the same space.

Marshall Swamp Tram, mile 36.9

Once carrying a narrow-gauge railroad deep into the swamps where the Silver River and the Ocklawaha River meet, this long, straight tramway lets hikers cross the wettest part of Marshall Swamp with dry feet while admiring the surrounding beauty reflected in its waters.

Observation Deck, mile 38.6

Built out over a marshy pond, it enables you to enjoy a tiny corner of a grand swamp. Marshall Swamp has trees of impressive size that create a dense canopy overhead. Starting near the deck, a short loop trail rounds this marsh.

Recommended Day Hikes

Mile 0.0

Dunnellon Trail / Blue Run, 3.7 miles round trip and loop

Mile 7.3

Pruitt to Ross Prairie, 6.2 miles linear

Mile 13.6

Ross Prairie to SW 49th, 6.5 miles linear

Mile 19.1

SW 49th to Land Bridge, 3.6 miles linear

Mile 22.4

Land Bridge Loop, 3.5-mile loop
Land Bridge to Santos, 7 miles linear

Mile 36.1

Marshall Swamp, 3 miles linear

Side Trip

At the eastern end of this section is one of the world's largest first-magnitude springs, **SILVER SPRINGS**. Protected as a Florida State Park, it is famed for both the depth and clarity of the spring and its unique glass-bottomed boats that showcase not just the head spring but dozens more along this beautiful waterway. floridahikes.com/silver-springs-state-park.

Silver Springs

Dunnellon Trail

22. Dunnellon Trail and Blue Run Park

3.7 MILES | DUNNELLON

Combining a walk on the paved Dunnellon Trail and a loop on natural footpaths through adjacent Blue Run Park, this gentle hike lets you experience the habitats surrounding the confluence of the Rainbow River with the Withlacoochee River.

Overview

One of Florida's most beautiful waterways, the Rainbow River is less than six miles long. Its primary source is a showy first-magnitude spring at the base of a steep bluff in Rainbow Springs State Park. From tiny bubblers to significant outflows, hundreds of springs add to its crystalline waters. In the 1890s, the town of Dunnellon sprouted along the Withlacoochee River where the two rivers meet.

Conceived more than two decades ago as a way to cross the Withlacoochee River using an old railroad route, the Dunnellon Trail bridged a gap for the Florida Trail. Paving the railbed allowed the Cross Florida Greenway to connect to the Withlacoochee State Trail. Many local residents cycle and walk the trail daily. It's an easy, mostly flat hike suitable for all ages. The paved portion is accessible and has benches placed along the route.

Trip Planning / Land Manager

See Cross Florida Greenway. Leashed dogs are welcome. Cyclists use all these trails but will be riding fastest on the paved portion of the route. Most of the hike is surrounded by swamps, so use insect repellent.

Directions

South of Dunnellon off US 41, the CR 39 trailhead [29.03125, -82.45610] is immediately east of the traffic light where the highways meet. Follow an access road to the parking area, where there is a kiosk with a trail map and sometimes a portable toilet. Blue Run Park has two trailheads off CR 484 east of downtown Dunnellon. The first [29.049122, -82.446777] is on the right just after you cross the Rainbow River on the highway bridge. It tends to be busy with people using the launch. The second is off the next right turn onto San Jose Blvd. Look for the large parking corral [29.0480, -82.4441] on the right after you make the turn.

Options

Since there are three parking areas along this route, start or end wherever you like. We prefer the CR 39 trailhead since your walk will cross the bridge over the Withlacoochee River both ways. While cyclists often ride to the Bridges Rd trailhead and back—an additional 2-mile round trip diverging from this route at the Blue Run Park junction—that paved path is less compelling as a hike. More significantly for cyclists, a new 1.2-mile paved connector with a tunnel under US 41 links the CR 39 trailhead to the northernmost trailhead of the Withlacoochee State Trail, Gulf Junction [29.026398, -82.471001]. This opens up a 45.3-mile linear ride to Dade City. The Florida Trail follows the same paved route 15.9 miles south, leaving the bike path at Whispering Pines Park in Inverness.

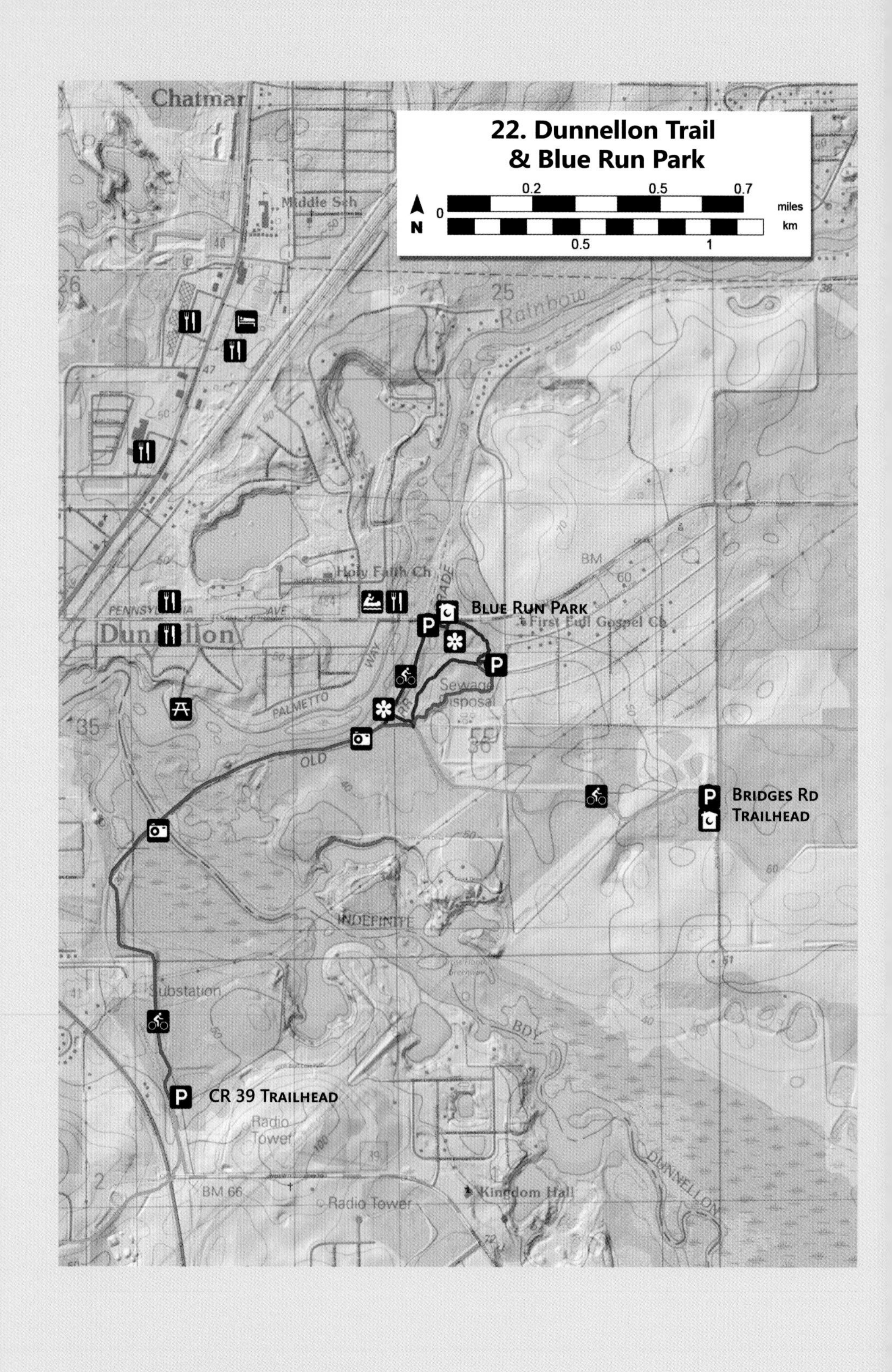
22. Dunnellon Trail
& Blue Run Park
0.2
0.5
0.7
0
miles
N
km
0.5
1
Chatmar
Middle Sch
Rainbow
Holy Faith Ch
Pennsylvania Ave
Dunnellon
Blue Run Park
First Full Gospel Ch
Palmetto Way
Sewage Disposal
Old
Bridges Rd Trailhead
Indefinite
Substation
BDY
CR 39 Trailhead
Radio Tower
BM 66
Kingdom Hall
Dunnellon

Hike

Starting at the CR 39 Dunnellon trailhead kiosk, join the paved path and turn right. It starts out flanked by a dense oak forest on both sides, which quickly gives way to the floodplain forests surrounding the Withlacoochee River. Rising from the Green Swamp and flowing northward, this river empties into the Gulf of Mexico less than 20 miles west of Dunnellon.

On both sides of the trail, pools of standing water reveal the location of pits excavated for phosphate over a century ago. Dunnellon became a mining boomtown after the first phosphate in Florida was discovered by Albertus Vogt not far downriver from this spot in 1889. The tree canopy closes in as you approach the Withlacoochee River. At 0.8 miles, the bridge crosses the river where the railroad trestle once stood. It's an exceptionally large and long bridge with observation decks built into its sides. From the top, enjoy views of the cypress-lined banks and lily-dotted coves. Not a visit goes by where we don't see a boater or paddler along this placid waterway. A launch is not far downriver at a park in downtown Dunnellon. A bench is built into the northwest end of the bridge.

North of the bridge, continue into a deeply shaded floodplain forest for the next half mile. Tree-topped mounds are

Sinkhole, Blue Run Park

Withlacoochee River

old phosphate-mining spoil piles. A few gates and fences prevent access off the trail to private property on the shoreline of the Rainbow River. The rivers meet at a confluence you can't see from the trail. But this path draws close enough to the Rainbow River for you to be able to glimpse its crystalline waters between palm fronds and tree trunks.

Where the paved path splits by a bench at 1.4 miles, make a left to leave the Florida Trail and walk into Blue Run Park. Cross a spring-fed waterway flowing toward the Rainbow River. Just past it is a natural footpath on the right, the Pond Trail. It leads to an oxbow pond cut off from the Rainbow River. While usually a greenish hue, it's an interesting waterway with a couple of benches along it for wildlife watching.

The Pond Trail returns you to the paved path within sight of the Blue Run trailhead. It's usually busy with paddlers carrying kayaks to the launch and people walking from the river with huge inner tubes. Because it's so clear, the Rainbow River is a popular tubing run. Rentals and shuttles can be arranged at an outfitter on the other side of the bridge from this trailhead.

Follow the signs to stay on the Pond Trail, which slips along the fence between the trailhead and the pond. At the far end of the parking area, walk around a retention area and down a side path. It leads to a small cove where blue flag iris blooms in springtime. Return to the Pond Trail. It tunnels into the shade while paralleling the pond, offering a few more views of the water before winding through the forest to the trailhead off San Jose Blvd. It edges the fence that corrals the parking area, reaching a kiosk with a trail map for Blue Run Park. Continue along the Pond Trail past it and make a left onto the Sandhill Loop Trail.

Under the shade of oaks and pines, this uplands trail curves through sandhill habitat. Don't be surprised to see a gopher tortoise making its way across the path to its burrow. Prickly pear cactus sport bright-yellow blooms beneath the pines. Meandering past several interpretive signs, the trail narrows as it follows a short ridge with a drop into a wetland on the left. An open area is just past a cabbage palm, along with the back side of a trail sign. Stepping into the clearing at 2.3 miles, meet the junction of the Sandhill Loop Trail, the Pond Trail, and the paved Dunnellon Trail. Walk to the paved trail and turn right. In just a couple of minutes, complete the loop around Blue Run Park at the bench at the original paved trail intersection.

Stick with the Dunnellon Trail as it curves into a straightaway, following the old railroad route. Notice the orange blazes painted on the pavement for the Florida Trail. Cross over the Withlacoochee River on the bridge, returning to the CR 39 trailhead after a 3.7-mile walk.

Hilly terrain near Shangri-La

23. Ross Prairie to SW 49th Ave

6.8 MILES | OCALA

Rolling hills aren't something you expect on a Florida Trail hike in Central Florida, but this segment along the Cross Florida Greenway offers them up for miles and miles.

Overview

Traversing a landscape altered more than fifty years beforehand by excavation work for the Cross Florida Barge Canal, this particular hike along the Florida Trail has something you don't see very often in Florida: boulders. Piles of boulders. Boulders with a thick mat of pine duff ferns growing on top of them. Boulders broken open to reveal the beauty of chert inside them. Boulders teetering along the edge of depressions and falling into sinkholes. Scrambling up and down bluffs created by this long-ago public works project, this hike provides a nice workout along with the unexpected rocks amid high, dry forests of sandhills and scrub.

Trip Planning / Land Manager

See Cross Florida Greenway. Leashed dogs welcome. Cyclists share the connector trail from the trailhead to the Florida Trail. You will cross the paved bike path several times along this hike, including sharing two underpasses under busy highways. The paved path also parallels the Florida Trail in several places.

Directions

Exit Interstate 75 at exit 324 (Belleview/Dunnellon) and drive west on CR 484 for 2.3 miles. For the trailhead at the end of this hike, turn right on Marion Oaks Course at the traffic light. Follow it 0.8 miles as it curves and becomes Marion Oaks Trail. Turn right onto SW 49th Ave and continue 0.4 miles to the SW 49th Ave trailhead [29.040916,-82.201057] on the right. For the starting point of the hike, return to CR 484 and continue west for 6.8 miles. Turn left onto SR 200 south. Drive 1.6 miles, crossing Ross Prairie before turning in at the Ross Prairie trailhead [29.038717, -82.295364]. Follow the entrance road past the Ross Prairie State Forest trailhead parking area and park at the trailhead adjoining the restrooms.

Options

Do a round trip from either end. Tack on another 3.6 linear miles to extend this route to Land Bridge trailhead to the east of Interstate 75, a 10-mile hike. Or shorten to a 4.3-mile linear hike using Shangri-La trailhead [29.038670, -82.239304] off Marion Oaks Trail as your end point.

Hike

At Ross Prairie trailhead, walk behind the restrooms and follow the fence between the campground and parking area to the right-hand corner. The blue-blazed connector trail, part of the Ross Prairie Loop, starts at a gap in the fence. Shaded by oaks in a sandhill habitat, the footpath winds its way along an arm of Ross Prairie before it reaches an

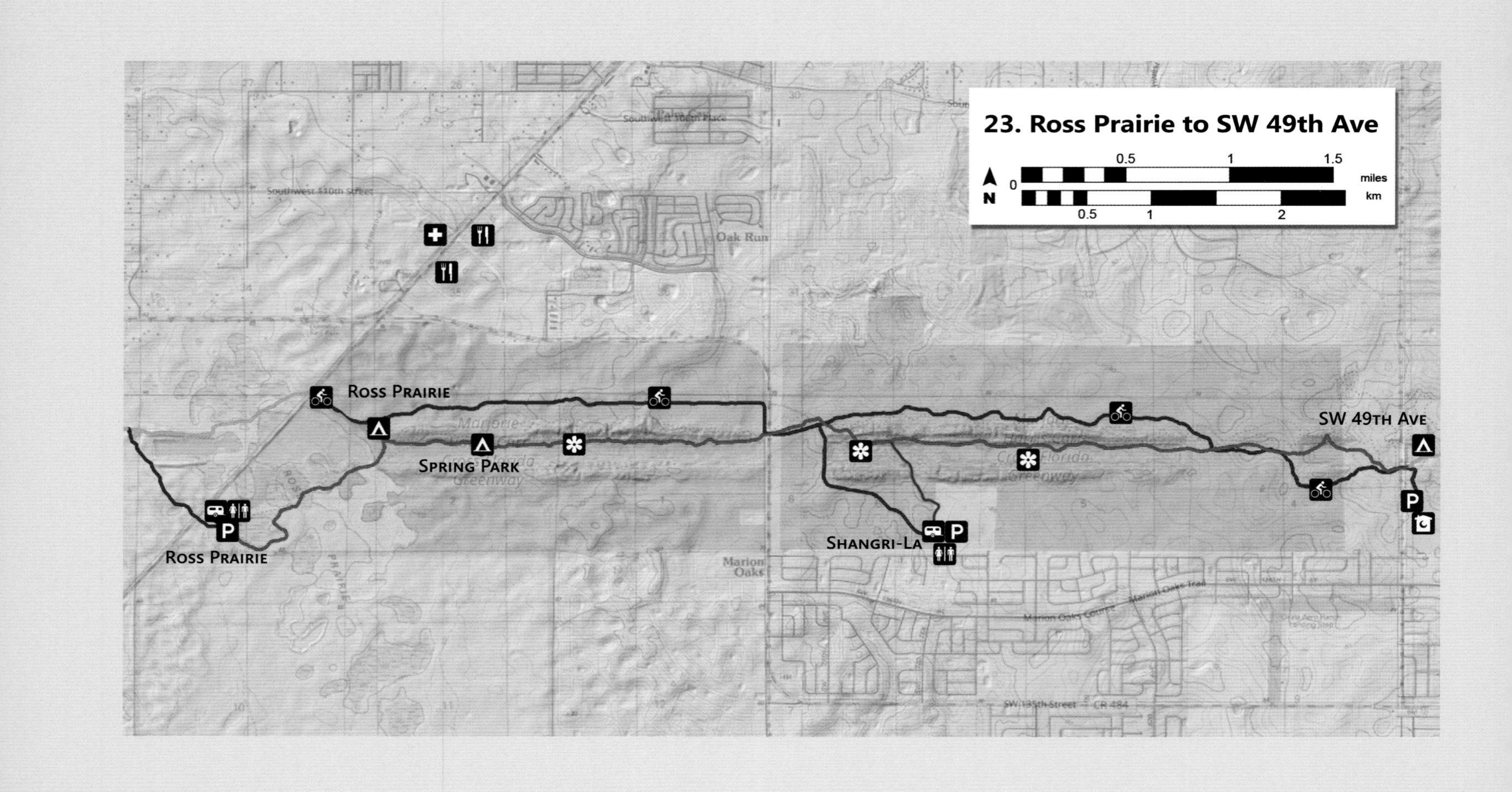
23. Ross Prairie to SW 49th Ave
0
0.5
1
1.5
miles
km
2
N
Ross Prairie
Spring Park
Ross Prairie
Shangri-La
SW 49th Ave
Southwest 110th Street
Oak Run
Marion Oaks
Marion Oaks Trail
Marion Oaks Course
SW 135th Street
CR 484

opening where it can cross it. A nearby jumble of boulders looks like a dinosaur's backbone.

Shared by equestrians, the next prairie crossing has soft sand. At times, we've found it wet here. A climb out of the prairie leads to the shade of an oak hammock before the blue blazes meet the Florida Trail at a signposted intersection after 1.2 miles. The Ross Prairie designated campsite is a short distance to the left. To continue toward your destination, turn right. For the next half mile, the trail corridor is in the bottom of the diggings of the Cross Florida Barge Canal. Topped in sand pines, a steep hill sweeps up to the left. On the right, a curvature through the trees is the other wall of the canal. The well-worn track is fringed with deer moss.

A beaten path descends into Spring Park equestrian campsite at 1.7 miles. Hikers are welcome to use this campsite, which has a picnic table, fire ring, and what was once a spring deep in the bottom of a sinkhole. Water at the bottom is now rare, but the sinkhole illustrates the unique geology of this region. Surface streams are nonexistent along this central portion of the Cross Florida Greenway because water flows underground through cavities in the karst bedrock—exactly why cutting a canal through these uplands wasn't smart. A cross section of karst looks like Swiss cheese. This is a landscape sculpted by the steady soaking of slightly acidic water into spongy limestone. The water etches pathways in the rock, eventually breaking it apart. This spring is inside a solution hole, a cylindrical sinkhole that looks like a natural pipe.

From Spring Park, backtrack uphill to find the orange blazes again. They lead to the first of the giant boulders. Unlike glacial deposits, these didn't form here, but were dug up during the original work on the Cross Florida Ship Canal—the predecessor to the Barge Canal—and left scattered on the canal bottom. Cross a natural bridge across a line of sinkholes that delineate an underground stream. More massive boulders are strewn along the forest floor. Shot through with smoothly eroded solution holes, they're cloaked in mosses and ferns, covered in pine needles, and support small trees.

SW 49th Ave campsite

Leaving this set of boulders, climb toward the top of the diggings before descending again. Scrub forest creeps in from the left, sand pines leaning from age and Chapman and myrtle oak in the understory. Grazing close to an equestrian trail, the Florida Trail ascends from the canal bottom under arches of sand live oak branches. On this uphill climb, the erosion to the canal walls is obvious. After a few pointless ups and downs, emerge at a two-track road. Turn sharply left past a very tall longleaf pine and what look like haystacks but are boulders swaddled in pine needles and ferns. More rocky mounds lie beyond.

Making another sharp left uphill, duck under a portal created by the sweeping limbs of a sand live oak. Climb a mossy slope out of the diggings to a high point before making a left. At the paved bike path, turn right and walk beneath CR 484 at 3.1 miles using the underpass. On the ascent beyond it, watch for hiker markers on posts on the left to guide you through a confusion of trail intersections leaving the paved trail. The worn footpath traverses an open, scrubby area where wildflowers are particularly showy in the fall.

Meet a limerock road and walk across it into a stretch of sand pine scrub. As the pines become taller, cross the paved bike path again. An oak hammock with mature sand live oaks casts deep shade over the climb into the next set of canal diggings. A thick layer of pine duff covers the forest floor. At the top of this steep climb, the footpath levels out for a short stretch, deeply shaded by tall pines and oaks. Then the workout begins. Up and down. Up and down. Over and over again, the trail scrambles in and out of divots atop this man-made ridge.

In one low spot, goldfoot fern sprouts from a boulder pile at 3.7 miles covered in pine needles. Around these boulders are some good examples of chert, crystallized limestone that Indigenous peoples once used to make arrowheads. The blue-blazed trail to the right connects to the Shangri-La trailhead and campground 0.7 miles east, a quiet choice for tent camping.

Ascending the next hill, the trail passes more boulder piles. Climbing up another steep slope, it makes a horseshoe curve around an eroded bluff before flattening out for a stretch. By 4.4 miles, overlook the forest below from a high bluff. You are now atop the highest terrace above what was the canal excavation below.

When the trail descends to the level of the sandhills where the bike path is located, it's almost a disappointment. But it's a very healthy stretch of sandhill habitat where you might spot a fox squirrel or an indigo snake, both endangered species we've seen here. After three crossings of the bike path at 5.6 miles, ascend one last ridge above it, tunneling into a stand of sand live oaks for a nice stretch. The ridge ends as you pop out at a promontory and overlook the underpass at SW 49th Ave. Descend past a covered bench to join the paved bike path at 6.4 miles. Go under the highway and keep left on the upslope to follow the orange blazes uphill.

Within a minute or two, reach a sign pointing to the SW 49th Ave trailhead. Follow the blue blazes along one last climb through a pine forest, up to the bike path and beyond it. Reach the trailhead at 6.8 miles.

24. Marshall Swamp

3.2 MILES | SILVER SPRINGS

A hauntingly beautiful natural landform along the Cross Florida Greenway, Marshall Swamp is a large floodplain forest near the confluence of the Silver River and the Ocklawaha River. The Florida Trail traverses it on historic tramways, boardwalks, and slightly raised ground.

Overview

This deeply shaded hike evokes the glory of Florida's cypress forests before timber companies discovered them more than a century ago. Some ancient cypress trees still stand because they had flaws that would ruin a sawmill blade. Clues to those removed include huge stumps and deep water-filled divots in the swamp. The remaining trees tower above, creating an impressive forest canopy overhead. Not all are cypress: sweetgum, hickory, red maple, and loblolly pine join the giants of Marshall Swamp.

Trip Planning / Land Manager

See Cross Florida Greenway. Leashed dogs are welcome. Cyclists share the trail. Most of this hike is shaded and surrounded by swamps, so you will want insect repellent. Alligators have been spotted in the swamps. A portable toilet is usually stationed at SE 64th Ave trailhead, and the Marshall Swamp trailhead has a restroom with flush toilets and water.

When this section of trail opened over twenty years ago, it was set atop a gravel bed to keep it out of the water. It was a sensible idea but very hard on the feet. The gravel is now covered in a dense layer of topsoil and pine duff, making for a more comfortable but very wild walk. If you encounter water over the trail near the pond at the north end (or beyond the first boardwalk at the south end), you will get your feet wet on this hike. It's not uncommon for the water levels to rise here after heavy rains, or as the river floodplains fill.

Directions

The southern access point is in Silver Springs Shores, roughly halfway between Silver Springs and Belleview, east of Ocala. From the intersection of CR 464 (Maricamp Rd) and CR 35 (Baseline Rd), drive east on CR 464 a half mile. Turn left on SE 64th Ave Rd. Follow it 2.1 miles. The SE 64th Ave Rd trailhead [29.1623, -82.0321] is on the left just before the road ends. The northern access point at Marshall Swamp trailhead [29.1833, -82.0162] is prominently signposted along Sharpes Ferry Rd 2.6 miles east of CR 35 in Silver Springs, immediately south of Silver Springs State Park.

Options

Staging two cars, you can walk all the way between trailheads. This is such a short and beautiful section that you might want to do most (if not all) of it as a round trip hike of up to 6.4 miles. Where this hike used to shine was in the old-growth swamp. A decade ago, an adjoining landowner clearcut a strip of ancient forest along the property line with the Cross Florida Greenway and erected a fence. The clearing and fence are along the middle of this hike, so hiking to the edge of that zone from either end offers the best natural scenery along the trail.

Marshall Swamp

Hike

From SE 64th Ave Rd trailhead, follow the paved bike path due west into a tunnel of trees. Note the blue blazes along it. Within a quarter mile is a small fence and a kiosk to the right along with an FT sign. Turn right and follow the blue blazes into the sandhills, which sport colorful blooms in the fall. After 0.2 miles, meet a T intersection with the orange blazes of the Florida Trail. Turn right. In just a few moments, reach the "Marshall Swamp Trail" sign. The character of the forest changes. No longer sandhills with an open understory, it remains well canopied by oaks, hickories, and pines but has dense thickets of saw palmetto surrounding the footpath.

A break in the forest reveals the end of SE 64th Ave Rd a quarter mile from the trailhead. If you're hiking out and back, it's a shortcut when you return—just not as nice as the walk in the woods. Passing two worn paths leading to the adjacent neighborhood and a footprint sign placed here when the trail was new, the footpath makes a sharp left and becomes more of a tunnel closed in by sand live oaks and scrub.

Turn a corner to meet an old narrow-gauge railroad tramway traversing the heart of Marshall Swamp. Particularly at dawn and dusk, the reflections of the trees in the water make the elevated walk through this landscape feel like you're inside a watercolor painting.

A Marion County Park sign and picnic table at 1.1 miles signal the next big change in the trail. Making a sharp left, it leaves the tramway at the picnic table and plunges into the swamp forest, where you may encounter puddles across the trail. The first boardwalk bridges a low area. The boardwalks through this swamp are normally blanketed in fallen leaves, so watch your footing.

Walking beneath a thickening canopy of floodplain trees like sweetgum, red maple, dahoon holly, and cypress, reach the next boardwalk, a much longer one traversing a significant stretch of swamp. South of this boardwalk you start to see the gap in the forest to the east created by the adjacent landowner. Turning around here nets a 2.6-mile round trip. Returning to the trailhead through the neighborhood cuts the distance to 2.4 miles.

Continuing north, parallel the fenceline. Focus on the forest to the left rather than the clearing to the right. Swaddled in mosses and fungi, the rootballs of cabbage palms swell in size. Every log is covered in lichens and fungi, with some forming natural planters for ferns. Pass an old bench. Sweetgum trees rain colorful leaves each fall into a sluggish stream.

A boardwalk at 2.1 miles arches past cypress knees so tall they seem out of proportion to the trees. Beyond it are some very old cypress stumps left behind from logging, partially hidden under the giant fronds of young cabbage palms. The next bench is past the stumps and signals where the trail pulls away from the property boundary. The lichens on tree trunks are extremely thick, as if painted on in multiple coats. Bromeliads thrive in the high branches.

While the trail is rarely soggy underfoot, you'll see low-lying spots on both sides where water collects in the remains of rotted-out rootballs. This is a humid place, where sphagnum moss

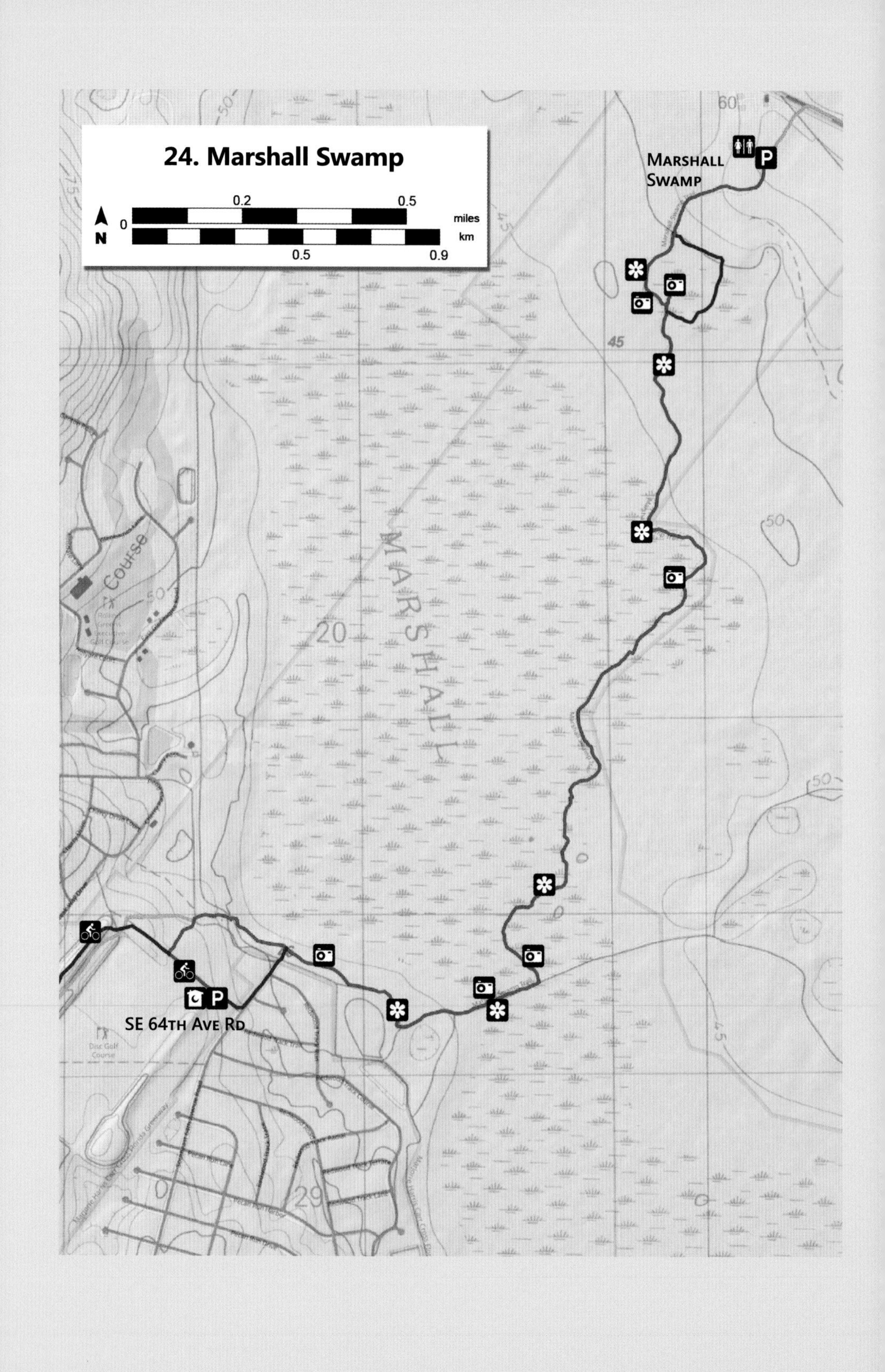

24. Marshall Swamp
0
0.2
0.5
miles
N
0.5
0.9
km
Marshall Swamp
SE 64th Ave Rd
Marshall

Cypress swamp along the tramway

swarms the trunks of cabbage palms and pine trees. Loblolly pines tower overhead, and grapevines as thick as a boa constrictor dangle above. This is truly Tarzan territory. Many of the Johnny Weissmuller movies were filmed just a few miles from here along the Silver River.

A massive swamp chestnut oak rises from the forest floor, with shaggy bark, huge leaves, and a buttressed trunk to anchor itself deep in the muck. Just beyond it is the hint of a former tramway veering into the woods on the right. Used by logging companies, narrow-gauge railroads on tramways carried the bounty of the cypress swamps to market. From historic photos, we know that some of Florida's virgin cypress approached the size of redwoods.

After 2.7 miles, reach the Loop Trail, marked with a sign. If you're hiking in and out from the Marshall Swamp trailhead, do the blue-blazed loop. Otherwise, the orange-blazed side of the loop is more picturesque. Either way, take the side trail to the observation deck. It overlooks a flag pond edged in alligator flag, a deeper expanse of open water than any other encountered in the swamp. Trees circling the pond are draped in lichens and bromeliads. Leopard frogs are common and alligators have been spotted.

Leaving this scenic spot, stay with the orange blazes. The trail winds through the swamp past deep divots filled with water. It crosses a long boardwalk over the outflow of this pond into the swamp forest, with a beautiful view framed by cypresses. Past the boardwalk, rise into more permanently dry ground under tall loblolly pines and oaks. The other end of the loop trail rejoins the main trail. As the understory opens up, the footpath is carpeted in leaves, yielding to a thick layer of pine needles as you approach the trailhead. Finish this linear hike at the Marshall Swamp trailhead kiosk after 3.2 miles.

Hiking near Clearwater Lake

Ocala Northeast

Spanning between two national forests, the Ocala and the Osceola, the first section of the Florida Trail to be blazed in the 1960s connects a string of public lands with intriguing natural features.

State Historic Marker at Clearwater Lake

BASE CAMPS

Astor

First a trading post along the St. Johns River above Lake George in 1763, Astor grew into its own as riverfront community a century later, with its sister village of Volusia across the river.

STAY

Castaways on the River 352-759-3422, 25131 Blackwater Ln.

Wildwoods Campground 352-759-3538, 22113 SR 40.

EAT

Castaways Restaurant 352-759-2494, 23525 SR 40.

Drifters Riverfront Bar & Grill 352-759-2802, 55716 Front St.

Sparky's Place 352-759-3551, 24646 SR 40.

SEE AND DO

Alexander Springs 352-669-3522, 49525 CR 445, Altoona.

Barberville Pioneer Settlement 386-749-2959, 1776 Lightfoot Ln, Barberville.

Lake George State Forest 386-985-7815, 5458 US 17, De Leon Springs.

Salt Springs

Surrounded by the Ocala National Forest and set between its namesake spring and Lake Kerr, the outdoorsy community of Salt Springs is a hub for outdoor recreation.

STAY

Bass Champions Lodge 352-685-2060, 25011 NE CR 314.

Elite RV Resort 352-685-1900, 14100 N SR 19.

Salt Springs Campground 1-877-444-6777, 13851 N SR 19.

Sportsman's Lodge 352-685-3224, 12959 NE 250th Ct.

EAT

Pop's Southern Buffet 352-685-0000, 25011 NE CR 314.

Square Meal 352-685-2288, 14100 N SR 19.

SEE AND DO

Salt Springs Marina 352-685-2255, 25711 NE 134th Pl.

Salt Springs Recreation Area 352-685-2048, 13851 N SR 19.

Palatka

With a charming historic downtown and riverwalk, Palatka ties together hiking, biking, and paddling with easy access to three trail systems. The Bartram National Recreation Trail along the St. Johns River traces the late 1700s travels of botanists John and William Bartram.

STAY

Crystal Cove Riverfront Resort 386-325-1055, 133 Crystal Cove Dr.

Hampton Inn Palatka 386-530-2420, 100 Memorial Pkwy.

Holiday Inn Express 386-325-2500, 3813 Reid St.

EAT

Angel's Dining Car 386-325-3927, 209 Reid St.

Corky Bell's 386-325-1094, 185 US 17.

The Magnolia Café 386-530-2740, 705 St. Johns Ave.

Mariachiles 386-530-2114, 318 St. Johns Ave.

Musselwhite's Seafood & Grill 386-326-9111, 125 US 17 S.

Niko's Pizza 386-328-8558, 804 SR 19.

SEE AND DO

Bronson-Mulholland House 386-329-0140, 100 Madison St.

David Browning Railroad Museum 386-328-0305, 222 N 11th St.

Ravine Gardens State Park 386-329-3721, 1600 Twigg St.

St. Johns River Center 386-916-5916, 102 N 1st St.

Keystone Heights

Developed in the 1920s as a winter resort, Keystone Heights drew visitors and new residents because of its many rounded lakes in the sandhills. The creation of one of Florida's first state parks at Gold Head started soon after.

STAY

Mike Roess Gold Head Branch State Park 352-262-8129, 6239 SR 21.

EAT

Johnny's Bar-B-Q 352-473-4445, 7411 SR 21.

Keystone Inn 352-473-3331, 208 SR 100.

SEE AND DO

Camp Blanding Museum 904-682-3196, 5629 SR 16 W.

Etoniah Creek State Forest 386-329-2552, 390 Holloway Rd.

Keystone Beach 352-473-4807, 565 S Lawrence Blvd.

Lake City

Incorporated in 1856, this city of many lakes became Lake City after a brief flirtation with the name Alligator, derived from the name of the Seminole chief of the village that preceded the pioneer settlement.

STAY

Best Western Plus 386-754-5944, 350 SW Florida Gateway Dr.

Holiday Inn Hotel & Suites 386-754-1411, 213 SW Commerce Dr.

Home2 Suites 386-487-9890, 414 SW Florida Gateway Dr.

Lake City Campground 386-752-9131, 4743 N US 441.

Ocean Pond Campground 1-877-444-6777, 24874 US 90, Sanderson.

EAT

Shirley's Restaurant 386-755-9130, 746 E Duval.

SEE AND DO

Alligator Lake 386-719-7545, 420 SE Alligator Glen.

Falling Creek Falls [30.257817, -82.668633] NW Falling Creek Rd.

Lake City Historical Museum 386-755-9096, 157 SE Hernando Ave.

Olustee Battlefield State Park 386-758-0400, 5815 Battlefield Trail Rd.

Osceola National Forest 386-752-2577, 24874 US 90.

Side Trip

A short walk down a nature trail from the swimming area at Juniper Springs Recreation Area, **FERN HAMMOCK SPRINGS** cradles pulsating pools of turquoise and gray that look like video screens on the bottom of the spring basin. floridahikes.com/juniper-springs.

Fern Hammock Springs

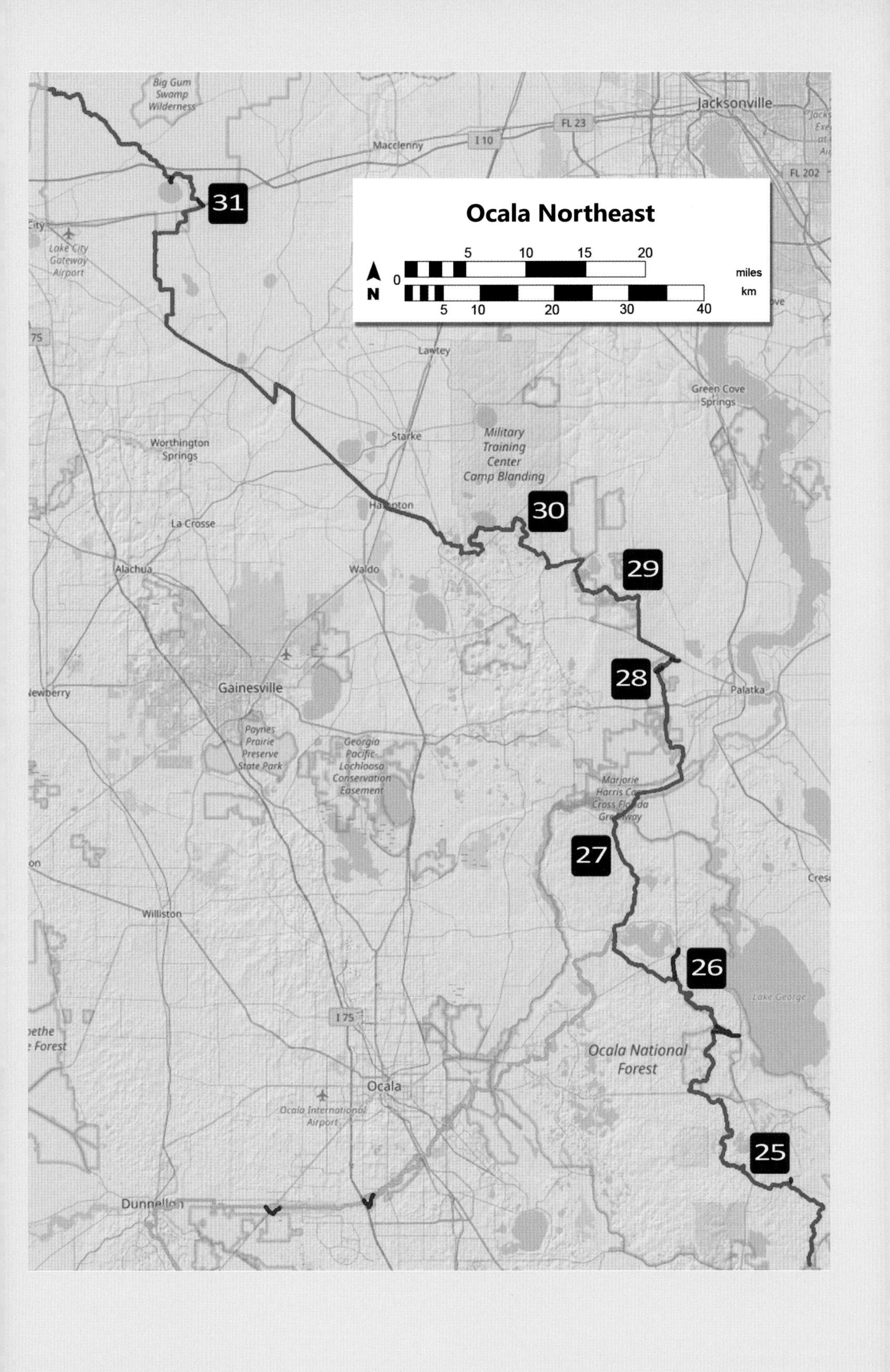
Ocala Northeast
0
5
10
15
20
miles
N
5
10
20
30
40
km
31
30
29
28
27
26
25
Big Gum Swamp Wilderness
Jacksonville
FL 23
I 10
Macclenny
FL 202
Lake City Gateway Airport
Lawtey
Green Cove Springs
Starke
Military Training Center Camp Blanding
Worthington Springs
La Crosse
Alachua
Waldo
Gainesville
Palatka
Paynes Prairie Preserve State Park
Georgia Pacific Lochloosa Conservation Easement
Williston
I 75
Lake George
Ocala National Forest
Ocala
Ocala International Airport
Dunnellon

Scrub corridor near Farles Prairie

Ocala National Forest

72.2 MILES | LAKE, MARION, AND PUTNAM COUNTIES

Along the oldest segment of the Florida Trail, hikers have worn a groove through the Ocala National Forest for over 50 years. Well-loved and easy to follow, it remains the most popular backpacker destination in Florida.

Overview

Established by President Theodore Roosevelt in 1908, the Ocala National Forest is the oldest national forest east of the Mississippi River in the continental United States. It protects the world's largest sand pine scrub forest, Big Scrub. It can be likened to a desert in places, its plants and animals adapted to soaking what nutrients they can from the rain that falls on these fine-grained sands. As the North American continent formed, ancient ridges along the spine of what would become Florida stood above the ocean, including ones found in this forest today. Unusual species live here, like the Florida sand skink—which swims beneath the sand—and several dozen plants found nowhere else but this well-drained scrub.

After attempts to build the Florida Trail elsewhere in the state in 1966, trail founder Jim Kern reached out to the Ocala National Forest to see about providing hikers with a backpacking route. On October 30, 1966, Jim and a small trail crew painted the trail's first official blazes northbound from Clearwater Lake. A state historic marker installed on the fiftieth anniversary of this event commemorates the south end of this section as the birthplace of the Florida Trail.

Throughout the forest, rolling hills topped with sand pine scrub or longleaf pine forest are broken up by low-lying prairie ecosystems that cradle lakes and ponds between the ridges. Wildlife abounds, with Florida black bears spotted more often here than anywhere else in the state. Florida scrub-jay thrive in the scrub forests, and endangered red-cockaded woodpeckers can be found in colonies in longleaf pine habitat.

A pleasure to hike, the Ocala section of the Florida Trail has side trails leading to the first-magnitude springs found throughout the forest. But it's not entirely inside the national forest. The northernmost 5.5 miles follow a discontinuous segment of the Cross Florida Greenway along a piece of the Cross Florida Barge Canal built in the 1960s, crossing it at Buckman Lock.

Trailheads

Trailheads behind the gates of popular recreation areas are connected to the Florida Trail via blue-blazed side trails. South to north, trailheads include:

0.0 CLEARWATER LAKE
Very small paved parking area outside recreation area gates.

10.0 ALEXANDER SPRINGS
0.5E. Large parking area inside springs recreation area. Fee.

13.5 SR 19
Small paved parking area along SR 19 at trail crossing.

18.1 FARLES PRAIRIE
Large grassy parking area at lake. Dirt road access. Vault toilet. Fee.

27.8 JUNIPER SPRINGS
0.5E. Large parking area inside springs recreation area. Fee.

36.6 PAT'S ISLAND
Small dirt lot off dirt forest road at north end of wilderness area.

38.4 HOPKINS PRAIRIE
Small dirt lot along dirt forest road outside seasonal campground.

45.0 SALT SPRINGS
2.9E. Dirt lot near marina in small community.

52.5 THE 88 STORE
Private business offering trail access and parking with permission.

53.0 CR 316
Site of old building and hunt check station off paved highway.

58.9 LAKE DELANCY WEST
Recreation area accessed by dirt roads. Vault toilet. Fee.

65.7 RODMAN
Large dirt parking area on west side of Kirkpatrick Dam.

66.4 RODMAN REC AREA
Small paved parking area on east side of dam. Restrooms and water.

67.5 RODMAN CAMPGROUND
0.2W. Parking permitted behind campground gates for a fee.

72.1 St. JOHNS SOUTH
Small campground adjoining Buckman Lock. Portable toilet.

Break-ins and vandalism have been reported at roadside trailheads in the Ocala National Forest. For peace of mind, consider leaving vehicles behind the gates of a recreation area, where a camp host is on duty 24/7.

Camping

Random camping is permitted year-round in Juniper Prairie Wilderness. It is also allowed throughout the Ocala National Forest except during general gun (deer hunting) season each fall. At that time you are required to use designated campsites, which charge a fee.

0.0 CLEARWATER LAKE
0.3W. Lakeside campground with tent and RV sites, bathhouse. Fee.

10.0 ALEXANDER SPRINGS
0.5E. Nicely wooded campground adjoining springs. Fee.

27.8 JUNIPER SPRINGS
0.5E. Deeply wooded campground with spring access. Fee.

29.0 JUNIPER PRAIRIE WILDERNESS
Random camping permitted at all times from mile 29 to 36.7.

38.4 HOPKINS PRAIRIE
Seasonal campground with vault toilet. Fee.

45.0 SALT SPRINGS
3.5E. Developed campground at springs north of trailhead. Fee.

52.5 88 STORE
Private camping area at popular bar and grill. Fee.

58.9 LAKE DELANCY WEST
Camping area with vault toilet. Water sometimes available. Fee.

67.5 RODMAN CAMPGROUND
Large campground, bathhouse and laundry. Fee.

72.1 St. JOHNS SOUTH
Tent campground adjoining Buckman Lock. Portable toilet. Fee.

For your safety, camp away from forest roads and avoid being anywhere near where you see tire tracks (including ATV tracks) as people do roam the forest freely in ATVs and other off-road vehicles after dark. It is mandatory to protect your food from bears by either hanging it properly or using a bear canister. Use a bear canister: bears have wised up to bear bags and hikers have had theirs stolen.

Trip Planning

Leashed dogs are welcome. This is one of the best destinations in Florida

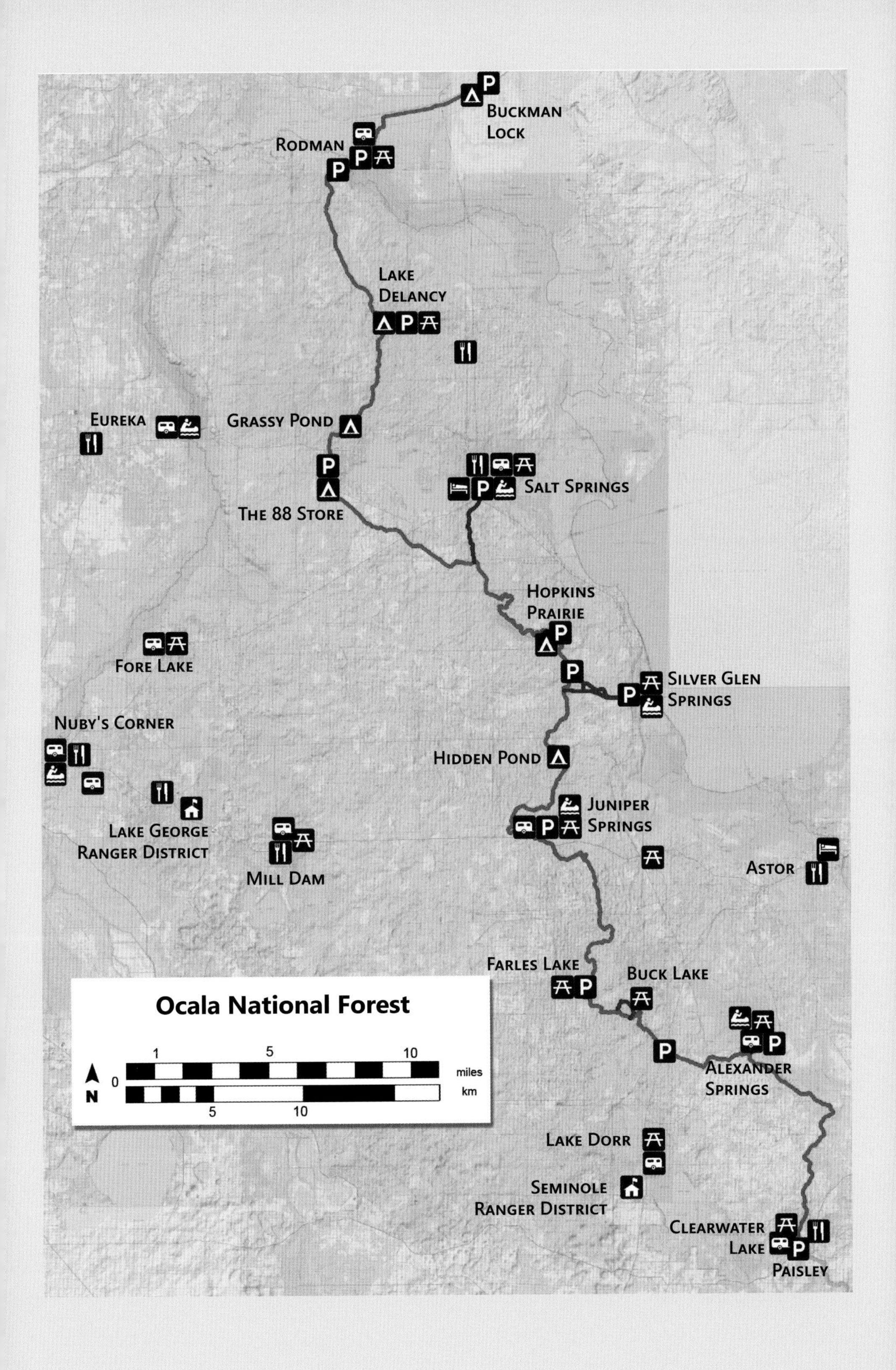
Buckman
Lock
Rodman
Lake
Delancy
Eureka
Grassy Pond
The 88 Store
Salt Springs
Hopkins
Prairie
Fore Lake
Silver Glen
Springs
Nuby's Corner
Hidden Pond
Juniper
Springs
Lake George
Ranger District
Mill Dam
Astor
Farles Lake
Buck Lake
Ocala National Forest
1
5
10
0
miles
N
km
5
10
Alexander
Springs
Lake Dorr
Seminole
Ranger District
Clearwater
Lake
Paisley

for hiking with your dog because it is mostly high, dry ground. Surface water sources are limited. The farther north you go, the tougher water is to find. Hunting is very popular here. Determine hunting season dates before making your plans. Wear bright-orange during hunting season. Random camping is not allowed during deer hunting season, which spans from November into January.

Planning a backpacking trip across the entire section? Determine where to start and end, how to get a shuttle, and where to stash your car while you hike. Contact the US Forest Service by phone or email for their list of shuttle providers. Volunteers who live in the area can help you get around. Leave a note on the Florida Trail Hikers Facebook group for shuttle assistance.

The Ocala National Forest has the highest population of bears in Florida. We've seen them in many different places throughout the forest and have come across bear tracks on the trail on almost every hike. Don't approach a bear if you see it. Wait for it to move on.

The Florida Trail in the Ocala National Forest is hiking only. Report incidents with vehicles (ATVs, Jeeps, or pickups), equestrians, or cyclists using the trail to the US Forest Service.

Land Manager

US Forest Service, National Forests in Florida
Seminole Ranger District
40929 SR 19, Umatilla
352-669-3153

Lake George Ranger District
17147 E SR 40, Silver Springs
352-625-2520
fs.usda.gov/florida

Highlights

Historic Marker, mile 0.0

It's a pretty big deal to have an official state historic marker acknowledging the founding of the Florida Trail more than 50 years ago, so stop in at the trailhead just south of Clearwater Lake Recreation Area to grab a photo.

Buck Lake, mile 16.2

Although the best views are off trail on a blue-blazed loop, Buck Lake is a beauty spot worth the detour. It's one of the prettiest lakes that the Florida Trail passes by in this section, and unlike the ponds along the trail, it doesn't dry out.

Farles Prairie, mile 18.2

One of the larger prairie systems that the Florida Trail works its way around, this is an ideal place to spot sandhill cranes, especially in winter. Beyond the permanent lake at its south end, sweeping views of the prairie occur at twists and turns of the trail over the next several miles.

Juniper Prairie Wilderness, mile 29.0

One of two wilderness areas within the Ocala National Forest, this has hilly terrain with ridges surrounding vast open prairies, sparkling wet prairies, lily-dotted ponds, and a stream crossing.

Pat's Island, mile 35.9

An island of longleaf pines surrounded by the scrub, Pat's Island is circled by the Yearling Trail, an interpretive walk through the pioneer settlement that once thrived atop its elevated ridge.

Big Sink, mile 37.8

An enormous, deep water-filled sinkhole sits east of the trail down a small side path.

Hopkins Prairie, mile 38.8

For more than five miles, the Florida Trail traces the shoreline of this extensive wet prairie, offering panoramic views in multiple directions.

The 88 Store, mile 52.5

A legendary watering hole along the Florida Trail, this popular trailside stop has a trail register behind the bar, a big porch to relax on and enjoy a cold drink or an ice cream, colorful characters to chat with, and camping on-site.

Riverside Island, mile 60.7

High ground topped with healthy longleaf pine savanna, once common throughout the Southeast but now seen more rarely, usually in carefully managed habitat.

Penner Ponds, mile 64.9

Cradled by scrub, a pair of picturesque ponds sits west of the trail on the edge of a former pioneer homestead. The grave of settler Arthur Pinner is nearby.

Recommended Day Hikes

Mile 0.0

Clearwater Lake to Alexander Springs, 10.5 miles linear

Mile 13.6

Buck Lake Loop, 6.4-mile round trip and loop

Mile 18.1

Farles Prairie to Juniper Springs, 9.7 miles linear

Mile 27.8

Juniper Prairie Wilderness, 8.8 miles linear

Mile 35.9

The Yearling Trail, 5.5-mile loop

Mile 36.6

Pat's Island to Hopkins Prairie, 3.6-mile round trip

Mile 38.4

Hopkins Prairie to CR 314, 9.7 miles linear

Mile 58.9

Lake Delancy to 88 Store, 6.9 miles linear

Mile 65.9

Rodman to Lake Delancy, 6.9 miles linear

Mile 67.5

Rodman Campground to Buckman Lock, 4.7 miles linear

Sand pine scrub near Farles Prairie

Dora Pond

25. Buck Lake Loop

6.4 MILES | ALTOONA

Combining a linear hike through typical Big Scrub habitat with a loop around scenic Buck Lake, this hike provides a satisfying walk in the woods from a major highway.

Overview

Between SR 19 and Buck Lake, the Florida Trail traverses scrub tunnels that are typical of the Big Scrub, where the crooked branches of rusty lyonia form an arch above, and densely packed scrub oaks—myrtle oak, Chapman oak, and scrub oak—fill the understory. Most of the hike is shaded, the footpath well defined. The loop around Buck Lake provides panoramic views from different vantage points.

Trip Planning / Land Manager

See Ocala National Forest. This hike is in the Seminole Ranger District. Leashed dogs are welcome. This hike is on high ground for the most part, until it dips to lake level around the group campground at Buck Lake Recreation Area, which has a vault toilet and picnic area.

Directions

SR 19 trailhead [29.0742, -81.6299] is 7.6 miles north of the traffic light in Altoona and 6.3 miles south of the traffic light at the intersection of SR 19 and SR 40 in the Ocala National Forest. With roadside signage pointing it out from both directions, it's easy to find.

Options

There has been vandalism to cars left overnight, so tackle this as a day hike. It's a good starting point along a major highway; unlike trailheads to the north and south, it charges no fee. If you'd prefer to park in a fee area, use Farles Prairie [29.10364, -81.674438] as a northerly approach to the loop portion for a 5.8-mile hike. The dirt road to the trailhead can be rough. Or begin your trek 4 miles south of SR 19 at Alexander Springs [29.079041, -81.577995] for a 14.4-mile day hike or an overnighter, camping between Railroad Grade and Dora Pond.

Hike

A short blue blaze connects the parking area to the Florida Trail. Turn left at the T intersection and immediately enter a tunnel of scrub. Changes in elevation are obvious as you hike the ancient sand dunes underlying the Big Scrub, the trail corridor inside a dense thicket of scrub-adapted myrtle and Chapman oaks and rusty lyonia. Limestone peeps from the sand near a pair of sinkholes hiding under the dense understory.

Drop into a small, showy clearing beneath the sand pines. Climb steadily from this low point through the scrub for a quarter mile. Passing under a power line, reach a graded road a few moments later. Railroad Grade (FR 57) is atop a former railbed.

Continue across it along a sand ridge circling a collection of residences to the southeast. The understory opens into a pine-shaded clearing with a view across a prairie and flat spots for random camping. Past a guardrail in the woods, the footpath curves toward water. Water isn't common in the Big Scrub, but

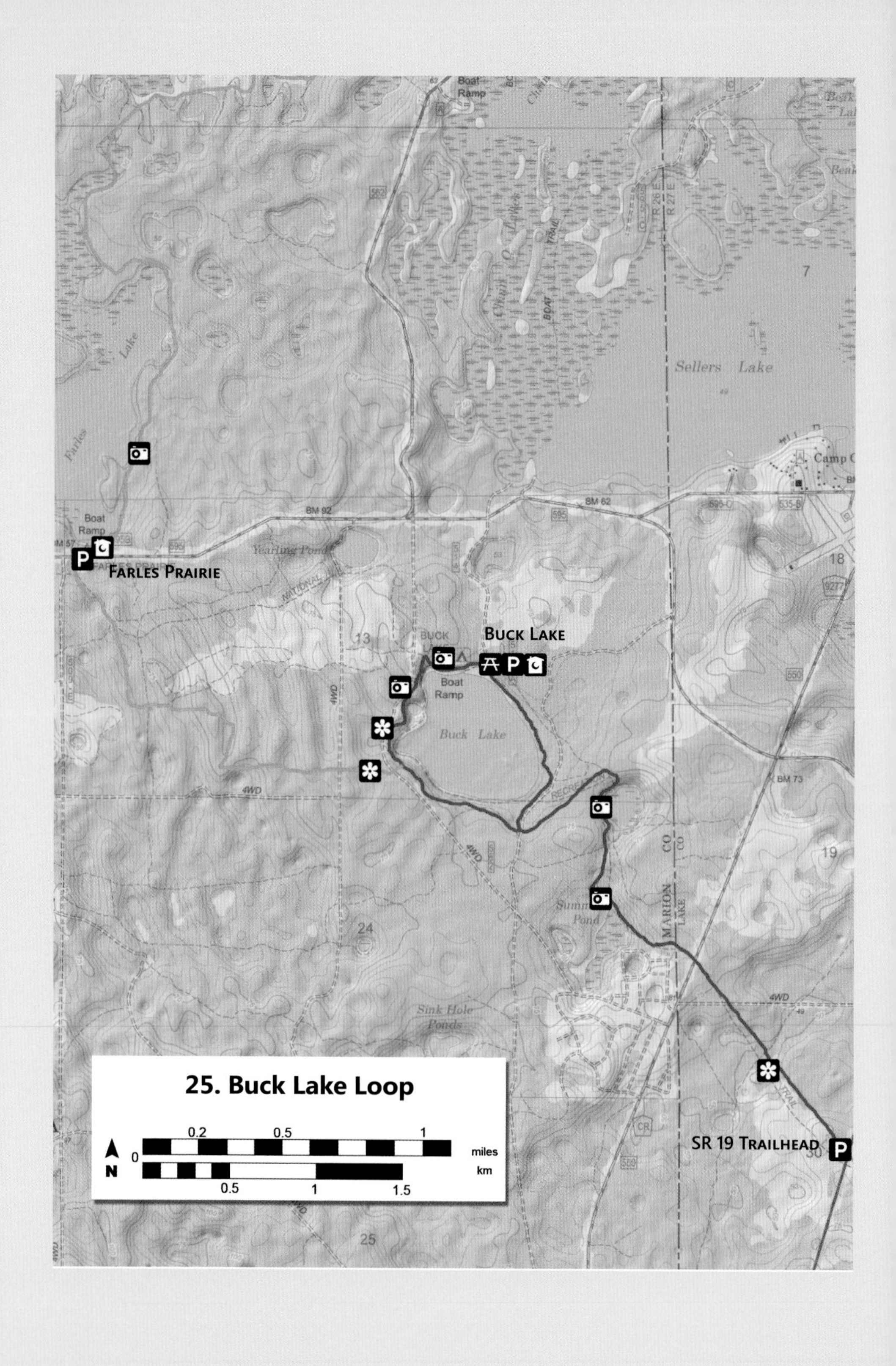

25. Buck Lake Loop
Farles Prairie
Buck Lake
SR 19 Trailhead
Sellers Lake
Buck Lake
Yearling Pond
Sink Hole Ponds
Boat Ramp
Boat Ramp
Boat Ramp
Farles Lake
Marion Co
Lake Co
0
0.2
0.5
1
miles
0.5
1
1.5
km
N

Buck Lake

where you find it, it's showy. At 1.7 miles, Dora Pond is surrounded by a small prairie. A clearing under the pines offers soft pine duff for camping.

Leave the pond to ascend through a low scrub forest. Meet the first junction of the Buck Lake Loop at 2.2 miles. Pass by it and continue the climb through the tunnel of scrub, catching glimpses through the trees of Buck Lake far below. Reach the second junction with the loop trail in a half mile, marked by a wooden sign. Turn right and follow the blue blazes.

Dense oak scrub yields to a sparser forest with views through the trees to the lake. With long, twisted trunks, sand live oaks and rusty lyonia knit together a canopy of shade. As the worn path starts downhill, enjoy more perspectives on Buck Lake, including a small cove at the base of this steep hill. At a four-way junction, turn right to descend to lake level, where tufts of sand cordgrass edge the lakeshore.

Join a forest road into Buck Lake Recreation Area, passing the campground and boat launch. The US Forest Service reserves this campground for group use, so if you want to camp here, plan a getaway with a bunch of friends and split the cost. Beyond the campground is a stop for a break, a picnic area with vault toilet at 3.6 miles.

The blue blazes continue along a forest road with sweeping views of the water. From this vantage point, the differing elevations surrounding the lake are obvious. The pine-topped ridge you traversed along the Florida Trail rises from the far shore of the lake.

When the trail diverges from the lakeshore, it aims for a stand of loblolly pines. Narrowing from a forest road to a footpath, it is swallowed up by the pine forest. Water seeps out of a nearby bayhead, making it mucky underfoot. Climbing from lake level up onto the ridge, enter the sand pine scrub. Reach the Florida Trail at the southern junction of the loop after 4.2 miles.

Turn left. The return route should be recognizable, or at least the landmarks along it: Dora Pond, the guardrail, the flat camping area by the prairie, and Railroad Grade. Enjoy the tunnel of scrub. The trail descends through it, reaching the turnoff and the SR 19 trailhead at 6.4 miles.

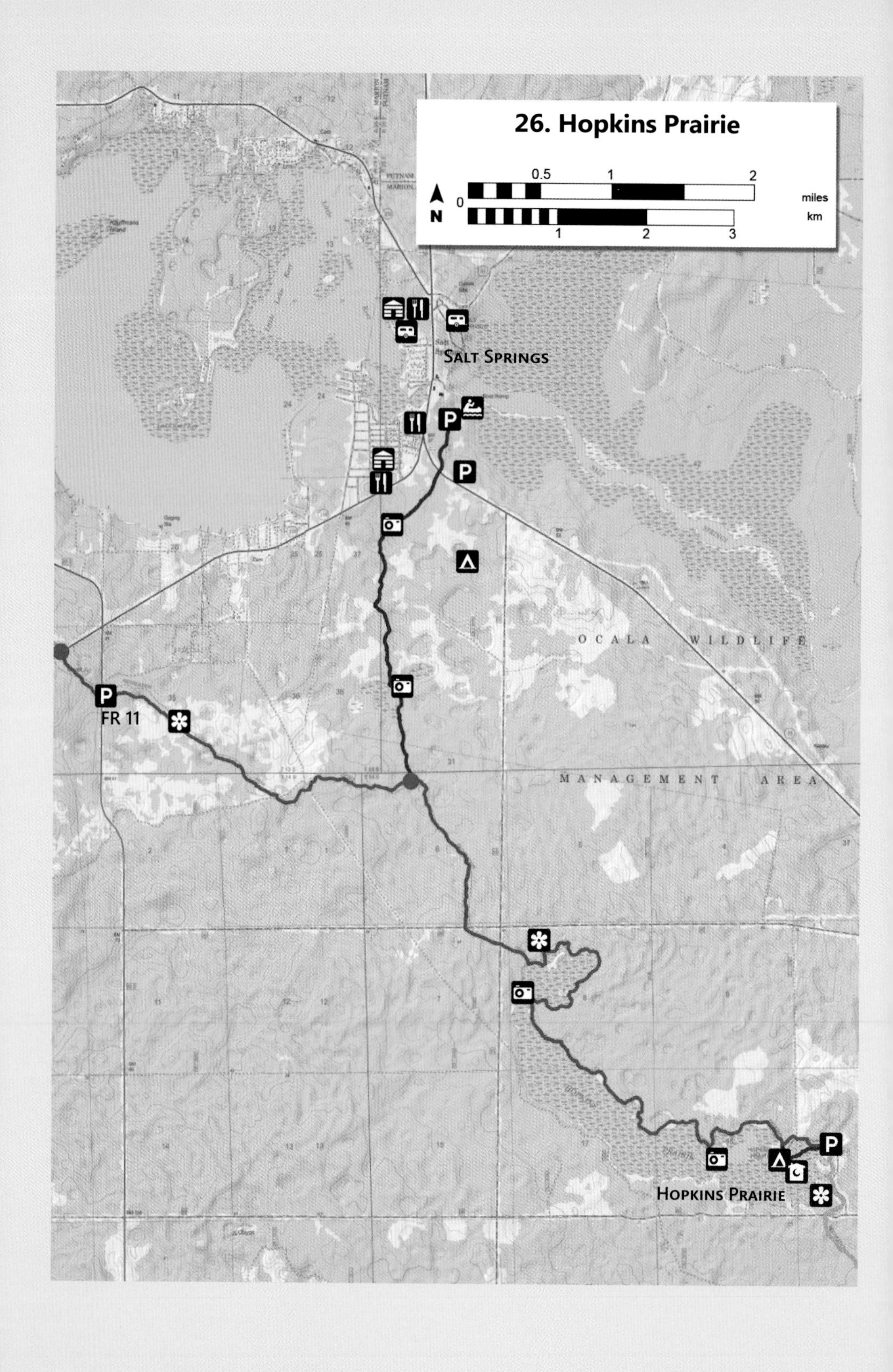
26. Hopkins Prairie
0.5
1
2
0
miles
N
km
1
2
3
Salt Springs
FR 11
OCALA WILDLIFE
MANAGEMENT AREA
Hopkins Prairie

26. Hopkins Prairie

9.7 MILES | SALT SPRINGS

Following the rim of one of the largest prairies in the Ocala National Forest, this segment of the Florida Trail offers scenic views for much of its length.

Overview

The Ocala National Forest has the largest expanse of sand pine scrub forest in the world. A lesser known facet of this national forest is its extensive wet prairies, each an oasis in the middle of the scrub. In these wide-open spaces, sandhill cranes gather, kingfishers buzz above small ponds, and eagles soar over the open landscape.

Hopkins Prairie is one of the biggest natural features in the Ocala National Forest. Portions of it are dry grasslands but it has many prairie ponds within it. If rainfall has been heavy for a season, the entire prairie can become a glassy lake. More than two-thirds of the distance of this hike follows the rim of Hopkins Prairie. At its northern end, the trail continues through sand pine scrub to reach Kerr Island, a promontory of pine savanna near Salt Springs.

Trip Planning / Land Manager

See Ocala National Forest. This hike is in the Lake George Ranger District. Leashed dogs are welcome, but this hike passes many ponds where alligators reside, so proceed with caution. There are times when the water creeps over the trail; on rare occasions, this hike becomes impassible due to high water. Provided that water levels are low to normal, there are a few nice places to set up camp along the prairie rim. Bears are common here. Protect your food: a bear canister is best. Hopkins Prairie campground is open October through May for tent camping for a fee.

Directions

For a linear hike, leave a vehicle near Salt Springs to hike toward. Backpackers should use the Salt Springs trailhead [29.34738, -81.733368] along the road to Salt Springs Marina off SR 19. Day hikers can spot a car at a pull-off near the trail crossing on FR 11 [29.320040, -81.773705] or along the eastern shoulder of CR 314 [29.324329, -81.778610] south of Salt Springs.

The starting point for the hike is Hopkins Prairie trailhead [29.27659, -81.688553]. From Salt Springs, follow SR 19 south past the turnoff for Shanty Pond campground. Once you get to a small community on both sides of the highway, about 9 miles south of Salt Springs, watch for a sign pointing to the right to Hopkins Prairie. Follow that road. Continue to follow the signs along bumpy dirt roads to the trailhead, which is outside the gates of the campground.

Options

Several different endings are possible for this hike. Although all of the route is pleasant, Hopkins Prairie is the highlight. A round-trip trek to the north rim and back is 9.6 miles. The pull-off at FR 11 lets you trim this linear hike to 9.2 miles. Or leave a car at the Salt Springs trailhead by the marina and hike to it along the blue-blazed side trail for a linear 9.6 miles.

From Hopkins Prairie trailhead, hike south on a 3.6-mile round trip to Pat's

Hopkins Prairie

Island trailhead [29.25738, -81.681137], Big Sink being a highlight. Tack on a walk around the inner Yearling Trail loop past Long Cemetery and Pat's Island sinkhole to make it a 6.9-mile hike.

Hike

Head straight into the woods in front of the parking area. It's a diminutive oak scrub, a delicate forest under a low canopy of sand live oaks with hanging gardens of lichen dripping from the branches. After a quarter mile, turn left to pass a sinkhole before crossing a forest road blocked off to vehicular traffic. Blueberry bushes line the footpath, reminding you that this is bear country. Don't be surprised to see bear footprints in the sand.

Emerging from a long corridor in the scrub, reach a T intersection on the edge of Hopkins Prairie at 0.4 miles. To the left is a bat house and campground access. Turn right to hike around this very large prairie. The walk along its rim is easy and gentle if it's not a wade. The sandy shore is obvious and the trail sticks close to it, dipping in and out of the scrub forest. Blazes can be sporadic, so side trails may lead you off the mark. Keep close to the prairie rim.

Passing a small pond close to the footpath a mile into the hike, the trail curves to offer its last glimpse of the peninsula where the campground is located. It then dips into an oak hammock and pops out on the other side to provide a different perspective on the prairie. Rounding two more ponds over the next mile, enter a stand of tall longleaf pines. This is a nice spot to set up camp. Smooth cordgrass blurs the near shoreline. Distant willows speak of deeper water.

Three miles into the hike, chirps arise from the grasses as dry prairie turns to marsh. Alive with a chorus of frogs, this marsh adjoins the trail for some distance. Duck through an oak hammock offering precious shade before circling the next marsh. This one is a symphony of textures rising to a crescendo in the middle, with wax myrtles and loblolly bay at its heart.

When the trail reaches the tip of the farthest arm of the prairie and starts to loop back on the other side, you can look across and see where you've been, a panorama stretching almost two miles. Rounding a cove covered in water lilies—the last reliable water source for nearly ten miles northbound—bid farewell to Hopkins Prairie at a series of posts blocking ATVs from driving to it, 4.8 miles into the hike.

Climbing into the sand pine scrub, cross a forest road where blue blazes come in from the left. That's the high-water bypass around the entire prairie. The trunks of surrounding pines are large in diameter in the next mature sand pine forest. Crossing FR 54, rejoin a tunnel through the scrub. As it leads downhill, reach a transition zone where scrub meets sandhill with longleaf pines and turkey oaks. There are more tiny prairies here. The first has an ephemeral pond at its heart and a flat area nearby for tenting.

After a dive into the scrub, snake around a string of small prairies before reaching the prominent Salt Springs junction with a sign and a bench at 6.6 miles. If your vehicle is parked at Salt Springs trailhead, follow the blue blazes east through the scrub forest. This 3-mile connector winds between picturesque prairie ponds and has many opportunities for random camping in beauty spots. Cross SR 19 and continue along the edge of the forest. Your hike ends at Salt Springs trailhead after 9.6 miles.

If you parked at FR 11 or CR 314, stay with the orange blazes. Around you are tall sand pines whose pine cones release when they burn, popping like popcorn. Past a two-track road, you're in the thick of lyonia and sand live oak beneath the sand pines, a two-tier forest, crowded and intimate. Jog left as the habitat transitions slowly to longleaf pine, the forest floor a yellow haze when wiregrass blooms in winter.

Crossing two forest roads where OHVs are allowed to roam, ascend Kerr Island around 8 miles. Like Pat's Island in the Juniper Prairie Wilderness, this is a biological island, a longleaf pine savanna surrounded by the Big Scrub. Where white bands are painted on pine trees, the candle-wax drip of sap down the bark is from nest holes drilled by red-cockaded woodpeckers. These endangered birds only nest in well-aged longleaf pine trees, preferably a century old.

The view of the landscape stretches on and on, thanks to the open understory under the high canopy created by the longleaf pines. Crossing a few more jeep trails, the trail drops through a depression like an old dry sinkhole. Traffic noise filters in as you approach FR 11. Keep alert for the sounds of birds, since a colony of red-cockaded woodpeckers is nearby.

Cross paved FR 11 at 9.2 miles. The last half mile through pine savanna atop Kerr Island has showy wildflowers in spring and fall. The end of this hike is the shoulder of CR 314 at 9.7 miles.

Longleaf pine savanna

27. Riverside Island

12.9 MILES | SALT SPRINGS

Traverse gently rolling hills topped with classic longleaf pine savanna to the east of the Ocklawaha River basin.

Overview

While the Ocala National Forest is widely known for its Big Scrub, its longleaf pine savannas are compellingly beautiful habitats to hike through. These islands in the scrub forest occur infrequently south of Salt Springs, but to the north and west of the "amazing crystal fountain" described by botanist William Bartram in his *Travels*, he walked among pine savannas in 1773, marveling at their splendor. You will too. The trade-off is a lack of surface streams on this high ground. Water sources for backpackers are ponds and lakes. This hike starts at the northern edge of Kerr Island, a pine island west of Lake Kerr, and crosses all of Riverside Island north of Lake Delancy. The low ground between the savannas is sand pine scrub, providing a contrast of habitats, with Grassy Pond a highlight in a deep sinkhole bowl in the scrub.

Trip Planning / Land Manager

See Ocala National Forest. This hike is in the Lake George Ranger District. Leashed dogs are welcome; this is an ideal section to hike with your dog. However, bears are extremely common. Protect your food: a bear canister is best. Lake Delancy West campground is open October through May for tent camping for a fee. ATV trails cross this part of the Florida Trail. If you see an ATV on the trail or ATV damage to the trail, please report it to the US Forest Service.

Directions

Drive 12 miles north along SR 19 from Salt Springs to Rodman Dam Rd. Turn left and continue 4 miles, crossing over the dam. In a quarter mile, the signposted Rodman trailhead [29.502291, -81.814079] is on the right. Leave a vehicle at Rodman. If you can handle graded forest roads with some soft sandy spots, it's a straight shot 9.5 miles south along FR 11 (formerly FR 88) from the ATV trailhead within view to CR 316. Otherwise backtrack to Salt Springs via SR 19 and take CR 316 west 6.8 miles to where FR 11 crosses. An old hunt check station [29.36622, -81.82066] is on the southwest corner. Park there.

Options

A hike to Grassy Pond from CR 316 is an easy 3.6-mile round trip, transitioning from sandhills to scrub. From Rodman trailhead south, the Penner Ponds overlook just north of FR 74 makes a nice 3.4-mile round-trip hike. There was formerly a marked loop around the ponds but we found no trace on our last visit. Continue south to the sinkhole just past the FR 11 crossing for an 8.8-mile round trip, or across Riverside Island to Lake Delancy West for a 13.6-mile round trip. Lake Delancy West is an intermediate trailhead near the middle of this hike with an adjacent campground open October to May. A day-use fee applies for parking; the road to it from SR 19 can be difficult to traverse at times.

If you plan to backpack this section and camp at Grassy Pond or random camp on Riverside Island, it's safest to leave vehicles at The 88 Store [29.359560, -81.820953] at the south end and Rodman Campground [29.519880, -81.799316] at the north end, extending your hike by 2.8 miles. Or use Lake Delancy West [29.428260, -81.788560] in the middle for a shorter trip. All three locations charge a parking fee.

Hike

Walk a tenth of a mile west along CR 316 from the parking area to where the Florida Trail crosses the highway at a prominent FNST sign. Enter the pine savanna on the north side of the highway, tall longleaf pines providing shade above an open understory carpeted in wiregrass. A jeep trail at an old wooden mileage sign marks the edge of Kerr Island, a sharp delineation between habitats at a half mile.

Join a tight corridor between a thicket of myrtle oaks and sand live oaks beneath sand pines, with turkey oaks infiltrating the scrub. Florida rosemary grows in clumps adjoining the white sand of the footpath. Walk along the edge of an older sand pine scrub with slender trunks. Cross the hard-packed surface of FR 11 at a mile. Don't be surprised to find bear prints or scat in the sand area, as the resident Florida black bear population uses the Florida Trail too. We've seen bears ambling along FR 11 in this vicinity. A trail marker confirms the crossing, the corridor a tunnel between and beneath scrub oaks.

Begin a gentle ascent, transitioning from dense scrub to fluffy sand pines and back again before emerging at an overlook atop the bluffs above Grassy Pond, centered in a prairie below in the middle of a very large depression in the sand pine scrub. At 1.7 miles, take a quarter mile round-trip side trip to visit this showy pond. Blue blazes descend to a level clearing perfect for camping. A path continues to the edge of the wet prairie, with the lily-dotted open water of the pond beyond a scrim of grasses. Return uphill to the junction and continue north along orange blazes through the sand pine scrub. Tall, skinny sand pines rise above a dense understory.

A series of ATV trail crossings marks a transition zone where scrub and sandhill habitats mingle. At 3 miles, cross NE 219 Terrace, a narrow sand road with a power line above it. Riverside Island begins, the footpath ascending from scrub into a forest of towering longleaf pines with an expansive open understory. After a half mile, drop into a mixed landscape of longleaf pine and wiregrass with scrub oaks in the understory. Young longleaf pines rise like giant green bottlebrushes from clearings dominated by wiregrass, interspersed between scattered tall pines. By 4.4 miles, enter a solid, showy stand of longleaf pine savanna, more magnificent in stature and understory the more the trail ascends over the next mile.

Loop around the upper rim of a sinkhole before starting a descent beneath the pines, clumps of saw palmetto and cabbage palms appearing in the forest as the trail draws close to Lake Delancy. Pass an ATV corral for ATV trail users at 5.8 miles. Continue around the edge of the recreation area through an oak hammock to reach FR 66, the graded east–west road leading to the entrance of Lake Delancy Recreation Area, 0.2 miles east. It's a fee area and the camp-

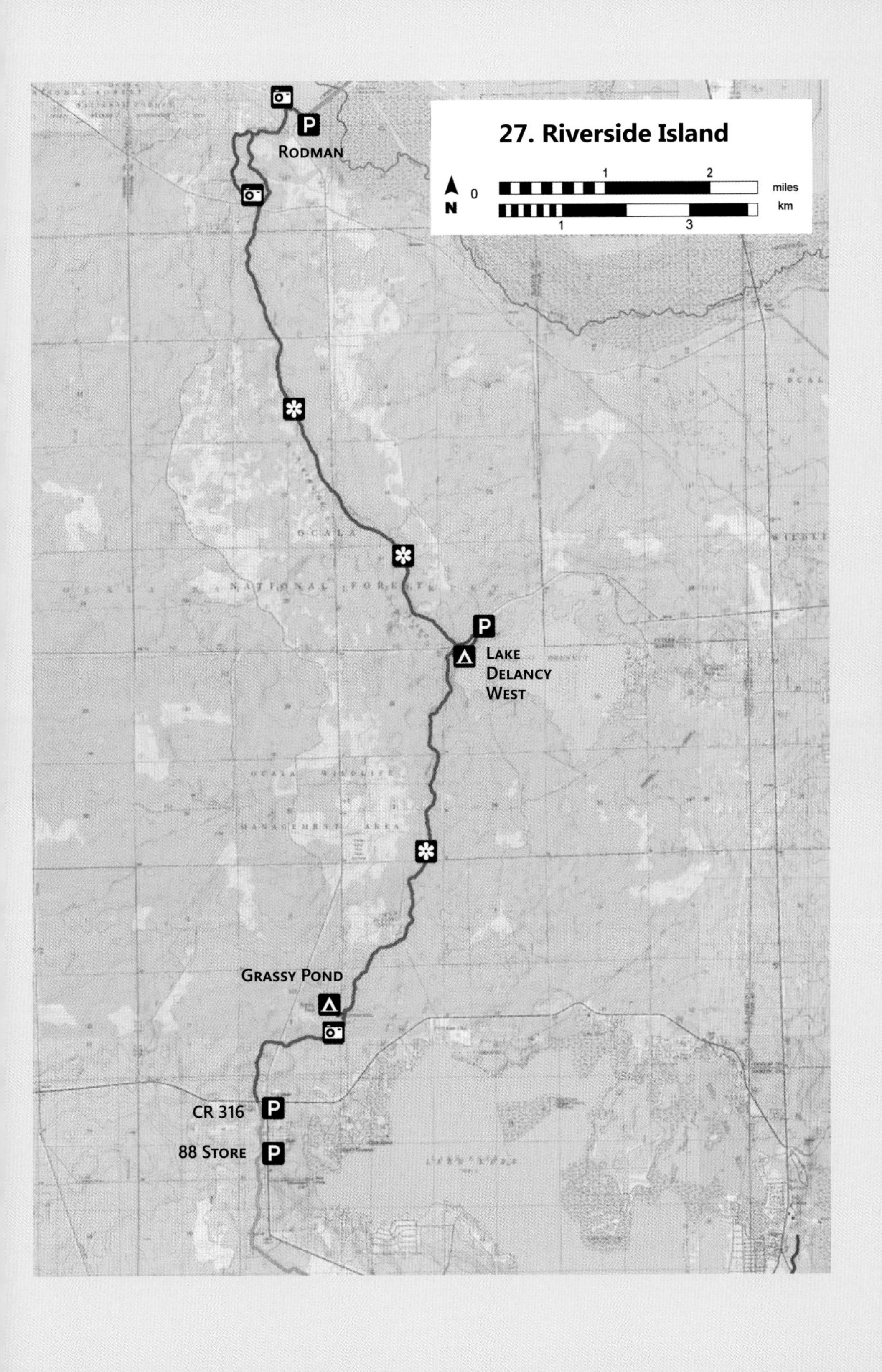
27. Riverside Island
0
1
2
miles
1
3
km
N
Rodman
Lake
Delancy
West
Grassy Pond
CR 316
88 Store
OCALA
OCALA NATIONAL FOREST
OCALA WILDLIFE
MANAGEMENT AREA

Rolling hills north of Lake Delancy

ground is seasonal. It has a picnic area and vault toilet. While it did have a pitcher pump—a crucial water source for backpackers headed north through these dry hills—it's been removed, and there is no easy way to reach the lake. It's best to carry all the water you need for an overnighter on this section.

Continue northbound from FR 66 into sandhill habitat, a forest of interspersed longleaf pines and skinny laurel oaks. Scattered copses of oaks made up of wavy-trunked sand live oaks provide tunnels of shade. Cross a Jeep trail at 7.2 miles. The forest opens up, its distant hilltops visible through the pines.

Beyond the next forest road, the grandeur of Riverside Island takes center stage, a longleaf pine forest spanning horizon to horizon. For the next mile, keep ascending and descending through this beautiful landscape, pausing to take in its colorful wildflowers. Paw-paw blossoms drape in spring. Pale pink roserush sways in a gentle breeze.

Dip through a natural bowl, a sinkhole edged by an oak hammock, before crossing graded FR 11 again at 8.3

miles. Another sinkhole is not far past the road. The immersive longleaf pine savanna continues, the high canopy of old-growth longleaf pines majestic. White-banded trees mark a colony of red-cockaded woodpeckers, the birds only boring their nests into longleaf pines a century or more old.

A shift of habitat occurs briefly at a forest road crossing. A small patch of oak scrub with large Florida rosemary and prickly pear cactus intrudes into the pine forest. The forest becomes dense with oaks before you cross FR 70 at 10 miles. Beyond it, the longleaf savanna resumes. It's not as open to the east, and more saw palmetto rise from the beds of wiregrass. Young longleaf pines and young turkey oaks compete for puddles of sunshine beneath the longleaf pine canopy.

As the understory becomes more crowded, the grand panoramas of Riverside Island end. Walk beneath a power line and emerge a few moments later at FR 74, the northernmost east–west forest road in this corner of the forest. A little to the west is the gravesite of early settler Arthur Pinner. Farther west, the riverfront community of Hog Valley begins.

Immediately north of FR 74 are the Penner Ponds, named for Pinner, whose homestead was along them. At 11.3 miles, follow the east edge of a prairie pond, your surroundings confirming a reimmersion in Big Scrub habitats. A loop trail once circled the ponds but has not been maintained. ATVs frequent this part of the forest. Cross a Jeep road and a sharply banked ATV trail in the scrub forest edging the ponds. At their north end, a trace of the old trail may be evident. Stay on the orange blazes for a half mile of immersion in the scrub, the trail a tunnel beneath the oaks and lyonia.

By 12.7 miles, the bright open expanse between the trees is the surface of the Rodman Reservoir, a controversial expanse of water also known as Lake Ocklawaha. Artificially formed by damming the Ocklawaha River and crushing its upstream forests during the 1960s revival of the Cross Florida Barge Canal, it is full of stumps and logs, which makes it a haven for anglers. But the depth of the water buries upstream springs and it is costly to maintain both Kirkpatrick Dam and Buckman Lock. Both also provide obstacles for aquatic life to migrate between the St. Johns River and upriver destinations off the Ocklawaha such as Silver Springs.

Follow the edge of the reservoir for your final footsteps of this hike, arriving at Rodman trailhead at 12.9 miles.

Trail adjoining Rice Creek

28. Rice Creek Loop

5.7 MILES | RICE CREEK CONSERVATION AREA, PALATKA

Deep in a swamp where settlers grew indigo and rice during the brief British rule of Florida, the Florida Trail slips between ancient trees towering over a vast floodplain.

Overview

As the headwaters of Rice Creek, this swamp remained relatively untouched after the eighteenth-century experiment of growing both rice and indigo, a native wildflower used for dyeing cloth. As in other parts of Florida, the virgin cypress fell to the logger's axe. But the lush hardwood forest was never cleared. It still contains trees that may have stood here during the plantation period. The levees built for attending to rice fields now serve as the footpath the Florida Trail follows. Despite many bridges and levees, you will get your feet wet and muddy. Know that up front. It's a small price to pay for immersion in one of the state's most stately swamp forests.

In the early days of the Florida Trail Association, Hudson Pulp & Paper Corporation executive Selmer Uhr convinced the company to preserve this grand swamp. Hudson dedicated Rice Creek Sanctuary in 1970 and closed it to hunting. FTA volunteers soon set to work building the loop trail. In 1976, the federal government bestowed a National Recreation Trail honor on the Rice Creek Loop, seven years before the Florida Trail attained National Scenic Trail status.

Trip Planning

No bicycles or equestrians are permitted. They may use paralleling forest roads and the equestrian trail, which is also very wet. Insect repellent is a must to keep away the perpetually persistent mosquitoes. Leashed dogs are allowed, but besides lots of tempting mud to roll in, there are alligators and venomous snakes, so beware. Water moccasins and pygmy rattlers are commonly seen. If the approach to the loop is flooded, turn back—or you might step off the levee into Rice Creek.

Land Manager

St. Johns River Water Mgt. District
4049 Reid St, Palatka 32177
386-329-4500
sjrwmd.com

Directions

From SR 19 in Palatka, follow SR 100 west for 4.2 miles. Passing the headquarters of St. Johns Water Management District, watch for the trailhead entrance on the left. Drive in the entrance road and park in the clearing on the right at the Rice Creek trailhead [29.682369, -81.736847].

Options

Extend this hike to Hoffman's Crossing, an extra 3.2-mile round trip from the south end of Rice Creek Loop for an 8.9-mile hike. A marvel of trail engineering, the narrow catwalk extends almost a half mile across the inky waters of the swamp. For a soggy 13.5-mile linear hike, follow the orange blazes from St. Johns North trailhead [29.546721, -81.728249] off SR 19 to Rice Creek trailhead. Backpackers can diverge from the orange blazes along the Oak Hammock Trail to Oak Hammock Camp, home to one of the Florida Trail's rare camping shelters, the "Rice Creek Hilton." It's a narrow two-story structure with a sleeping loft. Ample tent space surrounds it and a pitcher pump is provided.

Hike

Blue blazes beginning at the trailhead follow the entrance road into the preserve for a quarter mile before making a sharp right off the road due west into a longleaf pine restoration area. Head straight toward the distant treeline along Rice Creek. Meet the Florida Trail at a prominent trail junction after 0.7 miles. Sign the trail register and turn left. Saw palmetto provide a gateway to this section, standing at attention as if they were miniature cabbage palms. The forest is cool and damp, the corridor edged with saw palmetto. Crossing a grassy spot, you may find it damp and muddy. A bog boardwalk leads into denser forest, but expect more mud after it ends. Puddles appear in the footpath the closer you get to the swamp.

The forest is full of texture and light, from palm fronds at shoulder level to tree branches above cloaked with bromeliads. The footpath gets muddier. Trees of all types tower overhead, from red maples to cabbage palms to loblolly pines. It's easy to feel small.

Crossing a very long bog boardwalk over a flowing waterway in the swamp, enter a sparser forest where a bridge crosses a darkly stained creek. The next stretch of boardwalk is almost embedded in the mud. Gaining a little elevation as it joins a levee, the trail meets the north junction of the Rice Creek Loop at 1.6 miles at Bridge 1. Long ago, trail maintainers numbered these bridges to keep track of which ones needed repairs.

Cedar Swamp Trail starts at this junction. The signpost sports a hand-routed wooden map of the loop. Turn left. This levee along the floodplain's edge is more than 250 years old, the footpath a narrow leafy line weaving back and forth, the surroundings a mature forest. White blazes mark the route as it slips between sweetgum trees and dappled sunlight. While more at home in the Appalachians, deciduous tulip poplars grow tall in this forest.

Reach a trail junction at 1.9 miles. Cedar Swamp Trail turns right to go through the heart of the swamp for a quarter mile to meet the Florida Trail on the other side. Continue straight ahead to join the white-blazed Oak Hammock Trail in the uplands. Past a large live oak is a clearing sometimes used as a camping area for trail maintainers. It was the original trailhead for the Rice Creek Loop. At 2.1 miles, a short blue blaze leads to Oak Hammock Camp and its curious-looking shelter, tall and skinny and screened. Beyond it is a large clearing with space for tents, a pitcher pump, and benches facing the fire ring.

Leaving the campsite, continue along the white blazes. Oak Hammock Trail follows the eastern rim of the Rice Creek Swamp, marking the edge of William Panton's rice fields. A Scotsman and a principal in Panton, Leslie & Company, Panton made a fortune by opening up trading with Native American tribes throughout the South. During the British rule of Florida, Panton established this plantation in Florida's wilds soon after botanist William Bar-

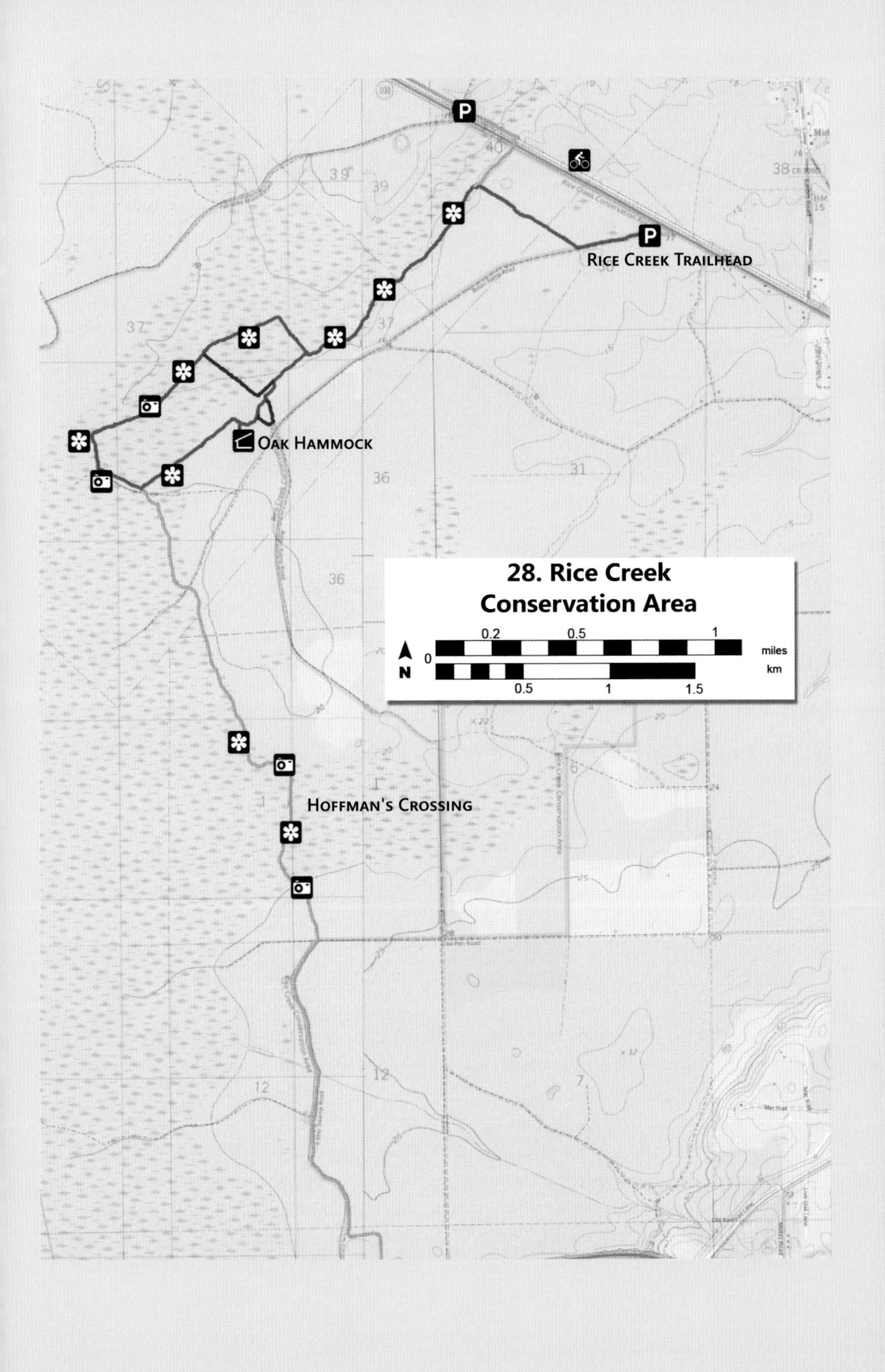

Rice Creek Trailhead
Oak Hammock
Hoffman's Crossing
28. Rice Creek
Conservation Area
0
0.2
0.5
1
miles
km
0.5
1
1.5
N

Oak Hammock Trail

tram documented the region's botanical riches. Nearly 125 acres were cleared and planted in rice after 1776. Then the British ceded Florida to Spain after the Revolutionary War. Panton abandoned this operation and left for Nassau. Hardwood swamp reclaimed the rice fields.

The only traces left are these levees the trails follow. Deeply shaded by tall oaks, Oak Hammock Trail crosses a low bridge before meeting the Florida Trail at the south junction of the Rice Creek Loop, marked by another hand-routed trail map.

If you have the time and energy to add an extra 3.2 miles of hiking to experience Hoffman's Crossing, make a left. Following Rice Creek briefly, the orange-blazed Florida Trail heading southbound emerges on a grassy road through a marsh. Be cautious of its swampy edges: we spotted a cottonmouth swimming in a soggy swale. Leaving the grassy road, the trail enters a swamp forest dense with tall trees. The footpath can get downright muddy. Reaching the catwalk into 9-Mile Swamp, take your time to walk Hoffman's Crossing. A nonslip surface and a railing help steady progress. A built-in bench provides a perch in the middle of the swamp. Return the way you came back to the south junction.

Take the orange blazes northbound from the south junction, which also has a routed wooden map, to continue the loop. The narrow berm feels like a natural landform. Trees grow from it and it skirts the spreading roots of swamp chestnut oaks and sweetgum. After several bridge crossings, the cypress swamp on the left is very prominent, with massive stumps of cypresses logged long ago emerging from its muck. At a tiny sign with a tree painted on it, turn left. This short boardwalk leads to an observation deck. Look into the swamp forest to pick out the giant towering above them all, a cypress that's the sixth largest documented in Florida. A "Record Setting Cypress" sign points toward it.

Return to the main trail and turn left. At 3 miles (6.2 if you did Hoffman's Crossing), make a sharp turn to stay on the levee. Cross Bridge 16 within sight of Rice Creek, which the hike parallels for the remainder of the loop. Tea-colored, the creek moves more swiftly than you'd expect in a swamp, eroding its channel between sandy banks. There is a succession of narrow bridges over gaps in the levee. One of the longest spans a floodplain where Rice Creek spills into Cedar Swamp. Walk past the base of a huge pine tree and views into the swamp open up on the right.

A double-trunked cypress breaks up the flow of the creek just before the trail approaches the charred base of a cypress trunk big enough to stand inside. After the next bridge, meet the other end of Cedar Swamp Trail at 3.5 miles. Its yellow blazes lead into a gauntlet of towering pines. Stay with the orange blazes and pass a bench.

In heavy shade, the waters of Rice Creek appear darker and swifter. The swamp beyond it stretches as far as you can see. Cross a series of bridges before reaching one that twists and winds around trees at a curve in the creek. Rice Creek picks up momentum, racing through cypress knees. At Bridge 5, a spring is sometimes visible near a confluence of creeks.

Large cypresses rise from the swamp west of the waterway at Bridge 3. The last two bridges lead into the uplands. Complete the loop by reaching the north junction at 4.1 miles, with Cedar Swamp Trail to the right. Walk past it and turn left, passing the sign stating the mileage to SR 100. Now you're on the return route.

Continue through the ancient forest, traversing the long boardwalks and bridges, to reach the trail junction with the trail register at 5 miles. Turn right and follow the blue blazes to the trailhead to wrap this 5.7-mile hike.

Oak Hammock campsite and shelter

Etoniah Ravine

29. Etoniah Creek

10.2 MILES | ETONIAH CREEK STATE FOREST, FLORAHOME

Walk along the edge of one of the deepest ravines in peninsular Florida on this well-shaded round-trip hike along Etoniah Creek and Falling Branch in Etoniah Creek State Forest.

Overview

As the Florida Trail connects public lands in Northeast Florida, it is broken into many small pieces connected by roadwalks and easements on private land. This particular section exists thanks to the kindness of a hunting club that has worked with the Florida Trail Association over the decades to provide access to Etoniah Ravine between two pieces of Etoniah Creek State Forest. A geologically significant landform for North Florida, the ravine is over 40 feet deep in places. For more than a mile, the trail stays close to the edge of the bluffs above it.

Built in the 1970s, this is one of the older pieces of the Florida Trail in this region, a well-defined footpath through mature forests. In addition to the ravine, Iron Bridge Shelter is a highlight, the roomiest camping shelter along the Florida Trail.

Trip Planning

Leashed dogs are permitted. Use insect repellent: this section of trail is mostly shaded. Pay the parking fee for Fieldhouse Rd trailhead online. It has flush toilets, potable water, and a picnic shelter with a grill. Restrooms are unlocked between 8 a.m. and 5 p.m. Less than 2 miles from the trailhead, Iron Bridge Shelter is a great place to camp. A large clearing and water source adjoin a large screened shelter. It tends to be busy on weekends during hiking season.

Check on hunting season dates for Etoniah Creek State Forest before hiking. Spring turkey and fall deer seasons are the most popular times for hunters. Since the trail passes through a private hunt camp past Iron Bridge, wear bright orange for this hike.

Land Manager

Etoniah Creek State Forest
390 Holloway Rd, Florahome 32140
386-329-2552
fdacs.gov

Directions

From SR 19 in Palatka, follow SR 100 for 12 miles west toward Keystone Heights. In Florahome, turn right onto Holloway Rd, crossing the paved Palatka-Lake Butler Trail. Continue 2.5 miles north on this graded road to a clearing where the Florida Trail crosses at Fieldhouse Rd. Turn right and drive Fieldhouse Rd past the trail sign and kiosk to Fieldhouse Rd trailhead [29.762154, -81.843422].

Options

As this is a round-trip hike, turn around when you like. Landmarks to shorten the hike include Iron Bridge Shelter for 4 miles and the bench above the ravine for 6.4 miles. A linear hike northbound through this section from Roberts Lane trailhead [29.705898, -81.780182] on the Palatka-Lake Butler Trail to Fieldhouse Rd trailhead is 9.2 miles. The Florida Trail leaves the paved bike path at Carraway to follow roads into private Rob-

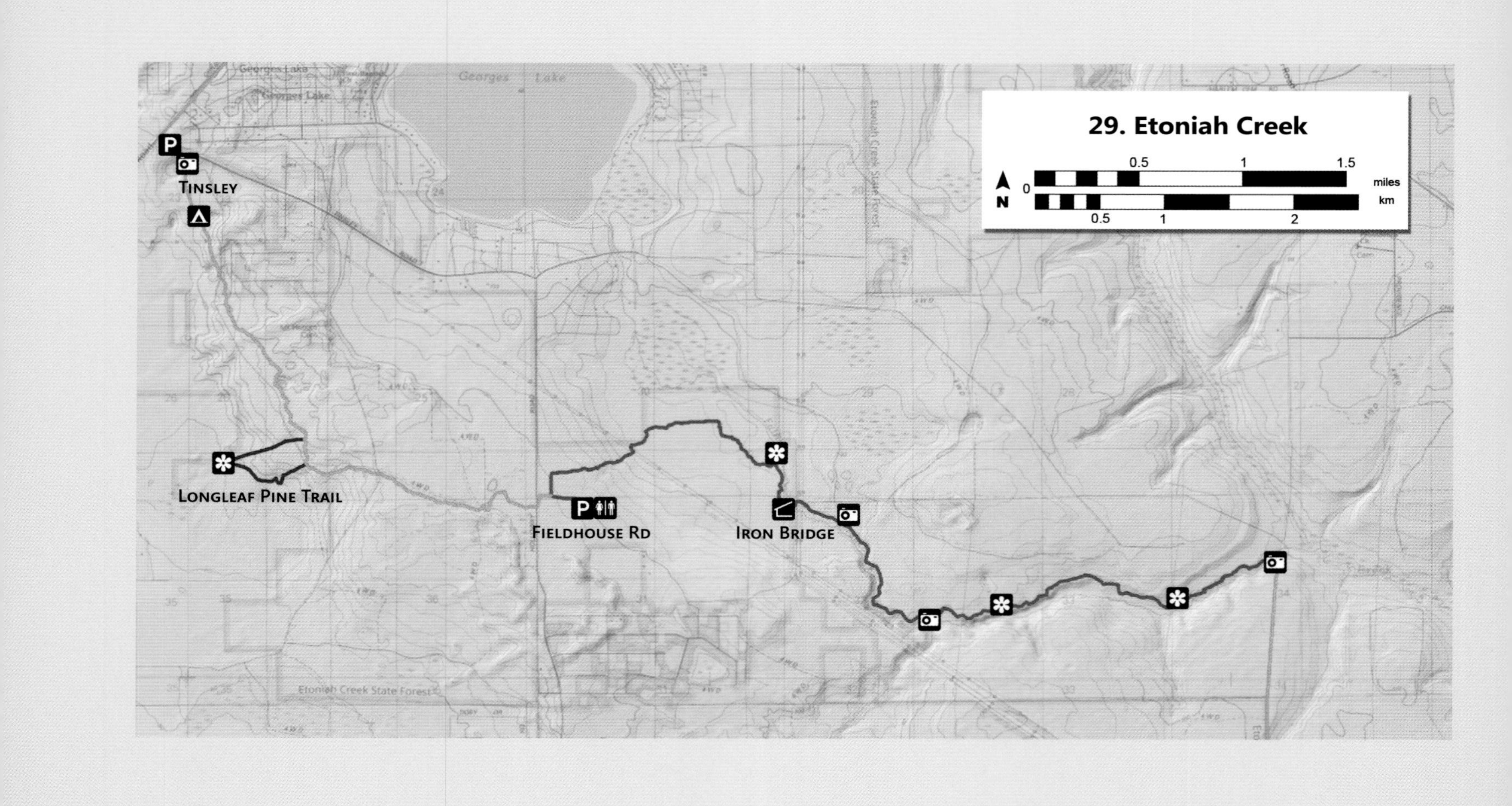
29. Etoniah Creek
0
0.5
1
1.5
miles
0.5
1
2
km
N
Tinsley
Longleaf Pine Trail
Fieldhouse Rd
Iron Bridge
Georges Lake
Etoniah Creek State Forest

Etoniah Creek at the turnaround point

ert's Hunt Club, reaching Etoniah Creek after 4 miles. No camping is permitted until you reach Iron Bridge.

A 3.4-mile segment of the Florida Trail north from Fieldhouse Rd to Tinsley Rd trailhead [29.78826, -81.876335] traverses sandhills and scrub with sinkholes. The Longleaf Pine Trail branches off 1.5 miles north. Use it to make a 4-mile round trip through a botanically significant stand of Etoniah rosemary. The Longleaf Pine Trail is a Florida State Forest Trailwalker Trail starting at Tinsley Rd trailhead, which can also be used as the start of a 10.2-mile round trip to Iron Bridge, or a 16.4-mile overnighter to the end of this section.

Hike

Backtrack along Fieldhouse Rd a quarter mile from the trailhead to where the Florida Trail enters the woods on the right and sign the trail register. A grassy corridor along a power line ushers you into the forest past an old mileage sign. A constellation of atamasco lilies rise from a damp spot each March. Turning away from the power line, continue under the shade of oaks and pines. Cross a power line easement at 0.8 miles and enter a damper habitat where cinnamon ferns rise in clusters from the dark earth.

Southern magnolia and hickory tower as your surroundings transition to bluff forest. Approach a winding waterway, crossing it on a small plank bridge. Fungi and ferns swarm across fallen logs in this fertile habitat. Overlook Falling Branch from a bluff at 1.6 miles at the sign "Saima's Point." A pioneer trailblazer known in Palatka as "Mother

Upper ravine

Nature," Saima Takken maintained this section of the Florida Trail in her twilight years.

Paralleling Falling Branch downstream, there are occasional glimpses into the deeply eroded ravine. A quarter mile past Saima's Point is the sign-posted side trail to Iron Bridge Shelter. Designed by FTA past president Dick Schuler (also responsible for the "Rice Creek Hilton"), it has two tiers of sleeping platforms on the inside. A porch, picnic bench, fire ring, and plenty of tenting space round out this popular overnight destination.

Immediately north of the shelter, cross Falling Branch on a bridge where two creeks merge within view. The former Iron Bridge crossing was a metal I-beam over the creek. Step into a broad easement where high-tension power lines slice through the landscape, marking the boundary between the state forest and a private hunt camp along Etoniah Ravine. Don't leave the trail or random camp on their private property. Hunters are permitted to drive ATVs along this portion of the trail. Enter a mature hardwood forest beyond the power lines and cross a small waterway on a bridge. The landscape drops sharply on the right.

A large pignut hickory shades a curve in Etoniah Creek at the first clear view of it at 2.3 miles. The trail slowly ascends as the ravine gets deeper below. There are several overlooks over the next mile, with a bench perched at one of the deepest drop-offs at 3.2 miles. The trail is in a narrow strip of mature forest surrounding the ravine from its bluffs to the bottom.

After passing a side road leading uphill, enter a sand pine scrub. Clumps of deer moss adjoin the footpath on sandy spots where reindeer lichen and sand-spike moss thrive, their backdrop short, gnarled rusty lyonia. Ascend a corridor of saw palmetto before crossing a long plank bridge. A tight corridor under the oaks and pines leads to additional bridges. While often dry underneath, the bridges are critical to prevent erosion along this slope.

Emerging into a clearing, walk under an odd-shaped radio tower at 4.2 miles. To its right, a road curves toward the hunt camp. Follow the forest road briefly, watching for the blazes to turn left onto a footpath. A narrow bridge perches over a small ravine. Ascending into an oak hammock, emerge into a sun-splashed sandhill. Showy sky-blue lupine blooms in spring, while Florida azaleas with soft-pink blooms dot the understory near the creek.

Return to the shade at a sharp left. A forest boundary sign marks a transition to public land. Rising into sandhills briefly before entering a bluff forest, draw close to the creek and cross a series of plank bridges. Past a towering pine, a sharp turn in the trail reveals the creek at the base of a small bluff. It remains visible briefly before clumps of saw palmetto obscure the view. Circle another massive pine and reach a wooden bridge over Etoniah Creek at 5.1 miles. It overlooks a showy series of curves in this tannic stream.

This is your turnaround point. The forest boundary ends at the clearing ahead. Return by the same route, pausing for views at the overlooks. By 7.1 miles, reach the bench above the ravine, and at 8.3 miles, cross Iron Bridge. Continue past Saima's Point. Wrap up this 10.2-mile hike at Fieldhouse Rd trailhead.

Devils Washbasin

30. Gold Head Branch and Camp Blanding

10.8 MILES | KEYSTONE HEIGHTS

Spotlighting the sandhills surrounding the many lakes of Keystone Heights, this hike from the middle of Gold Head Branch State Park through Camp Blanding sticks to dry, hilly terrain.

Overview

Designed to hit high points of scenic beauty, the central portion of the Florida Trail through Mike Roess Gold Head Branch State Park dates to the late 1960s. What was the trail's first camping shelter was replaced with a backcountry campsite away from the busy recreation areas and campgrounds of this popular park. It's one of Florida's oldest state parks—with pavilions, trails, and cabins established by the Civilian Conservation Corps in 1935—and centers on two natural features. A steep flight of stairs guides visitors into Gold Head, a steephead ravine where springs bubble up in a gully of ferns. Tiny streams merge to form Gold Head Branch, the waterway carving a deep ravine as it flowed toward a low spot in the sandhills, Little Lake Johnson. Cabins built by CCC Company 2444 perch above the lake and its natural shorelines.

Adjoining the state park, Camp Blanding served as an infantry training ground during World War II for more than 750,000 soldiers. Its 73,000 acres of forest are now held by the Florida National Guard for training exercises. The Florida Trail used to cross Camp Blanding to Crystal Lake but the route was blocked in a landowner dispute. The trail instead makes a sweeping curve through the southeast corner of the base, connecting scenic spots along major lakes. This change of route makes both linear and loop hikes possible from the state park.

Trip Planning

The Florida Trail is not open to cyclists or equestrians through this section. Leashed dogs permitted. Ticks are common in the sandhills; use insect repellent. There is a state park entrance fee for day-use and separate camping fees. There is no fee to walk through Camp Blanding, but you must sign in and out at their trailhead kiosks. If the prominent sign at either kiosk says the trail is closed, don't enter. The base closes the trail occasionally for military exercises and prescribed burns. Call Range Control at 904-682-3125 if you see munitions—including mortar shell casings, bombs, or grenades—along the trail.

Gold Head Branch State Park is along the Keystone Bike Path that starts in Keystone Heights not far north of the Palatka-Lake Butler Trail. With three campgrounds, modern cabins, and its well-maintained historic cabins, it makes a great base camp for outdoor activities. Reserve online. Active and retired military can also camp at Kingsley Lake in Camp Blanding. Call ahead.

Land Managers

Mike Roess Gold Head Branch State Park
6239 SR 21, Keystone Heights 32656
352-262-8129
floridastateparks.org

Camp Blanding
5629 SR 16 W, Starke 32091
904-682-3104
fl.ng.mil

Directions

From the junction of SR 21 and SR 100 in Keystone Heights, cross the Palatka-Lake Butler Trail and drive SR 21 north 4 miles to Treat Rd. To leave a vehicle for a linear hike, turn left. The end of this hike is on the right at the Camp Blanding kiosk [29.81337, -82.005562]. Space is limited.

Drive another 2 miles north to the state park entrance and pay your fee at the entrance station. To leave a vehicle for a loop hike through Camp Blanding, park at the trailhead [29.84742, -81.961472] on the left inside the entrance. For the start of the linear route, continue along the park road past Gold Head ravine and Sheelar Lake. Passing a campground entrance, park in the main parking area [29.826433, -81.952576] near the Recreation Hall, which has restrooms.

Options

This hike is described between two trailheads. If you're on your own, loop back from the Camp Blanding kiosk at Treat Rd using the Keystone Bike Path to the Florida Trail crossing along SR 21 and retrace your route along it inside the state park to your vehicle for a 17.7-mile round trip. To trim this, focus on a loop through Camp Blanding with only a little taste of Gold Head. Park at the trailhead inside the state park gate, follow the orange blazes through the sandhills across SR 21 into Camp Blanding, and return along the Keystone Bike Path to the park entrance for a 9.5-mile loop. Or rejoin the Florida Trail to the park entrance for a 10.1-mile loop.

Shorter hikes focus on round trips and loops inside the state park. One of the prettiest is a walk from the Recreation Hall north on the Florida Trail into the ravine on the Ravine Trail, returning downstream via the Loblolly Trail, a 4-mile hike with steep inclines. A round trip to Devils Washbasin is 4.2 miles. A 3-mile round trip to the back gate of Gold Head Branch along the orange blazes follows the shoreline of Little Lake Johnson before a ramble through the sandhills. The quarter-mile round trip nature trail to Sheelar Lake off the park road is pretty too.

Hike

Start at the Recreation Hall and descend toward Little Lake Johnson on a sidewalk that undulates over the hilly ground like a snake. Orange blazes cross just past a pair of signs. Turn left, following them from tree to tree below the old picnic grounds, enjoying lake views. After a quarter mile the trail joins a forest road and the Loblolly Trail, a loop along the lower portion of the ravine, soon branches to the left. The lake remains visible through the pine flatwoods. Puddles sometimes swamp this road after a rain.

Reach the crystalline waters of Gold Head Branch at a half mile, crossing on an old wooden road bridge next to a bench along the creek. Nearby pine

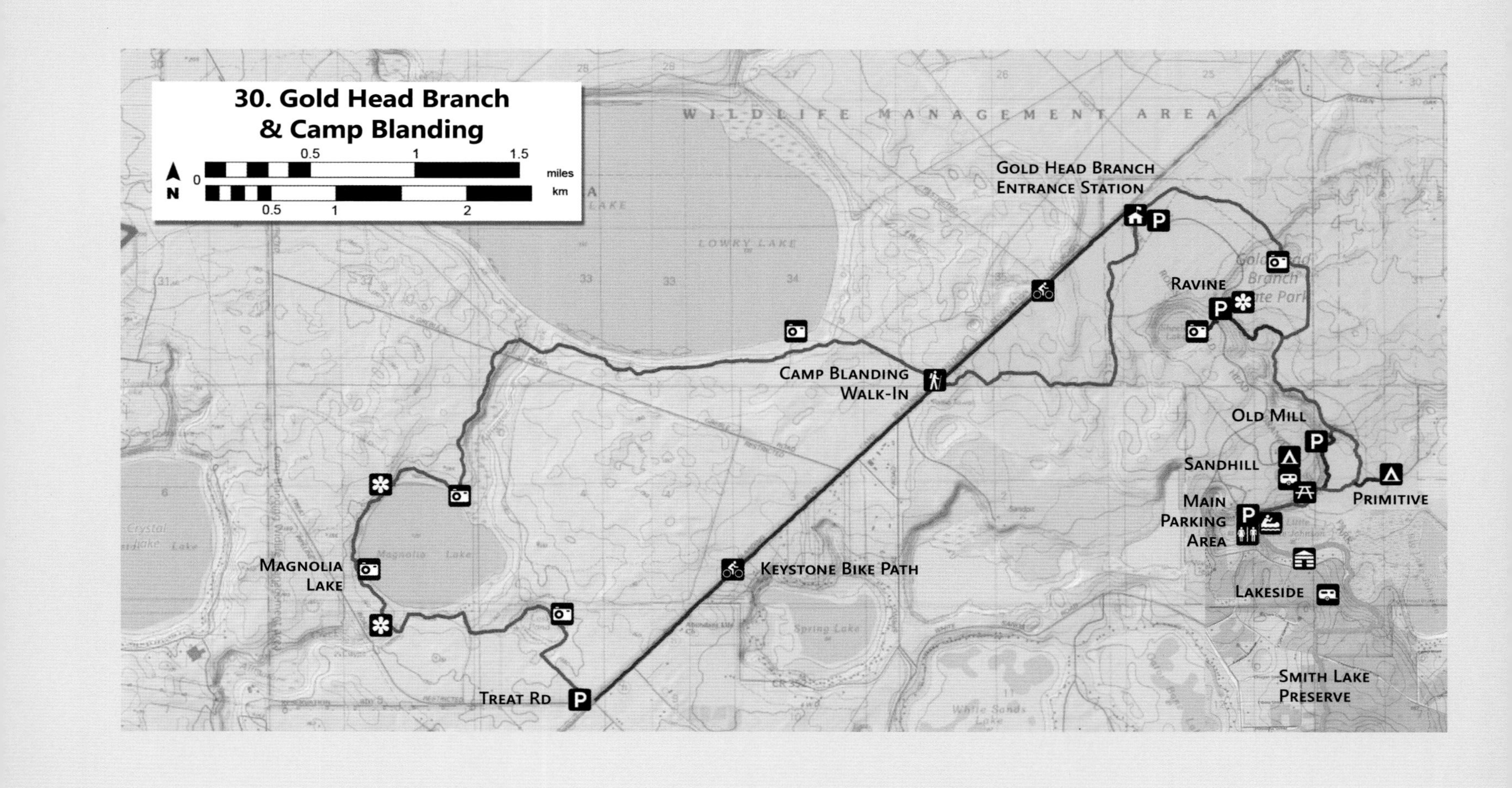
30. Gold Head Branch
& Camp Blanding
0
0.5
1
1.5
miles
N
0.5
1
2
km
WILDLIFE MANAGEMENT AREA
Lowry Lake
Gold Head Branch
Entrance Station
Ravine
Camp Blanding
Walk-In
Old Mill
Sandhill
Primitive
Main
Parking
Area
Lakeside
Magnolia
Lake
Keystone Bike Path
Treat Rd
Smith Lake
Preserve
Spring Lake
Crystal Lake

Tunnel of oaks, Camp Blanding

trees show deep catface gashes from being tapped for turpentine a century ago. Where the trail curves left, a blue blaze continues straight. The side trail leads a quarter mile to the primitive camping area, which has nice flat spots and a covered picnic shelter.

Becoming a narrow footpath shared with the Loblolly Trail, the Florida Trail meanders through scrubby flatwoods, following Gold Head Branch upstream. A curve reveals the creek behind the saw palmetto. Ascend into hardwoods with a higher forest canopy. The second junction with the Loblolly Trail crosses a bridge over the branch at 0.9 miles, with a side trail leading to a small parking area at an old mill site.

Signposted as the Ridge Trail at this junction, the Florida Trail does not cross the bridge. It ascends beneath sand live oaks in the sandhills above the ravine. Interpretive signs remind you this is part of the park's nature trail system. As the ravine widens, Gold Head Branch is deep at the bottom, the trail climbing to curve into a stand of pines and past a bench. At 1.5 miles, meet the junction with the Ravine Trail. Keep right to follow the orange blazes uphill.

Entering a healthy forest of longleaf pine and wiregrass, the footpath flattens out. Beyond a forest road used as a firebreak, immerse in the beauty of a pine savanna. Passing through an oak hammock, arrive at an overlook above showy Devils Washbasin at 2.1 miles, a giant sinkhole with water at the bottom. Curve along its near shore, pausing at a bench strategically placed to enjoy the view. Leaving the basin, ascend into a scrub forest that yields to more longleaf pine savanna broken up by groupings of sand live oaks, a pleasant walk through dappled shade. Expect to cross firebreaks. To keep this forest healthy, the park burns sections of it every year.

Beyond an interpretive sign about a historic tramway crossing this forest, the trail curves left and parallels SR 21, with traffic noise increasing as you reach the entrance station at 3 miles. Cross the park road and aim for the FT sign to pick up the blazes. While not as mature as the last mile of forest, this is a fine stretch of sandhills with turkey oaks dominating the understory and clusters of lupine in springtime. Two benches flank a forest road crossing. Dark green and rounded, Florida rosemary stand out on small sandy balds. Round the park's property boundary with a sand pit near a gate. Turning due west, pass a bench before descending a slope of pine savanna. Walk through a swale and emerge at its crest at the Keystone Bike Path and SR 21. Carefully cross the highway to Camp Blanding.

After 4.9 miles, sign in at the kiosk to start across Camp Blanding. A warning sign reminds you not to pick up munitions along the trail. Follow the graded

Sherman's fox squirrel

entrance road briefly before a narrow footpath leads into a sand pine scrub. On the other side of a road intersection with deep soft sand, the path narrows again. Scrub forest crowds closely on the ascent to a sand ridge, where a break in the vegetation provides a peek of Lowry Lake. Scrub yields to stands of sand live oaks, the forest floor decorated in lichens and mosses. A sand road at 5.6 miles provides access to the lake's marshy shoreline for an up-close view.

Past that turnoff, tall pines create a high canopy along the scrubby sand ridge. Reaching a welcoming corridor shaded by moss-draped sand live oaks, the footpath broadens and leads to a small bridge and monitoring station over Alligator Creek, which flows from Lowry Lake to Magnolia Lake. Ascend under a canopy of oaks and cross graded Greble Rd at 7.2 miles before the blazes follow Perry Rd. The range road ends and the footpath resumes, burrowing beneath curtains of Spanish moss in an oak hammock along the lakeshore. As the trail rounds the lake, it stays in the shade.

A bluff slopes to Magnolia Lake at 8.3 miles, proving a view of buildings on the far shore. For the next 1.7 miles, circle the lake through the oak hammocks toward that shore, crossing a boat ramp at the water's edge and another bridge over Alligator Creek at 9.2 miles. Streaks of aquatic grasses paint watercolor shimmers across the bottom of this clear waterway, broad and deep as it flows out of Magnolia Lake. A forested corridor leads to a sharp turn onto a long straightaway under moss-draped oaks. It emerges in what remains of Magnolia Lake State Park.

Opened in 1957, Magnolia Lake State Park was a segregated counterpart to Gold Head Branch State Park, one of four Florida State Parks built specifically for Blacks. When Florida integrated its state parks in 1964, Magnolia Lake became a swimming hole for the Keystone Heights community. It was turned over to Camp Blanding in the late 1970s. At 9.7 miles, a pavilion with a picnic table provides a rest break overlooking the lake. The expanse in front of you became part of the set of the 1997 movie *G.I. Jane*.

Following a fence, the trail exits the former state park complex. After a short stretch of sandhill habitat, a sweep of water glimmers to the right: Lost Pond. Circle the pond beneath the pines along its shoreline. Reach a bench overlooking a marshy peninsula at 10.2 miles. Past a collapsed spot in the limestone bluff above the pond, climb into the sandhills and join a forest road. Making a gentle ascent through longleaf pines and turkey oaks, this path narrows as it reaches the kiosk marking the end of the hike. Sign out and walk through the gap in the fence to complete a 10.8-mile linear hike.

31. Nice Wander Trail

1.6 MILES | OSCEOLA NATIONAL FOREST

An easy-to-reach hike off US 90 in the Osceola National Forest, this short loop adjacent to Olustee Battlefield State Park offers interesting botany and birding.

Overview

Developed as an easy loop along a portion of the Florida Trail that dates to the 1960s, the Nice Wander Trail joins the orange blazes north of the prominent Olustee trailhead and returns on a white-blazed route along a paralleling forest road. This immersion in a longleaf pine forest visits the heart of a habitat where endangered wildlife thrives, including indigo snakes, fox squirrels, and a nesting colony of red-cockaded woodpeckers.

Trip Planning

Open daily sunrise to sunset. Leashed dogs are permitted. No bicycles or horses are allowed. During hunting seasons, all recreational users must wear bright orange. Research hunt dates in advance. Access is more difficult but interesting during special events held at Olustee Battlefield, especially the annual reenactment each February. A parking fee is charged during events. There is a restroom at the state park visitor center and a picnic area immediately north of the trailhead.

Land Manager

US Forest Service, National Forests in Florida
Osceola Ranger District
24874 US 90, Olustee
386-752-2577
fs.usda.gov/florida

Directions

From Jacksonville, follow Interstate 10 west to the Sanderson exit for US 90. Continue west along US 90 toward Lake City. Seven miles later, there is a prominent sign at the entrance to Olustee Battlefield. Turn in, cross the railroad track, and make a left into the Olustee trailhead.

Options

Extend this hike by continuing north from the north end of the Nice Wander Trail loop to Cobb Hunt Camp, a 6.8-mile round trip. Or leave a vehicle at Cobb [30.246658, -82.409729] or Ocean Pond Recreation Area [30.239901, -82.43615] for linear hikes of 3.3 or 5.7 miles northbound through Osceola National Forest. Home to a popular lakefront campground, Ocean Pond also has a swimming beach and picnic area. Both trailheads are off paved CR 250-A.

Adjoining the Olustee trailhead, Olustee Battlefield Historic State Park has a 1.1-mile loop interpreting the clash between Union and Confederate troops during the Battle of Olustee, Florida's largest Civil War battle.

Hike

Cross a short bridge to the trailhead kiosk. Follow blue blazes past the fire tower and picnic grounds and along the edge of a historic cemetery next to

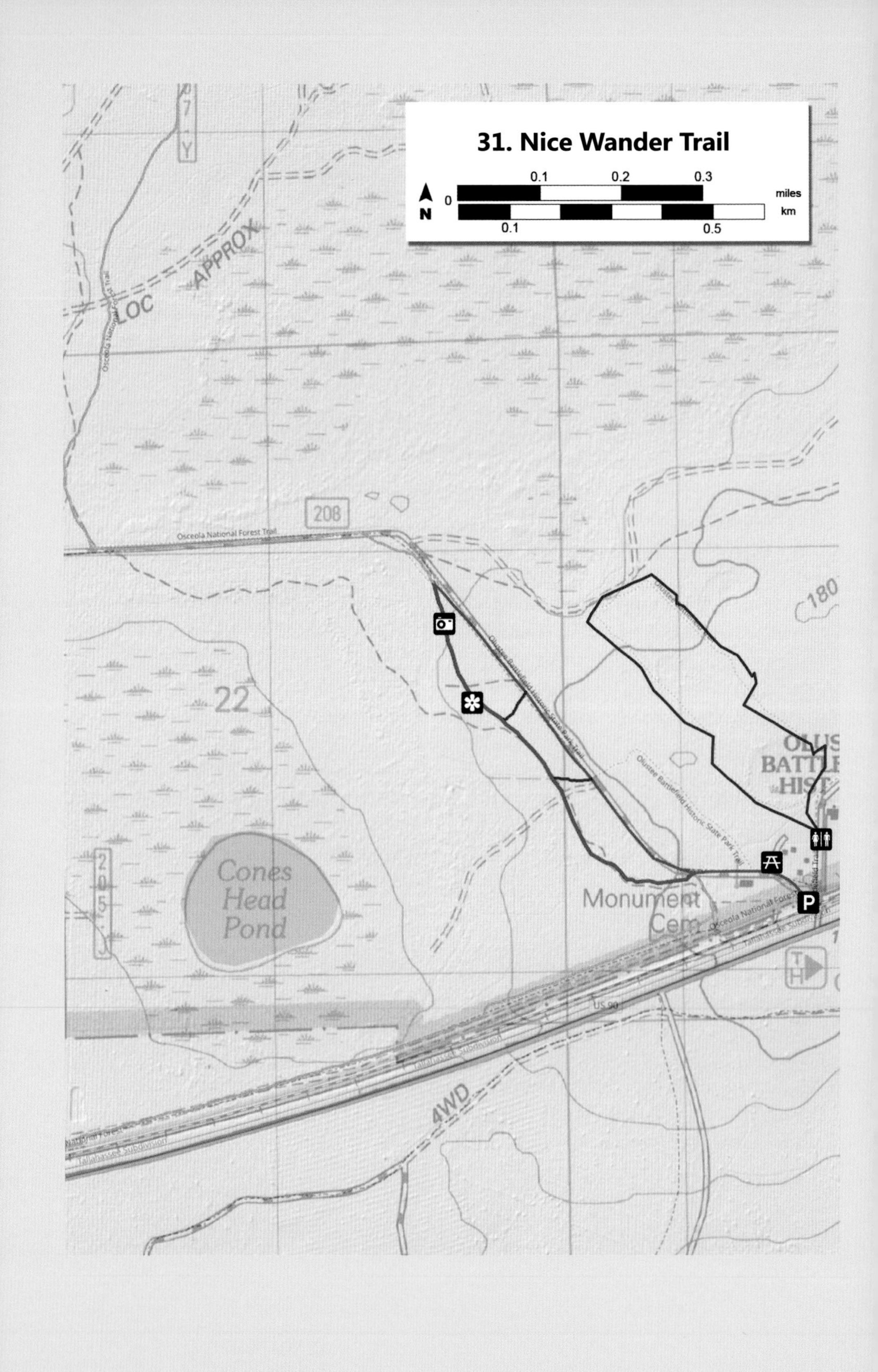

31. Nice Wander Trail
0
0.1
0.2
0.3
miles
0.1
0.5
km
N
LOC APPROX
Osceola National Forest Trail
208
22
Olustee Battlefield Historic State Park Trail
Cones Head Pond
Monument Cem
205
US 90
Tallahassee Subdivision
4WD
180

Nice Wander Trail

the railroad. Control of that rail line brought the two armies together at this spot in 1864. Blue blazes meet orange where the Florida Trail makes an arc past the cemetery and boomerangs northwest.

Join the orange and white blazes along the footpath into the longleaf pine forest, its understory very open with only scattered patches of saw palmetto. Listen for the tap of woodpeckers in the pines. The trail reaches an intersection with a two-track road and the "Loop A" sign pointing to the return route to the left. Only take that if you're looking for the shortest possible loop of 0.8 miles. Otherwise continue straight along the orange and white blazes.

Watch for white-banded pines. These are where the red-cockaded woodpeckers live, and you're most likely to see them active at dawn. This endangered species only nests in old-growth longleaf, and many of these banded trees are more than a century old. After a half mile, look up into the trees to see the sap dripping down the sides of the pines from the nest hole, looking much like candle wax. Red-cockaded woodpeckers do this to protect the entrance to their nests from predators such as rat snakes.

Continue straight where Loop B turns off to the right. A break in the trees to the left reveals a seasonal marsh. In this part of the pine forest, low damp spots host clusters of carnivorous plants, including the very elegant hooded pitcher plant.

Prescribed burn on the Nice Wander Trail

Hooded pitcher plants

Ascend a gently sloping boardwalk through a wet area. It has two benches on a broad platform, a nice place for a break. Past the platform, squeeze through a corridor of saw palmetto to emerge onto FR 208, a broad graded forest road. Orange and white blazes part ways at 0.9 miles.

To the left, the orange blazes of the Florida Trail lead northbound toward Cobb Hunt Camp and Ocean Pond Recreation Area. Turn right to follow the white blazes of the Nice Wander Trail along FR 208. The return walk along the forest road is straightforward along the edge of the longleaf pine forest and mostly in the sun.

Pass the Loop B crossover at 1.1 miles and the Loop A crossover at 1.3 miles. Walking by a set of cattle pens, continue through the gate and follow the forest road toward the picnic area at the tower. Watch for the bridge to the trailhead, finishing the hike after 1.6 miles.

Aucilla River rapids

Suwannee Big Bend

In a rural region where Florida's peninsula and panhandle meet, experience rugged and scenic terrain along the Suwannee and Aucilla Rivers and the Big Bend coastline.

BASE CAMPS

White Springs

A destination resort for spa-goers in the 1890s, White Springs is a charming historic village along a bend in the Suwannee River.

STAY

Kelly's RV Park 386-397-2616, 142 NW Kelly Ln.

White Springs B&B 386-397-4252, 16630 Spring St.

Stephen Foster Folk Culture Center State Park 800-326-3521, 11016 Lillian Saunders Dr.

EAT

Fat Belly's 386-397-2040, 16750 Spring St.

SEE AND DO

American Canoe Adventures 386-397-1309, 10610 Bridge St.

Big Shoals State Park 386-397-4331, 11330 SE SR 135.

Stephen Foster Folk Culture Center State Park 386-397-4331, 11016 Lillian Saunders Dr.

Suwannee Springs and Live Oak

A few minutes north of services at Interstate 10 in Live Oak, Suwannee Springs is the site of another late 1800s spa with a large camping and festival complex just across the highway.

STAY

Holiday Inn Express 386-362-2600, 6694 US 129 N.

Spirit of the Suwannee Music Park 386-364-1683, 3076 95th Dr.

EAT

Big Wood BBQ & Grill 386-362-7427, 314 72nd Trace.

Brown Lantern 386-362-1133, 417 E Howard St.

Dixie Grill & Steer Room 386-364-2810, 101 Dowling Ave SE.

SEE AND DO

Canoe Outpost Suwannee River 386-364-4991, 2461 95th Dr.

Suwannee County Historical Museum 386-362-1776, 208 Ohio Ave N.

Suwannee River State Park 386-362-2746, 3631 201st Path.

Suwannee Springs Recreation Area 386-362-1001, 3243 91st Dr.

Madison

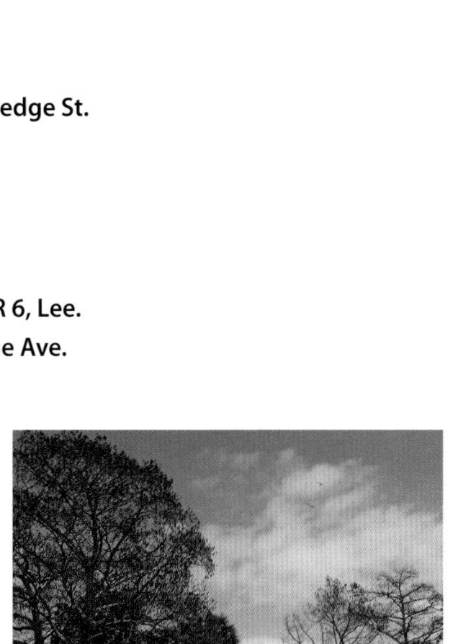

The county seat of rural Madison County, Madison has an architecturally impressive downtown historic district. Services are split between Interstate 10 and downtown, 6 miles north.

STAY

Best Western Plus Madison Inn 850-973-2020, 167 SE Bandit St.

Ragan's Family Campground 850-973-8269, 1051 Old St. Augustine Rd.

Unity House Bed and Breakfast 850-973-4556, 307 SW Dade St.

EAT

Rancho Grande 850-973-2363, 307 SW Pinckney St.

Cucinella's Brick Oven Pizzeria 850-973-3388, 201 SW Rutledge St.

Oneal's Country Buffet 850-973-6400, 558 W Base St.

Sunrise Coffee Shop 850-973-1381, 247 SW Rutledge St.

SEE AND DO

Historic downtown and residential Historic District.

Madison Blue Spring State Park 850-971-5003, 8300 NE SR 6, Lee.

Treasures of Madison County 850-973-3661, 200 SW Range Ave.

St. Marks

At the confluence of the St. Marks and Wakulla Rivers, St. Marks is one of Florida's oldest settlements, the site of a Spanish stockade in 1679. Bo-Lynn Grocery is on the National Register of Historic Places. Hikers must cross the St. Marks River by boat.

STAY

Newport Park 850-925-4530, 8046 Coastal Hwy, Crawfordville.

Shell Island Fish Camp 850-925-6226, 440 Shell Island Rd.

Sweet Magnolia Inn 850-755-3320, 803 Port Leon Dr.

EAT

Cooter Stew Cafe 850-925-9908, 859 Port Leon Dr.

Outz Too 850-925-6448, 7968 Coastal Hwy.

Riverside Cafe 850-925-5668, 69 Riverside Dr.

The Shack 850-810-5001, 23 Old Palmetto Path.

SEE AND DO

St. Marks Outfitters 850-510-7919, 721 Port Leon Dr.

San Marcos de Apalache Historic State Park 850-925-6216, 148 Old Fort Rd.

St. Marks National Wildlife Refuge 850-925-6121, 1255 Lighthouse Dr.

TnT Hideaway Outfitters 850-925-6412, 6527 Coastal Hwy.

Medart and Panacea

Along US 98 near the Florida Trail at the west end of St. Marks National Wildlife Refuge, these two small towns provide services south of the county seat at Crawfordville.

STAY

Best Western Wakulla Inn 850-926-3737, 3292 Coastal Hwy.

The Lodge at Wakulla Springs 850-421-2000, 550 Wakulla Park Dr.

Magnuson Hotel Wildwood Inn 850-926-4455, 3896 Coastal Hwy.

The Panacea Motel 850-745-4071, 1545 Coastal Hwy.

EAT

Hamaknockers BBQ 850-926-4737, 2837 Coastal Hwy.

Poseys Up the Creek Steam Room 850-984-5243, 1506 Coastal Hwy.

The Seinyard Rock Landing 850-713-0020, 99 Rock Landing Rd.

SEE AND DO

Gulf Specimen Aquarium 850-984-5297, 222 Clark Dr.

Wakulla Springs State Park 850-561-7276, 465 Wakulla Park Dr.

Wakulla Welcome Center 850-984-3966, 1493 Coastal Hwy.

St. Marks River crossing

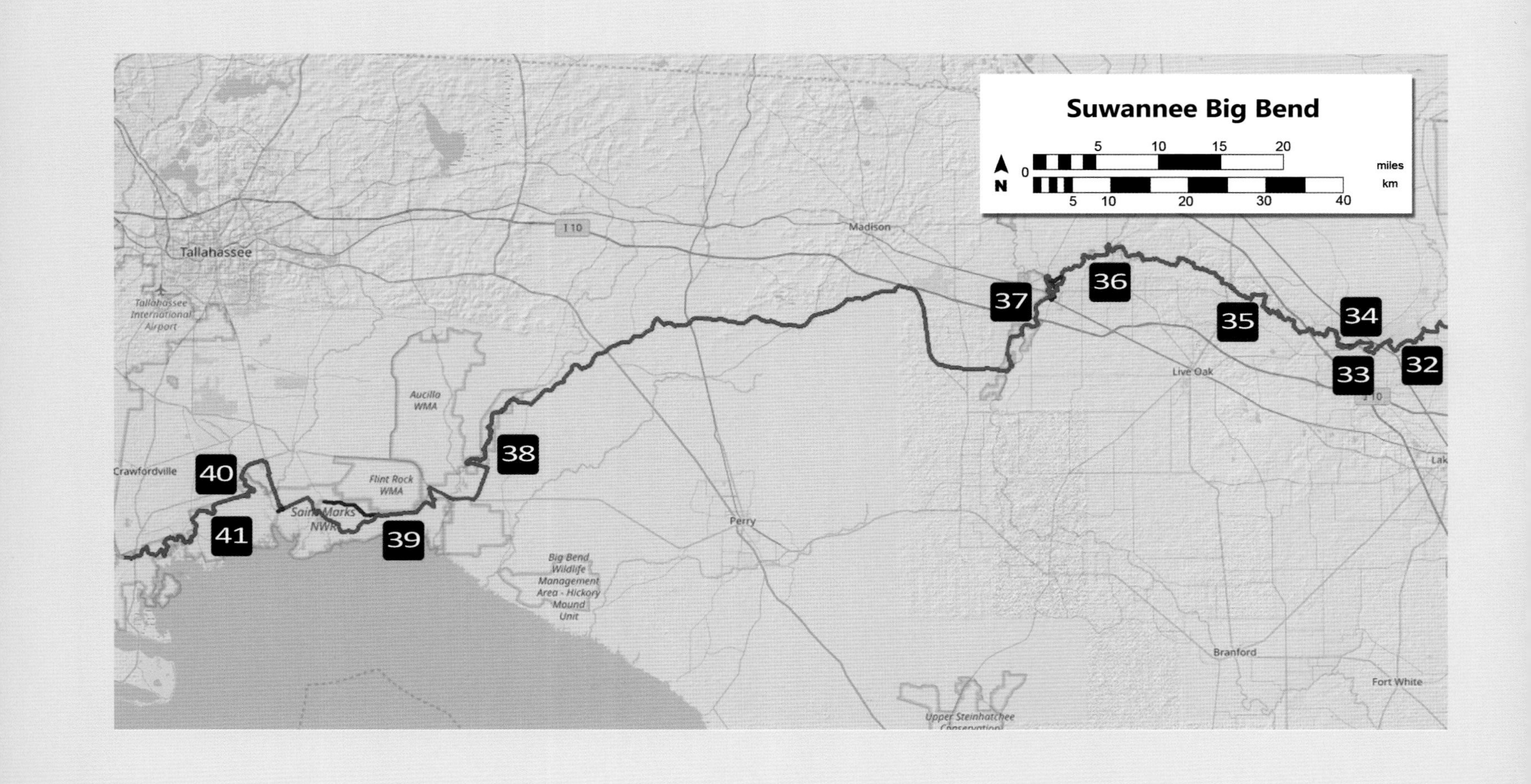
Suwannee Big Bend
N
0
5
10
15
20
miles
5
10
20
30
40
km
32
33
34
35
36
37
38
39
40
41
Tallahassee
Tallahassee International Airport
I 10
Madison
Live Oak
Perry
Crawfordville
Aucilla WMA
Flint Rock WMA
Saint Marks NWR
Big Bend Wildlife Management Area - Hickory Mound Unit
Branford
Fort White

Little Shoals of the Suwannee River

Suwannee

77.6 MILES | SUWANNEE RIVER

With a perfect combination of outstanding scenery and rugged terrain, the Suwannee section is a well-loved and well-worn hiking destination. Miles of sidehill with scenic river views and significant scrambles through ravines make for satisfying physically challenging hikes.

Overview

Along the Suwannee River, the Florida Trail clings to bluffs and plunges through chasms carved by the river and its tributaries. A portion of this route was built in 1966 but continues to be relocated a little farther from the river's edge as the Suwannee scours into its bluffs. Geological wonders abound, from Class III whitewater at Big Shoals to rapids, waterfalls, deep sinkholes, a whirlpool, and hundreds of springs. Side trails lead to natural wonders, including Florida's largest cypress trees. There are many designated campsites along the route, but when water levels are low the white sand beaches tempt as well. Shuttle services for paddlers on the Suwannee River Wilderness Trail make logistics easier for backpacking and linear day hikes.

In 2023, Hurricane Idalia devastated communities along this section of the Florida Trail. Call ahead before relying on a particular business to be open. Volunteer maintenance crews have reopened the trail, but expect a changed landscape. Many trees were toppled between White Springs and the Aucilla River.

Trailheads

The Florida Trail runs east to west along the south shore to the US 41 bridge at White Springs, crossing to the north shore and remaining there for the remainder of the section. The river flows south once it reaches Suwannee River State Park, so a northbound hike is then compass south along the west shore of the river. South to north, trailheads include:

0.0 DEEP CREEK
Tiny trailhead at the north end of Osceola National Forest.

8.0 BELL SPRINGS*
Large grassy trailhead off paved road.

11.4 LITTLE SHOALS*
Small trailhead at end of narrow dirt road off US 41.

12.8 US 41 WAYSIDE / WHITE SPRINGS TRACT*
Small parking corral accessed inside wayside park off US 41.

15.3 WHITE SPRINGS TRACT*
Small grassy parking area off dirt road.

16.3 WHITE SPRINGS
Parking lot at former visitor center. Day use only.

17.9 GAZEBO TRAILHEAD
Large paved lot inside state park. Secure spot. Fee.

21.0 CR 25A ACCESS
Grassy shoulder on unpaved road off CR 25A. Day use only.

22.6 SWIFT CREEK CA*
Small parking corral at end of rough dirt access road.

29.6 CAMP BRANCH CA*
Small parking corral 0.7E at end of narrow dirt access road.

36.0 SUWANNEE SPRINGS*
0.8W via old US 129 bridge. Large day-use parking at spring.

45.5 HOLTON CREEK RIVER CAMP*
At end of a long, sometimes-rough dirt road in WMA.

Swift Creek

47.8 HOLTON SPRING*
Along a dirt road near a first-magnitude spring.

49.7 HOLTON CREEK*
Larger unpaved parking corral at WMA entrance.

51.1 GIBSON PARK
Large paved parking area at county park with campground.

51.8 ALAPAHA PARKING*
Limited day-use parking under highway bridge.

58.6 BIG OAK PARKING
Small day-use parking area at boat ramp.

64.3 WITHLACOOCHEE RIVER
Small day-use grassy parking area.

66.5 SUWANNEE RIVER STATE PARK ANNEX
Small day-use lot off dead-end paved old US 90.

66.5 SUWANNEE RIVER STATE PARK
0.9 compass E via old US 90 bridge to secure paved parking at state park. Fee.

66.9 ELLAVILLE TRAILWALKER
Grassy lot in woods off US 90, 0.5 compass W of Cooper's Bluff via yellow blaze.

73.0 BLACK TRACT
Tiny grassy lot off dirt River Rd.

*Suwannee River Water Management District trailheads are day use only.

Camping

Random camping is allowed except at trailheads but the use of designated primitive campsites is encouraged. Most have benches, a fire ring, and access to water to filter. Noise can echo up and down the river at night, especially at campsites near Interstates 75 and 10. No permits or fees are required except at Holton Creek River Camp, which has screened shelters and restrooms with flush toilets and showers. Call ahead (800-326-3521) to secure a spot.

6.4 BIG SHOALS
Open area near shoals with benches and fire ring.

10.1 WALDRONS LANDING
Flat spot near river at the base of a steep climb.

11.0 DEEP GULLY
Flat spot with picnic table and river view.

17.4 CABLE CROSSING
State park riverfront primitive site. Full service campground 0.5E. Fee.

18.9 CATFISH HOLE
State park primitive campsite. Fee.

19.9 SUWANNEE OVERLOOK
State park primitive campsite. Fee.

21.5 SWIFT CREEK
Benches surround a fire ring, ample space for large groups.

24.9 HIDDEN SPRING
Small beauty spot with benches and fire ring. Spring 50 yards south.

32.0 CROOKED BRANCH
Benches and fire ring in a clearing.

45.6 HOLTON CREEK RIVER CAMP
Screened shelters and tent sites. Restrooms. Reserve. Fee.

46.7 RIVER BANKS
Clearing along Holton Creek with benches and fire ring.

47.6 HOLTON CREEK
Large clearing near Holton Spring suitable for groups.

51.1 GIBSON PARK
Developed campground with bathhouse. Fee.

53.0 ALAPAHA
Beauty spot at river confluence. Limited capacity.

61.5 CONFLUENCE CAMPSITE
Picnic bench near Big Oak peninsula. Train noise from nearby trestle.

65.2 WITHLACOOCHEE RIVER
Picnic tables overlook river, but close to a forest road.

66.5 SUWANNEE RIVER STATE PARK
0.9 compass east. Cabins and developed campground Reserve. Fee.

66.9 COOPER'S BLUFF
Covered picnic shelter and ample flat area for groups.

71.5 BLACK TRACT
Large flat area with picnic tables, access to river.

75.9 MILL CREEK NORTH
Small flat area with picnic table and paddler access.

When random camping, camp away from forest roads. Never camp at trailheads. If camping on a beach, keep in mind alligators live in the river. The river can rise suddenly due to rainfall at its source. Protect your food from bears by using a bear bag or a canister. Bears frequently roam through Holton Creek River Camp. From the Alapaha River south, call the Suwannee River Water Management District hotline before filtering river water. The city of Valdosta has spilled untreated sewage into the river system many times in recent years.

Suwannee River near Bell Springs

Trip Planning

Leashed dogs welcome. Parts of the trail are shared with cyclists and equestrians. Multiuse segments are normally clearly marked. Three parts of this section are open to hunting: Swift Creek Conservation Area, Holton Creek WMA, and Twin Rivers State Forest. Determine their hunting seasons in advance. If you hike during hunting season, wear bright orange and camp only at designated campsites for your own safety.

Backpackers are limited on where to leave a car because most trailheads are day use only. Stephen Foster and Suwannee River State Parks are the easiest options. These parks charge a fee. Shuttle services from American Canoe Adventures (386-397-1309) in White Springs and Canoe Outpost (386-364-4991) at Spirit of the Suwannee Music Park enable you to place a vehicle at the end of your hike and backpack toward it. You can arrange a hike or paddle loop along the river with the help of your outfitter: hike upriver and paddle downriver.

Ticks are troublesome along the Suwannee. Between April and June, you can be swarmed by hatchlings. Protect yourself by applying permethrin to your clothing in advance and using insect repellent. Light-colored clothes enable you to see ticks more easily.

The Suwannee is a floodplain river. Even when skies are clear overhead, waters can rise suddenly and silently if heavy rains fall in the Okefenokee Swamp, the river's source. Never hike into flowing water. Call the Suwannee River Water Management District hotline (386-362-6626) or check their website for current conditions on the Suwannee River and its major tributaries the Florida Trail also follows, the Alapaha and Withlacoochee.

Land Manager

Suwannee River Water Management District
9225 CR 49, Live Oak 32060
386-362-1001
mysuwanneeriver.com

Highlights

Big Shoals, mile 6.5

When the river is the right depth, water the color of root beer froths over limestone boulders and ledges through Class III rapids. Canoeists portage along the trail when the going gets rough.

Little Shoals, mile 11.3

Not far upriver from the Little Shoals trailhead, these permanent riffles in the Suwannee are a mellow version of their big brother upstream, with nicely framed views from the trail.

Sal Marie Branch, mile 20.5

Winding through a river bluff forest above the Suwannee, Sal Marie Branch carves showy meanders on its way to the river.

Swift Creek, mile 23.7

Inside a deep canyon in stone, Swift Creek flows beneath a high bridge through a canopied forest to unfurl into the Suwannee River.

No Name Creek, mile 29

Flowing through a deep cleft in the earth, No Name Creek is followed by a significant climb up a long staircase along a very scenic section of trail.

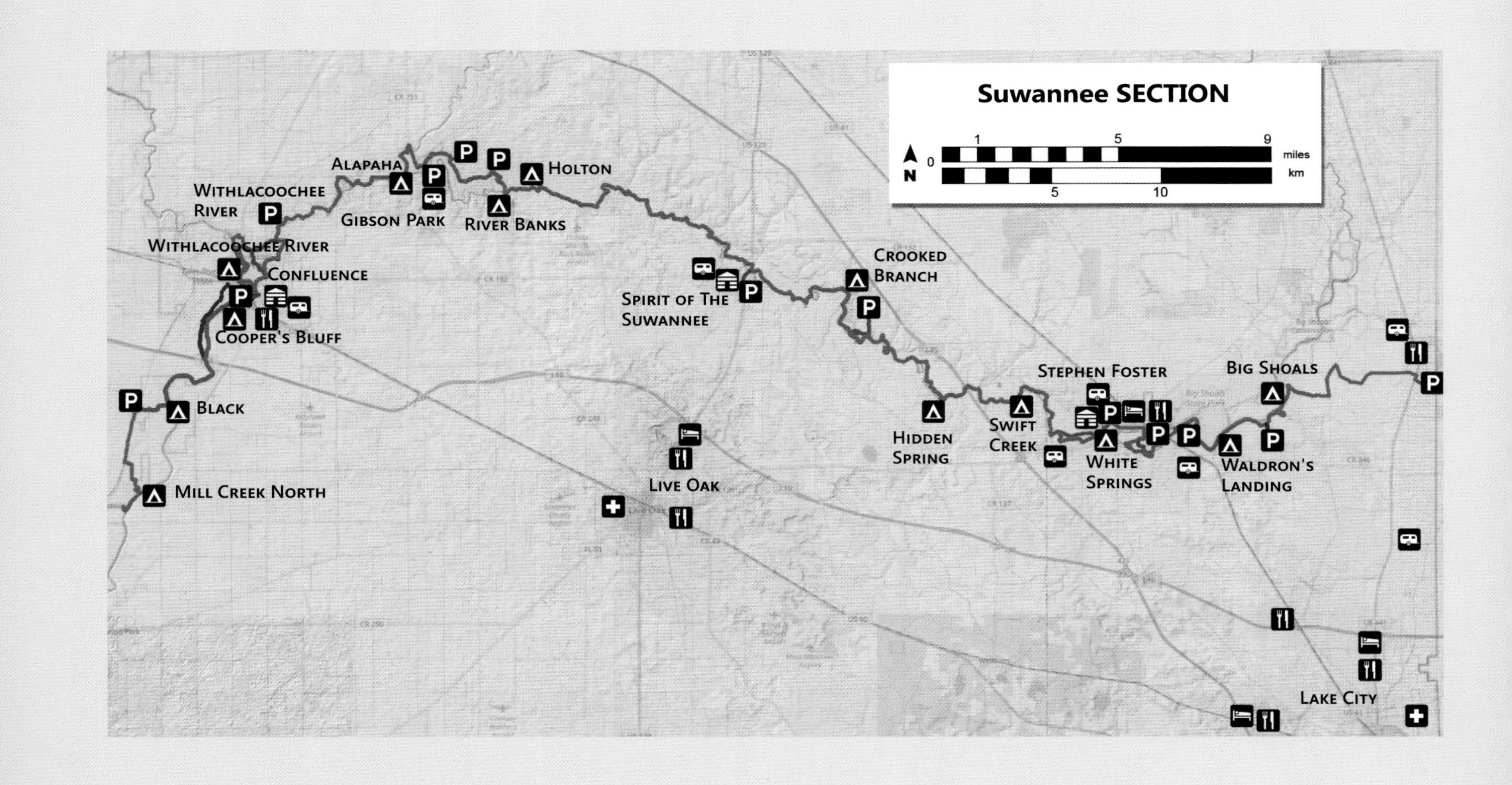
Suwannee SECTION
N
0
1
5
9
miles
5
10
km
Withlacoochee River
Alapaha
Gibson Park
River Banks
Holton
Withlacoochee River
Confluence
Cooper's Bluff
Black
Mill Creek North
Spirit of The Suwannee
Crooked Branch
Live Oak
Hidden Spring
Swift Creek
Stephen Foster
White Springs
Big Shoals
Waldron's Landing
Lake City

Disappearing Creek, mile 30.4

A short side trail off the trail toward the Camp Branch trailhead, a swallet gulps the sinuous flow of Camp Branch at the bottom of a deep sinkhole in a small canyon.

Devil's Mountain, mile 32.3

One of the steepest ascents on the Florida Trail, Devil's Mountain rises quickly from the banks of the Suwannee River up a slope made slippery by seepage springs in Greasy Gully.

Suwannee Whirlpool, mile 39.8

A permanent swirl at a sharp bend in the river, the whirlpool is a fascinating natural phenomenon you can see from the shore.

Guardian Cypress, mile 45.6

At the end of a blazed side trail at Holton Creek River Camp, Florida's two largest documented cypresses compete for attention towering from the bottom of a steep sinkhole.

Holton Spring, mile 47.8

Through a lush riverine forest, the Florida Trail circles this broad, steep and deep spring basin that is the source for Holton Creek.

Alapaha Confluence, mile 53

At the end of a slender stone peninsula just beyond the Alapaha River campsite, the Alapaha River flows into the Suwannee.

Big Oak, mile 60.8

One of Florida's landmark trees, the Big Oak is one of the state's tallest live oaks. It's along the Blue Trail 200 feet north of the Florida Trail.

Suwannacoochee Spring, mile 66.5

In the fading ruins of Ellaville, a once-prosperous riverside town, this gushing walled-in spring sits right along the river.

Recommended Day Hikes

Mile 8.0

Bell Springs to Big Shoals, 4.6-mile round trip
Bell Springs to Little Shoals, 3.4 miles linear

Mile 12.8

White Springs, 3.6 miles linear or loop

Mile 16.9

Stephen Foster to Sal Marie Branch, 7.2-mile round trip

Mile 22.6

Swift Creek to Camp Branch, 7.7 miles linear

Mile 29.8

Camp Branch to Suwannee Springs, 7.9 miles linear

Mile 49.7

Holton Creek WMA, 8.9-mile round trip

Mile 51.8

Alapaha Confluence, 2.6-mile round trip

Mile 58.6

Big Oak Trail, 6.9-mile loop

Mile 66.5

Ellaville North, 4.6-mile round trip
Ellaville South and Black Tract, 6.5 miles linear

32. Big Shoals

3.2 MILES | BELL SPRINGS TRACT AND BIG SHOALS STATE PARK, WHITE SPRINGS

On a round-trip hike from Bell Springs to the rapids of Big Shoals, watch the Suwannee roar across a challenging array of boulders beloved by generations of paddlers.

Overview

Big Shoals is Florida's only Class III whitewater. Leading to it, this rugged riverfront section of the Florida Trail is a geological delight. Follow the outflow of Bell Springs to a sandy beach along the Suwannee, glimpse "flowerpot" formations along limestone bluffs, and see Robinson Branch turn into a waterfall as it tumbles off an escarpment to river level. It's a delightful day hike to the portage above the rapids, with the opportunity to camp on the bluffs above the music of the shoals. Since the Suwannee is a floodplain river, sometimes it's dry enough to walk onto the big boulders, and sometimes the shoals are entirely submerged.

Trip Planning

See Suwannee. Leashed dogs are welcome. Hiking sticks help on rugged terrain and a water crossing. Check river levels before hiking. Don't attempt this section when the river is in flood stage. Turn back if you encounter water flowing across the trail.

Land Managers

Big Shoals State Park
18738 SE 94th St, White Springs 32096
386-397-4331
floridastateparks.org

Bell Springs run

Big Shoals

Suwannee River Water Management District
9225 CR 49, Live Oak 32060
386-362-1001
mysuwanneeriver.com

Directions

From the Interstate 10 interchange at US 41 between Lake City and White Springs, drive north 5.3 miles to Lassie Black Rd. Turn right and drive 1.8 miles. Turn left onto Morrell Dr. Follow this road to where it ends at a cul-de-sac in front of a house. Continue through the gate to Bell Springs trailhead [30.329298, -82.689613].

Options

From a drop-off point (no parking) at NW Cansa Rd [30.343201, -82.660599] it's 1.8 miles along the Florida Trail to the shoals and 3.4 miles to Bell Springs trailhead. Northbound hike 3.4 miles (6.8 miles round trip) to Little Shoals. It has a handful of climbs and great views, the riffling rapids at Little Shoals a highlight just before the trailhead. The access road to Little Shoals trailhead [30.332741, -82.723289] is in a low-lying area best crossed in a high-clearance vehicle. Shown in blue on the map, Big Shoals Trail [30.352167, -82.687617] overlooks the rapids from the river's north shore. A day-use fee applies.

Hike

Follow a forest road to a historic marker commemorating state senator W. E. Bishop and his wife, Virginia, who preserved this iconic natural area for future generations. At the junction with the orange blazes, continue north on the Florida Trail. It curves to the right and enters a hardwood forest surrounding Bell Springs.

The northernmost major spring along the Suwannee River, Bell Springs discharges more than 350 gallons per minute. Cross a bridge and turn downstream to parallel the spring run. At a sharp right, straight ahead is a beach along the Suwannee adjoining where the clear outflow of Bell Springs combines with the tannic river.

Ascend the forested bluffs and turn toward the river, emerging at a viewpoint near a very large oak tree and the remains of a log slide used by timber companies long ago to drop felled pines into the river. From this point on, the footpath is often rugged, rooty, and rocky. Mature trees tower over the trail, providing deep shade.

Cross a series of bog bridges over a small tributary before weaving in and out of the bluff forest. Follow the flow of the landscape, occasionally emerging along the bluffs at spectacular views. At 0.8 miles, Robinson Branch Falls echoes through the forest, its cascade tumbling over a steep limestone lip into a deep ravine. Turn to parallel Robinson Branch upstream to a ford above the falls. The water can be knee deep at times; use hiking poles for balance. Past the ford, follow the orange blazes along the creek downstream to the falls.

Make a sharp turn to rejoin the river bluffs, with a nice view to the northwest. Drop to the river's edge for a view upriver of the lower rapids, the first of several places to stop and savor the roar of whitewater. Climb and descend again, squeezing beneath a cage of roots under a towering pine tree along a narrow ledge.

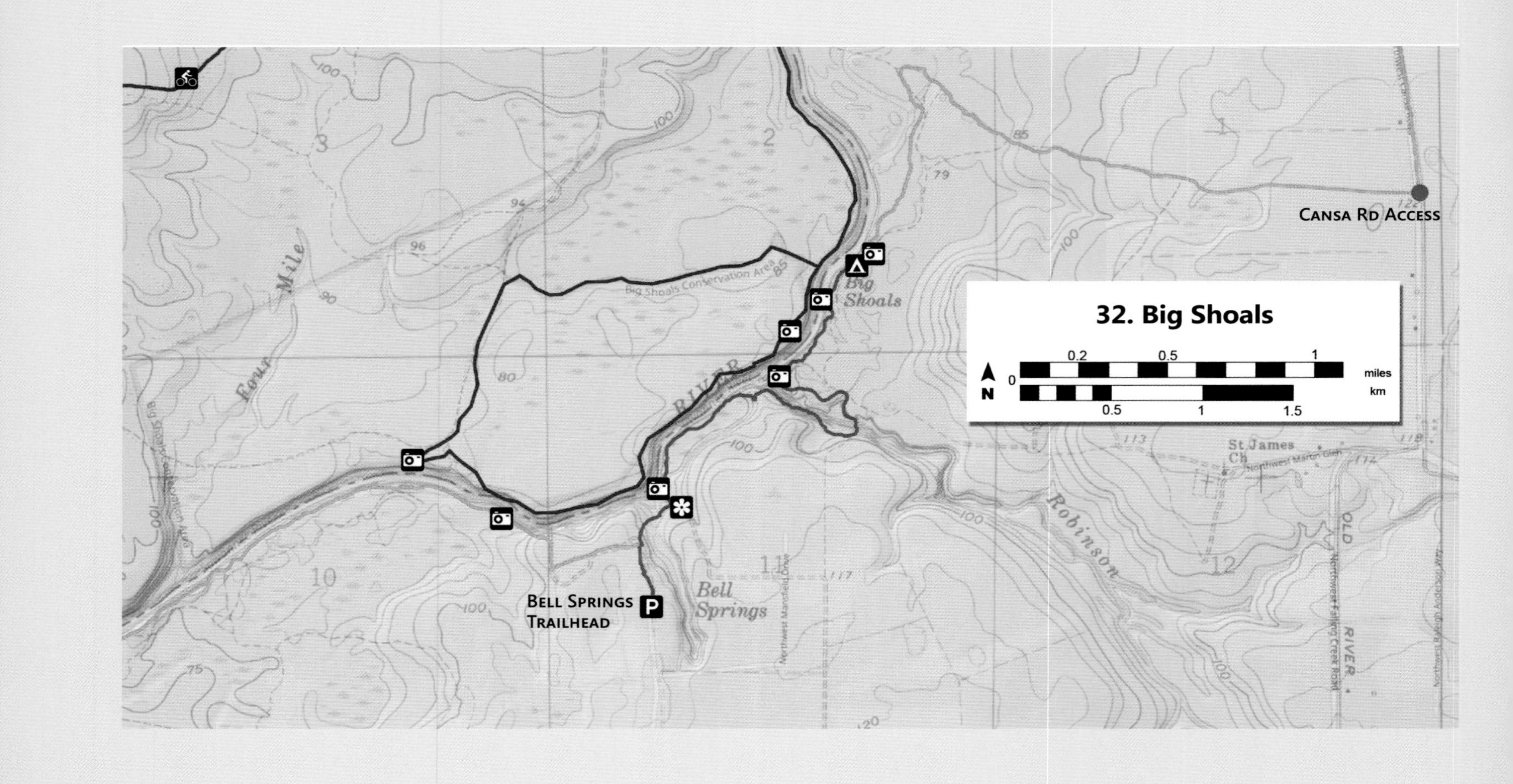

32. Big Shoals
0
0.2
0.5
1
miles
km
0.5
1
1.5
N
Cansa Rd Access
Big Shoals
Big Shoals Conservation Area
Bell Springs Trailhead
Bell Springs
St James Ch
Robinson
Four Mile
River
Old River
Northwest Falling Creek Road
Northwest Mansfield Drive
Northwest Martin Glen

Lose more elevation crossing a deep but narrow tributary draining into the river near a small rocky beach at the base of the shoals at 1.3 miles. Along a sweep of rapids around a curve in the river, it's a beauty spot with unusual erosional formations, limestone "flowerpots" along the bluff. Climb up into a forest of pines and saw palmetto, the trail now the width of a forest road to accommodate portage around the rapids. A campsite with benches sits above the take-out.

To see Big Shoals up close, scramble down to river level along the portage path. When river levels are ideal for whitewater, your perspective at waterline is of the tannic river rushing through limestone boulders. At 1.6 miles, this is your turnaround point.

A narrow path follows the water's edge. If it hasn't washed away, you can use it to gain different perspectives on the rapids. It used to rejoin the Florida Trail near the portage put-in but has eroded over time. Backtrack to the take-out and start your return hike. The view of Robinson Branch Falls is best on the return trip. Reaching the historic marker past the outflow of Bell Springs, leave the orange blazes for the blue-blazed trail straight ahead to Bell Springs trailhead to complete this 3.2-mile hike.

Below Big Shoals

Upland corridor

33. White Springs Tract

3.5 MILES | SWIFT CREEK CONSERVATION AREA, WHITE SPRINGS

Discover the beauty of the bluffs above the white sand banks of the Suwannee on your choice of two different loop hikes or a linear walk through the town of White Springs.

Overview

In a strip of public land buffering White Springs from the Suwannee River, the Florida Trail weaves between swamp forests cradled in old river channels, the bluffs above the river, and upland forests at higher elevations. After a landowner revoked access to the former Florida Trail route on the south side of the river, the orange blazes shifted to the Bridge-to-Bridge Trail on the north shore, initially constructed for off-road biking on the White Springs Tract of Swift Creek Conservation Area. Quiet on weekdays, busy on weekends, and generally broad and gentle for walking, this easy to access hike provides scenic river views and spring wildflowers.

Trip Planning / Land Manager

See Suwannee. Leashed dogs are welcome. When both blue and orange blazes are on the trees, the trail is shared with cyclists. Hikers should stick to the orange blazes where trails diverge, cyclists to blue. Keep alert where the trail narrows and is multiuse.

Directions

From Interstate 10 exit 301 for Lake City drive north on US 41 to White Springs.

Immediately after the Suwannee River bridge, make a left into US 41 Wayside Park. Follow the one-way loop through the picnic area. The trailhead entrance is on the right, leading to a parking corral with a "White Springs Tract" sign [30.32531, -82.739273].

Options

Two different loops are described in the text. For a 2.5-mile linear hike, leave a vehicle at the tiny White Springs Tract trailhead [30.326229, -82.74865], a left off US 41 onto Adams Memorial Circle a little north of the US 41 Wayside Park. For a 3.5-mile linear hike, leave a vehicle at the public parking area at the corner of SR 136 and US 41 [30.329895, -82.758987]. Reach the small White Springs Tract trailhead, turn left, and walk along Adams Memorial Circle past Riverside Cemetery and the ballfields to US 41. Turn left and follow the orange blazes along the sidewalk a mile through the historic town of White Springs, passing stores, restaurants, and grand homes along Spring Street. End at the parking area at US 41 and CR 136. To see historic White Sulphur Springs, the town's namesake, descend a staircase from the parking area to walk into the state park.

Hike

Follow a road from the trailhead toward the river bluffs, passing a blocky structure with a corrugated metal door. Side paths lead to views from the bluffs. At a gate, make a sharp right into the sandhills, undulating terrain with side

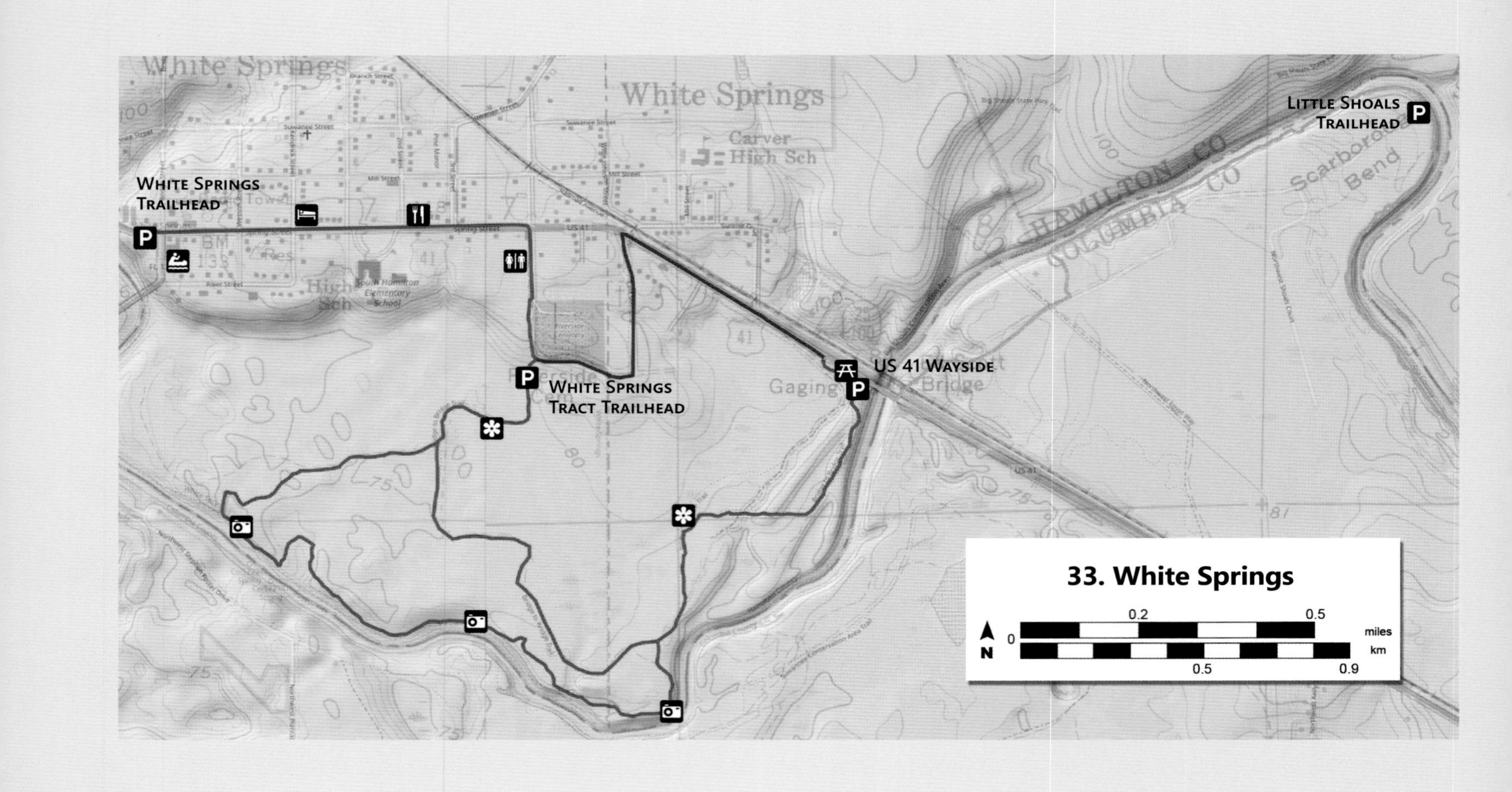
33. White Springs
White Springs Trailhead
White Springs Tract Trailhead
US 41 Wayside
Little Shoals Trailhead
White Springs
Carver High Sch
Hamilton Co
Columbia Co
Scarborough Bend
Gaging
Bridge
0
0.2
0.5
miles
0.5
0.9
km
N

channels carved by the river. One deep bowl is broad and flat beneath the pines. Ascend to face a cypress and tupelo swamp cradled in an oxbow pond abandoned by the river long ago. Turning left, follow this scenic swamp's edge. A large loblolly pine rises above the forest canopy.

Pass a gate on the left and meet a cross trail on the right at 0.6 miles. Depending on the route you choose, you may return along it later to this junction. Walking atop a natural terrace above the river, make a turn above a sand bluff with a beach below. Depending on recent erosion, it might be possible to scramble to the water's edge. Along most of this hike, beaches aren't accessible—the bluffs are too high and steep.

At a Y intersection, the blue-blazed Bridge-to-Bridge Trail veers right. The Florida Trail keeps you on the bluffs above the river in an old river channel shaded by oaks and pines. Clumps of saw palmetto line the footpath. The trails merge again as the forest becomes denser, the footpath deeply worn as it tunnels through the forest. The Suwannee burbles below, but it's impossible to see from the perspective of hiking inside a half-pipe bowl of the old river channel.

By 1.2 miles, return to the bluffs, with river views through the sparse understory before easing into a moss-draped canopy of trees with several overlooks. The tall, arching shrubs with peeling red bark are sparkleberry, a variety of blueberry also known as huckleberry. It's not exactly tasty eaten right off the plant, but people make jam or wine from the berries.

Leaving the bluffs, curve through a low basin in a pine forest where young pines are so closely crowded together they look like bamboo from a distance. Ascending the bluffs, the trail curves around a wooden railing directing cyclists away from the trees. Beneath tall pines and a lower canopy of bluff

Shady river bluff forest

forest, there are more views of the river through the trees.

At the next Y intersection, trails diverge. The Bridge-to-Bridge Trail stays along the bluffs. Turn right to follow the Florida Trail straight down a forested corridor. It rejoins the blue-blazed trail at a T intersection. Make a right, and the trails diverge again soon after. Stay with the orange blazes, quickly reaching a T intersection with a forest road. Turn right and walk into an open clearing for the forest road between the oaks and pines.

A marker with white disks and a wooden "Bridge-to-Bridge Trail" sign point to the cross trail at 2.2 miles. For a 3.5-mile loop entirely in the forest, turn here. Shared with cyclists, the cross-trail trail winds through upland forest 0.7 miles to the trail junction you passed early in this hike. Turn left at that junction to retrace your walk back to the trailhead.

The next 3.5-mile loop is ahead. The forest crowds closer to the forest road and water collects in swales edged by cinnamon ferns beneath the loblolly pines. Paw-paw sports draping ivory blooms each spring. Dappled shade replaces the open feel. Reach a kiosk and the tiny parking area for the White Springs Tract at 2.5 miles.

If you haven't left a vehicle here or near White Sulphur Springs for a linear hike, circle back to yours by turning right to walk up little-used Adams Memorial Circle. This dirt road leads to US 41 in a quarter mile, passing a community playground. At the highway, turn right. Follow the sidewalk to the US 41 Wayside Park and walk through it to the trailhead to complete the hike.

Alternatively, backtrack to the cross trail for a 4.1-mile round trip and loop, or simply follow the orange blazes all the way back to the trailhead for a 5-mile round trip.

34. Stephen Foster to Sal Marie Branch

7.2 MILES | STEPHEN FOSTER FOLK CULTURE CENTER STATE PARK, WHITE SPRINGS

Ancient live oaks, river views, and the sweet scent of wild azalea in spring will tempt you into this undulating hike along the Suwannee at Stephen Foster Folk Culture Center State Park.

Overview

This popular piece of the Florida Trail scrambles in and out of ravines and climbs up and down eroded bluffs created by the Suwannee River over geologic time. From the heart of Stephen Foster Folk Culture Center State Park, this round-trip hike continues a mile past the park boundary to a deep ravine carved by a creek flowing toward the Suwannee River.

In addition to a campground, riverfront cabins, and the unmistakable bells of its carillon ringing music across the landscape, the state park has a permanent Craft Square where visiting artisans demonstrate weaving, pottery making, blacksmithing, and other traditional crafts. Items made are sold in Cousin Thelma Boltin's Craft and Gift Shop, just north of the River Gazebo, the starting point for this hike. Hosting major festivals and events all year, the park's legacy is music, named for a famous 1800s songwriter. Folk musicians gather from across the state for the Florida Folk Festival annually on Memorial Day weekend.

Trip Planning

See Suwannee. Leashed dogs are welcome. An entrance fee is charged at the state park. Bring a hiking stick for steep pitches and rugged climbs. Check river levels prior to hiking. Never enter flowing water or hike when the river is at flood stage. While the last mile of trail is within Suwannee River Water Management District lands, most of the hike is in the state park.

Land Manager

Stephen Foster Folk Culture Center State Park
11016 Lillian Sanders Dr., White Springs 32096
386-397-2733
floridastateparks.org

Directions

From Interstate 75 exit 439 north of Lake City, follow SR 136 east 3 miles into White Springs. Turn left at the blinker onto US 41. At the curve, turn left into the park entrance to Stephen Foster Folk Culture State Park. Pay your entrance fee at the entrance station and follow the one-way loop around the park. Past the Carillon Tower is a road on the right. Park in the lot on the left adjoining the River Gazebo [30.3296, -82.7669].

Options

Inside the state park, use Foster's Hammock Trail to make a loop. Or extend your hike by starting at the Spring House just inside the park gate instead of the gazebo, which adds 0.8 miles to your round trip. White Sulphur Springs is the big spring which the town was named after and is surrounded by a structure constructed as a destination

Sal Marie Branch

spa during the turn-of-the-last-century mineral spa boom in the United States.

If you plan a linear hike, drop a vehicle at the end point. It's not an official trailhead, just day-use parking along a neighborhood access road off CR 25A [30.3458, -82.8016]. To reach it from White Springs, drive past the park entrance up the hill and make a left on CR 25A. Continue 2 miles to a turnoff on the left. A landmark we've used for the turnoff when driving westbound is turn left after a house on the right with a wagon wheel out front.

Hike

Follow the ramp or staircase from the parking area to the River Gazebo below. A large structure, it's one of many venues for folk music during the Florida Folk Festival. Approaching this clearing from White Sulphur Springs, the orange blazes pass the gazebo and lead you along the bluffs above the river past the first of many scenic views. A sweet scent perfumes the hike in March as native Florida azalea blossoms in pale pink against the light greens of new growth.

The first physical challenge of the hike comes up quickly. Drop into a deep ravine carved by the river in the past when it overflowed its banks and scramble out up a rather steep bluff that's easy to climb down on the return trip. After a meander along the bluffs, make a sharp right at a split-rail fence with a view of a boat launch. Paddlers put in here to tackle the Suwannee River Wilderness Trail or take out to relax for a night in the cabins or at the campground. Beyond the launch, continue through a deeply shaded bluff forest.

Meet a trail junction at a power line in a clearing. To the right a trail follows the power line a half mile to the campground. Along it is a connection to Foster's Hammock Trail, a big multiuse loop inside the park. Continue straight across the clearing and walk by the Cable Crossing designated primitive camping area on the bluff. It's cheaper and more tent-friendly than the campground.

Edging close to the bluffs in the forest, make a sharp right and drop steeply into the Dip, a crescent-shaped waterfront hollow usually filled with sand. A mile into the hike, it's one of the first features to flood when the river rises above its normal levels. We've had to turn back at this point more than once. A massive oak tree leans over this depression on the far side. Scramble up the sharp incline to continue along the bluffs, where several houses are visible across the river.

Passing an immense loblolly pine perhaps six feet around the base, continue walking under large live oaks to a scenic spot where during low water, islands appear in the river. A large cluster of azaleas tops the next section of bluffs. A tricky traverse lies ahead, a steep slope curving upward to the top of the river bank. After another bend in the river, a tiny forest of cypress knees appears below, some forming natural arches along the riverbank. The trail clings close to the rim of the river bluff, rounding a large floodplain area to the left.

Ascend from river level to reach Catfish Hole at 1.9 miles at the first intersection of the park's major trails. Foster's Hammock Trail leads east and west. Taking a right on it makes a loop back towards Cable Crossing. The Florida Trail sticks with the river bluff. Within

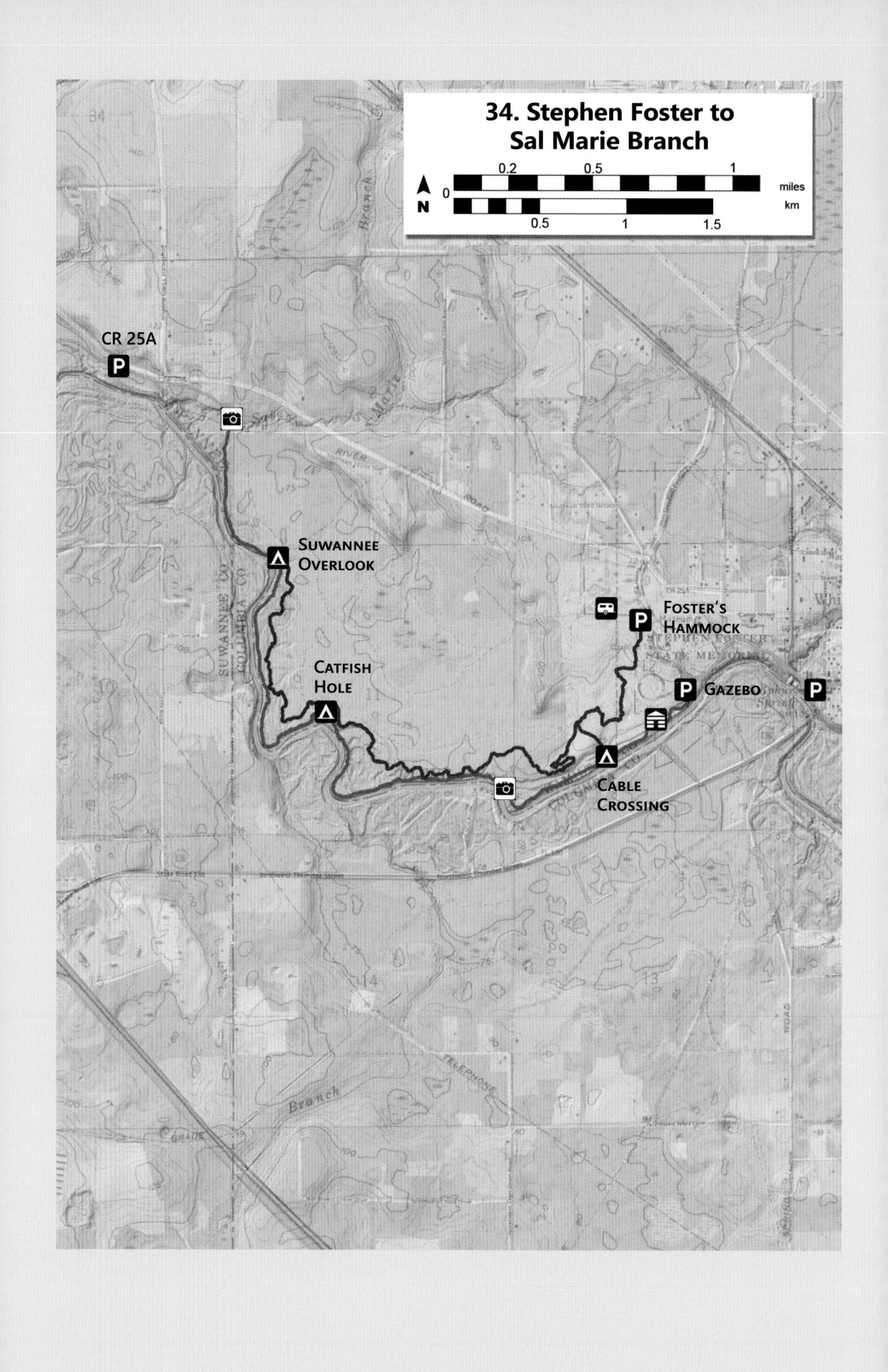
34. Stephen Foster to
Sal Marie Branch
0.2
0.5
1
0
miles
N
km
0.5
1
1.5
CR 25A
Suwannee
Overlook
Catfish
Hole
Foster's
Hammock
Gazebo
Cable
Crossing

a quarter mile, savor a scenic view beneath the big oaks. More azaleas fill the forest with a heavenly aroma.

Follow the curve of the bluff, passing a gigantic live oak leaning over the river. The trail drops to river level on a low forested terrace. This basin fills with water easily when the river splashes over its banks, so there may be puddles to wade through. If the terrace itself is under water, turn around.

Across the river, occasional residences are obvious where a staircase drops to the river or a long skid provides a place to launch a boat from the bluff. Creating natural sculptures, cypress roots cling tightly to the limestone walls of the river basin. The bluff narrows sharply, the trail crossing rocky overhangs and crevices. Watch your step. An accumulation of pine needles provides a deep cushion underfoot briefly. Then a deep ravine provides a challenge to climb in and out of. Follow the worn switchbacks and take your time.

Hugging close to the river, this section of the trail is a wonderland of green giants. Some of the pines have deep catface gashes cut by axes and metal flashing embedded in their trunks, once used to funnel sap for turpentine production. One tree trunk is so fat it looks like it's bursting at the seams. At 2.9 miles, reach Suwannee Overlook, the final junction with Foster's Hammock Trail.

At 3.2 miles, the river may rumble a little. A short stretch of whitewater we call Tiny Shoals appears here when water levels are low. Caves gape from the river bluffs on the far shore. Grab a few glimpses of the Suwannee through gaps in the trees before the trail turns away from it. Descending from the pine forest, enter a grassy clearing with native plum trees, followed by a bluff forest magical when rain-kissed, with ferns glistening and the tips of pine needles tipping drops of water toward the ground.

Sparkleberry and saw palmetto dominate the understory as you draw within earshot of this hike's destination, Sal Marie Branch. This sinuous stream carved a deep hollow through the hills behind the river bluffs. Its rushing waters echo in a stony passageway below. A switchback leads into the hollow to a bridge across the creek.

The Sal Marie bridge washes out easily. If the bridge is in place, cross the creek to climb to a panoramic view of it from the bluffs on the other side.

This viewpoint at 3.6 miles is the turnaround point for this hike unless you're walking to a vehicle parked off CR 25A. If so, keep climbing the hill through the forest above Sal Marie Branch until you run out of woods. Turn left onto a power line easement. Orange blazes on telephone poles confirm the route, which becomes a grassy double-track through a small neighborhood. Reach your vehicle at 4 miles.

Returning to the River Gazebo? Scramble down the bluff and cross the bridge. Continue toward the trailhead the same way you hiked here. On the return trip the river is to your right, offering better views. At both Suwannee Overlook and Catfish Hole you can use Foster's Hammock Trail to loop back toward Cable Crossing. For river views, stick with the orange blazes. End at the River Gazebo parking area after 7.2 miles.

Camp Branch

35. Camp Branch to Suwannee Springs

7.9 MILES | CAMP BRANCH AND SUGAR CREEK TRACTS, SUWANNEE SPRINGS

Rugged climbs through abandoned river channels to the highest elevations along the Suwannee River make this hike a serious roller-coaster through river bluff forests and sandy beaches.

Overview

While the Florida Trail along the Suwannee River is notable for rough terrain, this particular piece of the trail serves it up more than most. Anchored by Camp Branch—where Disappearing Creek Loop makes a fascinating side trip—this hike offers not just river views and beaches but challenging ravines and sandy slopes with sidehill. One of its highlights is the climb up Devil's Mountain. At 126 feet above sea level, it's not the highest point of the Florida Trail, but one of its highest. It's all downhill from the top since Suwannee Springs is at river level. Expect a serious workout along a challenging course of ascents and descents, with footpath edging steep drop-offs along sandy river banks and diving into deeply carved ravines through which waterways cascade to the Suwannee River. Not all of those waterways are bridged. Enjoy ample opportunities to drink in the ever-changing river views and expect wet feet.

Trip Planning / Land Manager

See Suwannee. Leashed dogs are welcome. Hiking poles help for rugged traverses and waterway crossings. Many slopes are muddy and slippery when wet, particularly the climb to Devil's Mountain. Check river levels prior to hiking. Don't attempt this section when the river is at flood stage. Never enter flowing water.

Directions

The trailheads at the ends of this hike are 15 minutes apart by road. To leave a vehicle at the end, leave Interstate 10 at exit 283 Live Oak and drive 4.1 miles north on US 129 to Suwannee Springs [30.394106, -82.934105], its entrance road marked by a brown sign on the right across from Spirit of the Suwannee Music Park. Suwannee Springs is a day-use area that closes at 6 p.m. and is a quarter mile from the trail at the old US 129 bridge. For the starting point, cross the Suwannee River on US 129 and turn right on CR 132. In 1.5 miles, turn right on CR 25A. It crosses Camp Branch on a highway bridge at 2.5 miles. In 0.7 miles, after a curve and just past the weigh station on Interstate 75, turn onto a narrow two-track road on the right with a small sign for Camp Branch. Drive this one-lane dirt road a half mile to Camp Branch trailhead [30.378094, -82.878853].

Options

To extend this to an overnighter, check in at the agricultural check station on US 129 (someone is on duty 24/7) or Spirit of the Suwannee Music Park about parking a vehicle to hike toward. Arrange with the Suwannee Canoe Outpost to shuttle you to the start point. Get dropped off at Swift Creek trailhead [30.342037, -82.816193] off CR 25A for

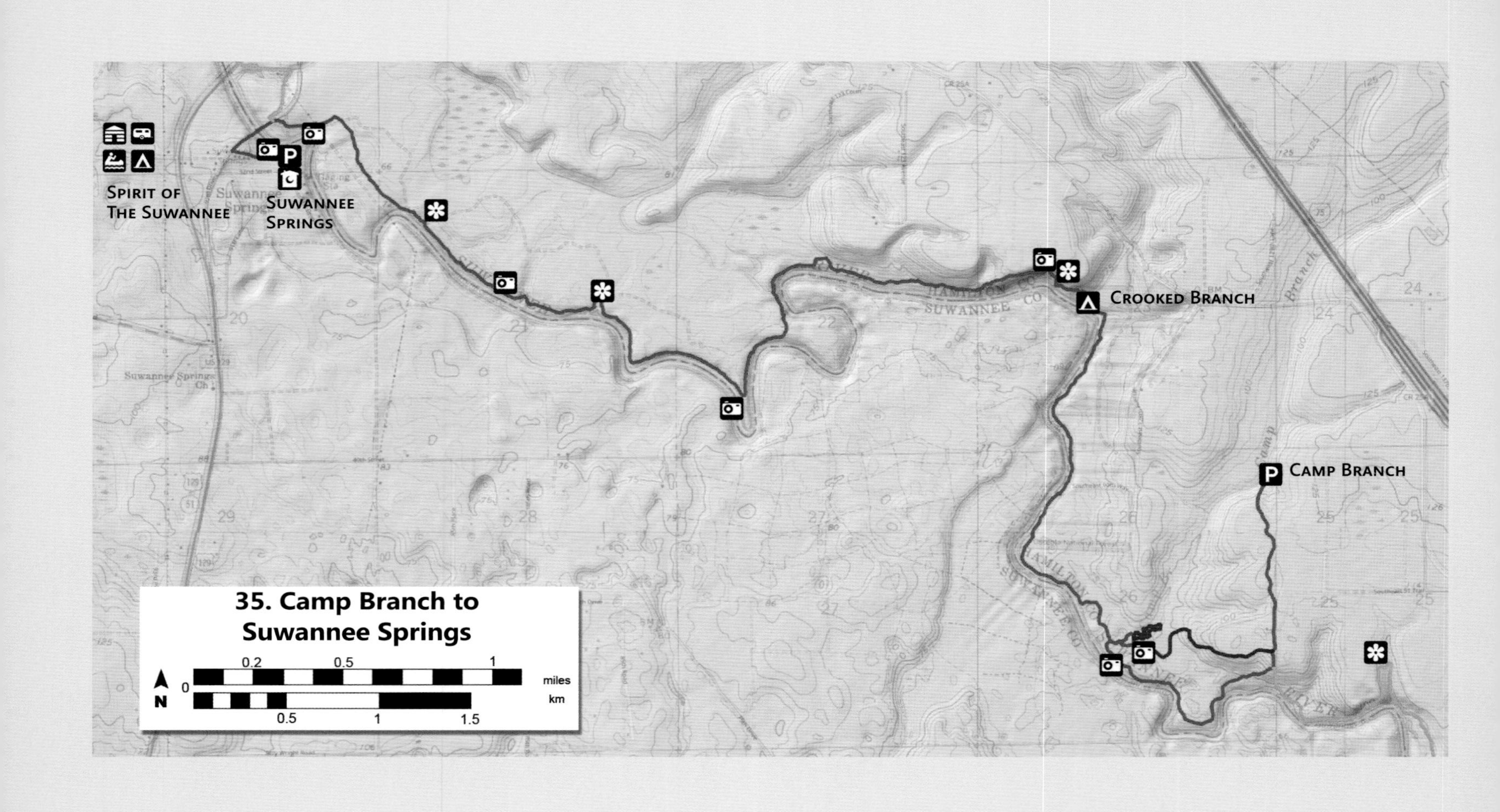
35. Camp Branch to Suwannee Springs
Spirit of The Suwannee
Suwannee Springs
Crooked Branch
Camp Branch
0
0.2
0.5
1
miles
0.5
1
1.5
km
N

a 13.4-mile hike or the River Gazebo parking area [30.329321, -82.767349] at Stephen Foster Folk Culture State Park for a 19.1-mile hike, plus the walk to where your vehicle is parked. Or arrange a shuttle to Camp Branch trailhead to tackle this linear day hike, returning to your car at the end.

For the most rugged round trip, go from Suwannee Springs to the top of Devil's Mountain and return, 9 miles. For a shorter and easier day hike, follow the route as described from Camp Branch trailhead but turn off onto the Disappearing Creek Trail after 1.5 miles. Hike Disappearing Creek Loop and return to Camp Branch trailhead via the Camp Branch Trail for a 4.5-mile double loop. Shorten that hike to 3.2 miles by just visiting the swallet overlook along Disappearing Creek Loop instead of doing that whole loop.

Hike

From Camp Branch trailhead, follow the white-blazed forest road down a very steep hill. Leveling out, meet a Y intersection. Take the blue-blazed trail to the left to quickly reach the orange-blazed Florida Trail at a T intersection at 0.7 miles. Turn right. Cross a small stream as the trail climbs, turning toward the bluffs with views of the river. Reach the junction with Disappearing Creek Trail at 1.5 miles.

If you haven't seen Disappearing Creek, add a quarter mile side trip to see the steep-sided canyon where Camp Branch vanishes into a swallet. Hiking the full Disappearing Creek Loop adds another half mile. This trail also leads to the other fork of the Camp Branch Trail back to the trailhead.

Past the junction is an overlook facing a narrow natural bridge near the river's edge. Camp Branch emerges as a spring in the Suwannee River within view, but you can only see it flowing when the river is low. The footpath enters a corridor of saw palmetto in the bluff forest, passing Crooked Branch Ranch and a privately owned camping shelter before reaching Crooked Branch campsite at 3.1 miles. After the trail crosses the creek on a bridge and dips near river level, it's time to ascend.

From the base of Devil's Mountain, it's usually slippery up to the top. The ascent is steeply pitched, rising through the bluff forest and its devil's walkingsticks (*Aralia spinosa*) that grow along the slopes, giving this hill its name. A fern-lined chasm with a trickle of seepage springs just below the crest is called Greasy Gully for a reason. Beware of slipping off the hill in the mud. Views extend across the river from the bluffs.

The high point at 128 feet, Devil's Mountain is relatively flat on top. In winter, it's obvious just how low the bluffs are on the south side of the river. It's all downhill from here, but far from flat. Starting at 3.4 miles, the descent is nowhere near as steep as the ascent but provides panoramas across the bluff forest on the way down to a gully with a clear sand-bottomed stream flowing through it, a good water source. Like this sandy stream, most of the waterways crossed along the remainder of this hike aren't bridged. Their drainages carved deep, often steep ravines to clamber in and out of.

Reaching the river bluffs after the next ravine, walk atop deposited sand that drops sharply into the river below.

A tributary flows between palmettos in the next low basin. Climb up to a flat, scrubby area where the footpath is edged with moss and lichens. Periodic flooding deposited deep sand along the next riverbank. Plowing through deep sand in spots, the footpath clings to its sharp vertical pitch as sidehill.

Reenter the bluff forest. After 4.2 miles, make a sharp turn at a horseshoe bend in the bluff, the river both in front of and in back of you. Continue along high forested bluffs with views between the trees before a gentle descent a half mile later to a showy and broad, crescent-shaped beach, a nice spot for a break. Turning away from the river, tackle a gully where tannic waters flow between the cypress knees, a half-log bridge providing passage.

It's a steep descent into another gully at 5.3 miles where water sometimes rushes through the bottom, with a sometimes slippery scramble to climb back out of it. Return to high sand bluffs where wild azalea bloom in spring, walking under a low canopy of sparkleberry and rusty lyonia. The footpath occasionally winds into old river channels behind the bluffs. A handful of river

Stream crossing north of Devil's Mountain

views open up from level spots before trail and river part ways at a view of a river bend.

Ascend into a bluff forest on the worn footpath, swarms of saw palmetto defining the corridor wherever it drops through swales. Draped in streamers of Spanish moss, the low canopy changes as you gain more elevation, becoming a tunnel of scrub oaks at 6.7 miles decorated with a curious gray-green lichen called old man's beard. Shorter and stiffer than Spanish moss, it infuses this passageway with an eerie glow. An ephemeral waterway rushes through the low spot of the next palmetto-dense swale.

Emerge from the forest past a very old wooden Florida Trail sign into a sun-drenched power line easement. Past a bluff a few steps off the trail with a very nice view of the shoreline of Suwannee Rivers, the well-defined footpath broadens. At 7.1 miles, an old concrete bridge formerly used by US 129 marks the end of this segment.

Climb the steep blue-blazed trail and turn left to cross the old highway bridge, now covered in colorful graffiti. Some call it the "Hippy Bridge" for the spontaneous and ever-changing artwork by festivalgoers attending concerts nearby, but it has a more sinister past as the site of the 1944 murder of fifteen-year-old Willie James Howard. The young black man's "crime" was to send a card signed with affection to the daughter of a local state legislator.

On the south shore, a left on the blue blaze leads to Suwannee Springs. Straight ahead, the road leads to US 129 at the agricultural check station across from Spirit of the Suwannee Music Park. Making a left, follow the trail to the recreation area, where a historic spring house still surrounds the outflow of Suwannee Springs to the river.

Hotels adjoined the springs in the 1830s and after 1880 up until 1925, drawing visitors seeking to rejuvenate their health in the slightly sulfuric waters. You can still "take the waters" with a brisk swim in the spring or from a white sand beach along the river. Reaching the parking area adjoining the spring, complete a 7.9-mile hike.

Holton Spring

36. Holton Creek

8.9 MILES | HOLTON CREEK WMA, LIVE OAK

Crossing an unusual wonderland where yawning sinkholes and giant trees provide both depth and height to undulating terrain, this fascinating piece of the Florida Trail leads to showy Holton Spring, spilling fast-moving Holton Creek into a rugged landscape shaped by karst.

Overview

Every time we visit Holton Creek, another surprise awaits. On one of the earliest trips backpacking this segment, it was the fog rising up and out of the spring basin on a cool winter morning. A day hike in spring after heavy rains highlighted uncommon plants like green dragon and trillium as well as the half-hidden forms of turpentine collecting basins. An expedition to find Florida's largest cypress tree led us to two outstanding specimens in the bottom of a sinkhole. Any time of year, the amenities of Holton Creek River Camp are cause for applause.

Using a well-worn footpath, this round-trip hike leads you under enormous trees and around the edges of deep sinkholes. Although only a small part of this hike is along the Suwannee River, the richly forested landscape offers up its own delights.

Trip Planning / Land Manager

See Suwannee. Leashed dogs are welcome. It is perpetually humid here. Poison ivy grows profusely, swarming across the forest floor and up tree trunks. Cell phones don't work well. If you're using yours to navigate to the trailhead, lock in directions before leaving Live Oak.

Check river levels prior to hiking and don't hike here when the Suwannee or Alapaha are at flood stage. Floodwaters can rise from below into the crevices and sinkholes along the trail. Don't hike into water—turn around. Research hunt dates for Holton Creek WMA and wear bright orange if you hike during hunting season.

Built as one of a series of riverside campsites for paddlers on the Suwannee River Wilderness Trail, Holton Creek River Camp is plush by backpacker standards, a destination campsite. It has screened pavilions for camping as well as tent sites, restrooms with flush toilets and hot showers, and is perched on a curve along the river with a sandy beach and canoe rentals. Call 800-326-3521 to make a reservation; a camping fee is charged and a camp host is on duty. Other primitive campsites are free. At all campsites, secure your food from bears.

Directions

From Interstate 10 exit 283 for Live Oak, drive north along US 129 for 4 miles to CR 132, Stagecoach Rd. Take CR 132 west to CR 249. Continue north along CR 249, crossing the Suwannee River at Gibson Park. Take the first right past the agricultural check station and drive a little over a mile to the Holton Creek sign on the right. A narrow dirt road leads to Holton Creek trailhead [30.44342, -83.076553] at the WMA gate.

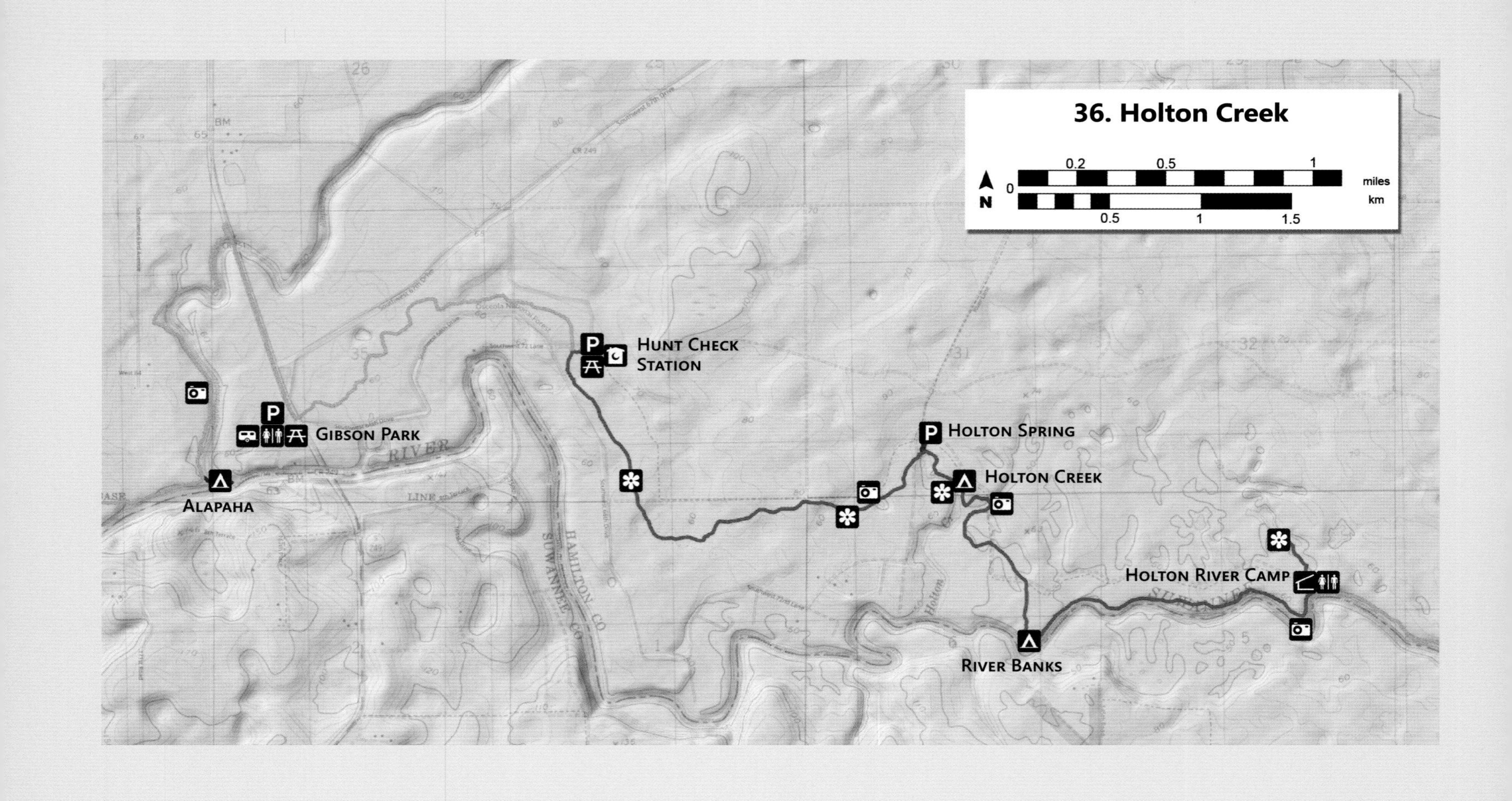
36. Holton Creek
0
0.2
0.5
1
miles
0.5
1
1.5
km
N
Hunt Check Station
Gibson Park
River
Alapaha
Hamilton Co
Suwannee Co
Holton Spring
Holton Creek
Holton River Camp
River Banks

Options

All three trailheads at Holton Creek WMA are along a narrow, sometimes-rough access road roughly paralleling the Florida Trail. It's possible to stage vehicles along it, but easier to make a round trip from the main trailhead at the hunt check station at the gate, which has picnic tables and a portable toilet. A round trip to Holton Spring is 4 miles.

The first trailhead inside the gates is near Holton Spring [30.4389, -83.057213], past the worst bumps, puddles, and low spots of the access road. The small River Camp trailhead [30.43181, -83.036903] is at the end of the road. For a 4.2-mile linear hike, leave a vehicle at the hunt check station to hike toward from River Camp. Vehicles cannot be left overnight at these trailheads. Backpackers, start at Gibson Park [30.438841, -83.093002] off CR 751. It has a large paved parking area and a riverfront campground. Let the camp host know you're parking overnight. Cross CR 751 behind the agricultural check station to hike into Holton Creek WMA. It's an 11.2-mile round trip from Gibson Park to River Camp, a fun family overnighter.

Hike

The "Entering 100 Year Floodplain" sign on the fence may give you pause, since the Suwannee River is nowhere to be seen. But beneath the leaf litter of this forest floor, the bedrock is porous. Water oozes up from below. You'll see it pool in unexpected places as you walk this section of the trail. Follow a short blue-blazed connector from the trailhead under magnolias and oaks to reach the Florida Trail at a T intersection. Turn left.

Very little sunlight filters through the bluff forest canopy. Some of the oaks are quite old and stout, and a few sport shaggy bark. Giant grapevines dangle from overhead limbs and ivy carpets the forest floor. Dozens of straight-angled shapes poke out of the leaf litter, crumpled metal basins that are curious reminders of the past. Older pines in this forest bear the scars of where they were cut by an axe and the basin mounted to collect pine sap to make turpentine.

Stepping over a log, note the profusion of plants. Poison ivy thrives, but so does Virginia creeper and green dragon. Yucca grows in open spots. Towering Florida dogwood trees rain soft white petals across the footpath in spring. After the trail crosses two forest roads near the end of the first mile, the character of the forest changes.

Grass sprouts beneath a dense collection of younger trees. The first of several sinkholes reflects the forest canopy in a pool of water. Drawing close to the ribbon of access road, signposts and fence and gate to the left, descend into a lush bluff forest. The landscape undulates downhill to the right. Slender fronds of bluestem palms waggle along the footpath. A rivulet vanishes into a deep cleft in the earth, its sinkhole bottom out of sight.

The round gleam of green at 1.7 miles is Green Sink, a karst window exposing the water table. A large clearing beyond it was once used for camping. Past the sink, the forest floor drops off in many directions, plunging into crevices and sinkholes. At a stand of bamboo, reach the rim of Holton Spring, the trail cir-

Trailside sinkhole

cling it on a high rocky bluff with a precipitous drop-off. Large and clear, the spring reflects the sky on its placid surface. It forms Holton Creek, up to 500 cubic feet of water per second creating a powerful natural current for this Suwannee tributary.

Circling the bluffs, pass a water monitoring station and reach a blue-blazed side trail to Holton Spring trailhead at 1.9 miles. Edging from the bluffs to avoid their erosion, the footpath slips into the forest and loses elevation among more bluestem palms wagging in the slightest breeze. The approach at spring level is an unmarked path to the water's edge amid clusters of atamasco lilies. While the beach is tempting to walk on, it's mucky. The spring outflow pours past this peninsula.

Turning away from the spring, follow Holton Creek downstream. Worn side paths lead to the creek's mucky edge. One ancient cypress towers from the middle of the creek within view of a large flat area, the former Holton Creek campsite. Leaving the creek, make a sharp left and cross a natural causeway between two long, thin sinkholes. Join the access road briefly to circle them at 2.4 miles, the footpath resuming on the opposite side of the sinks. The trail parts ways with Holton Creek soon after. Cross the access road at the base of an enormous swamp chestnut oak.

Round a sinkhole edged by cypress knees and cross the road one last time, reaching the Suwannee River bluffs. A small peninsula at 3 miles defines River Banks campsite, a beauty spot with its own little beach. Hugging river bluffs for the remainder of the hike, the trail provides views across the Suwannee. This well-shaded route reaches the next peninsula with a sandy bluff at Holton Creek River Camp. Canoes are stacked by the river for use. The Florida Trail goes right past the screened shelters and restrooms at 4.2 miles.

This is the far end of the round-trip hike, but one more side trip is a must: a walk to the Guardian Cypress. A blue-blazed trail connects the trailhead at the end of the access road into another stretch of undulating karst terrain, circling several large sinkholes. It's a quarter mile to the rim of the big sinkhole where the Florida champion bald cypress rises 84 feet from the bottom. From above it may not seem impressive, but if the sinkhole is dry, a careful descent to the base of the tree puts everything in perspective—it's more than 46 feet around.

After marveling at these giants of the forest, return the same way you hiked to River Camp to complete an 8.9-mile round trip. Or walk the access road to your vehicle for a different perspective on the forest, a 7.7-mile loop.

At the base of the Guardian Cypress

Grandfather oak, Ellaville Tract

37. Ellaville to Black Tract

6.8 MILES | TWIN RIVERS STATE FOREST, MADISON

Starting near the confluence of the Withlacoochee and Suwannee Rivers, this segment of the Florida Trail follows river bluffs from a ghost town through an old-growth oak forest battered by Hurricane Idalia in 2023.

Overview

A bustling timber town of more than a thousand people, Ellaville centered around Florida's largest sawmill, established immediately after the Civil War by George Franklin Drew. A newly built railroad spanned to the town of Columbus across the river. Steamboats navigated the Suwannee to the docks. A successful businessman, Drew was elected Florida's governor in 1876. After his term, he returned to Ellaville and his timber business. Ellaville thrived for decades, but the bottom fell out—as it always does—once the loggers felled the old-growth pine and cypress along the river basins. Having developed no other industry, Ellaville and Columbus faded away as residents sought jobs elsewhere. Ellaville's post office closed in 1942.

Tracing the flow of the Suwannee downriver through Twin Rivers State Forest from the DeSoto Annex of Suwannee River State Park, the Florida Trail connects the remnants of Ellaville with a walk along the forested bluffs and side channels of the Suwannee, ending at the Black Tract trailhead near a pioneer cemetery.

Trip Planning

See Suwannee. Leashed dogs are welcome. The trail from Coopers Bluff to the southern tip of the Ellaville Trail is shared with off-road cyclists and equestrians. Research hunt dates for Twin Rivers State Forest before hiking and wear bright orange if you hike during hunting season.

Check river levels prior to hiking. The Suwannee won't just swamp the trail in flood stage, but floodwaters also can rise from crevices and sinkholes along the trail, making hiking dangerous. If there is water across the trail, turn around.

For your safety, don't leave cars overnight at trailheads along this section. Backpackers should park behind the gates of Suwannee River State Park and use its connector trail to reach the Florida Trail across the old US 90 bridge. There is a fee for parking at the state park.

Land Managers

Suwannee River State Park
3631 201st Path, Live Oak FL 32060
386-362-2746
floridastateparks.org

Twin Rivers State Forest
3019 McCulley Farm Rd, Jasper FL 32052
386-208-1460
fdacs.gov

Directions

From Interstate 10 westbound, use exit 275, Live Oak/Lee. Eastbound, use exit 262 at Lee, following CR 255 north several miles to US 90. Either way, it's close to 8 miles to where US 90 and the Suwannee River meet.

To leave a vehicle at the end of this hike, turn south onto River Rd on the west side of the river. Drive 4.2 miles.

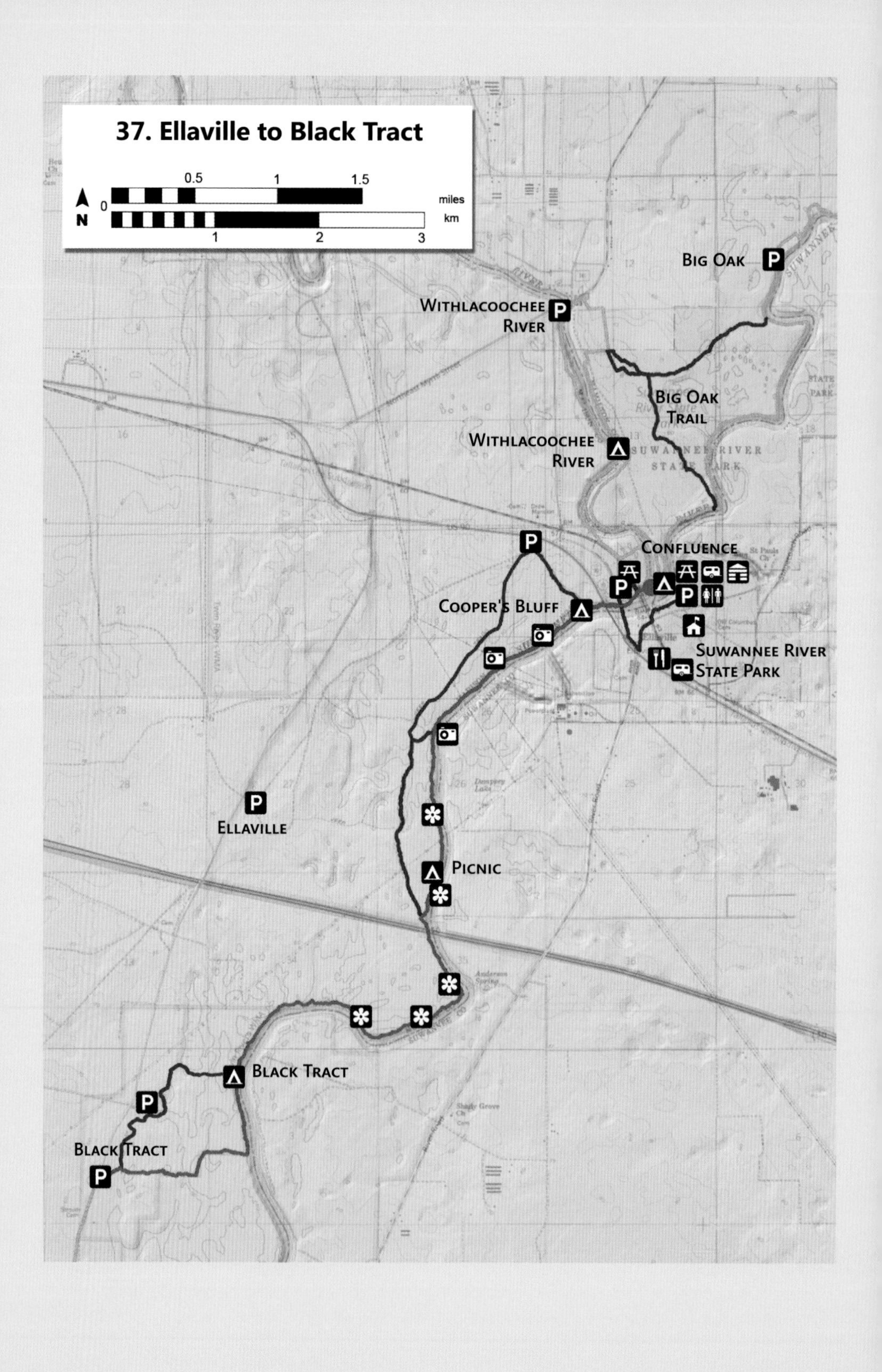

37. Ellaville to Black Tract
0.5
1
1.5
0
miles
N
km
1
2
3
Big Oak
Withlacoochee
River
Big Oak
Trail
Withlacoochee
River
Confluence
Cooper's Bluff
Suwannee River
State Park
Ellaville
Picnic
Black Tract
Black Tract

Past Interstate 10, River Rd turns to a graded dirt road. Look for an FNST sign and a small parking area for Black Tract [30.337395, -83.226959] on the left under a large oak tree. Drive back up River Rd to US 90 and turn right.

Immediately after passing a trailhead on the right, make a left onto old US 90. Follow it to a dead end at Suwannee River State Park Annex [30.386771, -83.175193]. The old wayside park provides access to the Florida Trail and the Ellaville Trail on the south side of US 90.

Options

The trail system at Twin Rivers State Forest interconnects with the trails of Suwannee River State Park on the east side of the river using a 0.9-mile blazed connector trail across the old US 90 bridge. With a shaded campground and cabins, the park makes a great base camp to explore all of the trails in this area, starting with its Suwannee River Trail near the campground.

One of the park's more popular trails is the Big Oak Trail, a 12.5-mile round trip and loop from the ranger station. Signposts follow the blue-blazed connector to DeSoto Annex. Join the Florida Trail southbound (compass north) to CR 141 and cross the Withlacoochee River on the highway bridge. On the east side of the river, the Big Oak Trail loops around a peninsula where the two rivers meet. The riverside walk is also the orange-blazed Florida Trail. Backpackers can camp at Confluence campsite at the tip of the peninsula, but you will hear passing trains.

The 5-mile Ellaville Trail loop is part of Florida State Forests' Trailwalker program. Walk from DeSoto Annex to Cooper's Bluff to hop on it. Following the Florida Trail from Cooper's Bluff to just shy of Interstate 10, it returns along yellow-blazed forest roads, passing through the Ellaville Trailwalker trailhead [30.389759, -83.183403] off US 90. Similarly, the yellow-blazed 3.1-mile Black Tract Loop passes through the main Black Tract trailhead [30.344046, -83.223434] off River Rd but also starts 0.2 miles in from the Florida Trail trailhead. It uses the Florida Trail past Black Tract campsite for the riverside part of its loop.

Round-trip hikes are easy from DeSoto Annex Picnic Area. Upriver to Withlacoochee River campsite is a 3-mile round trip through the ruins of Ellaville, largely engulfed by the forest. Downriver, turn around at the picnic table north of the second Ellaville Trail junction for 5 miles. Or continue along the river bluffs to Black Tract campsite and return for 10.2 miles.

Hike

At DeSoto Annex trailhead, skirt around the gate and follow the blue-blazed forest road, passing by where the two-story Drew Mansion once stood, the ruins now reclaimed by nature. Blue blazes meet orange in front of the railroad tracks that once served Ellaville. Walk through the underpass to a kiosk with historical information, including a map of where the mansion and other buildings stood. Ellaville stretched north along the Withlacoochee River from this point. The remains of foundations and some of the docks can be seen on a hike upriver.

Take the side trail downhill in front of the kiosk to visit Suwannacoochee

Spring. A rock wall divides the small, deep spring from the Suwannee River's flow. Return to the kiosk and backtrack to the junction on the other side of the railroad underpass, starting your downriver hike at 0.3 miles. Turn left to follow the orange blazes along the riverfront of the old wayside park. Connector trails lead uphill past the picnic tables to the trailhead.

Pass beneath the old US 90 bridge. A chimney stands trailside amid the ruins of a home. In the 1960s, a small roadside attraction drew tourists in with alligators on display, and its legacy is the dense bamboo thicket in this river bluff forest. Walk under the US 90 bridge. A large clearing under the pines opens up at 0.7 miles at Cooper's Bluff, the first junction with the Ellaville Trail. A bench overlooks the river. The campsite has a roofed picnic shelter and an ample flat area for pitching tents. Over a small rise past the campsite, a steep trail descends to the river's edge for filtering water. Walk under a set of high-tension power lines, the first of several spanning overhead from a power plant on the east side of the river.

River views open up as the trail sticks close to the bluff. The next set of power lines intrudes at 1.3 miles. Join a corridor lined with saw palmetto into a swale of an old river channel, curving and descending into another floodplain where ancient oaks reach for the sky. Worn paths lead up the bluff to river overlooks. Walk through a stand of very old oaks and cross a grassy power line easement. Enter a much denser forest. A sinkhole yawns beneath a bower of massive live oaks. Drop through an old side channel which can get soggy inside. Boulders emerge from a depression; karst bedrock is close to the surface here.

Circling a cove where anglers can reach the river from a forest road, pass a midpoint junction with the Ellaville Trail at 1.8 miles. A warning sign tells horses and bicycles to stay off the Florida Trail. Rejoin the river bluffs for more great views of the Suwannee. Native bamboo grows in clumps. Sinkholes gape below the trees. One immense live oak leans over the river from the bluffs. Easily centuries old, ancient trees are the norm in this stretch of forest. Perhaps the timber company's removal of the tall "yellow pine" for the Ellaville sawmill helped the oaks and hickories attain these sizes.

Beyond a final power line easement at 2.5 miles, continue through a sparse bluff forest with towering oak trees. A quarter mile later, a picnic table provides a scenic perch high above the river, with large live oaks forming the forest canopy. The footpath joins an old river channel behind the bluffs. A waterway flows between cypress knees from a swamp on a terrace.

Climbing uphill, reach the final junction with the Ellaville Trail at 3 miles. Descend to a grassy underpass beneath Interstate 10. Traffic noise echoes up and down the river basin. Join a forest road briefly. A double blaze points left to a footpath into the hardwood forest. Return to the bluffs for a new array of river views, including a grassy clearing at 3.4 miles across the river from Anderson Springs.

Even in winter, saw palmetto and the shiny green leaves of American holly and Southern magnolia brighten up this stretch on a high bluff above an elbow in the Suwannee. Ancient oaks make up an impressive forest canopy, but the oaks aren't the only giants here. With smaller, scrubbier-looking needles and cones than loblolly pines, spruce pines also tower. Most of the big trees adjoin former river channels in swales between the footpath and the rest of the forest.

After a small hill is a rare peek at a home on the far shore. It's a steep drop from this high bluff to the river. The forest thins near a property boundary with a private landowner at 4.7 miles. Reach a hitching post at a blue-blazed equestrian trail. Join it for a quarter mile before returning to the river bluffs. Red and yellow blazes appear at this junction, the yellow marking where the Black Tract Loop joins the Florida Trail. Past a thicket of holly, cross a stream bed plunging toward river level. Emerge into a large clearing for Black Tract campsite at 5.3 miles.

Adjoining a forest road that vehicles can access, this designated campsite is a large flat area on the bluff with picnic tables and a brick-lined fire ring. A rough path leads to the rocky rim of the river, where a spring bubbles beneath limestone boulders. Pass the picnic tables and continue the walk along the bluff with views to the far shore. The trunk of a live oak arches overhead before you reach a sinkhole forming beneath the base of several trees.

At 5.7 miles the trail turns due west, leaving the river bluffs for the last time. Cross the blue-blazed equestrian trail twice more and meander through the dappled shade of pine flatwoods restored from pine plantation. The final equestrian trail crossing is at 6.4 miles. Within a quarter mile, a "Black Tract Loop" sign adjoins a double yellow blaze under the pines. Stay on the orange blazes to reach the trailhead at 6.8 miles.

The Florida Trail joins River Rd to connect to the Mill Creek Tract of Twin Rivers State Forest downriver. Stroud Cemetery is a quarter mile along the orange blazes. Established after the Civil War, it includes more than a dozen burials. Georgia native James Stroud was an early settler in Madison County. One of his family members ran a hotel in Madison back when Ellaville was in its prime.

Suwannee River at Black Tract camp

Aucilla River

38. Aucilla River and Sinks

14.7 MILES | AUCILLA WMA, AUCILLA

Threading through a wonderland of unusual geologic features, the Aucilla section of the Florida Trail is one of the finest hikes in the National Scenic Trail system.

Overview

Tumbling through limestone boulders edged by cypress knees, the Aucilla River races toward the Gulf of Mexico as the Florida Trail follows it through a fascinating landscape. Swallowed whole at a river sink called the Vortex, the river vanishes into a karst plain topped by a primordial forest. The ghosts of antiquity are strong at the earliest known site of human occupation in the southeastern United States, where pre-Clovis peoples settled when the river was more than a hundred miles from the coast. Ripples reflect against pockmarked limestone walls where the flowing river appears briefly at the bottom of yawning sinkholes. Since 1902, archaeologists have removed a treasure trove of artifacts from these sinks, including the oldest known work of art in the Americas, a carved ivory tusk. Finds in this century included a double-edged stone knife along with the tusk it cleaved from a mastodon skull. With dense palm fronds obscuring sudden drop-offs, narrow natural bridges, burrow-like caves, karst windows, and boulders, hiking along the Aucilla is quite an adventure.

Trip Planning

Built in 1983, this trail segment is hiking only and has three designated campsites. The path is well worn. Be cautious of stepping off it: deep pits used to trap mastodons adjoin the footpath. Vegetation grows riotously in this humid environment. If you leave the trail, you may have a hard time finding it again. While leashed dogs are welcome, unless you can tightly control your pet you shouldn't bring them here. The same goes for small children.

Check river levels before hiking: see water.weather.gov station LAMF1. This is a very dangerous area when the Aucilla River floods, as the river rises through the porous limestone. When flooded, it's impossible to determine the footpath from the deep holes around it. Don't wade along this trail—turn back if it's under water.

Research hunting seasons for Aucilla WMA and wear bright orange if you hike during hunting season. A mile of trail between the Vortex and Long Sink (including Goose Pasture trailhead) is posted year-round as a no-hunting zone. Closed during fall deer hunting season, Goose Pasture is a free, no-frills campground 2.6 miles west on the Wacissa River.

Compass and trail directions are exact opposites along this section. A southbound hike leads north along the Aucilla River. A northbound hike leads to the south end of the Aucilla Sinks. We use compass directions in the hike description for that reason.

Land Manager

Suwannee River Water Management District
9225 CR 49, Live Oak FL 32060
386-362-1001
mysuwanneeriver.com

Directions

Drive east along US 98 from Newport for 16 miles, crossing the Aucilla River and passing JR's Aucilla River Store. Turn left onto Powell Hammock Grade and drive north for 4.3 miles. The pavement ends but the road keeps going. Pass a sign for Aucilla WMA on the left. The next major left is Goose Pasture Rd. Goose Pasture trailhead [30.20092, -83.92469] is 1.1 miles west on the right, room for a few cars. Use caution: puddles on this dirt road may be deep.

An alternative access point is a clearing at Longsuffering Road [30.185217, -83.9374] via the unmarked road in front of the Aucilla WMA sign, depending on the condition of that road. The Florida Trail exits Aucilla Sinks 0.9 miles west of Powell Hammock Grade along this road. Use this as a place to drop a vehicle to hike to, or to hike compass north into Aucilla Sinks. If you have a high-clearance vehicle, consult a map of Aucilla WMA to find other places to access the Aucilla River via side roads off Powell Hammock Grade. We have seen trucks at River Bend and several other numbered river access roads.

The northernmost access point for this section is along CR 14 [30.255878, -83.863892] south of Lamont off US 27 east of Tallahassee. In the middle of private timberlands, it can only be used as a drop-off or pickup point. The land is leased to a hunt club. Because of ongoing logging, it can be difficult to follow the blazes the 2.2 miles it takes to reach Upper Aucilla Camp.

Options

As the trail passes through private timberlands under a year-round hunting lease, only section or thru-hikers will want to walk in from CR 14 for a 9.7-mile linear hike along the Aucilla River to Goose Pasture Rd, or 13.7 miles to Long Suffering Rd. Day hikers and backpackers should otherwise round trip from Goose Pasture Rd to whichever feature is of interest. Compass north along the Aucilla River, worthy destinations are River Bend (4.2 miles), Aucilla River Rapids (9.6 miles) and Upper Aucilla Camp (14.4 miles). Compass south into Aucilla Sinks, a 5.8-mile round trip to Twin Sinks provides the best of this unusual landscape. The most unusual sinks are an easy walk from Goose Pasture trailhead. It's a 1.2-mile round trip to the solution hole cave near Long Sink, and only a 0.8-mile round trip to the Vortex, where the Aucilla River vanishes underground in a swirl of debris.

Hike

While the Aucilla section is a linear 14.7 miles between CR 14 and Powell Hammock Grade, the round-trip mileage for these two hikes totals 22.4 miles.

Aucilla Sinks

Follow the orange blazes compass south into the bluff forest to the right of the trail kiosk on Goose Pasture Rd. Sinkholes adjoin both sides of the trail. Sometimes the water flow is obvious in

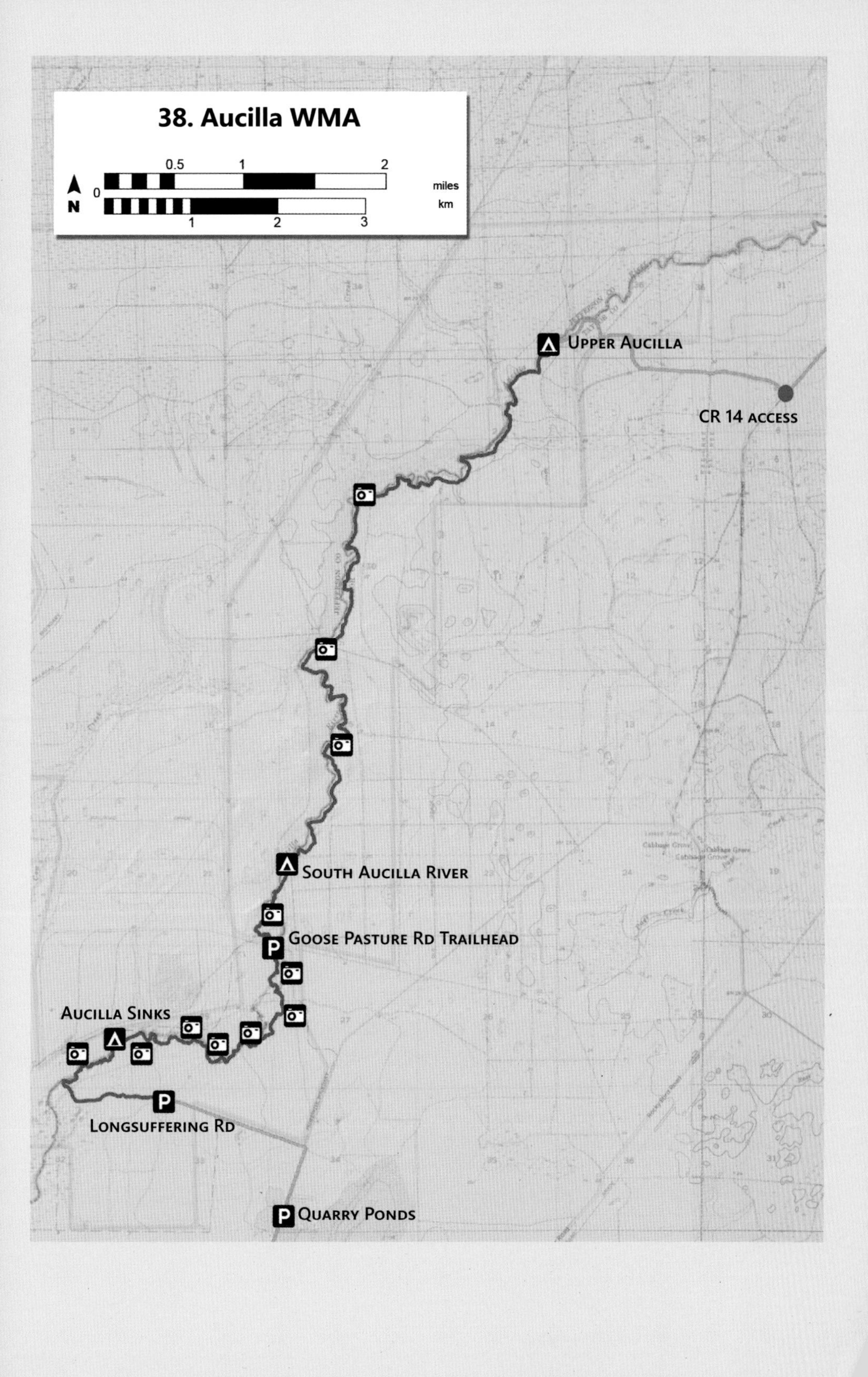
38. Aucilla WMA
0
0.5
1
2
miles
km
N
1
2
3
Upper Aucilla
CR 14 access
South Aucilla River
Goose Pasture Rd Trailhead
Aucilla Sinks
Longsuffering Rd
Quarry Ponds

Breakdown Sinks

the sinkhole on the left on the approach to Breakdown Sinks. The trail snakes between a long, linear deep gash in the earth on the left and a series of newer sinkholes forming on the right. A footbridge spans a crevice at the north end of these sinks. Cross a forest road into a dense bluff forest a half mile in. Sinkholes slice through the forest floor.

In another quarter mile reach the edge of Long Sink, a linear sinkhole that looks like a section of the river. It is, but it has a distinct beginning and end, which makes it a sinkhole. Traverse a natural bridge—a slender slice of rock between two sinkholes—and two footbridges. After circling a pair of large sinkholes, look for a solution hole cave shaped like it was bored into the earth by some prehistoric giant armadillo.

The trail returns to the rim of Long Sink. Passing Sunshine Sink and Frink Sink in quick succession, cross a forest road at 1.1 miles. There is a nice view of a linear sinkhole with caves at water level on its far shore. It, like many of the other sinks coming up, looks like a river basin.

We compared the shape of the sinks to the original 1980s map of the trail to guess at their names. The large sinkhole with a pine forest on its far shore is likely Long Suffering Sink at 1.7 miles, with a gently sloped bank to the water's edge. Beyond a forest road where a pine tree is swallowing a small FNST sign, the next sink may be Kitchen Sink since it's perfectly round. Colorful fungi like yellow-tipped coral and jelly leaf thrive in the leaf litter on the forest floor. Cracks and crevices in the karst are half-hidden by palm fronds.

Round a deep sink on the left. A short blue blaze at 2.4 miles ends at Aucilla Sinks Camp, a small designated campsite with a bench and a fire ring. Within sight of the next forest road, make a sharp left to parallel it, passing a series of sinkholes before circling a broad, shallow basin with cypress trees in the middle. Cross the forest road and a sharp left guides the trail around Sarasinks, a showy area with a natural bridge between two smaller sinks. The footpath is right along their rim. At the next long sink, there's a "sink inside the sink" on the right with a rock bluff inside it. It's an unusual geologic formation we think is Twin Sinks at 2.9 miles.

By 3.2 miles, turn away from the sinks to slip between boulders placed to keep vehicles out of the fragile karst. Cross a dirt road to join a forest road briefly on the other side. Make a sharp left. Bluestem palm thrives in the understory of this lush forest beneath tall oaks and cabbage palms. Dip through two swales, sinkholes-in-training above where the river runs underground.

The last of the Aucilla Sinks is on the right where you emerge onto a forest road at 4 miles. A beaten path provides a look from its rim into the sink. Beyond it is a clearing where several forest roads meet at Longsuffering Rd. Proceed to the vehicle you left in the clearing to finish a linear hike or backtrack to Goose Pasture Rd for an 8-mile round trip.

Aucilla River

Walk west briefly along Goose Pasture Rd to circle Roadside Sink, a steep drop into the aquifer. Turn right to follow orange blazes compass north into a lush bluff forest where unusual sinks abound. Shaped like a crescent moon, Half Moon Sink has water flowing through its bottom. Surrounded by chunky boulders, Overflow Sink mirrors the sky, a portal into another world.

Beneath a canopy formed by ancient trees, approach the Vortex at 0.4 miles. Here, the entire Aucilla River gets sucked into a swallet. A perpetual whirlpool of debris on its surface is choked with logs, leaves, and trash that floated downriver. Circling the Vortex, turn to parallel the eastern bluffs of the Aucilla upriver. Pass a land management boundary sign at the end of the no-hunting zone. For the next quarter mile, enjoy expansive river views.

A bench above a side channel and a sign mark South Aucilla River Camp at 0.8 miles. The only flat ground for tenting is inside the side channel below, an interesting perspective near water level. At RA (River Access Road) 34, which ends atop this bluff, cross a limerock road. Views open up again, deeply shaded by bluff forest.

Reach River Bend at 2.1 miles, a beauty spot with a boat launch at the end of RA 36 and a rope swing from a large flat rock. Car campers are often here on weekends. Scramble through a deep cut in the bluffs in another mile, with an intermittent tributary trickling through it. Climb out of the cut to another fabulous view across the river.

A railroad trestle once crossed the Aucilla River at Burnt Bridge, 3.4 miles into the hike. The concrete abutment remains, a sheer drop to the water below. From its name and location, it's highly likely this is the bridge a Union sympathizer set on fire near the end of the Civil War while a train was crossing it.

Continue along the high bluffs. A cove forms off the main flow of the river, a whirlpool of waters pouring through it. Dark tannic waters surround an island in the river. Glimpse riffles of rapids through dense vegetation as the sound of rushing water echoes through the forest. Emerge on a rocky bluff at 4.8 miles and scramble through the cut to the water's edge for the showy display of Aucilla River Rapids. The river churns and bubbles in a rootbeer-colored froth

Overflow Sink

between limestone boulders edged by cypress knees. It's such an unusual and compelling sight that you'll want to linger.

North of a road paved with crushed limestone, the trail passes one final sinkhole nearly obscured by the forest. Cross RA 41, the northernmost river access road inside Aucilla WMA. Circle a cypress swamp with towering trees a mile north of the rapids. In winter, this is a "rainbow swamp." When the trees are bare and the angle of sunlight is just right, pastel hues caused by the oils from the cypress create a subtle rainbow across the swamp's surface.

Logs provide a tricky bridge over a deceptively deep tributary at 6.2 miles. Scramble through several deep dips along the river's edge before rounding a second cypress swamp with remarkably large trees. The footpath levels out to a gentle walk through a deciduous forest. Reach Upper Aucilla Camp at 7.2 miles, a pleasantly situated clearing near the river with easy access for filtering water.

Use Upper Aucilla Camp as your turnaround point for a 14.4-mile day hike or overnighter. The Florida Trail continues compass north and east another 2.5 miles to CR 14 but is on forest roads across private land leased to hunters year-round. Don't tackle the linear hike unless you're a Florida Trail Association member and dressed in orange.

Stoney Bayou

St. Marks National Wildlife Refuge

47.3 MILES | WAKULLA AND JEFFERSON COUNTIES

Protecting 70,000 acres in the Big Bend, St. Marks National Wildlife Refuge has one of Florida's longest wild shorelines, more than 43 miles across three counties. Edging a rich estuary along the shallows of the Gulf of Mexico, it is affected by tides, fed by major rivers, and fringed by coastal pine forests and palm hammocks. Established in 1931 to protect migratory birds, the refuge has vast impoundments built by the Civilian Conservation Corps.

Overview

Passing through two federally designated wilderness areas, the Florida Trail spans the full width of the refuge. Although many miles follow levees and forest roads, there are spectacular coastal panoramas visible nowhere else along Florida's Big Bend. Forested portions of the trail are deeply shaded and weave through many coastal swamps, sometimes plunging right into them. Other delights are dense palm hammocks, healthy longleaf pine savannas, and a large spring.

Trailheads

The Florida Trail runs compass east to west across the refuge, broken into two by the St. Marks River. Trailheads generally have only enough space for a few cars. South to north, they include the following.

0.0 AUCILLA WMA
Room for a couple of cars off Aucilla Small Game Rd.

13.4 LIGHTHOUSE RD EAST*
Limited roadside parking. Fee.

13.8 LIGHTHOUSE RD WEST*
Limited roadside parking. Fee.

15.4 VISITOR CENTER*
Paved day-use parking, 0.9-mile blue blaze to trail. Fee.

19.4 ST. MARKS
Downtown parking lot adjoining trail.

22.2 COASTAL TRAIL
Bike path parking area off US 98.

24.7 THOMPSON HOUSE
Small dirt trailhead off US 98 west of the Wakulla River.

28.9 WAKULLA*
Small dirt trailhead at Wakulla Beach Rd.

34.7 SPRING CREEK
Small grassy trailhead along Spring Creek Hwy.

44.0 PURIFY BAY*
Tiny dirt trailhead down long dirt road that can flood.

47.3 CARRAWAY CUTOFF*
Small lot off dirt road off US 319 between Medart and Sopchoppy.

**Day use parking only.*

Camping

Backpackers must obtain a permit in advance, cross the refuge in one trip, and use designated campsites. A small camping fee applies. Because of the ongoing closure at Spring Creek, you can't reach Marsh Point campsite without backtracking; the 5-mile bypass roadwalk skips it entirely.

4.2 PINHOOK RIVER
Large clearing in coastal hammock near Pinhook River. Benches.

10.3 RING DIKE
Small open flat spots with the best view from a tent on the Florida Trail.

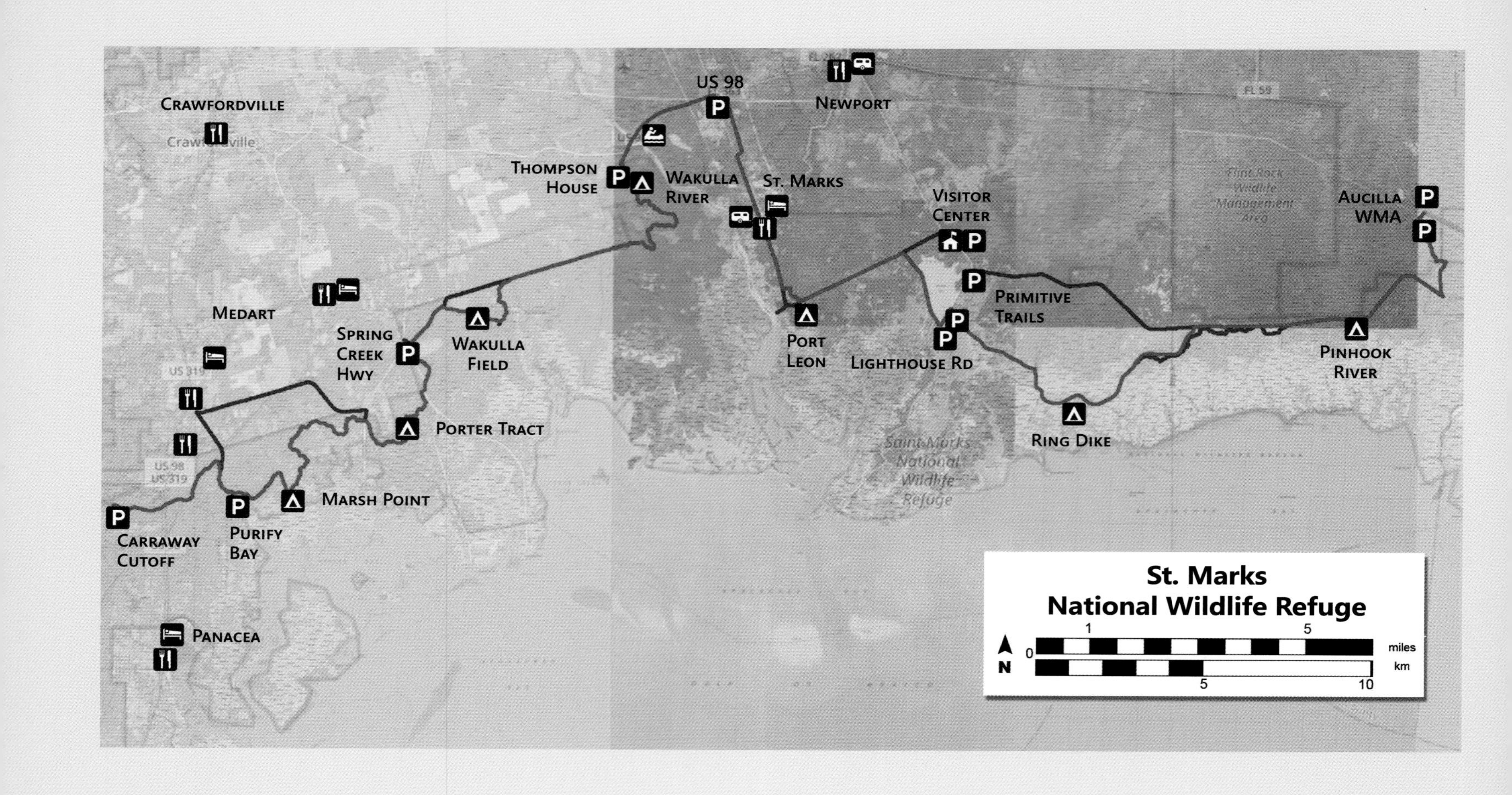
St. Marks
National Wildlife Refuge
Crawfordville
Medart
Spring Creek Hwy
Wakulla Field
Porter Tract
Marsh Point
Purify Bay
Carraway Cutoff
Panacea
Thompson House
Wakulla River
US 98
Newport
St. Marks
Port Leon
Visitor Center
Lighthouse Rd
Primitive Trails
Ring Dike
Pinhook River
Aucilla WMA
Flint Rock Wildlife Management Area
Saint Marks National Wildlife Refuge
US 319
US 98
FL 59
N
0
1
5
miles
km
5
10

17.5 PORT LEON
Ample clearing in a pine forest with benches and fire ring.
24.7 WAKULLA RIVER
Tiny clearing with benches, fire ring, and a nearby water spigot.
33.1 WAKULLA FIELD
Large clearing in pine flatwoods with benches and fire ring.
36.7 PORTER TRACT
Small site on old road between two swamps. Benches.
42.0 MARSH POINT
Beauty spot on a peninsula under the pines, with benches and fire ring.

Bears roam the refuge. Bear bag or use a bear canister. Finding surface water to filter is a major problem since saltwater intrusion has crept far inland. The refuge suggests you use potable water sources, which are few and far between: the Visitor Center (1.8-mile round trip, limited hours) on Lighthouse Rd, the town of St. Marks, and Thompson House. Once a reliable water source, Shepherd Spring is now brackish.

Trip Planning

For most day hikes in the refuge, no permits or fees are required. The exception is when using Lighthouse Rd to access the Florida Trail segments at Apalachee Bay, Deep Creek, and Port Leon. Day passes and annual passes are available. The refuge accepts National Public Lands passes.

To do the entire St. Marks section, you'll need a ride across the St. Marks River. The trail ends on the south shore and resumes on the north shore, joining the paved Tallahassee-St. Marks Historic Railroad State Trail. Swimming the deep tidal river isn't an option. Some hikers wave down passing boats. Shell Island Fish Camp (850-925-6226) will ferry you for free if you stay with them, otherwise there's a fee. Within sight of the crossing, Shields Marina (850-925-6158) also provides transport. Either way, tip your captain. There's no dock, so it's rough on boats.

Although much of the trail is on levees and forest roads, it also enter swamps where you must wade. Depending on tides, the wilderness area at the east end of the refuge and Cathedral of Palms can be wet and muddy to traverse. For over a decade the Spring Creek estuary has been impassable, and replacement boardwalks have yet to be built. Don't try to wade the estuary—deep mud can trap you. Hikers must roadwalk around the closure.

Research hunting season dates and wear bright orange if you hike during hunting season. Wakulla Field and Marsh Point campsites are closed during hunting season. Hiking season is prime season for prescribed burns. Call the Visitor Center the morning of your hike and ask about the status of the area you plan to hike.

Land Manager

US Fish & Wildlife Service
1255 Lighthouse Rd, St. Marks 32355
850-925-6121
fws.gov/refuge/st-marks

Highlights

Pinhook River, mile 4.0

A wooden bridge crosses this scenic tidal river, offering hikers a unique glimpse of the estuary.

Swamp Hammock Trail, mile 6.0

Plunging into a dense palm hammock, an optional immersion into coastal swamps adding a half mile to the otherwise easy levee route.

Big Bend Panorama, mile 9.2

A long curve in the levee offers an outstanding sweeping view across vast estuaries where Florida's Panhandle and peninsula meet.

Stoney Bayou, mile 11.4

Extraordinarily scenic for a levee walk, Stoney Bayou provides near-shore wildlife watching and panoramas of a distant shoreline edged by ancient cypresses and cabbage palms.

Port Leon, mile 17.5

At the end of a blue blaze off the Florida Trail, the original site of Refuge headquarters sits on the scenic estuary where Leon Creek seeps into the Wakulla River.

Pine flatwoods near Purify Bay

Cathedral of Palms, mile 32.0

A notable destination for day hikers, the Cathedral of Palms impresses with towering cabbage palms that rustle in the wind along the coast.

Shepherd Spring, mile 32.4

A boardwalk and bench provide access to a showy third-magnitude spring in a floodplain forest, clear enough to see schools of fish darting through its depths.

Marsh Point, mile 42.2

A protrusion of land into the estuary enables a walk into a vast needlerush marsh at low tide for an expansive view of the coastline at Oyster Bay.

Recommended Day Hikes

Mile 0.0

Apalachee Bay, 14 miles linear

Mile 13.4

Stoney Bayou, 4-mile round trip

Mile 15.4

Port Leon, 7-mile round trip from Visitor Center

Mile 25.3

Wakulla River, 4.3 miles linear

Mile 29.6

Cathedral of Palms, 6 miles linear

Mile 44.1

Purify Bay to Marsh Point, 3.6-mile round trip

Mile 44.1

Purify Bay to Carraway Cutoff, 3.3 miles linear

39. Apalachee Bay

13.4 MILES | ST. MARKS NATIONAL WILDLIFE REFUGE, NEWPORT

Emerging from a jungle-like floodplain forest in the Aucilla River basin to open estuaries along Apalachee Bay, traverse miles of the most breathtaking panoramas along the Florida Trail.

Overview

The sweep of Florida's Big Bend provides a stunning backdrop to a hike through natural habitats along the coastal shallows of the Gulf of Mexico on Apalachee Bay. While the designated wilderness area at the start of this hike requires some wayfinding skill and wading through a swamp, the showiest portions of the hike use old tramways and levees topped with unpaved roads. Elevated above the surrounding landscape, you're treated to horizon-to-horizon views of estuaries and floodplain forests in a part of Florida few people ever see. Crossing vast wetlands also means tallying the largest number of alligators per day along the Florida Trail.

Trip Planning / Land Manager

See St. Marks National Wildlife Refuge. Leashed dogs are permitted but alligators are ridiculously common along this trail. Avoid getting within twenty feet of any alligator you see. The levee portions of the Florida Trail are open to bicycles. Bicycles are not permitted on the Swamp Hammock Trail or Rookery Trail or in the designated wilderness area. Research hunting seasons for Aucilla WMA, since the first mile of trail is inside it. Wear bright orange during hunting season.

Check the weather forecast before hiking. Shade is minimal west of the wilderness area, and the last five miles of this hike are entirely exposed to the elements. Use sun protection and carry plenty of water. Hiking poles help for balance on swamp wades and to keep a good stride atop the levees. Insect repellent is a must. Backpackers may want a bug net. Mosquitoes and no-see-ums can be torturous at dusk and dawn.

Directions

Both access points are off US 98 east of St. Marks. For the end point, turn off US 98 onto Lighthouse Rd across from Newport Park. Gates open at 6:00 a.m. A fee applies, but a National Public Lands pass scores free entry. Continue 1.8 miles past the Visitor Center to a small pull-off [30.13031, -84.14489] near the open waters of Stoney Bayou Pool. If it's full, continue a quarter mile to another on the right adjoining the Florida Trail kiosk [30.125759, -84.148094]. Avoid blocking any gates.

For the starting point, return to US 98 and turn right. Drive 11.8 miles east, past Flint Rock WMA, SR 59, and signs for Aucilla WMA. Turn onto Small Game Rd—a narrow one-lane dirt road through the swamp forest—and follow it a quarter mile. It can be soft or muddy under the power lines. Find solid ground uphill near the FNST [30.1556, -83.99935] and park, but don't block the road. If the gate off US 98 into Small Game Rd is closed, the next nearby parking area is Aucilla WMA picnic area [30.1629, -84.0032]. Return west along US 98 for 0.5 miles and turn

Apalachee Bay estuary

on Western Sloughs Rd. Park near the picnic pavilion. Walk back along US 98 to Small Game Rd. Starting at the picnic area adds 0.7 miles to your hike.

Options

Round trips make good day hikes from both trailheads. At Aucilla WMA, tackle 5.2 miles entirely inside the wilderness area, turning back at the clearing at Aucilla Tram Rd. Or continue to the scenic Pinhook River, turning around after a rest break at Pinhook River campsite for 8.4 miles. From Lighthouse Rd, a 4-mile round trip along Stoney Bayou to the trail turnoff offers outstanding scenery and wildlife watching. An easy 1.2 miles northbound on the Florida Trail from Lighthouse Rd crosses a spillway to scenic views of salt marsh punctuated by pine islands.

Grab a copy of the Primitive Trails map at the Visitor Center to work out options using its loops that interconnect with the Florida Trail: 6.5 miles along Stoney Bayou Trail and 12 miles along Deep Creek Trail. Each uses part of this hike on its return loop. The Deep Creek loop includes the outstanding Big Bend panorama and scenic Ring Dike campsite.

Hike

Begin at the FNST sign on Small Game Rd in Aucilla WMA and follow the edge of coastal marshes dominated by needlerush and edged with sawgrass. Tides may push salt water into the footpath. Once the trail leaves the marsh, enter a floodplain forest of cabbage palms, sweetgum, maples, and cypress nourished by swamps surrounding Oyster Creek. Tannic water puddles or flows across the trail.

After a mile, reach the St. Marks National Wildlife Refuge sign. This swamp forest is a federally designated wilderness area. The deeper into it you go, the more primordial it feels. Focus on following the blazes.

Two-plank boardwalks span Oyster Creek and one of its tributaries. Join a tramway briefly before a break in it forces a wade in the swamp. The tramway meets another at a T intersection. Make a sharp right. The trail almost doubles back on itself joining the railbed of the former Live Oak, Perry & Gulf Railroad at 1.9 miles. Known as the "Lopin' Gopher," the railroad connected the long-vanished timbering town of Flintrock with sawmills in Perry. Railroad trestles bridge swampy gaps.

After 2.6 miles, emerge from the swamp forest to a broad open grassy area where several forest roads meet at the western boundary of the wilderness area. Keep left to follow Aucilla Tram Rd atop a levee. Flanked on both sides by floodplain forests, it has little shade. Start counting alligators. They tend to lay just out of the water at the base of the levee.

Cedars and cabbage palms line the trail until the landscape opens up at the Pinhook River bridge at 4 miles. With a sweeping view of needlerush marsh edged by palms, this picturesque wooden bridge was built decades ago atop the original train trestle. Just past it, take a break on a bench at Pinhook River campsite across a plank bridge on the right. Edged by sawgrass marsh, its flat tent sites are shaded by cabbage palms.

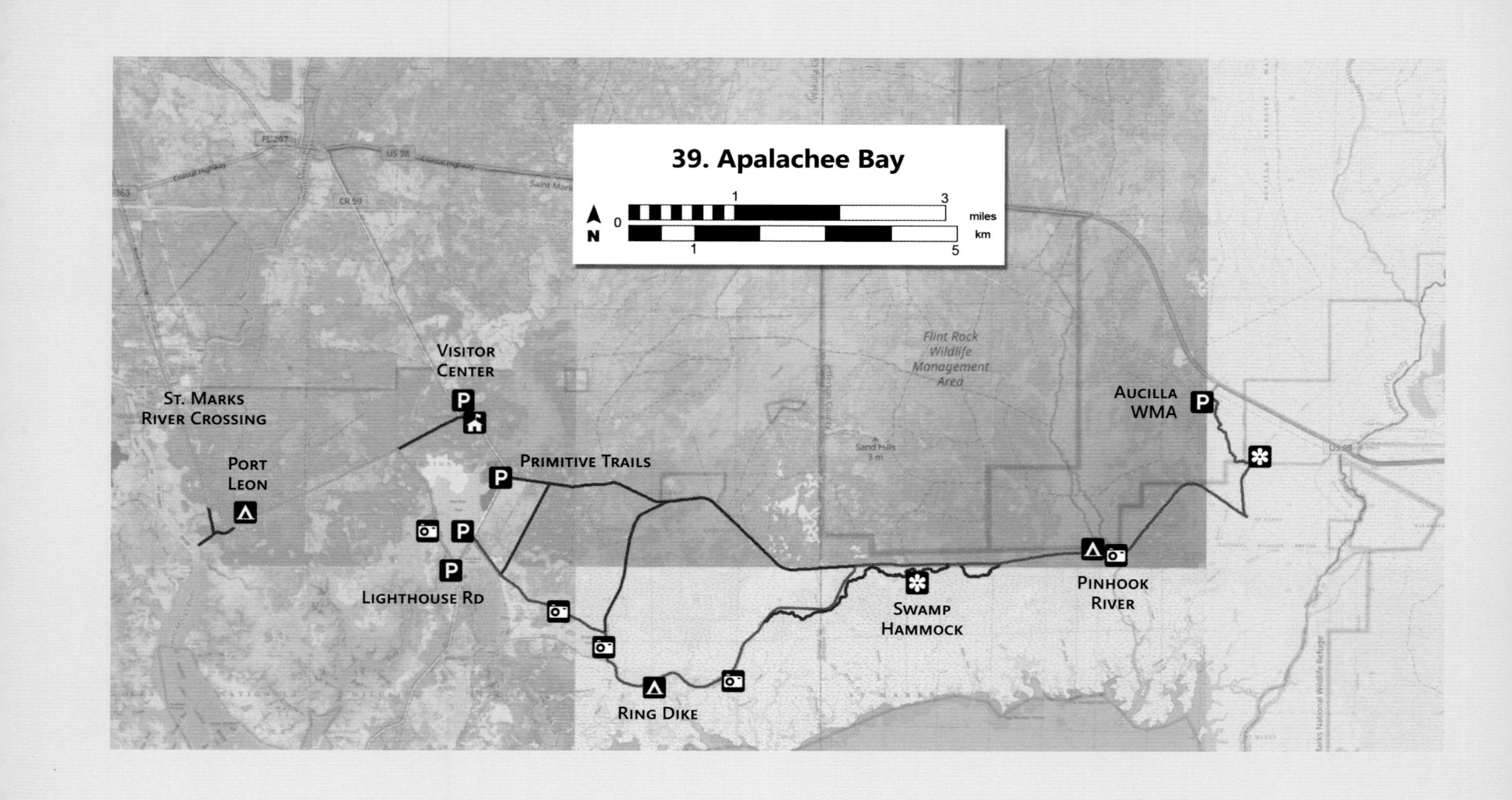
39. Apalachee Bay
0
1
3
miles
1
5
km
N
St. Marks
River Crossing
Port
Leon
Visitor
Center
Primitive Trails
Lighthouse Rd
Ring Dike
Swamp
Hammock
Pinhook
River
Aucilla
WMA
Flint Rock
Wildlife
Management
Area
US 98
CR 59
FL 267

Pinhook River bridge

The trail becomes a broad straightaway crossing two old highway bridges. Dark tannic waters flow in culverts below into the palm hammocks. Just past a set of culverts at 5.3 miles, a blue blaze marks the 0.7-mile Rookery Loop, an alternate route the Florida Trail detours onto whenever biologists determine nesting birds might be bothered by hikers. If there are no signs, continue straight ahead. Within a half mile, Rookery Loop rejoins Aucilla Tram Rd at a highway bridge with guardrails.

On the opposite side of the bridge is the Swamp Hammock Trail. Over the past two decades its blazes have sometimes been blue, sometimes orange. Hikers attest the footpath is usually mucky and difficult to follow through the palm hammocks. If you decide to take it, it adds a half mile to this hike. It also skips the Deep Creek Trail junction. Unless you're up for the challenge, stay on Aucilla Tram Rd.

Over the next 1.1 miles, pass two forest roads before meeting Deep Creek Trail at a broad junction. Here's where weather comes into play. The remainder of the hike provides the best scenery, but it's also fully in the open and *you* may be the high point for miles around. If thunderstorms threaten, Deep Creek Trail makes a 4.5-mile beeline through forests to Lighthouse Rd, reaching it at a parking area 0.8 miles north of the Florida Trail.

Turn left to stay on the Florida Trail, Deep Creek Trail joining in to make its loop. Reach the west end of the Swamp Hammock Trail at a bench in the shade at 8.5 miles. Take advantage of this stop as the remainder of the hike is in full sun. Within the next half mile, an extraordinary view opens up at the approach to a grated bridge over a gated outflow from the marshes. Salt marshes extend to the eastern horizon.

A sweeping panorama of the Big Bend starts around 9.2 miles and continues as you walk, becoming more extensive and captivating across Apalachee Bay. The views on the right side of the levee are beautiful, too, salt marshes and oyster beds a foreground to the distant scrim of forest. Cross two large spillways the next quarter mile.

At 10.3 miles, Ring Dike campsite has the distinction of being entirely circled by salt marsh, making for outstanding views and starry skies. Shared with the Florida Circumnavigational Saltwater Paddling Trail, it's the most beautiful campsite on the Florida Trail but hellish when mosquitoes and no-see-ums swarm. Be prepared.

Affording an excellent view of Apalachee Bay, a bench sits in the shade along the levee past the campsite. With open water on both sides of the trail, it's easy to watch birds and spot alligators. At 11 miles, the Florida Trail makes a sharp right at an intersection of levees to follow the rim of Stoney Bayou. At this end, the bayou is shallow. Expect plenty of alligators along its edge.

Within a quarter mile, reach the junction where the Stoney Bayou Trail comes in from the north. Turn left to stay along the bayou. Scenic panoramas surround the trail. At 12.2 miles, pass beneath a lone pine tree. Ancient cypresses soon call attention to the beautiful floodplain forest along the distant horizon to your right.

Trails meet at a junction of levees within sight of Lighthouse Rd at 12.8 miles. The Deep Creek Trail turns north to complete its loop. The levee to the left is favored by birders as it heads toward the salt flats. Flanked by marshes, the Florida Trail continues straight ahead. Finish this 13.4-mile hike at Lighthouse Rd.

Ring Dike campsite

40. Wakulla River

4.3 MILES | ST. MARKS NATIONAL WILDLIFE REFUGE, ST. MARKS

Following the floodplain of the Wakulla River basin, this short, sweet hike includes limestone boulders, quiet cypress swamps, and a big bouncy sawdust pile buried deep in the forest.

Overview

The Florida Trail along the west side of the Wakulla River never gets within sight of the river. Instead, it traverses the swamp forests that drain into the tidal waterway, surprisingly scenic in their own right. Towering trees provide deep shade. A footpath for most of its length, it makes a pleasant day hike.

Trip Planning / Land Manager

See St. Marks National Wildlife Refuge. Leashed dogs are welcome. Bicycles are not permitted. Trailheads have limited parking. Expect to get your shoes wet. Hiking poles are helpful for balance when you need to wade. Bring insect repellent or a bug net.

If you are backpacking, Wakulla River campsite is a key stop even if you don't camp there. It has critical access to potable water for northbound hikers. A forest road runs compass west from the campsite to Thompson House, where there is an external spigot on the main building.

Directions

Both access points are off US 98 west of St. Marks. Thompson House trailhead [30.169408, -84.247194] is along US 98 just west of the Wakulla River on the south side of the highway. Look for the large FNST sign at the driveway. Wakulla Beach Rd is the next left west along US 98. Wakulla Beach Rd trailhead [30.145603, -84.254211] is one mile down the road on the right side. It's small, so avoid blocking the gate.

Options

Make a round trip from Thompson House trailhead. Three landmarks for turnaround points: Sawdust Hill for 2.2 miles; the boardwalk for 3.4 miles; and the boulders for 5.2 miles. It's a much wetter hike if you approach these landmarks from Wakulla Beach Rd. The hike north to Cathedral of Palms from that trailhead is described in the next chapter. Connect the two hikes together for a 10.4-mile linear hike between the Thompson House and Spring Creek Highway.

Hike

A short blue blaze leads from Thompson House trailhead to a T with the orange blazes of the Florida Trail coming in from the Coastal Trail bike path along US 98. Turn right and pass a pond in an old borrow pit. Candyroot thrives along the pine duff on its edge. A quarter mile in, reach a T intersection with a forest road, the small Wakulla River campsite with two benches to your right. Campsites usually aren't this close to a trailhead, but there's a critical potable water source nearby. Turn left.

Culverts shuffle swamp water beneath the forest road, but there's a spot where clear water drains across the trail. The flow is usually narrow enough to hop across. Past a junction of forest roads,

Sawdust Hill

the trail narrows to a footpath in the pines. If the pine duff is soggy, a basin swamp ahead may be flowing into the footpath at the half-mile mark. It's a large, picturesque cypress swamp with open water in the center, ringed with cypress knees beneath towering cypress trees. Fallen leaves, pollen, and floating cypress needles create the illusion of a solid surface atop dark waters.

Gaining elevation leaving the swamp, the footpath is needle-strewn and grassy under the pines. Cross the faded track of an old forest road and enter towering rows of planted slash pine. After a forest road at a mile, transition into natural pine flatwoods. Walk beneath Southern magnolia on a descent to the river floodplain. Pines yield to a hardwood forest.

At a curve at 1.1 miles, Sawdust Hill looms to the right. It's a remnant of a compacted sawdust pile from a long-ago sawmill. Scramble up top along its bouncy surface to a crest with a view into the forest canopy below. The steep pitch of Sawdust Hill is more obvious on your descent. North of it, the woods have an open understory.

A line of cabbage palms draws attention to the swirling surface of a floodplain swamp. Enter a corridor defined by dense clumps of saw palmetto. Some are very old, their trunks standing upright like miniature cabbage palms. Older slash pines bear scars from turpentine tapping.

A boardwalk spans a sluggish creek at 1.7 miles. Cypress knees rise from water the color of iced tea. The creek drains a floodplain forest into the Wakulla River estuary. Perched on a rise above the swamp, a bench is a welcome dry spot. Beneath tall Southern magnolias and a thicket of native bamboo, ascend into a hardwood forest. As vegetation crowds in, pass a massive oak with multiple gaps through its thick trunk and walk through a large clearing under the pines.

Beyond the next stands of bamboo, puddles form across the trail. At first they are easy to skirt, but in a palm hammock at 2.1 miles, the footpath is the low spot where water collects. Rise into a hardwood forest, passing a palm hammock fringed with sawgrass. As cabbage palms intersperse with the pines and oaks, walk beneath tall slash pines. A corridor of saw palmetto again lines the trail, bamboo growing beneath hickory trees in damp areas. We crossed swampy puddles by balancing on fallen tree trunks laid out like bridges.

Towering pines shelter the climb out of this low area, leading to an unusual collection of limestone boulders worn smooth as if polished into sculptures. Strewn across the forest floor, they resemble miniature megaliths, some topped with pine needles, others with small palms. Two ancient civilizations called this basin home in nearby Byrd Hammock, but these may be of much newer origin since they're near a forest road.

Cross the road and continue under the pines. Slipping past a cypress swamp, rise into uplands with a largely open understory beneath the oaks, magnolias, and American holly, clumps of saw palmetto dotted throughout the forest. At 3.2 miles step over a ditch onto a two-track road. Look carefully for the next blaze. It's on the other side of

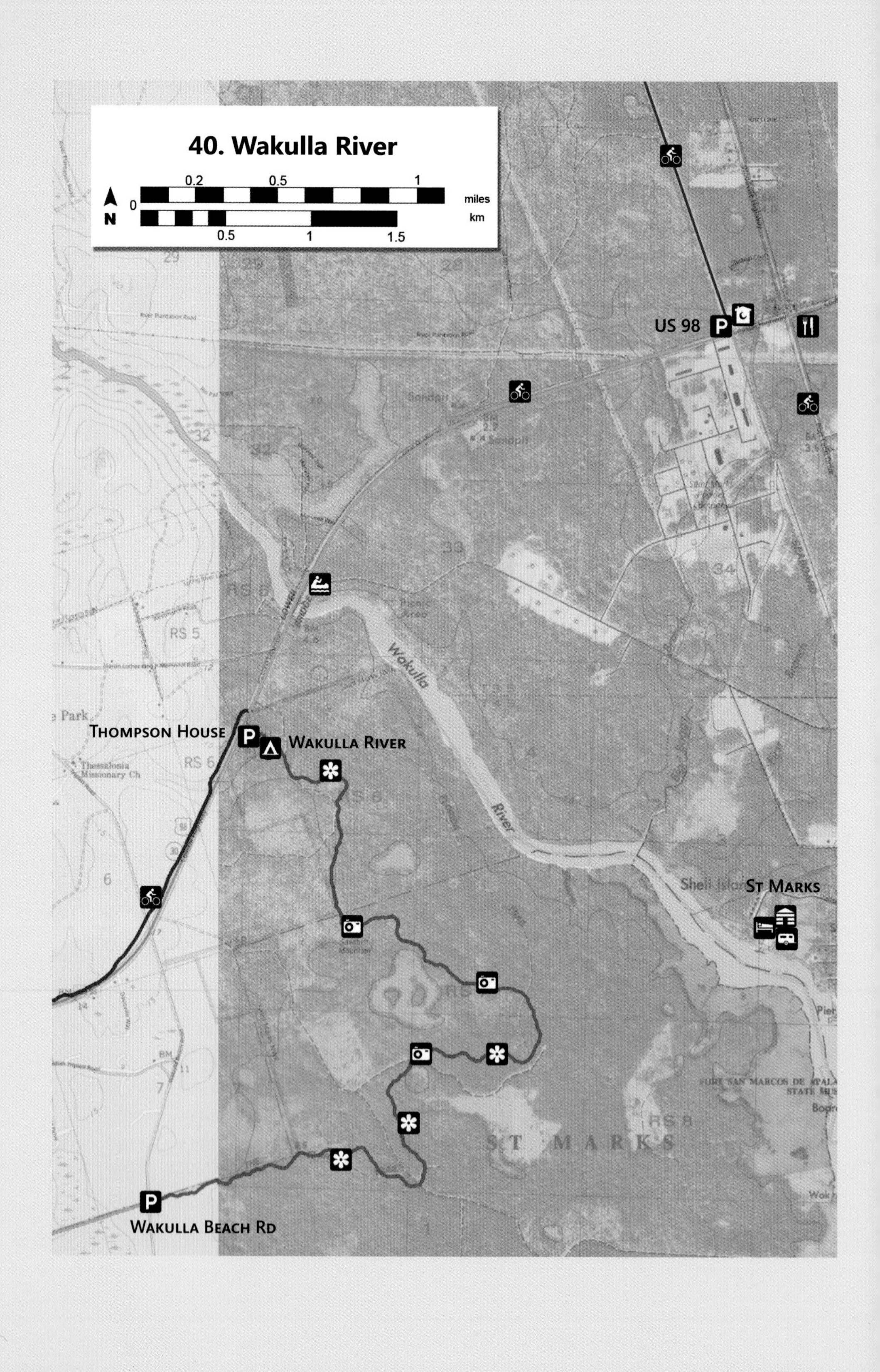

40. Wakulla River
0.2
0.5
1
0
miles
N
km
0.5
1
1.5
US 98
Thompson House
Wakulla River
Wakulla
River
St Marks
Wakulla Beach Rd

Cypress swamp

a ditch adjoining the road, a ditch that can be deep at the crossing point. Scout for a shallower crossing.

Entering pine-palm flatwoods, follow the footpath winding between the trees. It becomes a well-defined corridor again when mature Southern magnolias and slash pines form the high canopy. Gain a little elevation and enter a drier forest.

Descending from that high ground, circle the rim of a vast basin swamp around 4 miles. It's similar to the one at the beginning of the hike, and sometimes spills into the footpath. A gap of open water reveals the floodplain forest beyond.

Join a firebreak along a property boundary fence to skirt the rest of the swamp, passing under a loblolly pine of incredible size. Rejoin a footpath through the forest. End the hike by crossing Wakulla Beach Rd to the trailhead at 4.3 miles.

Canopied forest road

41. Cathedral of Palms

6.1 MILES | ST. MARKS NATIONAL WILDLIFE REFUGE, SPRING CREEK

Plunging into one of the showiest palm hammocks on the Florida Trail, this hike centers on the Cathedral of Palms and Shepherd Spring, natural treasures along the coast of Wakulla County.

Overview

On one of the more popular segments of the Florida Trail in this region, this hike ties together an easy stroll on forest roads with a sometimes-tough traverse of a muddy but spectacular coastal palm hammock, the Cathedral of Palms. The prize beyond it is Shepherd Spring, a looking glass of clear water in a floodplain forest. In spring, redbud trees lend a hint of pink to the emerging fresh green leaves of deciduous trees. In late fall and early winter, red maples, sweetgum, and hickories sport crimson, purple, and gold. Alligators lounge on logs and raccoons shuffle through the understory. The hike isn't far from US 98 as the crow flies, but it's a whole different world exploring the coastal swamps on foot.

Trip Planning / Land Manager

See St. Marks National Wildlife Refuge. Expect wet, muddy shoes on this hike. Hiking poles help for balance. Bring insect repellent or a bug net for this deeply shaded hike. Leashed dogs are welcome, but they will get muddy too. The trail uses forest roads open to cyclists. Bicycles are not permitted on the footpath sections. Trailheads have limited parking.

Directions

Both access points are off US 98. From the intersection of US 319 and US 98 south of Crawfordville at Medart, drive east 4.9 miles on US 98 to Spring Creek Hwy. For the end point of this hike, turn right and continue 1.4 miles to Spring Creek trailhead [30.121129, -84.314977] on the left. For the starting point of the hike, continue east 3.8 miles along US 98 to Wakulla Beach Rd. The small Wakulla Beach Rd trailhead [30.145603, -84.254211] is a mile south on the right. Don't block the gate.

Options

Round trip from either trailhead to the highlights of the hike: 7 miles from Wakulla Beach Rd trailhead to Shepherd Spring via the Cathedral of Palms, or 5.6 miles from Spring Creek trailhead to the Cathedral of Palms via Shepherd Spring. From either direction, connecting forest roads (the high-water bypass shown in blue on the map) enable a loop hike back to where you parked.

Hike

Leaving the trailhead, the trail follows a forest road due west as far as the eye can see. The reason is immediately obvious—a vast cypress swamp flanks the road. Within the first mile, a canopy of towering trees forms a beautiful tunnel. Where the swamp often flows across the road, you may have to wade if it's too wide to jump. A sluggish stream parallels on the south side of the trail.

After a second swamp drains across

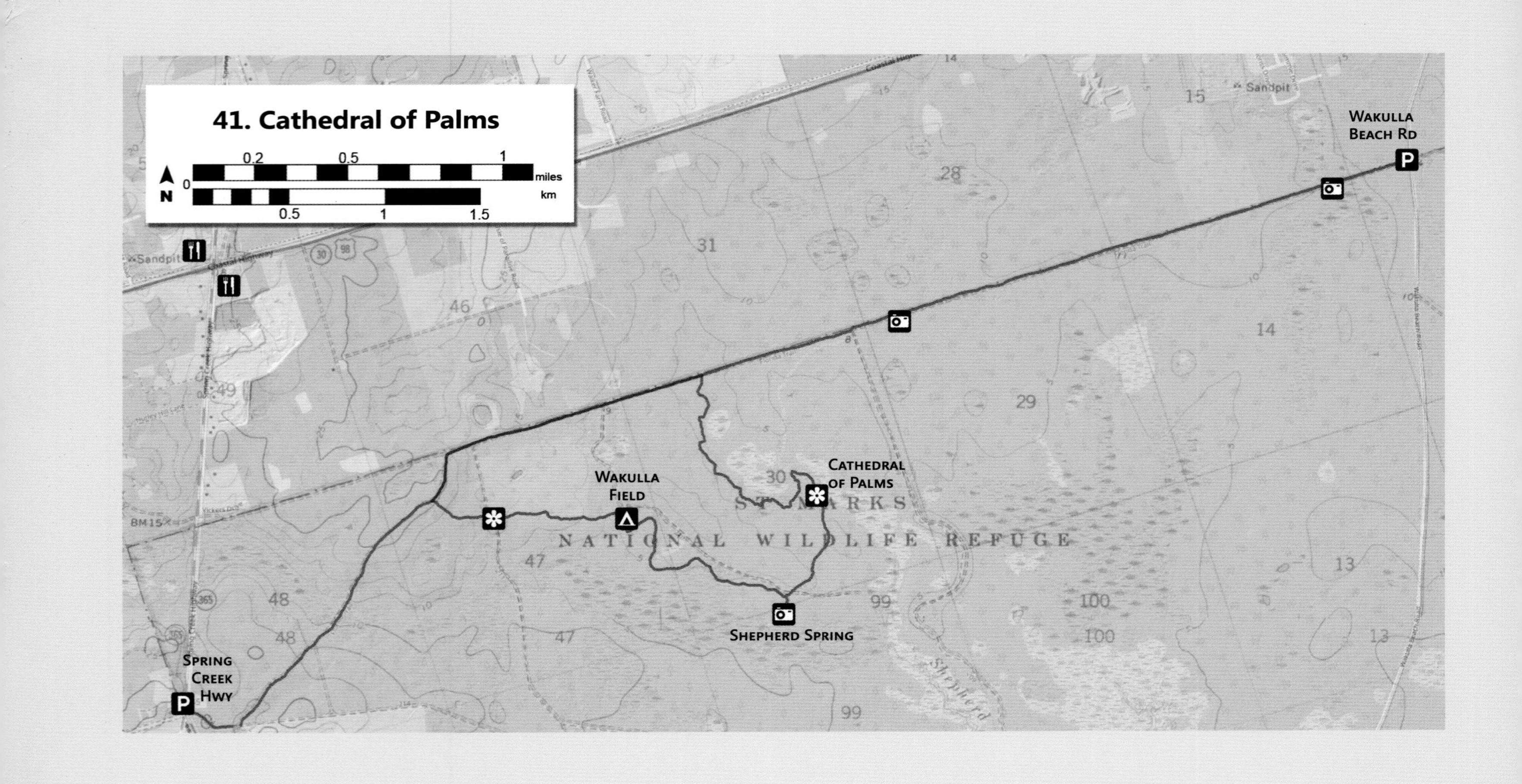
41. Cathedral of Palms
0
0.2
0.5
1
miles
0.5
1
1.5
km
N
Wakulla Beach Rd
Cathedral of Palms
Wakulla Field
Shepherd Spring
Spring Creek Hwy
NATIONAL WILDLIFE REFUGE
Sandpit

the road, pass FR 209 at 1.8 miles. Relocated from its original route due to the rise of coastal waters, the FNST turns into the woods on the left almost a half mile later. The footpath now edges the west side of the coastal marshes instead of crossing them.

The ground remains soggy and muddy except in times of drought. Perpetual dampness encourages fungi to flourish on fallen logs and tree trunks. Jelly leaf swarms across mossy surfaces, violet corts rise from leaf litter, and oyster fungi stairsteps up fallen logs.

At 3.2 miles, the forest closes in. There is no mistaking the Cathedral of Palms, the cabbage palm trunks rising like columns in every direction. Dodge deep mud holes and puddles where the estuary along its edge spills over at high tide into this grand forest. Ancient oaks snake thick limbs between the palms in their search for sunlight above the fronds.

The footpath gets muddier and sloppier as the palms thin out. Crossing a forest road, reach a bench carved as a set of directional signs: "Trail" to the right and "Spring" to the left. Turn left to visit Shepherd Spring. A boardwalk through the floodplain forest ends at an overlook with a bench. Twenty-five feet deep, the spring has a large resident alligator. Schools of mullet swirl through the clear water.

Follow the blazes straight past the bench at 3.6 miles and enter a native bamboo thicket in the understory of a pine and oak forest, with longleaf pines of significant girth and height. Pass through a showy stand of southern magnolia before the turnoff to Wakulla Field campsite, a large clearing with a couple of benches. Circle it at 4.4 miles along the edge of the pine forest. Cross FR 211 diagonally beneath towering longleaf pines. Enter an oak hammock dominated by one mature oak tree spreading its limbs widely.

Ascend into a healthy longleaf pine forest with a dense understory of saw palmetto. The footpath meets FR 210 at a T intersection at 5 miles. This is where you can make an 8.2-mile loop to your starting point by following FR 210 east to the next forest road junction, then east again to rejoin the straightaway tunnel through the woods to Wakulla Beach Rd.

The Florida Trail northbound turns left on FR 210, leading through a nice stand of longleaf pines. Descend to a causeway flanked by swamp forest, where tannic waters flow beneath the trail in a culvert. Rising back into pine forest, reach a Y intersection with FR 206. Keep right.

In a clearing, forest roads intersect at 5.9 miles. Orange blazes continue straight ahead toward the Porter Tract of St. Marks National Wildlife Refuge. Turn right and follow blue blazes along a forest road through sandhills. Pass a sheltered kiosk with a bench, emerging at Spring Creek trailhead at 6.1 miles.

Cathedral of Palms

Titi thicket, Apalachicola

Eastern Panhandle

Spanning two time zones and two major rivers, this region of the Florida Trail provides contrasts between Florida's largest national forest and the rural heartland of northwest Florida.

Lafayette Creek floodplain, Nokuse

BASE CAMPS

Sopchoppy

A quirky little town along its namesake river and the edge of the Apalachicola National Forest, Sopchoppy is a jumping-off point for outdoor adventures in the region. A paved bike path through St. Marks National Wildlife Refuge connects Sopchoppy to the Gulf of Mexico; a network of bike paths spans to St. Marks and Tallahassee.

STAY

Holiday Campground 850-984-5757, 14 Coastal Hwy, Panacea.

Myron B. Hodge City Park Campground 850-962-4611, 220 Park Ave.

The Oaks RV Resort & Motel 850-713-0175, 54 Coastal Hwy, Panacea.

Ochlockonee River State Park 800-326-3521, 429 State Park Rd.

Tiny Treehouse on the Sopchoppy, 850-524-6216, Sopchoppy.

EAT

Angelo's Seafood Restaurant 850-984-5168, 5 Mashes Sands Rd, Panacea.

La Palmas, 850-524-0914, 460 Coastal Hwy, Panacea.

SEE AND DO

Civic Brewing Co. 850-696-6790, 106 Municipal Ave.

George Griffin Pottery 850-962-9311, 1 Suncat Ridge.

Mashes Sands Beach 850-926-7227, 801 Mashes Sands Rd, Panacea.

Ochlockonee River State Park 850-962-2771, 429 State Park Rd.

Sopchoppy Opry 850-962-3711, 164 Yellow Jacket Rd.

Bristol

The county seat of Liberty County, Bristol is on the eastern bluffs of the Apalachicola River, a gateway to the Apalachicola National Forest. The Florida Trail follows sidewalks through this small town.

STAY

Camel Lake Campground 1-877-444-6777, 23239 FR 105.

Snowbird Motel 850-643-2330, 10758 NW SR 20 E.

Torreya State Park 800-326-3521, 2576 NW Torreya Park Rd.

EAT

Apalachee Restaurant 850-643-2264, 10536 SR 20.

TJ's Country Store 850-643-1006, 15447 NW CR 12.

SEE AND DO

Apalachee Savannas Scenic Byway CR 12 S to CR 379 S.

Apalachicola Bluffs and Ravines [30.454700, -84.970433] Garden of Eden Rd.

Torreya State Park 850-643-2674, 2576 NW Torreya Park Rd.

Veterans Memorial Park Railroad 850-643-6646, 10561 NW Theo Jacobs Wy.

Blountstown

On the western bluffs of the Apalachicola River, Blountstown is the county seat of Calhoun County and home to the Panhandle Pioneer Settlement, providing insight into rural life. The Florida Trail follows the paved Blountstown Greenway through this compact small town.

STAY

The Calhoun Motor Lodge 850-447-2347, 20228 W Central Ave.

EAT

El Jalisco 850-674-3411, 16919 N Pear St.

Fiddler's Steam House & Oyster Bar 850-237-1243, 17415 Main St S.

SEE AND DO

Ocheesee Creamery 850-674-1573, 28367 SR 69, Grand Ridge.

Panhandle Pioneer Settlement / Sam Atkins Park 850-674-2777, 17869 NW Pioneer Settlement Rd.

Marianna

A half hour north of where the Florida Trail crosses Calhoun and Washington counties, Marianna is one of the region's largest towns. On the Chipola River and Merritt's Mill Pond, it's home to numerous springs and Florida's only show cave, Florida Caverns. Some outdoor activities are summer season only.

STAY

Florida Caverns RV Resort 850-482-5583, 4820 US 90.

Hinson House Bed & Breakfast 850-526-1500, 4338 Lafayette St.

EAT

The Waffle Iron of Marianna 850-526-5055, 4509 Lafayette St.

Mashawy Grill 850-526-1578, 3297 Caverns Rd.

The Oaks Restaurant 850-526-1114, 4727 US 90.

The Wharf Casual Seafood 850-526-1955, 4767 US 90.

SEE AND DO

Bear Paw Adventures 850-482-4948, 2100 Bear Paw Ln.

Blue Springs Recreation Area 850-718-0437, 5461 Blue Springs Rd.

Florida Caverns State Park 850-482-1228, 3345 Caverns Rd.

Lilypad Adventures 850-326-4884, 3150 SR 2, Campbellton.

Choctawhatchee River Basin

On opposite sides of the Choctawhatchee River, the tiny crossroads of Ebro and Bruce are ten minutes apart along SR 20. Ponce De Leon is a half hour north of Bruce. Vernon is 20 minutes north of Ebro.

STAY

Ebro Motel 850-535-2499, 5312 Captain Fritz Rd, Ebro.

Sand Pond Campground 1-877-879- 3859, 5583-A Longleaf Rd, Ebro.

Dead River Landing 850-539-5999, 2207 Dead River Rd, Ponce de Leon.

Vortex Spring 850-836-4979, 1517 Vortex Springs Lane, Ponce de Leon.

EAT

Bruce Cafe 850-835-2946, 10417 SR 20, Bruce.

Dee's Restaurant 850-535-6449, 3730 Roche Ave, Vernon.

SEE AND DO

Cypress Springs Adventures 850-535-2004, 3324 SR 277, Vernon.

Morrison Springs 850-892-8108, 874 Morrison Springs Rd.

Muscogee Nation of Florida 850-835-2078, 278 Church Rd, Bruce.

Pine Log State Forest 850-535-2888, 5583-A Longleaf Rd, Ebro.

Ponce De Leon Springs 850-836-4281, 2860 Ponce de Leon Springs Rd.

Seacrest Wolf Preserve 850-773-2897, 3449 Bonnett Pond Rd, Chipley.

Freeport

Established 1830 along a bayou on the north shore of Choctawhatchee Bay, this small town sits along the eastern edge of Eglin Air Force Base, with services spread along SR 20 and US 331.

STAY

Calypso Cove RV Park 850-835-4606, 18655 US 331.

Live Oak Landing 1-877-436-5063, 229 Pitts Ave.

EAT

Nick's Seafood Restaurant 850-835-2222, 7585 SR 20 W.

SEE AND DO

E.O. Wilson Biophilia Center 850-835-1824, 4956 SR 20 E.

Eden Gardens State Park 850-267-8320, 181 Eden Gardens Rd.

Point Washington State Forest 850-267-8325, 5865 E US 98.

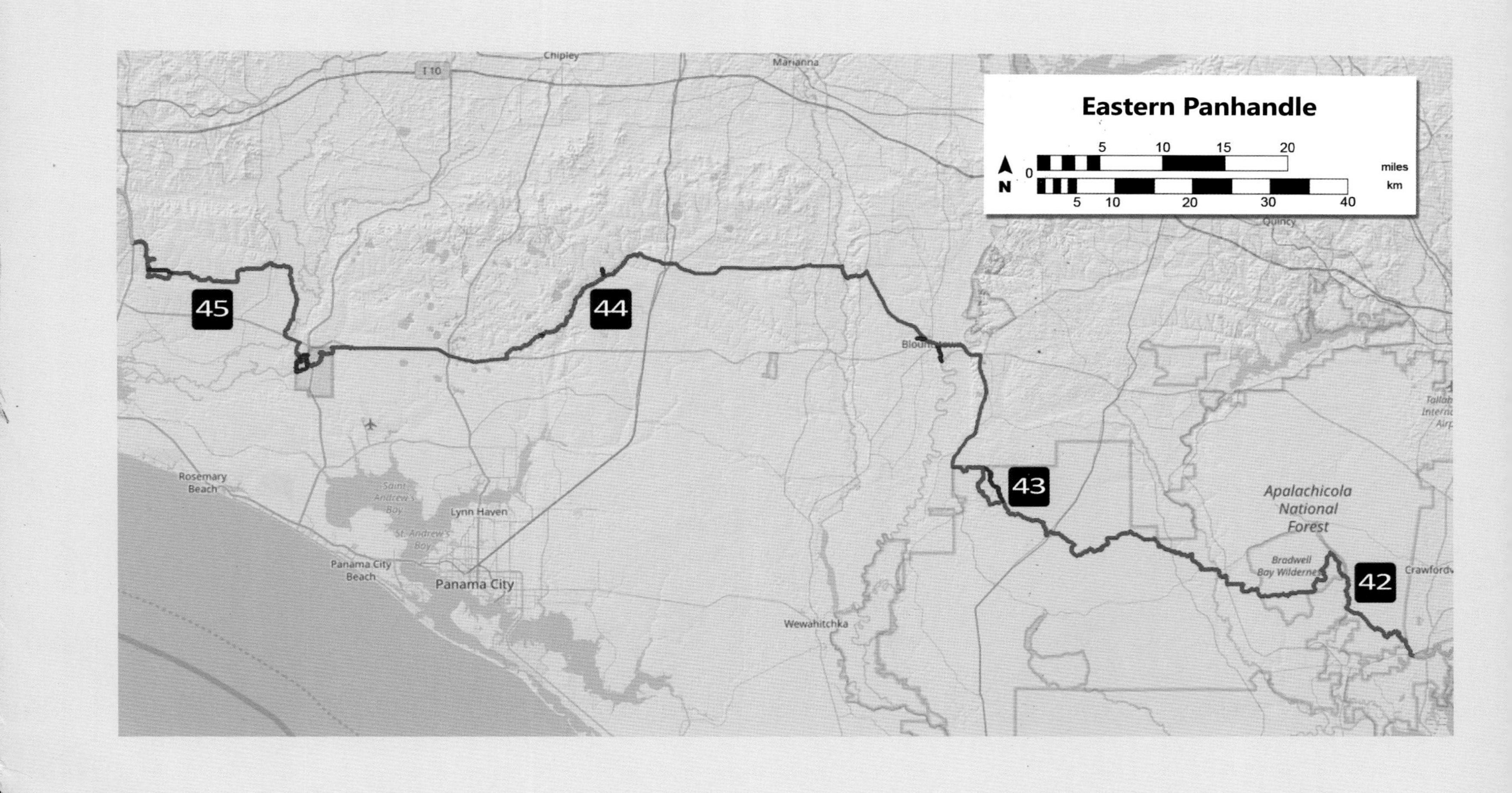

Eastern Panhandle
0
5
10
15
20
miles
N
5
10
20
30
40
km
Chipley
I 10
Marianna
Quincy
45
44
43
42
Rosemary Beach
Saint Andrew's Bay
St. Andrew's Bay
Lynn Haven
Panama City Beach
Panama City
Wewahitchka
Apalachicola National Forest
Bradwell Bay Wilderness

Pine flatwoods near Sopchoppy

Apalachicola National Forest

66.2 MILES | WAKULLA AND LIBERTY COUNTIES

In Florida's largest national forest, expect to get your feet wet. Protecting 989 square miles near Tallahassee, the Apalachicola National Forest is renowned for its botanical diversity.

Overview

Basin swamps, baygalls, cypress strands, floodplain forests, pine savannas, gum swamps, titi thickets—across the Apalachicola section of the Florida Trail, it's wet. Pine flatwoods, pine plantations, and sandhill break up the damper terrain, and the bluffs above the Sopchoppy River provide a fine contrast to soggy habitats. The centerpiece of this section is legendary Bradwell Bay, a massive basin swamp surrounding a virgin forest. When wet—which is often—it's the toughest piece of trail outside of Big Cypress Swamp, best tackled with a friend.

This is the second most remote section of the Florida Trail after Big Cypress. But over the past decade, the Apalachee Chapter of the Florida Trail Association has added many pleasant, well-spaced designated campsites on always-dry land, making this a backpacker's destination. Most pleasant in spring, when wildflower blooms are at their peak, it's far from your average walk in the woods.

Trailheads

The Florida Trail makes a rough diagonal across the forest southeast to northwest, with a series of well-marked trailheads providing access, three along paved roads. Forest roads can be challenging for passenger vehicles, particularly when muddy or sandy. High-clearance vehicles and/or 4WD will have an easier time reaching the more remote trailheads, especially near Bradwell Bay. South to north, trailheads include the following.

0.0 CARRAWAY CUTOFF
Off dirt road off US 319 near Sopchoppy. Small lot. Day use only.

8.9 OAK PARK
Dirt road access north of Sopchoppy. Very large lot.

13.0 FR 329
Dirt road access east side Bradwell Bay Wilderness.

18.3 MONKEY CREEK
Dirt road access edging Bradwell Bay Wilderness.

20.7 BRADWELL BAY SOUTH
Dirt road access east side Bradwell Bay Swamp.

25.2 BRADWELL BAY WEST
Rough dirt road access west side Bradwell Bay Swamp.

29.1 LANGSTON HOUSE
Paved access along CR 329 with side trail to pioneer homestead.

31.8 PORTER LAKE
Paved access along FR 13.

36.3 JEWEL
Paved access along CR 67 at old fire tower location.

50.6 VILAS
Short drive down dirt road off SR 65 south of Hosford and Telogia.

60.9 CAMEL LAKE
Lengthy graded dirt road access off CR 12 south of Bristol. Fee.

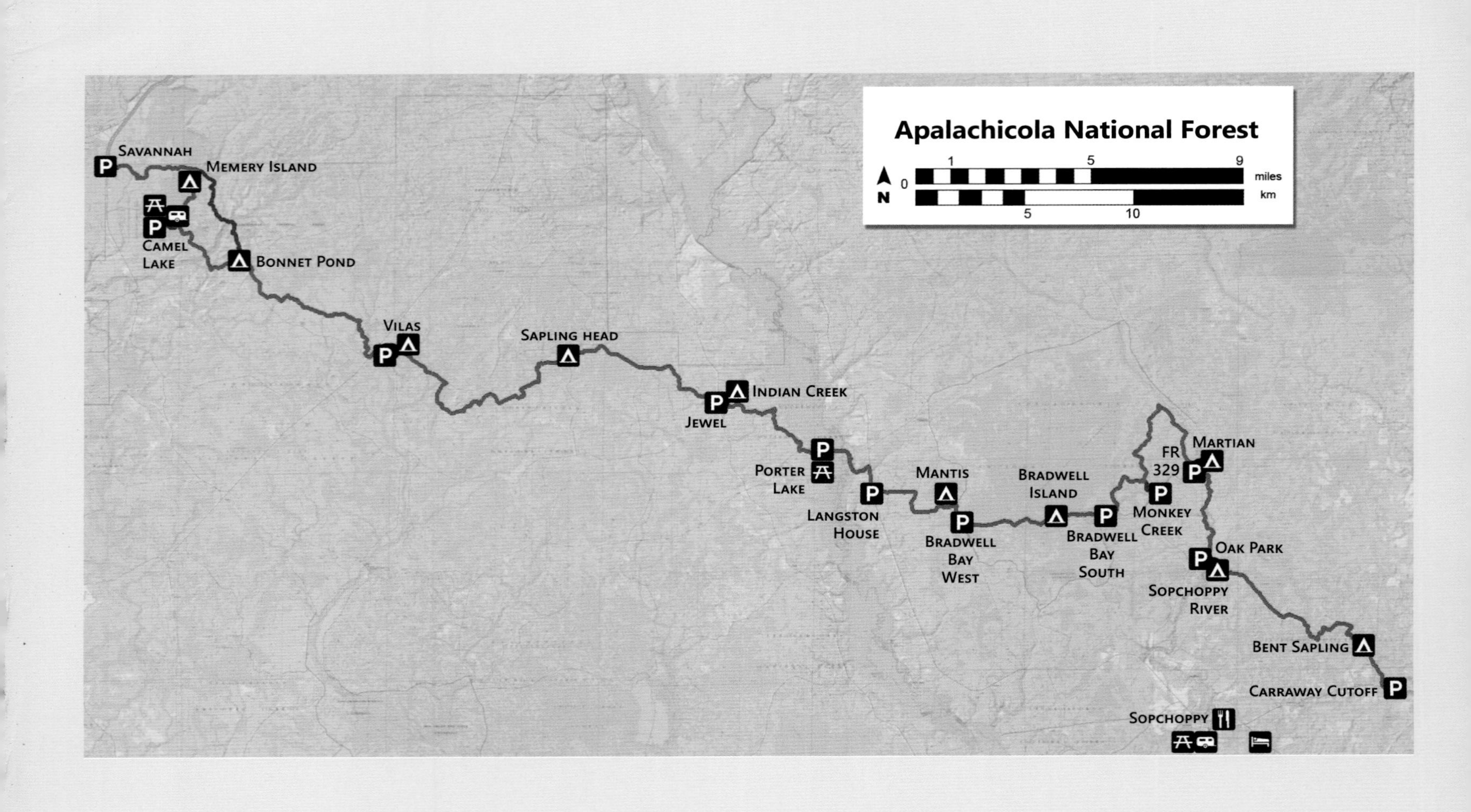
Apalachicola National Forest
0
1
5
9
miles
N
5
10
km
Savannah
Memery Island
Camel Lake
Bonnet Pond
Vilas
Sapling head
Indian Creek
Jewel
Porter Lake
Langston House
Mantis
Bradwell Bay West
Bradwell Island
Bradwell Bay South
Monkey Creek
FR 329
Martian
Oak Park
Sopchoppy River
Bent Sapling
Carraway Cutoff
Sopchoppy

66.2 SAVANNAH
Rough dirt road entrance off paved CR 12 with small grassy corral.

Camping

Random camping is permitted except during fall deer hunting season when you must use designated campsites. South to north, campsites include the following.

1.9 BENT SAPLING CAMP
Pleasant pine forest with ample tent spaces, bench and fire ring. Nearby creek.

8.6 SOPCHOPPY RIVER CAMP
Clearing with benches and fire ring atop river bluffs. Nearby river access.

12.8 MARTIAN CAMP
Small campsite with benches and fire ring. No water nearby.

22.1 BRADWELL ISLAND CAMP
A "desperation" piece of slightly higher ground in the swamp forest. Don't plan to use it unless you must. May be overgrown or underwater.

26.0 MANTIS CAMP
Dry clearing in palmettos under pines with a bench and fire ring. Water from nearby ditches.

36.2 INDIAN CREEK CAMP
Ample tenting in a natural bowl in the sandhills, benches and fire ring. Nearby creek. Quiet spot.

41.8 SAPLING HEAD CAMP
Small dry area carved out of wet pine flatwoods. Benches and fire ring. No water nearby.

50.5 VILAS CAMP
Pleasant campsite under tall pines. Benches and fire ring. No water nearby.

57.7 BONNET POND CAMP
Modest clearing with bench and fire ring, ample tenting in open sandhills nearby. Water from pond.

60.9 CAMEL LAKE CAMPGROUND
Recreation area campground with lake views, bathhouse, restrooms. Reserve in advance. Fee.

62.9 MEMERY ISLAND CAMP
Secluded site in sandhills. Benches and fire ring. Nearby stream.

No permits required. All backpackers must bear bag or use a bear canister. Flowing water sources are generally plentiful and preferable to standing water.

Trip Planning

Expect to squish, slosh, and wade. Although many creeks are bridged, swamps are generally not. Wet shoes and socks are the norm. Leashed dogs are welcome but you may not want your pup to put up with miles of wet feet. Alligators reside in Bradwell Bay and other deep swamps.

Gum swamp east of Vilas

Pitcher plants, Apalachee Savannas

Prime months for backpacking are also prime season for prescribed burns. To help avoid getting caught in one, call the Forest Service the morning of your hike and ask about the area you plan to hike. Research hunting seasons and wear bright orange if you hike during hunt dates. This is a popular destination for fall deer hunting.

Paved roads are few. Day hikers shuttling cars to tackle linear segments should plan for long drives between some of the trailheads. Cell service is very spotty throughout the forest.

Land Manager

US Forest Service, National Forests in Florida
Apalachicola Ranger District
11152 NW SR 20, Bristol 32321
850-643-2282

Wakulla Ranger District
57 Taff Dr., Crawfordville 32327
850-926-3561
fs.usda.gov/florida

Highlights

Sopchoppy River, mile 9.3

Following deeply folded bluffs along this tannic waterway, the trail is physically challenging and scenic, showcasing ancient cypress in the river basin.

Bradwell Bay, mile 18.3

Florida's toughest day hike is a deep swamp wade to a rare island of virgin forest. It's one of those hikes you shouldn't tackle solo, which is why the Apalachee chapter of FTA leads an annual Bradwell Bay Swamp Tromp in early March.

Hickory Branch, mile 34.8

While the trail crosses this major waterway by using FR 142, along the footpath are abundant wild azalea with fragrant blooms late February through early March. Scattered bogs northbound have several showy species of carnivorous plants.

Great Wall of Titi, mile 42.7

You have to be a glutton for swamp wading to get to this spot, but it's so unusual we wanted to call your attention to it. Flanking Bay Creek Swamp, dense titi (pronounced tie-tie) shrubs form a continuous thicket at the edge of the pine forest for 0.7 miles. Their white blooms fill the air with a cloyingly sweet scent in springtime.

New River Swamp, mile 52.4

Just west of SR 65, the Florida Trail hops on and off a forest road before plunging into a tangled corridor where island-hopping over flowing tannic waters is necessary. As the trail rises out of the water, it enters a pitcher plant bog.

Shuler Bay, mile 55.1

A trio of boardwalks form a nearly half-mile bridge across Shuler Bay in a deeply shaded floodplain that echoes Bradwell Bay. It's a tricky traverse through a haunting place.

Bonnet Pond, mile 57.6

Named for the water lilies floating on its surface, this sparkling cypress-lined pond is one of the forest's true beauty spots. The Trail of Lakes Loop out of Camel Lake showcases several ponds. This one is at the eastern junction of the loop, with a waterfront bench and nearby campsite.

Recommended Day Hikes

Mile 0.0

Sopchoppy, 8.9 miles linear

Mile 8.9

Sopchoppy River, 4.1 miles linear

Mile 29.1

Langston House, 0.6-mile round trip

Mile 31.8

Porter Lake to Jewel, 4.6 miles linear

Mile 36.3

Jewel to Hickory Branch, 3.2-mile round trip

Mile 50.6

Vilas to Sapling Head Swamp, 6-mile round trip

Vilas to Camel Lake, 10.3 miles linear

Mile 60.9

Camel Lake to Savannah trailhead, 5.3 miles linear

Trail of Lakes, 9.4-mile loop

Side Trip

South of the Savannah trailhead, the **APALACHEE SAVANNAS SCENIC BYWAY** showcases the very best of the savannas, with pitcher plants growing in roadside ditches. The best swarms are just north of Sumatra on the east side of the highway. Drive CR 12 and CR 379 south to Sumatra. Follow SR 65 north to CR 12 north for a 47-mile driving loop. floridahikes.com/apalachee-savannas-scenic-byway.

Sopchoppy River

42. Sopchoppy River

4.1 MILES | APALACHICOLA NATIONAL FOREST, SOPCHOPPY

Follow the gentle curves of the Sopchoppy River as it carves deeply into the bedrock of the Apalachicola National Forest, hiking river bluffs with fabulous views of ancient cypresses.

Overview

Rising from the swamps of the Apalachicola National Forest, the Sopchoppy River snakes through a wilderness landscape for much of its 46 miles, emptying into the Ochlockonee River south of the town of Sopchoppy. This hike provides the best perspective of the river other than from a kayak. It dips in and out of floodplain channels, so there are steep climbs and a lot of drop-offs into the rocky river basin. But that's part of the fun.

Trip Planning / Land Manager

See Apalachicola National Forest. This hike is in the Wakulla Ranger District. Leashed dogs are welcome. Check river levels before hiking: water.weather.gov station SOPF1. If you encounter flowing water across the trail—or if Monkey Creek has topped the footbridge—turn back. A designated campsite is at the north end of this hike.

Directions

Oak Park trailhead [30.130432, -84.495514] is 6.3 miles north of downtown Sopchoppy. Follow Railroad Avenue north. Entering the rural community of Oak Park, it becomes Oak Park Rd, which turns to dirt as FR 365 as it enters the Apalachicola National Forest. Turn left on FR 343. Across the Sopchoppy River bridge, the trailhead has an enormous parking area on the right.

The end point, FR 329 trailhead [30.168764, -84.500664], is along the edge of Bradwell Bay Wilderness. It can be difficult to get to. Avoid driving through mud puddles on these forest roads as there is no way to gauge their depth. Follow the above directions, but don't turn onto FR 343. Continue north another 0.9 miles and bear left onto FR 349, leaving FR 365. Drive 1.8 miles to a T intersection with FR 348. Turn left. Turn left onto FR 329 in 0.6 miles. Cross the Sopchoppy River on Martian Bridge. After 0.4 miles, the trailhead is on the right.

Options

Since the FR 329 trailhead can be hard to drive to and this is a short, scenic section, try a round trip from Oak Park trailhead. Up to FR 329 and back is 7.8 miles, or to Monkey Creek bridge, 3.6 miles. The 8.9-mile Sopchoppy segment extends southeast from the Oak Park trailhead to Carraway Cutoff trailhead [30.074890, -84.404846] in St. Marks National Wildlife Refuge. Largely in pine flatwoods, it has a few tricky titi swamp crossings, a handful of boardwalks, and two designated campsites along its route.

Hike

Leaving Oak Park trailhead northbound, stay left at the junction; the trail to the right is a dead end to where a bridge used to be. Descend steeply along a tannic tributary to a suspension bridge

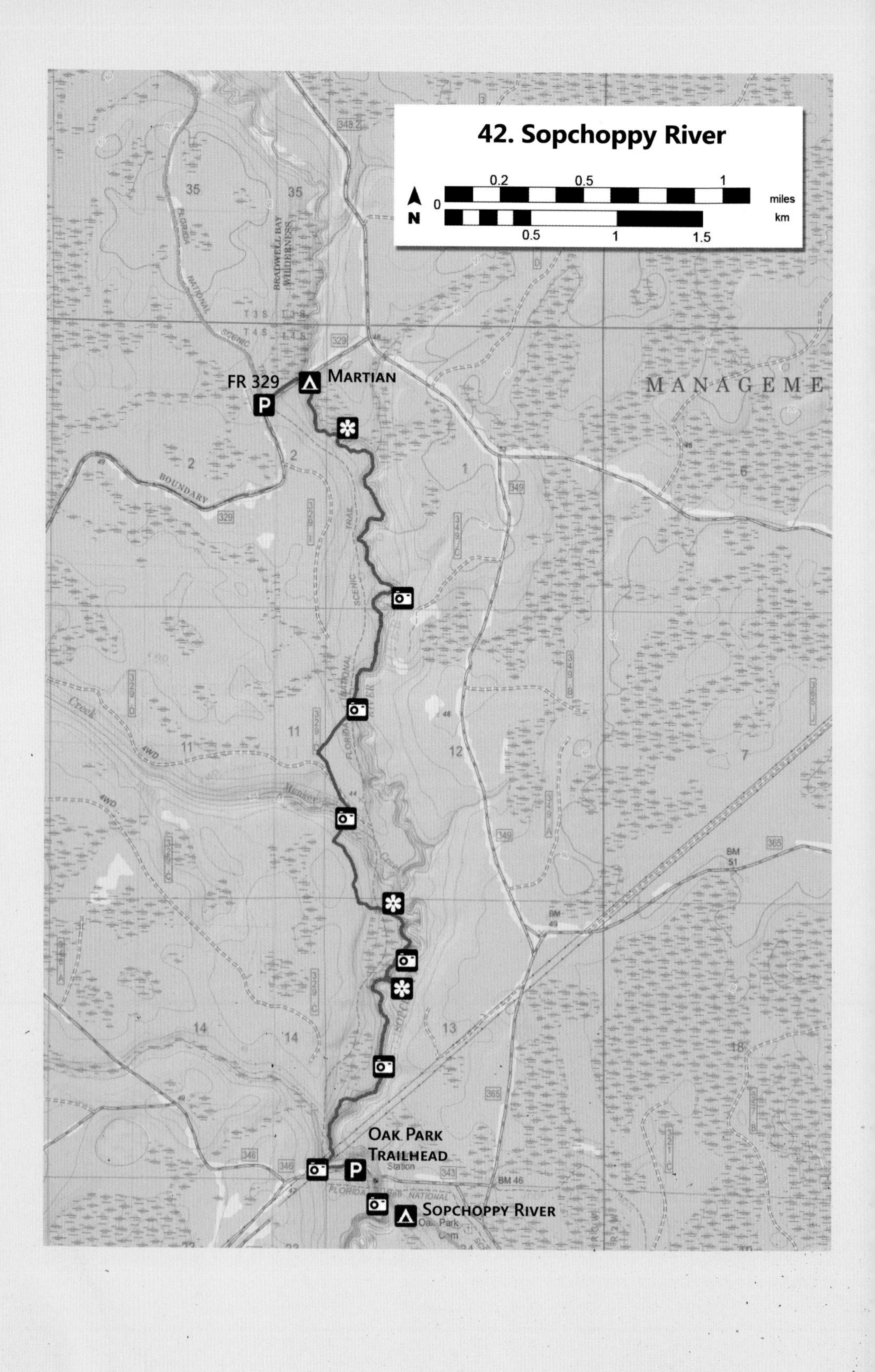

42. Sopchoppy River
0.2
0.5
1
miles
km
0
N
0.5
1
1.5
FR 329
Martian
Oak Park
Trailhead
Sopchoppy River
MANAGEME

with cascades far below. Pass under power transmission lines and through a patch of scrub forest. Emerge above the Sopchoppy River at 0.4 miles. Follow the footpath along the bluffs, with occasional climbs in and out of small ravines.

Notice the many unusual cypress trees along this river. One has a base as flat as the bottom of a shovel, another with a strangely twisted trunk, and yet another blocks the river's flow with a broad base like a giant hoop skirt at about a mile. There's a cypress with a heart-shaped hole in its trunk, too. Oddly shaped cypress knees define portions of the river's generally steep-sided shoreline.

Overlook a peninsula jutting into the river as it rounds a bend. The orange blazes leave the river, leading into a tunnel of titi. It's sometimes soggy underfoot. When titi, a buckwheat tree, blooms in spring, its cloying scent can be almost overwhelming. Emerge from the titi thicket to climb into dry pine flatwoods. Walk beneath a majestic canopy of pines for the next half mile.

At 1.8 miles, descend a slope to meet the Monkey Creek bridge. A path adjoining the bridge leads to water level. As the sole drainage for Bradwell Bay, the water levels of Monkey Creek under this bridge speak to how deep the swamp is right now. Normally, the bridge is high above a deep, narrow ravine punctuated by cypress knees.

Traversing a short stretch of pine flatwoods and scrub, rejoin the river bluffs at 2.3 miles. Views are partly obscured by vegetation, but you can hear the

Bridge along the Sopchoppy

burble of a cascade dropping into the river. Over the next half mile, descend to a couple of natural sand beaches. Wild azalea blooms in spring with soft-pink flowers and an attractive fragrance. The footpath remains close to the river as it climbs in and out of dips carved by tributaries.

An ancient cypress with an enormous base occupies much of the river channel at 3.6 miles, towering above the forest around you. A quarter mile later the trail leaves the river, hooking west through Martian Camp, the one designated campsite along this section.

Its name comes from the nearby highway bridge over the river, which you'll see as the trail reaches FR 329. Martian Bridge sits to the east where the trail goes in the opposite direction. Over two decades ago, the guardrail had a long amusing story scrawled on it about an alien abduction. There isn't anything left to see, but locals still joke about it.

Following the dirt road west briefly, this segment ends at FR 329 trailhead, the eastern gateway to the Bradwell Bay Wilderness, after a 4.1-mile hike.

Shuler Bay boardwalk

43. Vilas to Camel Lake

10.3 MILES | APALACHICOLA NATIONAL FOREST, HOSFORD

An ever-shifting focus from landscape to macro—from vistas of towering pines to pitcher plant bogs, rolling sandhills to leafy titi tunnels—makes this the best hike to experience the botanical diversity of the Apalachicola National Forest.

Overview

A sense of perspective pervades this long, linear day hike thanks to the many habitats it traverses. Pine flatwoods and swamps of all sorts dominate but are particularly beautiful in this part of the forest. Starting with tricky footwork through the gnarly New River Swamp and ending in high, dry sandhills punctuated by a cedar swamp, the hike offers many contrasts. It includes a lengthy traverse of Shuler Bay, the second largest basin swamp along the Florida Trail in the Apalachicola National Forest, via narrow puncheon boardwalks. Lovely Bonnet Pond is a major highlight and a place to linger, either on a bench overlooking its cypress-lined waters or overnight in the only designated campsite along this section.

Trip Planning / Land Manager

See Apalachicola National Forest. This hike is in the Apalachicola Ranger District. Leashed dogs are welcome. The eastern end of this hike is generally very wet. Check the level of the New River before hiking: water.weather.gov station SNWF1. New River Swamp and Shuler Bay aren't safe to cross when the river is high. At the end of this hike, Camel Lake Recreation Area has a swimming beach and restrooms with potable water in its day-use area, where a fee is charged for parking. Beneath a forest canopy, its campground offers beautiful views and restrooms with hot showers. Camping reservations must be made online in advance on recreation.gov. A camp host is normally in residence. If you are camping, the day-use fee is waived.

Directions

To leave a vehicle at the end of this hike, drive south 11.5 miles on CR 12 from SR 20 in Bristol to a left on FR 105, an often-bumpy dirt road. Drive 2 miles to Camel Lake Recreation Area [30.276987, -84.987236] and park in the day-use area. To continue to the start of the hike, return to CR 12 and drive north toward Bristol but turn east onto CR 379 across from the Rex Lumber Mill. After 1.4 miles, turn right on CR 67 and follow this rural paved highway 9.4 miles to Telogia. Turn right onto CR 65. Drive 10.4 miles south to FR 120, a left turn onto a dirt road just before the New River bridge. Vilas trailhead [30.21903, -84.885719] is on the right in a half mile, just past the railroad tracks. It has space for three or four cars.

Options

Camel Lake Recreation Area is a gateway to a variety of hikes. A round trip east to Bonnet Pond is a pleasant and mostly dry 6.6 miles. A bounty of carnivorous plants and colorful wildflowers awaits on a 5.3-mile linear trek west to Savannah trailhead, with wades through swamps. For a soggy full-day

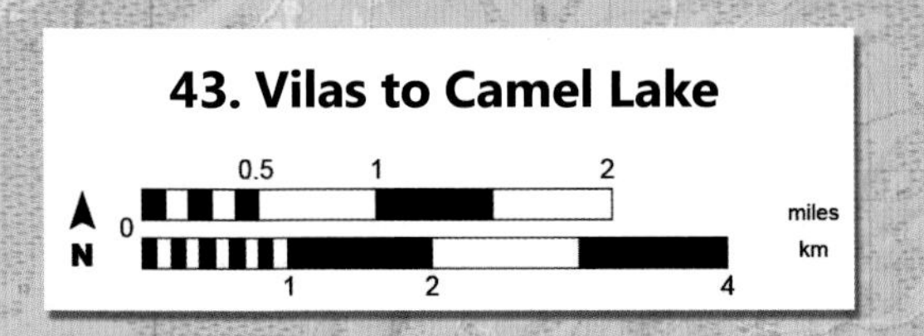
43. Vilas to Camel Lake
0.5
1
2
0
miles
km
N
1
2
4

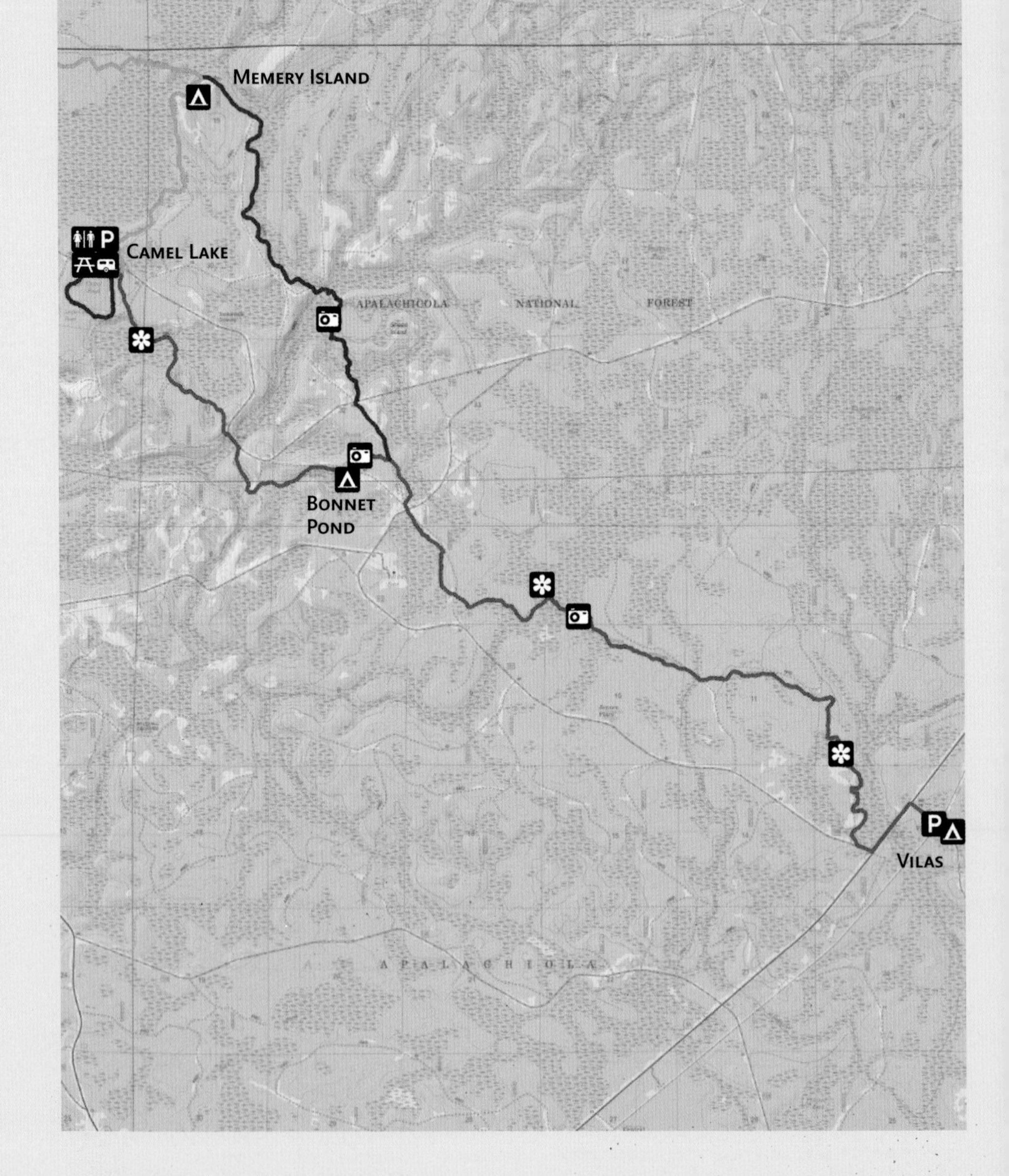
Memery Island
Camel Lake
APALACHICOLA
NATIONAL
FOREST
Bonnet
Pond
Vilas
APALACHICOLA

Pine flatwoods edged by titi thicket

hike, tackle the 9.4-mile Trail of Lakes Loop in either direction. A high and dry 1.1-mile loop circles Camel Pond itself. Soggy and scenic, a hike from Vilas trailhead northbound to the far end of the Shuler Bay boardwalk is a 9.6-mile round trip. If you're dropped off at the start of this hike instead of staging two cars, shave off a 0.7-mile roadwalk by starting just south of the New River bridge where FR 112 turns off SR 65.

Hike

Leaving Vilas trailhead, follow FR 120 west over the railroad tracks to SR 65. Pitcher plants bloom in roadside ditches in April. Use the crosswalk at SR 65 to cross the not-so-busy high-speed two-lane highway. Walk the highway bridge over New River. The trail joins FR 112 to the right immediately after the bridge. At 0.8 miles, enter the forest through a stile.

For the next mile, follow an ecotone where pine flatwoods meets titi swamps, hopping on and off forest roads to skirt the titi. At 1.8 miles the footpath gets squishy, then wet, then goes underwater in the New River Swamp. Figure out a route between the roots and deep holes, then ascend through the sloppy muck of a pitcher plant bog on the other side. The habitat opens into pine flatwoods but remains very boggy and soggy. Carnivorous butterwort and sundew thrive among the grasses.

Join FR 112-H to cross the Hostage Branch floodplain at 3.4 miles. Follow the forest road for a quarter mile before entering towering pine flatwoods on the left. Immerse in this habitat for more than a mile until the trail descends, slipping into a tunnel through a titi thicket. The first gum swamp marks the eastern edge of Shuler Bay.

Traverse three back-to-back boardwalks across this vast, densely canopied basin swamp. In its middle, Bracel Branch flows beneath the boardwalk at 4.7 miles. An unexpected open patch of shallow savanna cradles a collection of white-topped pitcher plants. Rounding it, the boardwalk plunges into gum swamp for another short stretch. When the boardwalk ends, so does Shuler Bay.

Ascend into a majestic stand of longleaf pine. At 5.6 miles cross FR 108-D (also marked as FR 112-L), one of the few major forest roads through this area. There is a small parking area east of the trail crossing. Keep your attention on the orange blazes over the next mile.

Join FR 112-K briefly as the trail corridor squeezes between private property and a stream edged with titi swamp. Cross a small creek along FR 112-K within sight of FR 108-D. Watch for a 90-degree turn west plunging through a wall of titi to reach an expansive sandhill forest dense with turkey oaks.

Meet FR 108-D at a major intersection of forest roads at 6.4 miles. Continue straight across and immediately take the right fork past the intersection. A blazed right turn at a large oak tree marks a transition into scrub habitat. Make an arc to the west above a well-defined baygall with towering loblolly bay trees. A colorful sign marks the Trail of Lakes junction at 6.8 miles. Stay on the orange blazes toward Bonnet Pond, which shimmers through a screen of cypress trees.

Stop at the water's edge to watch the lilies drift across this placid pond. Bonnet Pond Camp, with benches and a fire ring, is just up the hill. For the next mile and a half, hike through sandhills with an open understory. In autumn, the turkey oak leaves turn orange and crimson. At 7.9 miles, circle a shallow grassy sinkhole with pines in the middle before returning to the rolling sandhills.

Emerging onto the white limerock surface of FR 105 at 8.5 miles, the trail uses the forest road to cross Big Gully Creek. It's a steep dip into the creek basin and a climb back out again. Watch for blazing—the trail makes two very quick turns to leave the forest road and ascend into a longleaf pine savanna. Pass by and cross a number of two-track roads. A mile beyond the creek, a sudden plunge into a titi thicket leads to a swamp crossing, the stream in the middle of this gum swamp bridged by a plank.

After another traverse of sandhill habitat, drop into an Atlantic white cedar swamp at 9.8 miles. This uncommon swamp of towering trees is nourished by seepage springs in the uplands. A thick layer of sphagnum moss beneath the trees is always moist. Atlantic white cedar (*Chamaecyparis thyoides*) has a distinctive spiraled bark.

Crossing several more forest roads in the pine flatwoods, the trail reaches a large FNST sign near the edge of the campground at Camel Lake. A side path connects to campsites within view. Wait until you get to the official trail junction before turning off on the side trail that passes the camp host's site. It leads to the entrance road. Walk straight ahead to the parking lot at the day-use area, ending this hike after 10.3 miles.

44. Econfina Creek

19.2 MILES | ECONFINA CREEK WATER MANAGEMENT AREA, FOUNTAIN

Surprisingly rugged and delightfully diverse, the Florida Trail along Econfina Creek is a delight. Suspension bridges, scrambles and sidehill through ravines, the sounds of cascades and rapids, and high bluffs above the spring-fed creek showcase the region's geology.

Overview

Until Hurricane Michael upended the forests north of Panama City in October 2018, we considered Econfina Creek one of the best overnighters in Florida. It has a concentrated diversity of landscapes ranging from high bluffs to deep ravines, low swamps, and rolling sandhills. And it was just plain scenic. Not so much once Michael messed with it, but nature is resilient. Geologic features remained intact. Rattlesnake Lake expanded in size, some tributaries shifted, and although the beech-magnolia forests atop the river bluffs lost a tremendous number of trees, sunlight reaching the understory brought on riotous growth.

Florida Trail Association volunteers spent several years clearing the route and restoring trail infrastructure. To proof our data for *The Florida Trail Guide* and app once the trail reopened, Chris and Chelsey Stevens backpacked this section as we'd done before the hurricane. Necessary reroutes lengthened the trail. State efforts to replace sand pine plantation with longleaf savanna accelerated. Econfina Creek is once again well worth a weekend in the woods.

Trip Planning

Leashed dogs are permitted. Several primitive campsites and developed camping areas are along the route; the latter require a free permit available online from the land manager. Research hunt dates for Econfina Creek WMA in advance and wear bright orange during hunting seasons. Check the level of Econfina Creek before hiking: water.weather.gov station ECBF1. The gauge is downstream from the trail. If the creek is in flood stage at that location, don't attempt this hike.

Land Manager

Northwest Florida Water Management District
81 Water Management Dr., Havana FL 32333
850-722-9919
nwfwater.com

Directions

US 231 and SR 20 intersect 37 miles north of Panama City and 22.5 miles south of Interstate 10 at Cottondale. To reach the western trailhead from this intersection to leave a car, follow SR 20 west for 11 miles to SR 20 trailhead [30.428308, -85.609680]. For the start of the hike, backtrack to US 231 and drive north 7.4 miles. Turn left on Scott Rd. Bear right in 0.6 miles. Continue 2 miles through a rural residential area north of Fountain. Make a left at the trailhead sign and follow a narrow dirt road a quarter mile to Scott Road trailhead [30.548933, -85.435780].

Two Penny Bridge

Options

This is an isolated segment of the Florida Trail with lengthy roadwalks to its east and west. Rough and sandy roads make it tricky for most vehicles to drive into the WMA, but if yours is capable, Walsingham Park [30.481993, -85.523338] makes a good central location from which to reach The Bluffs and Horseshoe Bend as well as Devil's Hole and Tupelo Spring.

Scott Road trailhead provides quick access to the bluffs above Econfina Creek, with small cascades to cross and overlooks along the creek. A round trip to Two Penny Bridge is 3.6 miles; beyond it is Econfina Falls at 4.8 miles. Hiking north from the SR 20 trailhead, enjoy scenic rolling hills topped with restored pine savanna. A round trip to a view of Mabel Porter Pond is 2.2 miles; the campsite at Little Porter Lake is a 4.8-mile round-trip.

Hike

From the kiosk at Scott Road trailhead, walk through the gap in the fence to follow a narrow footpath through a stand of young longleaf pines. Veer right at the large wooden sign with mileage posted to various points along the trail. The path descends into the regrowth of a beech-magnolia forest that lost its old-growth trees. The sound of water rushing over Stairstep Shoal fills the air at 0.9 miles at an overlook of the rapids. Cross numerous plank bridges over tributaries, some of which form cascades into the creek. At 1.8 miles, blue blazes lead to Two Penny campsite, a designated primitive campsite with room for several tents. The first large suspension bridge, Two Penny Bridge, sways as you cross Econfina Creek far below.

Large toppled trees crisscross the bluffs, a path cut between them by FTA volunteers. The creek flows swiftly, rippling across limestone bedrock. At 2.4 miles, Sweetwater Branch plunges over the lip of a cliff on the south bluffs, creating Econfina Falls. The strength of the cascade depends on recent rains. Cross Branning Branch on sturdy Apple Bridge before climbing in and out of dips and ravines, some rather steep. On these slopes, mountain laurel sport fragrant blooms in early spring. The flow of Econfina Creek quickens as surface limestone becomes more prevalent, the creek pouring through near-vertical walls of rock in a canyon below.

By a bridge at 4.3 miles, the landscape flattens out into a regrowth of pine flatwoods. A sign points out the half-mile blue blaze to Trap Pond campsite just before the swaying Fender Bridge over Econfina Creek. A spring run of crystalline water flows beneath a small bridge, an easy-to-reach water source. After an easement for power transmission lines a quarter mile later, walk on sidehill along a long slope above the creek, beneath towering magnolia trees that survived the hurricane. The winding creek is visible over steep edges.

The terrain becomes more rugged 6 miles into the hike, traversing deep, steep dips across tributaries, some bridged. A flat bluff high above the creek provides a panorama and a place to pitch a tent. Beyond it, resume intense climbs in and out of ravines, reaching a geologic feature known as The Bluffs at 7.8 miles. Part sand, part clay, they're eroding down a sharp

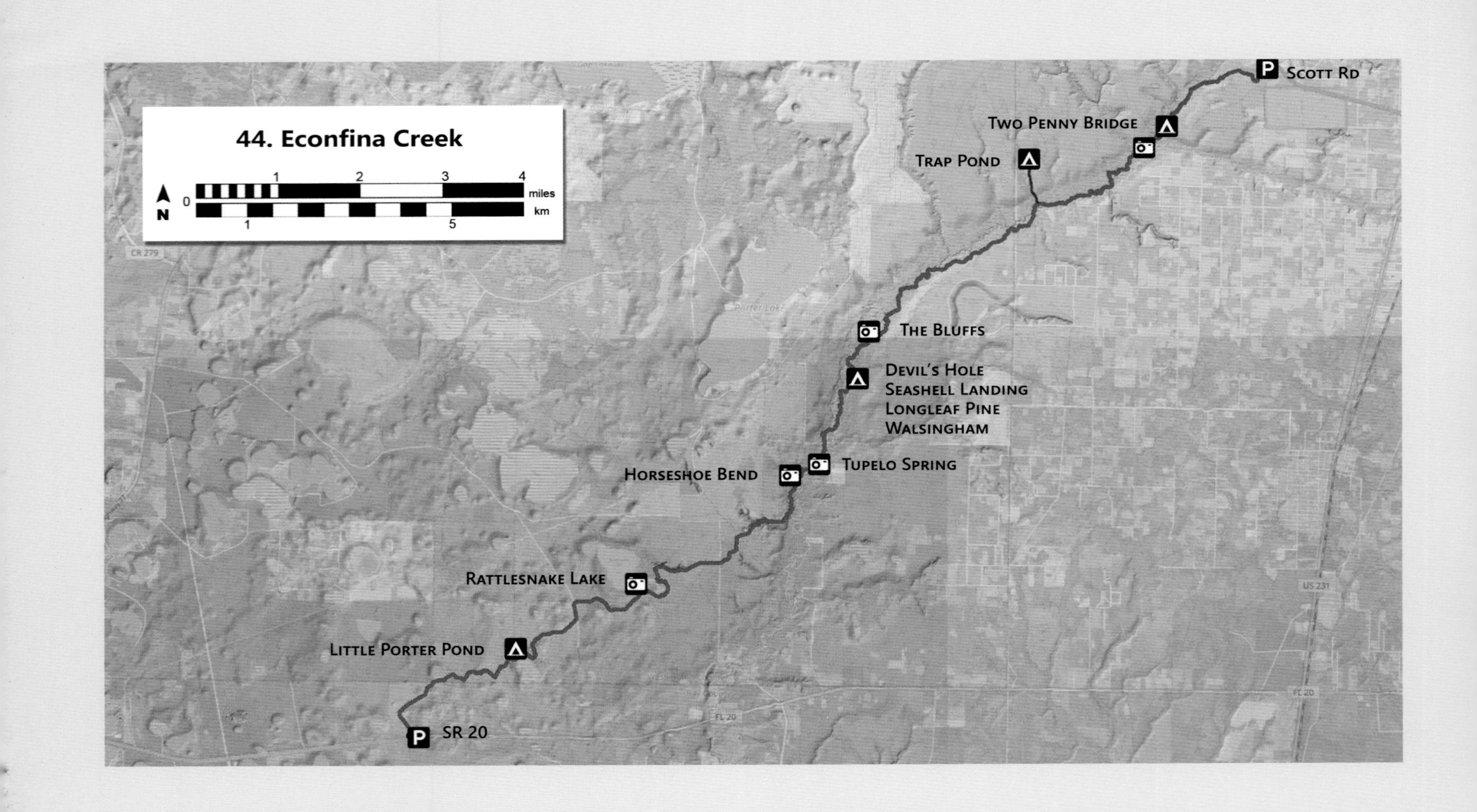
44. Econfina Creek
N
0
1
2
3
4
miles
1
5
km
Scott Rd
Two Penny Bridge
Trap Pond
The Bluffs
Devil's Hole
Seashell Landing
Longleaf Pine
Walsingham
Tupelo Spring
Horseshoe Bend
Rattlesnake Lake
Little Porter Pond
SR 20
CR 279
US 231
FL 20

Longleaf pine savanna

slope toward a bend in Econfina Creek. Descend soon after, reaching a lazy meander around cypress swamps and sinkholes in the floodplain up to Devil's Hole at 8.8 miles.

Devil's Hole is the first of a string of water management recreation areas along the next mile of trail; camping at these must be reserved online. This steep-sided basin is a karst window, a sinkhole that's been used as a swimming hole and water source, but its water quality dropped from clear to murky after the hurricane. Pass through Seashell Landing and Longleaf Pine Recreation Areas along Econfina Creek on the way to Walsingham Bridge. In the opposite direction from the bridge is Walsingham Park at 9.9 miles.

Cross Walsingham Bridge and walk under power lines to enter a hardwood forest bordering the creek's western shore. When a glint of turquoise appears through the trees, slip to the water's edge to see gorgeous Tupelo Spring at 10.5 miles. A half mile later, leave the creek to climb to the rim of tall sandy bluffs along Horseshoe Bend, facing a panorama you'd never expect in Florida with a curve in Econfina Creek far, far below.

A steady climb from this point puts Econfina Creek permanently behind you. One last dive into a ravine reaches Quail Farm Spring Run at 12 miles, an excellent water source. The ascent from it is the steepest along this hike, leaving the ravine's hardwood forest for rolling

Tupelo Spring

sandhills. Formerly blanketed with sand pines planted for pulpwood, most of the forests along the remainder of the hike were clearcut or toppled by hurricanes. Or both. Replanted in longleaf pine and wiregrass, they are slowly transforming to expansive longleaf pine savannas.

At 12.8 miles, cross unpaved Strickland Rd. Sidehill keeps the trail near the top of the steep slope of Rattlesnake Spring Ravine; the spring run at the bottom flows toward Rattlesnake Lake. Since the hurricane the lake expanded, dunking popular Rattlesnake Pond Recreation Area. Take a side trip at 14.6 miles for lakeshore views and picnic tables.

Past Econfina Rd, rolling hills overlook depressions filled with distant prairie ponds. Little Porter Lake campsite is along one of these little gems, with scenic surroundings and easy access to water at 16.8 miles. Leaving the campsite, climb a switchback to a forest road.

Over the next mile of relatively open expanse, the footpath can be tricky to follow. It aims for a depression in the distance, jumping onto a forest road before dropping into the dry sinkhole. A wall of titi thicket shields a stream flowing from a swamp at a higher elevation at 17.6 miles. Cross this quickly on concrete chunks in the water and ascend into an open expanse sloped toward a large wet prairie.

Reaching a copse of sand live oaks along the prairie rim, cross a forest road atop a high sand ridge a half mile later. Mabel Porter Pond glimmers at the bottom of a large sinkhole. From this promontory, the footpath descends through a shimmering savanna of wiregrass and scattered longleaf pines, where showy sky-blue lupine blooms in spring. This is the oldest and finest part of the longleaf savanna restoration along the hike.

The SR 20 trailhead is visible from some distance. Reach the end of this hike at the parking corral at 19.2 miles.

45. Nokuse

27.5 MILES | NOKUSE PLANTATION, FREEPORT

Spanning from the Choctawhatchee River to rolling hills along the eastern boundary of Eglin Air Force Base, the Nokuse section is a compelling destination. It offers physically challenging terrain, outstanding natural features, and botanical beauty along the way.

Overview

In the early 2000s, entrepreneur M. C. Davis purchased more than 53,000 acres of agricultural land in Walton County—pine plantations and sod farms at risk of becoming future subdivisions. With a plan to restore the grand longleaf pine savannas of his youth, he established a private conservancy, Nokuse Plantation. Arranging a permanent conservation easement for the Florida Trail, he ensured the future of the trail would be tied to restoration of this landscape.

Pronounced Nah-Go-Say, Nokuse means "bear" in the Creek language. They definitely roam these hills, but you're far more likely to see white-tailed deer, foxes, turkeys, fox squirrels, and gopher tortoises. Along with a heartening amount of wildlife, you'll see the full spectrum of habitat restoration along this hike, from young candle-stage pines sprouting from tall grasses to a towering canopy of pines with an open understory that stretches on to the horizon.

Trip Planning

Nokuse is broken into three named sections: Choctawhatchee River, Forgotten Creek, and Lafayette Creek. Only foot travel is permitted. Leashed dogs welcome. Backpackers *must* use one of the four designated campsites. No permits are required. Protect your food from bears. Flowing streams provide ample water sources for filtering.

This trail traverses floodplains. Check water levels before hiking: water.weather.gov station BRUF1. A blue-blazed high-water route skirts the Lafayette Creek floodplain, which is tricky to traverse even on a perfect day. Don't enter flowing waters. If the Cypress Creek boardwalk is underwater, turn around.

Hunting is not permitted in Nokuse Plantation, but the trail weaves in and out of water management district lands where it is. All campsites are inside those public lands. Research hunting seasons for Choctawhatchee River WMA and Lafayette Creek WMA. Dress in bright orange if you hike during hunting season.

Prescribed burns are an important part of managing longleaf pine habitat. Call the water management district to determine whether any are planned when you intend to hike. Closures due to burns or flooding are posted at the trailheads.

Land Managers

Nokuse Plantation
13292 CR 3280, Bruce FL 32455
850-835-2457
nokuse.org

Northwest Florida Water Management District
81 Water Management Dr., Havana FL 32333
850-722-9919
nwfwater.com

Longleaf pine restoration at Nokuse

Directions

East to west (trail south to north), the following trailheads are along paved roads.

Choctawhatchee River [30.450644, -85.899513] has a large parking area with restrooms and a picnic shelter west of Ebro off SR 20 at a boat ramp on the west bank of the river.

Seven Runs [30.539318, -85.92038] SR 81 north of Bruce, is on the northwest side of Seven Runs bridge.

Lafayette Creek [30.526541, -86.048592] is at the end of J. W. Hollingsworth Rd off SR 20 east of Freeport.

Owls Head [30.561478, -86.107490] is along US 331 southbound where the Florida Trail enters Eglin Air Force Base. The access point to Nokuse [30.561817, -86.106552] is a stile on the east side of US 331. In between are four lanes of 60 mph traffic and a median. Use caution while crossing the highway.

Options

For an overnighter, arrange a drop-off at US 331 after leaving your car under the bridge near the Choctawhatchee River Boat Ramp and hike to it. Camp at Forgotten Creek after 11.5 miles or River Bend after 19.3. Backpacking southbound lets you tackle the toughest terrain first.

Satisfying short round-trip hikes include Cypress Creek boardwalk from the Choctawhatchee River at 3.2 miles, and a walk through Boggy Head Creek steephead from Seven Runs trailhead at 3 miles. For a surprisingly challenging 6.4-mile loop, head north from Lafayette Creek trailhead into the Lafayette Creek basin and return along the blue-blazed high-water trail. Add an extra 3.4 miles to make it an overnighter with a stay at Steephead campsite. Not as scenic, a round trip south to Forgotten Creek campsite is 4.5 miles, with Red Doe Creek as a highlight.

For a hike and paddle option, drop your kayak or canoe at Dead River Landing [30.541915, -85.890757], a campground a mile off the trail. Backpack from Cowford Landing, a county park with camping shelters for paddlers and hikers immediately south of the Choctawhatchee River Boat Ramp. Spend a night at Dead River Landing. Paddle downriver to Cowford Landing the next day. Paddling the Choctawhatchee takes navigational skill and experience with paddling broad rivers because of its mazy channels and swift currents.

Hike

This narrative stitches together all three sections of Nokuse as a backpacker or section hiker would hike end-to-end northbound. Each can also be day hiked between trailheads.

Choctawhatchee River Section

Park under the Choctawhatchee River bridge adjoining the boat ramp and walk under the bridge. Follow the low grassy shoulder below SR 20 westbound, crossing Howell Bluff Rd. After a quarter mile, look for a gap in the fenceline below the large FNST road sign along SR 20. A plank boardwalk enters Nokuse Plantation. Boardwalks traverse sometimes-squishy spots in a slender strand of swamp forest. At 1.2 miles, join a forest road briefly between stands of longleaf pine of different ages. The trail leaves it, heading due north.

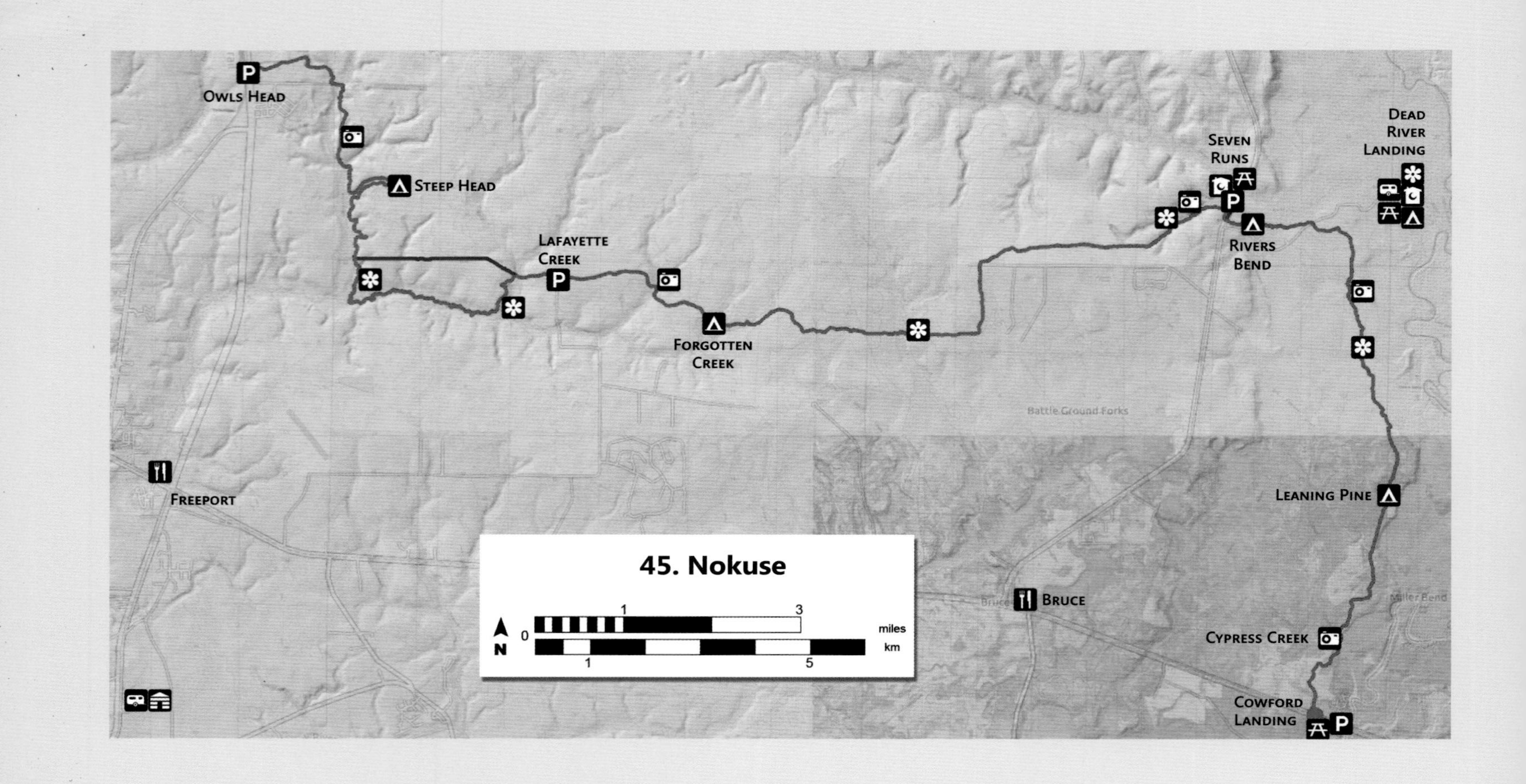

Owls Head
Steep Head
Lafayette Creek
Forgotten Creek
Seven Runs
Rivers Bend
Dead River Landing
Battle Ground Forks
Leaning Pine
Freeport
Bruce
Miller Bend
Cypress Creek
Cowford Landing
45. Nokuse
0
1
3
miles
N
1
5
km

Walking along a deeply forested floodplain, reach the picturesque Cypress Creek boardwalk at 1.6 miles. Savor the reflections of the cypress swamp. If camping at Leaning Pine, obtain water here. Climb into the pine forest beyond the creek. Near the edge of a mature longleaf pine forest, slip through a soggy drainage under tupelo trees. Past this sloppy stuff, the forest is much younger. Beyond two forest road crossings, the landscape opens up at 2.6 miles into an immersive panorama of grassy prairie. Walk through it to reach the distant stand of longleaf pines. A quarter mile later is a gopher tortoise preserve at a T intersection of forest roads. Follow the orange blazes past Jasper Pond, a large pond edged with pine forest.

Past a gate for Choctawhatchee River WMA, the trail leaves the forest road for the woods. Blue blazes at 3.5 miles lead to Leaning Pine campsite, a small clearing with a fire ring and park benches. Beyond it, reenter Nokuse Plantation. Within a mile, the trail draws close to the floodplain of the Choctawhatchee, now visible as a dense wall of trees at the eastern edge of the pine forest. Join a forest road to cross the outflow of a pond at 4.6 miles where tannic waters tip into the road and flow across the gravel before dropping off a concrete lip into a creek. Cross several small drainages within the pine forest. Some are bridged with planks, but one is not.

Descend a sudden slope to cross a natural bridge between two sinkholes at 6.3 miles, the larger of the pair cradling a dark gum swamp. A forest road leads to an old concrete road bridge spanning a waterway. A quarter mile later, a forest road marks the boundary of a place of grandeur, a mature longleaf pine forest with an open understory. The footpath through it has soggy spots. Pines tower above until the next forest road, where the habitat transitions to sandhills. Reach paved Dead River Rd at 7.4 miles. A mile east along it is a primitive campground and launch along the Dead River, noted for its ancient cypresses.

Leave Nokuse Plantation to reenter Choctawhatchee River WMA along the Seven Runs basin. In a half mile, water gushes out of the hill below the footpath like a spring. Two quick 90-degree turns lead to a reservoir berm with lots of private property signs. Deer stands in surrounding trees are occupied during fall hunting season. A sharp right off the berm returns the footpath to the woods. Step across a small creek.

Reach an overlook on Seven Runs Creek at 8.2 miles. Tannic and sand-bottomed, it's the water source for Rivers Bend campsite. Past the sharp turn and uphill, the campsite is to the left down a blue blaze and has park benches and a fire ring. Leaving the floodplain, climb through sandhills where young longleaf pines fill clearings in a former pine plantation. Emerge onto the shoulder of SR 81 at 8.5 miles. Cross the highway, which has sporadic high-speed traffic.

Forgotten Creek Section

Subtract 8.3 miles from the following mileages for day hiking from Seven Runs trailhead, 0.2 miles north of the trail crossing along SR 81; there is a picnic table and portable toilet. Day hikers walk south along the shoulder of SR 81 to reach the trail crossing.

Rejoining the Seven Runs floodplain

a quarter mile past SR 81, hike along a bluff with views of the braided streams. Enter a steephead ravine, a cool and shady habitat. Follow the edge of the clear burbling creek, with access to filter water a mile in. Florida anise (*Illicium floridanum*) appears in the understory and mountain laurel adds its clusters of fragrant blossoms each spring. A plank bridge spans Boggy Head Creek at 9.5 miles. Ascending, the footpath parallels the waterway past burbling cascades. Climb steeply out of the steephead ravine into sandhills with a dense growth of gopher apple around the saw palmettos. Gopher tortoises frequent these drier uplands, their burrows visible from the trail.

Cross a sand road at 10.1 miles. To the west is a gate to Airport Rd, the final access point by public road to the eastern end of Nokuse. There won't be another until the Lafayette Creek trailhead. The trail enters a longleaf pine restoration area with unusual artifacts that M. C. Davis explicitly left in place for hikers to find—sod sprinklers. The first one has odd bicycle-like metal wheels. Walk beneath the thick pipes of the second one at 10.8 miles. Hike through restoration areas for the next two miles, crossing three forest roads. There may be clear cuts, grading, or replanting through this section. Watch for orange blazes.

Descend into a gum and titi floodplain along Black Creek at 13.5 miles. Expect muck and damp spots. Filter water from a sandy curve in the creek before crossing the bridge over it. Walk a plank over Little Black Slough, which flows through the wall of titi defining both sides of the trail. Climb out of the floodplain to reach a sand road at 14 miles. Entering the next longleaf pine restoration area, the trail hops on and off roads used as firebreaks.

Drop from a corridor edged by saw palmettos in the sandhills into a titi tunnel to walk a plank over Little Black Creek. Rising out of the titi, return to the restoration area. Cross a few more firebreaks before entering Lafayette Creek WMA, marked by a boundary sign at 15.1 miles. Descend through a gauntlet of splayed tupelo trees into a murky floodplain. Lafayette Creek, a ribbon of tannic water, curls through this rough-bottomed swamp. Although the waterway is bridged, the approaches to the bridge are not and may be sloppy. Pick your way between deep mud holes carefully. Once out of the goo, follow blazes through a thicket of understory. Cross a forest road before the trail descends to Forgotten Creek.

Adjoining the footpath at 16 miles, Forgotten Creek campsite has small benches and a fire ring. The hillside plummets to the creek just past the campsite. Cradled by a bowl of gum swamp, Forgotten Creek isn't easy to get to. The creek is bridged but the swamp extends well beyond the span, a titi tunnel leading to pine flatwoods on higher ground. Cross two forest roads in the pine flatwoods over the next quarter mile before joining the rim of a steephead ravine. A sharp downhill leads to Red Doe Creek at the bottom, a beauty spot at 17 miles. It's bridged by a broad plank, but the uphill scramble can be slippery.

Emerge from this steephead to an extensive longleaf pine restoration area on relatively flat ground. Spend the next mile in this young forest. An overhead

Cypress Creek reflections

power line roughly marks its midpoint. At 18.2 miles, a sign at a forest road points to Lafayette Creek trailhead.

Lafayette Creek Section

Lafayette Creek trailhead is 250 feet compass south of the trail. It's a small dirt parking area with a kiosk. Subtract 18.2 miles from the following mileages for day hiking from this trailhead.

Wind through a longleaf pine restoration area in the first half mile before a steep slope into the Wolf Creek floodplain. Clusters of white-topped pitcher plants rise from pine duff on the forest floor. Emerging on a forest road, cross a bridge over Wolf Creek. Meet the eastern junction with the blue-blazed Lafayette Creek bypass at 18.7 miles. Return to it if Lafayette Creek is flooded.

The orange blazes turn sharply left at the junction to enter a restoration area. Along a deeply eroded forest road, swing around a horseshoe curve along the lip of a narrow steephead ravine. Passing a perched seepage bog where pitcher plants thrive farther downslope, plunge into the Lafayette Creek floodplain at 19.5 miles. If water is flowing across the trail at *any* point, turn back and use the bypass. Although not broad, Lafayette Creek is deep and swift. You don't want to accidentally step into it.

Within the next quarter mile, the rough stuff begins with a difficult route through a floodplain swamp. The forest floor isn't solid ground, but moss-rimmed puddles and muck and slippery roots. Wayfinding takes some skill. Keep the orange blazes in sight but don't as-

Boggy Head Creek

sume following them is the best path. Sometimes there is a less direct but drier route.

Reach a solid white sand bluff tossed into the floodplain whenever Lafayette Creek spills over its banks. Cross Little Creek on a footbridge at 20 miles. Climbing out of the floodplain briefly, enjoy brief upland vistas. Descending a bluff along an oxbow pond, curve through a patch of scrub habitat before settling into the swamp forest of the Lafayette Creek floodplain.

It's tricky navigating across slippery roots and sloppy, muddy, leafy pools of water. A plank footbridge spans Tom Turtle Creek at 20.7 miles. On the other side, enter another tough stretch of swamp forest along Lafayette Creek. Deep mossy puddles are trapped between tree roots and you have to figure out how to get around them.

Bamboo appears in the understory near the swampy confluence of Magnolia and Lafayette Creeks at 21.5 miles. More gooey mud awaits as the footpath tunnels through a titi swamp. At the white sand bank, breathe a sigh of relief. That's it for the Lafayette Creek floodplain. Ascend the bluff from Magnolia Creek and cross Snake Eating Creek on a boardwalk. Emerge from the bluff forest at the western junction with the blue-blazed bypass route at 22.1 miles.

Slipping around an old barbed wire fence, parallel Magnolia Creek upstream. A half mile later, descend into a ravine to cross Little Coyote Creek on a plank footbridge. Follow this creek downstream, with a sharper descent to Missing Creek, a shallow, crystalline waterway. On the ascent, look back and admire the view. The trail becomes sidehill, tracing the curve of the ravine you exited. At 23.2 miles, cross two shallow creeks on a series of puncheons.

Emerge from a stand of sand live oaks. A planted prairie of wiregrass edges the rim of Steep Head. Steepheads are formed by groundwater erosion. As the ravine deepens around the stream flowing from it, it becomes cooler inside than the habitats along its rim. This one hosts a lush hardwood forest with old-growth trees and is an excellent example of the geologic process. Steephead campsite adjoins the trail at 24.1 miles. This small designated campsite has a fire ring and benches in a cleared area with wiregrass clumps.

Descending sharply after the campsite, reach the bottom of Steep Head to cross a thick plank bridge, the stream the closest water source for the campsite. Climbing out of the ravine, follow sidehill for the next half mile. Leaving the edge of Steep Head, ascend toward a young longleaf pine forest before a drop into the ravine surrounding Magnolia Creek, where Southern magnolias thrive. Following a curving descent, listen to the tiny cascades at Little Falls Creek at 24.9 miles. Half-hidden by forest, they are hard to see until you cross the bridge and look behind you. Meet the floodplain of Magnolia Creek, drawing close to its sandy banks. Expect muddy spots and hummock hopping.

Climbing from Magnolia Creek, crest a windswept hilltop of young longleaf pine forest with a panorama of ridges to the north. This part of Florida has some of the state's highest elevations. Descending sharply from the ridge, cross Minnow Creek on a plank bridge. Climb out of its steephead and the trail descends again, with a low span over Sweet Spot Creek at 25.8 miles. If you are backpacking into Eglin Air Force Base after finishing Nokuse, filter water here. This is your last guaranteed water source for the next six miles.

Emerging onto an crumbling paved road, make a sharp left to cross Magnolia Creek on a road bridge high above the water at 26.1 miles. Blazes lead down a slope on the northwest side of the bridge, where the trail parallels the west side of the ravine. Once it climbs out of the Magnolia Creek basin for the last time, it edges its west side for a stretch.

Leaving the shade of the oaks near the ravine, make a compass southwest turn to cross a longleaf pine restoration area on a former sod farm. Blaze posts mark the route. Exit Nokuse Plantation at a gap between a wooden fence and a locked gate along the east side of US 331. Cross the sometimes-busy highway to reach Owl's Head trailhead on its west side, finishing this 27.5-mile hike.

Sandhill habitat, Eglin

Western Panhandle

With folded hills and ridges just north of the white sand beaches of the Gulf of Mexico, the northwest corner of Florida provides dramatic topography and scenery for hikers to enjoy.

Juniper Creek basin, Blackwater

BASE CAMPS

DeFuniak Springs

Established in 1881 along the L&N Railroad, DeFuniak Springs had its heyday as a grand cultural center. The southernmost camp of the Chautauqua movement still retains its Victorian flair and is home to the state's oldest library.

STAY

Best Western Crossroads Inn 850-892-5111, 2343 US 331 S.

Holiday Inn Express 850-520-4660, 326 Coy Burgess Loop.

Hotel DeFuniak 850-610-8800, 400 E Nelson Ave.

Sapphire Island Camping & RV Park 850-520-4757, 5687 US 331 S.

EAT

4C BBQ 850-892-4227, 1045 US 331.

Bogie's Bar & Restaurant 850-951-2233, 660 Baldwin Ave.

Ed's Restaurant 850-892-5839, 1324 US 90 W.

La Rumba 850-951-2174, 1317 US 331.

SEE AND DO

Historic downtown and residential district.

Chautauqua Winery 850-892-5887, 364 Hugh Adams Rd.

Florida's High Point (345′) at Britton Hill [30.986008, -86.281109].

Walton County Heritage Museum 850-401-2060, 1140 Circle Dr.

Crestview

Atop a high ridge north of the Shoal and Yellow Rivers, Crestview sits between Eglin Air Force Base and Blackwater River State Forest. The Florida Trail goes right through its business districts and historic downtown.

STAY

Comfort Inn & Suites 850-801-3681, 900 Southcrest Dr.

Hampton Inn 850-409-3360, 112 John King Rd.

Holiday Inn Express 850-398-8100, 125 Cracker Barrel Rd.

River's Edge Campground 850-537-2267, 4001 Log Lake Rd, Holt.

EAT

Desi's Downtown Restaurant 850-682-7477, 197 N Main St.

Pepper's Mexican Grill and Cantina 850-398-5042, 1900 S Ferdon Blvd.

Pounders Hawaiian Grill 850-306-2451, 6276 Old Bethel Rd.

SEE AND DO

Historic downtown shops and murals.

Milton

Incorporated in 1884, Milton grew up along the Blackwater River, a transportation artery of that time. Its history is reflected in downtown buildings, museums, and murals throughout this riverfront town.

STAY

Gulf Pines KOA 850-623-0808, 8700 Gulf Pines Dr.

Blackwater River State Park 800-326-3521, 7720 Deaton Bridge Rd.

Coldwater Gardens 850-426-1300, 7009 Creek Stone Rd.

Holiday Inn Express 850-626-9060, 8510 Keshav Taylor Dr.

Old School House Inn 850-623-6197, 8974 Tomahawk Landing Rd.

EAT

Ace's Restaurant 850-623-3611, 6583 Caroline St.

Blackwater Bistro 850-623-1105, 5147 Elmira St.

David's Catfish House 850-626-1500, 5129 Dogwood Dr.

SEE AND DO

Blackwater Canoe Rental 850-623-0235, 6974 Deaton Bridge Rd.

Adventures Unlimited 850-623-6197, 8974 Tomahawk Landing Rd.

Arcadia Mill Archaeological Site 850-626-3084, 5709 Mill Pond Ln.

Blackwater Heritage State Trail 850-983-5338, 5533 Alabama St.

West Florida Railroad Museum 850-623-3645, 5003 Henry St.

Navarre and Navarre Beach

Named for a province of Spain, these two communities face each other on Santa Rosa Sound, which the Florida Trail crosses on the pedestrian walkway of the CR 399 highway bridge.

STAY

Hampton Inn 850-939-4848, 7710 Navarre Pkwy.

Best Western Navarre Waterfront 850-939-9400, 8697 Navarre Pkwy.

Navarre Beach Campground 850-939-2188, 9201 Navarre Pkwy.

Springhill Suites by Marriott 850-939-0010, 8375 Gulf Blvd.

EAT

Alphy's Catfish House 850-515-1201, 1900 SR 87.

Sailors' Grill 850-939-1092, 1451 Navarre Beach Cswy.

SEE AND DO

Navarre Pier 850-710-3239, 8579 Gulf Blvd.

Gulf Breeze Zoo 866-620-1825, 5701 Gulf Breeze Pkwy, Gulf Breeze.

Pensacola Beach

Sandwiched between miles of natural beaches protected as Gulf Islands National Seashore, Pensacola Beach is a residential community just a few blocks wide with a tight core of hotels and restaurants in its center.

STAY

Fort Pickens Campground 877-444-6777, 1400 Fort Pickens Rd.

Margaritaville Beach Hotel 850-916-9755, 165 Fort Pickens Rd.

Paradise Inn 850-932-2319, 21 Via De Luna Dr.

Pensacola Beach RV Resort 850-932-4670, 17 Via De Luna Dr. *No tents.*

Surf and Sand Hotel 850-934-5400, 40 Fort Pickens Rd.

EAT

Flounder's Chowder House 850-932-2003, 800 Quietwater Beach Rd.

Native Cafe 850-934-4848, 45 Via De Luna Dr. A.

Peg Leg Pete's 850-932-4139, 1010 Fort Pickens Rd.

SEE AND DO

Fort Barrancas, 850-455-5167, 3182 Taylor Rd.

Fort Pickens, 850-934-2600, 1400 Fort Pickens Rd.

Historic Pensacola Village 850-595-5993, 205 Zaragoza St, Pensacola.

National Naval Aviation Museum 850-452-3604, 1750 Radford Blvd, Pensacola.

Naval Live Oaks Preserve 850-934-2600, 1801 Gulf Breeze Pkwy, Gulf Breeze.

Blue Angels practicing over Fort Pickens

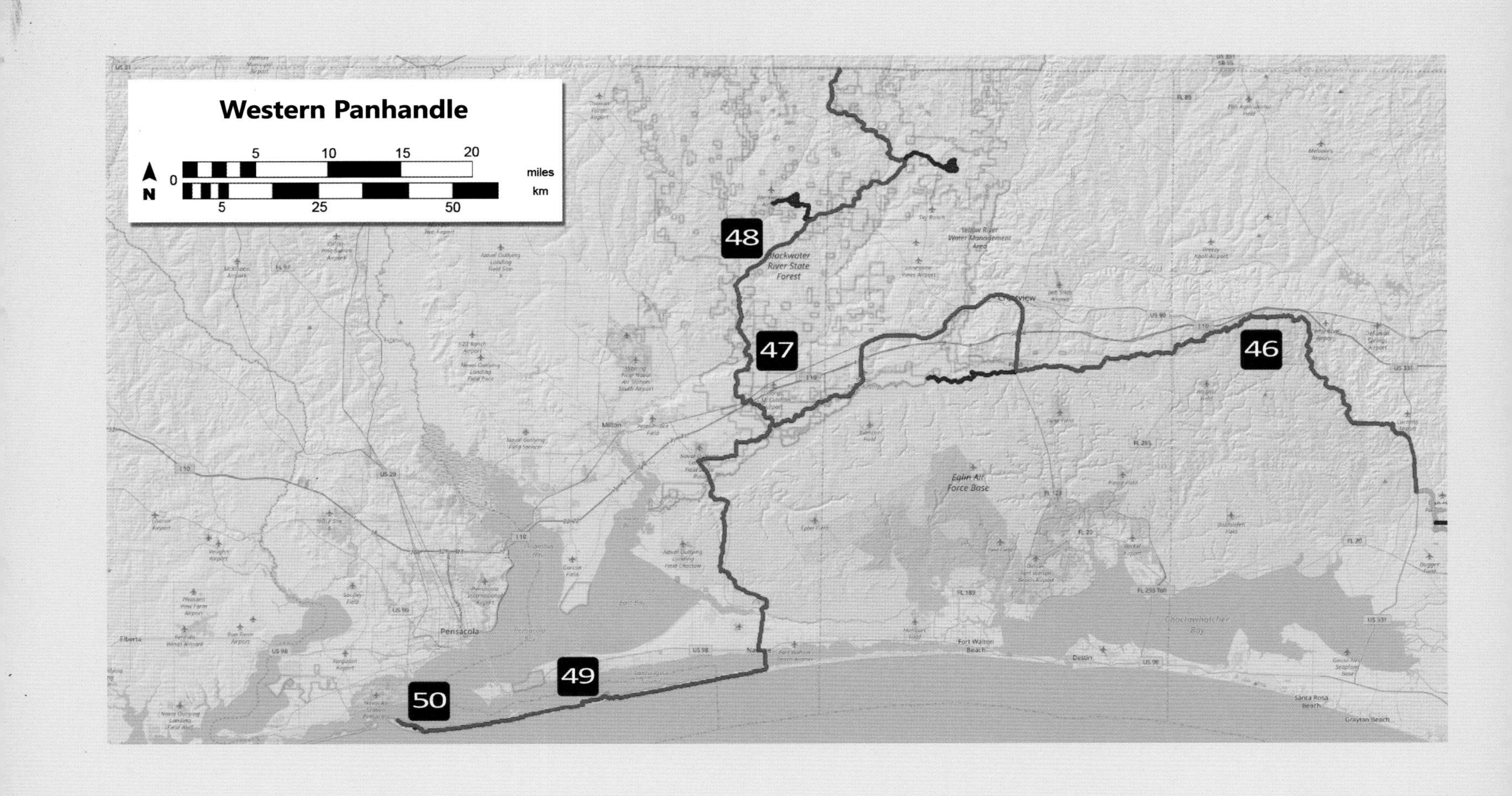
Western Panhandle
0
5
10
15
20
miles
5
25
50
km
N
48
47
46
49
50
Blackwater River State Forest
Yellow River Water Management Area
Eglin Air Force Base
Milton
Pensacola
Fort Walton Beach
Destin
Choctawhatchee Bay
Santa Rosa Beach
Grayton Beach
Elberta

Anise Creek, Catface section

46. Eglin

41.9 MILES | EGLIN AIR FORCE BASE, NICEVILLE

Steep descents. Immersive forests. Burbling waterways. A high suspension bridge. These are some of the many elements that make the Florida Trail on Eglin Air Force Base a compelling destination for day hikers and backpackers alike.

Overview

Established concurrently with the Ocala National Forest in 1908, Choctawhatchee National Forest was a vast swath of old-growth longleaf pine forest tapped for turpentine and timber. Ceded to the War Department in 1940, the forest allowed Eglin Field in Valparaiso to expand from 1,460 acres to over 384,000 acres. Crucial for training Army Air Force fighter pilots for World War II, Eglin grew into a nationally important military aviation testing center for aircraft and armament. Covering 724 square miles, Eglin Air Force Base is the largest military base in Florida. Outdoor recreation is overseen by the Jackson Guard.

Of six distinct Florida Trail segments across the base, the three showiest—Alaqua, Catface, and Titi—make a continuous route from DeFuniak Springs to Crestview, with trailheads easily accessed from Interstate 10. Well defined and pleasant to hike, this portion of the Florida Trail across Eglin Air Force Base is one of the trail's best hikes statewide.

Trip Planning

Hikers must obtain a required recreation permit at the Eglin Natural Resources Office (open from Monday to Friday, 7:30 a.m. to 4:30 p.m., closed federal holidays) or online at eglin.isportsman.net before hiking at Eglin Air Force Base. Day-use permits are $5, annual permits $30. Thru-hikers should call the Natural Resources Office before reaching Eglin to arrange a free permit.

Portions of the base may close at any time. Check the Public Access Map (PAM) before hiking to avoid entering active military operations or prescribed burns. It shows an advance closure forecast for the next three or four days. Review PAM at eglinlife.com/jg/ or call 850-882-4164 to ensure where you plan to hike will be open. Recheck the morning of your hike. One exception: if the PAM shows closures between Eglin Portal trailhead (US 331) and Roger Nelson Rd (RR 208) in Alaqua section, you can hike that 7.7-mile segment unless it is signposted closed.

Leashed dogs are welcome. Bicycles are not. The Florida Trail is hiking only in Eglin. Never stray from the trail corridor—unexploded ordinance lurks in these woods. If you see a rocket, bomb, or hand grenade, don't approach it. Call the 96th Force Support Squadron (850-882-2502) to report the location. You may encounter military personnel or equipment. During hunting seasons, wear bright orange. Hunt dates are posted on the iSportsman website. Expect to see hunters with dogs any time of year in a dog-training area along the Catface section.

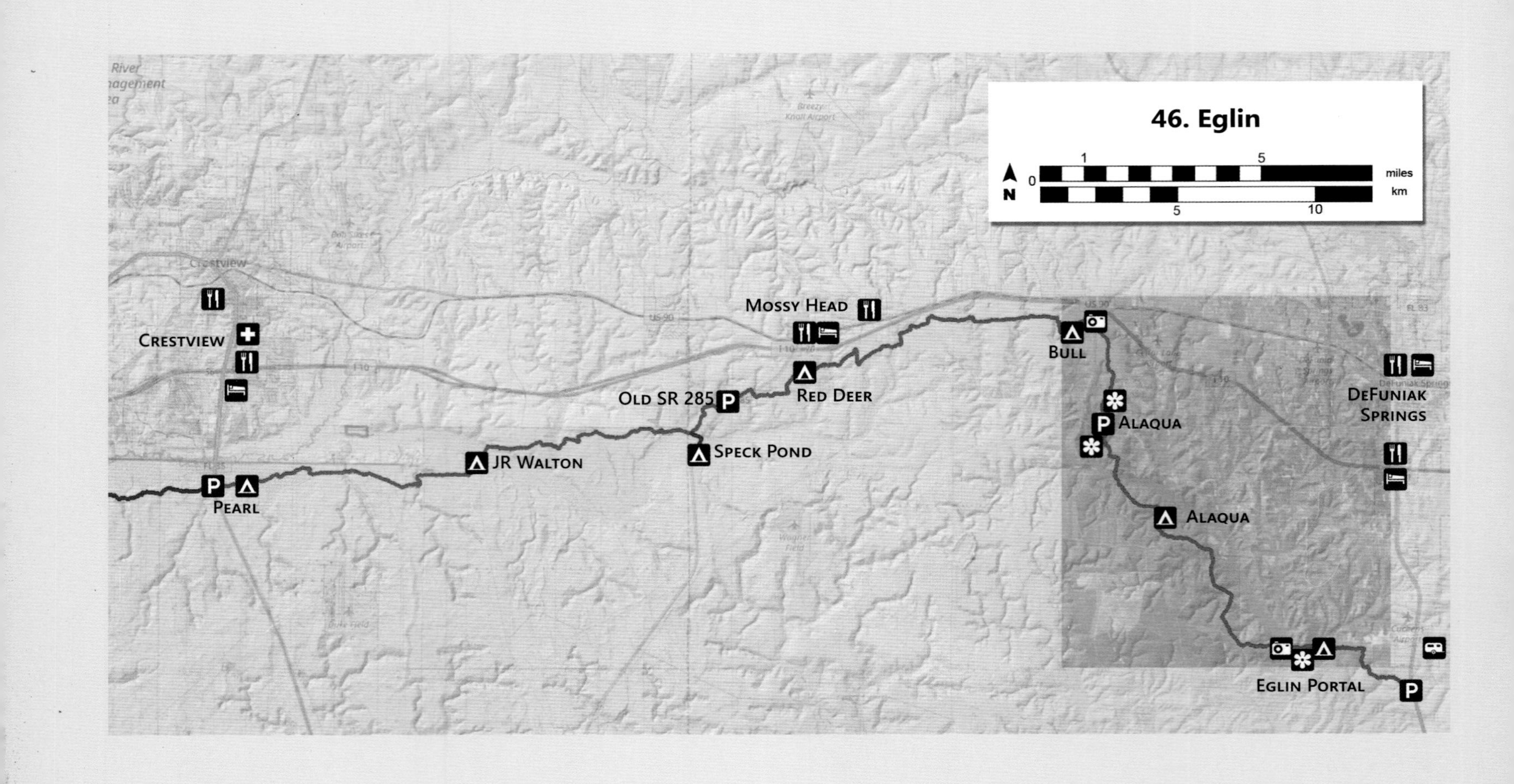
46. Eglin
0
1
5
miles
km
5
10
N
Crestview
Pearl
JR Walton
Speck Pond
Old SR 285
Red Deer
Mossy Head
Bull
Alaqua
Alaqua
Eglin Portal
DeFuniak
Springs
Breezy Knoll Airport
US 90
I-10

Designated campsites must be used. Visit the Natural Resources Office to obtain camping permits. Ground water sources are abundant but must be filtered. Expect the sounds of artillery fire and bombs dropping at night. Traffic noise from Interstate 10 echoes across the Bull, Red Deer, and Pearl campsites. Bring earplugs. Bear bag or use a bear canister.

The Alaqua Creek basin is treacherous when flooded. Check water levels in advance: water.weather.gov station ALQF1. Turn back if you encounter flowing water.

Land Manager

Eglin Air Force Base
Natural Resources Office
107 SR 85 N, Niceville 32578
850-882-4165 or 850-882-4166
eglin.isportsman.net

Directions

East to west (trail south to north), these are the trailheads for this hike. All are off paved roads but are simply dirt parking areas at a kiosk. Some are very small.

Eglin Portal [30.618299, -86.117218] Follow US 331 south from Interstate 10 at DeFuniak Springs for 5.1 miles. The trailhead is on the west side of the highway across from a fire station.

Alaqua [30.706369, -86.233582] Follow Bob Sikes Rd for 6.6 miles west from the traffic light with US 331 in DeFuniak Springs. The trailhead is on the left on a slope.

Old SR 285 [30.714701, -86.376221] Take SR 285 south for 2 miles from Interstate 10 exit 70. The trailhead is on the right.

Pearl [30.687201, -86.571892] Trailhead is a few miles south of Interstate 10 at SR 85 in Crestview and north of Colonel Greg Malloy Rd. It is accessed by a short dirt road off the northbound lanes of SR 85. Look for the FNST sign.

Options

Logistics for backpacking can be tricky due to base closures, but excellent round-trip hikes abound. A must is the 7.8 miles from Eglin Portal trailhead to Alaqua Creek and back. Past Eglin Portal campsite, it descends into an ancient beech-magnolia forest; the scenery keeps improving all the way to the suspension bridge. Hiking southbound to Alaqua campsite from Alaqua trailhead has both challenging climbs and boardwalks through lush swamps across 6.4 miles. Northbound, a mile-round trip to Anise Creek immerses you in botanical beauty. Keep going to reach the Florida Trail's high point with a 6.2-mile round trip or turn around at Bull campsite for 7.4 miles. Don't miss the blue blaze downhill to Cascade Grotto.

From Old SR 285 trailhead, a 10.4-mile round trip northbound to Big Fork Creek crosses crystalline streams and rolling hills with some steep descents. Trim that hike by turning around at Dog Creek after 4.6 miles or the end of the Gum Creek boardwalk after 3.6 miles. Pretty Pearl Creek is a 1.6-mile round trip from Pearl trailhead that tunnels through titi. It may be soggy underfoot. Continue to colorful Institution Branch and back for 5.2 miles.

Park along the shoulder at the trail crossing on Colonel Greg Malloy Rd for day hikes. Moore Creek is a nice 1.8-mile round trip northbound, and Silver Creek and Honey Creek are scenic turnaround points southbound for 1.6 and 5.2 miles respectively.

Hike

This narrative stitches together all three contiguous sections as a backpacker or section hiker would tackle it end-to-end northbound. Each can be day hiked between trailheads.

Alaqua Section

At Eglin Portal trailhead, enter a sand pine forest with increasingly taller trees the deeper in you get. Sand pines yield to longleaf, providing a high canopy with an open understory and comfortable pine duff. Within a half mile drop into a swale to cross shallow Switch Cane Branch, a clear sand-bottomed stream, on a plank. Walk beneath tall pines to emerge at an open area bisected by power lines. Cross the grassy slope and reenter the pine forest.

Dense vegetation frames the approach to a plank bridge over Moccasin Creek at 1.3 miles. Slightly broader than Switch Cane Branch, this creek has a darker bottom but clear water. A boardwalk spans a gum swamp before the trail rises into a longleaf pine forest. Over the next half mile, the habitat transitions to sand pine scrub. Cross Forrest Oak Rd at 1.9 miles, a sand road connecting to US 331 east through a residential area.

Pass an ancient, towering Choctawhatchee sand pine amid the immersive sand pine forest stretching on nearly a mile. Losing elevation through a thicket of sparkleberry, enter a dense beech-magnolia forest. At 2.8 miles, Eglin Portal campsite is an appealing flat perch on a bluff. A blue-blazed trail leads to its water source, a clear stream.

Quickly descending through the beech-magnolia forest, reach Trapper Bridge, a plank bridge over a horseshoe bend in a waterway. Walking through more showy forest, reach a long beam bridge at 3.2 miles over shallow, clear Blount Creek. It's a balancing act with a guy wire to steady your crossing.

On the other side, hike past gigantic trees in a dense beech-magnolia forest. After a ladder leads to the top of a unique geologic uplift, drop into the Alaqua Creek floodplain. Traverse a broad swampy area on a series of boardwalks. With just the right angle of sunlight and lack of shade in winter, a "rainbow swamp" effect appears on the swamps on the left.

Following the banks of Alaqua Creek, reach a sturdy suspension bridge over the swift, deep waterway at 3.9 miles. Scramble out of its floodplain and cross Turpentine Branch, a clear fast-flowing stream, a half mile later. By 5.5 miles, reach a strange tangle of uprooted pine tree roots, the Alaqua Dragon.

Enter an extensive sand pine forest, walking beneath two sets of power transmission lines over the next mile. Clumps of deer moss rise from the carpet of pine needles on the forest floor. At 6.6 miles, descend a long, steep slope through a beech-magnolia forest to reach bog bridges leading to a span over crystalline Sparkleberry Creek. Climb into more sand pine forest, crossing two faint two-track roads among the trees.

Descend a steep slope thickly covered in pine needles through a stand of Florida anise to walk along Oakie Creek. A sturdy bridge spans this waterway, leading to bog boardwalks zigzagging through a gum swamp in the floodplain. Climb out of the swamp to cross Roger Nelson Rd, a broad clay road at 7.8 miles. Pines dominate the next mile. Is-

Beech-magnolia forest, Alaqua section

lands of longleaf break up the vast sand pine scrub.

At 9.1 miles, curve downhill to Lyonia Branch, a clear sand-bottomed stream. A gentle dip in the forest marks the basin of Dykes Branch, a shallower waterway. The sand pine forest continues west of these creeks, making it easy to spot Alaqua campsite at 9.6 miles. It's the largest of the campsites along in Eglin and can accommodate groups on its soft pine duff. Amenities include benches and a fire ring, a full-sized picnic bench, and a permanent grill. Just beyond it, Hellfire Creek serves as its water source. Ascend past it to traverse an expanse of clayhill forest—sandhills on clay—where turkey oaks wave their leaves at eye level. This is the flattest part of the Alaqua section. Jump Across Creek is as cute as its name: a plank bridge crosses a narrow waterway at 10.7 miles.

Long boardwalks leading into a gum swamp end at Little Alaqua Creek at 11.3 miles. Swift and deep, it is crossed by a substantial bridge. Climb steeply through a beech-magnolia forest on the other side. A mile later, descend from the shade of turkey oaks and sand pines and traverse the White Top Creek basin via a series of boardwalks across the floodplain. Its name comes from rare white-topped pitcher plants. A few sprout right along the steep ascent from the creek, the footpath muddy and slippery from the flow of seepage springs.

Reach the top of White Top Hill and walk along its bluff. Downslope, natural terraces hold a showy array of pitcher plant bogs fed by seepage springs. Make a sharp right to follow the orange blazes uphill beneath longleaf pines. Emerge at Alaqua trailhead above Bob Sikes Rd at 12.9 miles.

Silver Creek, Titi section

Catface Section

Subtract 12.9 miles from the following mileages for day hiking north from Alaqua trailhead.

Descend steeply from Bob Sikes Rd through a beech-magnolia forest to a rare wonderland of Florida anise. Sporting red starburst blossoms in early spring, they surround Anise Creek at 13.4 miles. Bog boardwalks lead to a climb out of its basin. Follow the footpath through a tunnel of yaupon holly into a sand pine forest with scattered Southern magnolia trees.

A mile past Anise Creek, meet an intersection of range roads. Continue through sand pine and magnolia forest for nearly a mile and a half, crossing numerous sand roads in the dog-training area for hunters. The trail has steadily climbed since the creek.

It's almost a surprise to reach the High Point sign and bench at 15.9 miles since there isn't a distinguishing hill in this pine forest. At 271 feet above sea level, this is the highest elevation along the entire Florida Trail.

Bull campsite sits atop a significant ridge at 16.5 miles. The blue-blazed trail to and through it descends steeply to its water source. Burbling waters fill Cascade Grotto, a beauty spot worth the extra mile round trip to visit. Past the campsite turnoff, an abrupt descent leads to Bullhide Creek, a clear stream crossed on a plank. Climb a staircase up the steep hill on its other side.

Crossing several dirt roads on a continuing ascent through pine forests, meet the next rugged descent at Buck Branch at 17.9 miles. A boardwalk traverses the floodplain that surrounds the waterway. Climb uphill into clayhill forest to walk along a ridge above a ravine.

After a long, steep switchback, cross Live Oak Creek at 19.3 miles. Stairs snake up the hillside past older pines sporting catfaces—deep gashes made long ago to tap their sap for turpentine production. Scattered shards of clay turpentine cups lay among the leaf litter. Following another ridge above a ravine, turn sharply a mile after the creek crossing, revealing a view down a pitched slope into the steephead below. Steephead ravines are formed by seepage springs that gradually carve out a bowl in the landscape as they trickle together to form a creek.

Descending from the forest of oaks and pines, cross bog bridges through the Cowpen Branch floodplain at 21.6 miles. The creek in the middle of the swamp is a clear, sand-bottomed waterway suitable for filtering water. Climb through a deciduous forest into the pine flatwoods. Round a sun-drenched longleaf pine restoration area with tall grasses waving in the sun. Cross two range roads immediately north of it.

At 22.8 miles, RR 214 is a rare exit point between trailheads. Should you need to bail, US 90 at Mossy Head is 1.5 miles north. Step over an abandoned railroad line immediately north of this broad clay road. In this vicinity is the "Thousand Mile Bench," commemorating that achievement for thru-hikers who started at Big Cypress and headed north. After a long stretch of pine flatwoods, traverse the swampy floodplain of Hog Creek East on a series of boardwalks at 23.9 miles. Rising through the pines to cross a sand road, continue along a second set of boardwalks through Hog Creek West.

A short blue-blazed trail leads to Red Deer campsite at 24.6 miles. It's a beauty spot under the pines with benches and a fire ring, its tent sites nicely cushioned by pine duff. It's also close enough to Interstate 10 for traffic noise to echo all night. Red Deer Creek provides a water source. Cross a long plank boardwalk through the titi swamp on the other side of the waterway.

Beyond the next stretch of pine forest is a short descent to Wise Creek, a clear stream at 26.3 miles. Climb out of the creek basin to cross SR 285 near the highway bridge over the creek. Use caution: it's a high-speed highway and motorists do not expect hikers crossing here. Following a short walk through sand pine scrub, join the crumbling pavement of Old SR 285. Where a gate is across the pavement, the trailhead is straight ahead at 27.1 miles. The trail makes a sharp right turn at the gate.

Titi Section

Subtract 27.1 miles from the following mileages for day hiking north from Old SR 285 trailhead.

Dense myrtle oaks and sand live oaks yield to an open understory with tall Choctawhatchee sand pines. A slope drops into a creek basin on the right which the trail parallels for some time. Scrub yields to mature longleaf pines and the footpath becomes thickly carpeted with pine needles. At 28.3 miles, cross RR 207, a broad clay road used for military and recreational traffic. Within a quarter mile, reach the junction with the 0.7-mile blue-blazed trail to Speck Pond Recreation Area, a vehicle-accessible camping area along SR 285. It has no facilities.

Following a steep descent from the trail junction, bog bridges cross the Gum Creek floodplain. Winding through the damp forest, they lead to a footbridge over the creek and end along a sand bank. Climb out of the floodplain into clayhills topped with longleaf pines and turkey oaks. At 29.3 miles, drop downslope under turkey oaks to the floodplain of Dog Creek, crossed by a plank footbridge through a bamboo thicket. Ascend into pine flatwoods.

A mile later, past RR 531E, a glimmer of water appears from a long, linear marshy pond with longleaf pines along its rim. The trail curves around it for nearly a half mile, the pond sometimes overflowing and making the footpath soggy. Beyond the pond, the forest becomes denser, with larger oaks and American holly trees. On the north side of a sand road, a delightful stand of "wiggly trees"—sand live oaks with wavy trunks—provides deep shade at 30.8 miles.

Descend for some time through mature longleaf pine savanna to reach scenic Big Fork Creek at 32.2 miles, spanned by a large bridge. Continue on plank boardwalks another quarter mile through the floodplain, returning to the pine savanna. The landscape slopes toward a creek to the south. Cross a sand road. The trail remains in this pine forest long enough that a certain sameness permeates your surroundings. Finally descending through laurel oaks, reach RR 220. Turn left on this clay road to cross Titi Creek using the road bridge at 34.1 miles.

The trail stays on RR 220, reaching a road junction at JR Walton Pond Recreation Area, which has campsites with picnic tables and fire ring at 34.5 miles. All are first-come, first-served to anyone with a camping permit. The earthen dam forming a pond from Blue Moon Creek collapsed in 2020. The orange blazes follow the waterway upstream on its east side to a crossing. A mile past the recreation area, cross RR 561, a sand road leading toward an open grassy prairie on the horizon. Cross another sand road before the forest becomes dense again.

A slope carpeted with pine needles leads to a large bridge over Honey Creek at 36.5 miles. Benches on both sides of the creek encourage a break. After the ascent from creek basin to forest cross several range roads, including RR 573 at 37.2 miles. The habitat shifts from longleaf pine and turkey oaks to scrub and back again over the next mile. A descent through the pines leads to bog boardwalks through titi, ending at the bridge over Silver Creek at 38.3 miles. One of the showier spots in this section, this scenic, broad creek is both glassy and grassy. Climb a gentle slope after the bridge.

West of RR 571, enter a sand pine scrub with towering Choctawhatchee sand pines. Emerge at Colonel Greg Malloy Rd at 39.1 miles. Benches are on the west side of this paved road, a gateway to a pretty sandhill forest where a showy white fringetree (*Chionanthus virginicus*) stands out in sharp contrast to its surroundings when it blooms each spring. Descend gently to the floodplain of Institution Branch. Bog bridges lead to the crossing of this red-tinted creek.

A stretch of pine flatwoods follows. Descend to puncheons through a gum swamp surrounding Moore Creek. Loblolly bay trees line the ascent. Pop out into full sun at a broad easement for a power transmission line. Compass north is a clear view to traffic on a road in Crestview. Traffic noise affects the remainder of the hike.

At 41 miles, Pearl campsite sits just west of the trail in a small clearing with benches and fire ring. Its water source, Pearl Creek, is the next stop. From the boardwalk across it, you can see through the crystal-clear water to the ripples in the sand bottom of the creek. Tunneling through titi, you may splash through puddles on the approach to the final patch of pine flatwoods surrounding Pearl trailhead. Reach this parking area off busy SR 85 after 41.9 miles.

Thru-hikers follow the orange blazes of the Florida Trail along the highway on a roadwalk into Crestview. Blue blazes on the trailhead kiosk call attention to the Cimmaron section, a hoped-for future routing of the Florida Trail along the Yellow River basin. For now, the spur trail provides a scenic 17-mile round trip from the west side of SR 85 to the river, with one designated campsite along it, Duck Pond.

Pearl Creek

Jackson Red Ground Trail

Blackwater River State Forest

45.4 MILES | BLACKWATER RIVER STATE FOREST, MILTON

An official connector trail, the Blackwater section takes a blue-blazed branch of the Florida Trail to the Alabama state line to link up with the Alabama Hiking Trail and the greater Eastern Continental Trail.

Overview

Florida's largest state forest, Blackwater River State Forest encompasses 211,100 acres of pine flatwoods and clayhills along the scenic Blackwater River and its tributaries. As one of the best places in Florida to immerse in longleaf pine savanna, the central portion of this section—the Jackson Red Ground Trail—has been a destination for backpackers since 1970.

The state forest surrounds Blackwater River State Park. North of the park, the route follows three named hiking trails in the forest: the Juniper Creek Trail, the Jackson Red Ground Trail, and the Wiregrass Trail. South of Deaton Bridge, the trail traverses the newer Hutton Unit and Burnt Grocery Unit, both with steephead ravines and showy pitcher plant bogs.

Trailheads

This spur off the orange-blazed Florida Trail runs north from a prominent junction near Deer Lake Rd in the Yellow River basin to the Alabama state line. South to north, trailheads include the following.

2.9 MILLER BLUFF RD
Rough small dirt area adjoining Interstate 10 bridge.

3.9 US 90
Parking for 1-2 cars off US 90 at Hutton Unit sign.

7.6 HUTTON UNIT
Large grassy parking area 0.5E at Deaton Bridge Rd.

9.0 DEATON BRIDGE
Large paved parking area at state park. Fee.

9.1 PICNIC AREA
Small paved parking area in state park. Restrooms. Fee.

16.5 RED ROCK RD
Small parking area uphill from trail crossing.

23.4 BEAR LAKE
Recreation Area 3.5W with campground. Fee.

33.1 SOUTH KARICK LAKE
Recreation Area 4.2E with campground. Fee.

33.1 NORTH KARICK LAKE
Recreation Area 4.8E with campground. Fee.

37.3 KENNEDY BRIDGE RD
Day use only, very small parking area.

38.3 SOUTH HURRICANE LAKE
Recreation Area 0.4W with primitive camping.

39.2 NORTH HURRICANE LAKE
Small parking area just outside campground gate.

For day hiking, park next to trail crossings along the road shoulder at Deer Lake Rd, Indian Ford Rd, Sandy Forest Rd, Old Martin Rd, McVay Rd, and several points along Beaver Creek Rd.

Camping

The forest rangers and Boy Scouts who designed and built the Jackson Red Ground Trail in the 1970s took their inspiration from the Appalachian Trail: it has camping shelters. One burned down in a forest fire but two remain. All three locations have benches and a fire ring, as does Burnt Grocery Creek campsite. Fee sites at state forest recreation areas and at Blackwater River State Park offer more amenities but must be reserved in advance online.

Random camping is permitted in the state forest but not in the state park. Backpackers should bear bag or use a bear canister. Since this section is largely dry, it's a good choice for backpacking with your dog. North of Sandy Forest Rd, surface water sources are infrequent in the rolling hills. South to north, designated campsites include the following.

1.9 BURNT GROCERY CREEK
Picnic bench, fire ring, and water access.

9.9 BLACKWATER RIVER STATE PARK
Campground with gravel pads, bathhouse, and laundry. Fee. Reserve.

14.0 FOOTBALL FIELD
Unimproved clearing with river access.

15.2 BLUFFS CAMPSITE
Beauty spot with trail shelter and ample tenting.

23.0 BLACKWATER SHELTER 2*
No shelter. No water. Picnic bench and ample tenting in sandhill.

29.1 BLACKWATER SHELTER*
Trail shelter not far from flowing creek.

38.3 SOUTH HURRICANE LAKE
Primitive campground for tenting. Fee.

39.1 NORTH HURRICANE LAKE
Developed campground with bathhouse and hot showers. Fee.

* Avoid these campsites on weekends. They are close to forest roads. Backpackers have reported trouble on weekends with being hassled by nonhikers and having gear stolen at these locations.

Trip Planning

Leashed dogs are welcome. Instead of orange blazes, this section is blazed blue as an official side trail of the Florida National Scenic Trail. Spring is the most pleasant time of year to hike Blackwater, when flowering trees and a profusion of less common wildflowers—including Gulf Coast lupine, mountain laurel, and white-topped pitcher plants—are in bloom.

The forest is managed through the use of frequent prescribed burns. Expect at least a portion of your hike to be through recently burned forest. To avoid walking into an active fire, call 850-957-5700 to check on burns along the Florida Trail. Inform the rangers where you're headed if planning a multi-day backpacking trip.

Research hunting seasons and dress in bright orange if you hike during hunting season. During fall deer hunting season, it's safest to camp at designated campsites.

Check river levels before hiking: water.weather.gov station BAKF1. The Wiregrass Trail dips into the Blackwater River floodplain and Juniper Creek Trail is largely in the Juniper Creek floodplain, a major tributary for the river. During severe floods, Blackwater River has topped Deaton Bridge and entirely swamped the state park.

Fees are charged at Blackwater River State Park and all state forest recreation areas. A designated parking area inside the state park gates is the safest place to leave a car while backpacking; arrange at the ranger station. Or park at one of the state forest recreation areas where a camp host is present. The fee is worth the peace of mind. We've received reports of cars being broken into when left overnight at other trailheads.

Land Managers

Blackwater River State Forest
11650 Munson Highway, Milton FL 32570
850-957-5701
fdacs.gov

Blackwater River State Park
7720 Deaton Bridge Rd, Milton FL 32564
850-983-5363
floridastateparks.org

Highlights

Burnt Grocery Creek, mile 1.0

This tannic waterway winds its way toward the Yellow River. Overlooks offer perspectives of tall white-topped pitcher plants, a cedar swamp, and shallows at the campsite.

Hutton Summit, mile 6.8

From this high point of 132 feet, ridges are visible on the northwest horizon. Descending northbound, an immense pitcher plant bog covers the slope of the hill on the right.

Blackwater River, mile 9.0

Cross the Blackwater River using the pedestrian walkway on Deaton Bridge. This tannic river makes gentle curves through the forest, depositing white sand beaches. At the state park, the recreation area provides swimming access at a large river beach.

Juniper Creek Beach, mile 15.2

While Juniper Creek has quite a few white sand beaches, this one is worth a stop. In spring, mountain laurel blooms frame the view; at all times, there is easy access to the water.

Red Rock Bluffs, mile 16.1

Made of clay, not rock, this erosional feature fools the eye. It rises 68 feet over Juniper Creek, a truly unique perspective from the Florida Trail.

Charlie Foster Roadcut, mile 22.0

Colorful layers of sandstone are exposed in a deep roadcut along an unpaved section of Charlie Foster Rd that the trail follows out of the Blue Creek floodplain.

Hurricane Lake, mile 38.8

From the dam crossing on the east side of the lake to the sweeping arc the trail makes north of North Hurricane Lake Campground, views of the lake go on for almost two miles.

Longleaf Pines, mile 41.5

Experience the best of the longleaf pine savanna between the two northernmost road crossings of Beaver Creek Rd.

Recommended Day Hikes

Mile 2.9

Miller Bluff to Wild Azalea Camp, 11.4-mile round trip

Mile 9.1

Juniper Creek Trail, 7.8 miles linear

Mile 16.5

Juniper Creek Trail to Red Rock Bluffs, 1.3-mile round trip
Juniper Creek Trail to Bluffs Camp, 2.6-mile round trip
Jackson Trail to Bear Lake Junction, 6.9 miles linear

Mile 37.2

Kennedy Bridge to Jackson and Wiregrass junction, 8.4-mile round trip

Mile 39.2

Hurricane Lake to Alabama State Line, 12.4-mile round trip

Coldwater Creek

Side Trip

West of Blackwater State Forest, **COLDWATER GARDENS**, a private nature retreat, hugs clear sand-bottomed Coldwater Creek for several miles. Centered on an organic farm, it has cabins, safari-style "glamping" tents, and primitive sites by the creek, all connected by forest roads and trails. Tent camp on the broad sandy beaches along the creek. Bring kayaks and tubes to enjoy the waterway. Reserve ahead online or by phone at 850-426-1300. Dogs are not permitted. floridahikes.com/coldwater-gardens.

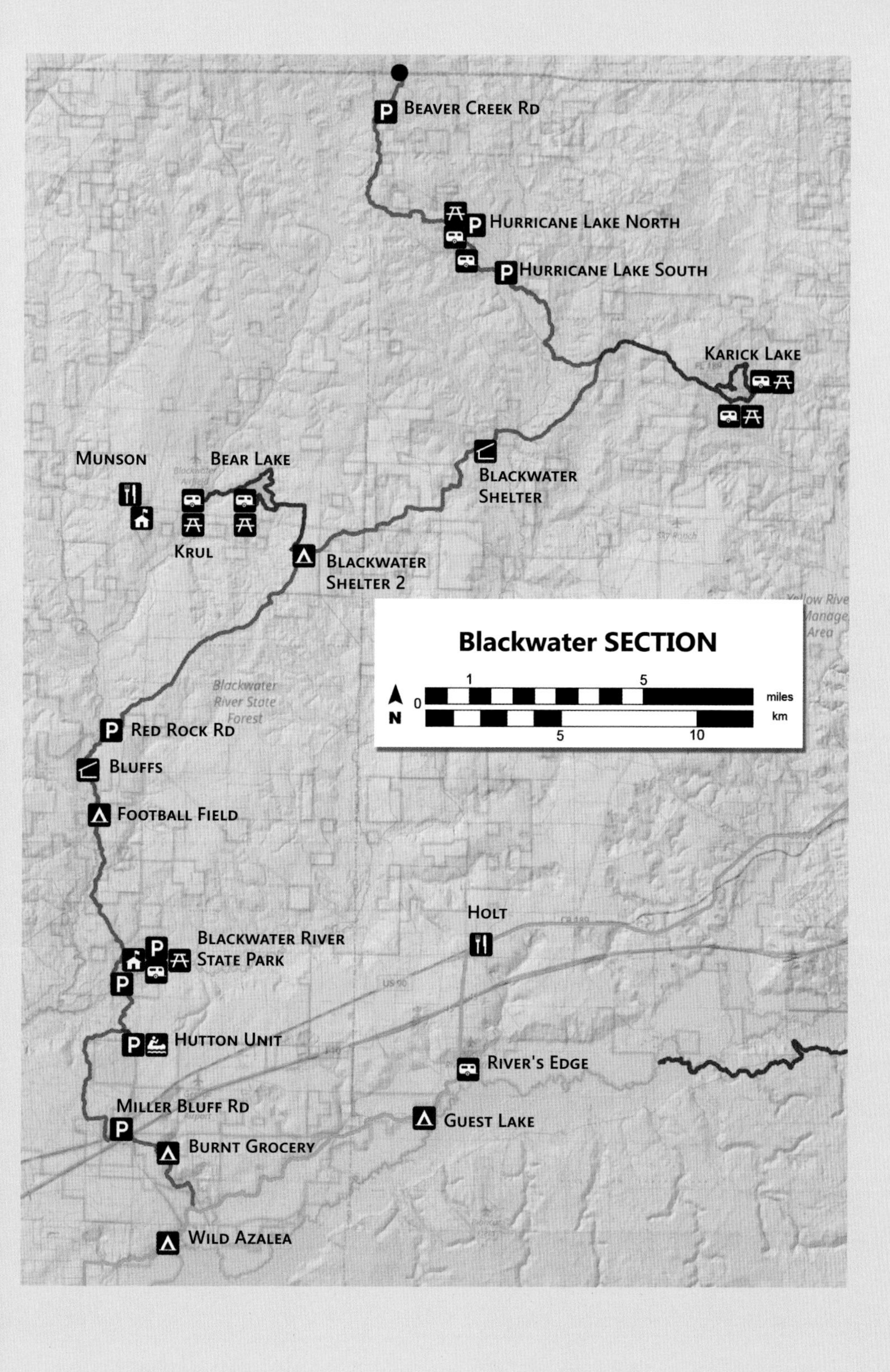
Beaver Creek Rd
Hurricane Lake North
Hurricane Lake South
Karick Lake
Blackwater Shelter
Munson
Bear Lake
Krul
Blackwater Shelter 2
Blackwater SECTION
1
5
0
miles
N
km
5
10
Blackwater River State Forest
Red Rock Rd
Bluffs
Football Field
Holt
Blackwater River State Park
Hutton Unit
River's Edge
Miller Bluff Rd
Guest Lake
Burnt Grocery
Wild Azalea

Red Rock Bluffs

47. Juniper Creek Trail

7.8 MILES | BLACKWATER RIVER STATE PARK AND STATE FOREST, MILTON

A scenic destination year-round, the Juniper Creek Trail shines in springtime when mountain laurel blooms in both pink and white atop the crumbling bluffs at Red Rocks.

Overview

Starting within sight of the Blackwater River at a picnic area inside Blackwater River State Park, the trail crosses bogs and flatwoods along the park's boundary before entering Blackwater River State Forest for the remainder of the hike. North of Indian Ford Creek, it parallels the river's largest tributary. Showy sandy beaches mark lazy curves in Juniper Creek. Side trails lead to several beaches. Some of the state's tallest Atlantic white cedars rise from cedar swamps along this hike. Gaining elevation in longleaf pine savannas at the northern end of the journey, the trail provides panoramas from the bluffs at Bluffs Campsite and a stunning view at Red Rock Bluffs, more than 65 feet above Juniper Creek.

Trip Planning / Land Managers

See Blackwater. Leashed dogs are welcome. Don't attempt this trail when Blackwater River floods. Expect to get your feet wet in wet flatwoods and titi swamps, particularly in the first mile. March and April are the best months to hike this section. The mountain laurel between Bluffs Campsite and Red Rock Bluffs blooms in March. Pitcher plants blossom in early to mid-April.

Blackwater River State Park charges a day-use fee for parking unless you are camping in their campground. Campsites must be reserved in advance. No permit or reservation is needed for Bluffs Campsite, but it is popular on weekends.

Directions

To leave a vehicle at the end of this hike, follow SR 191 north from downtown Milton toward Munson. Turn at the turnoff for Red Rock Picnic Area. Cross the bridge and continue a half mile to the Red Rock Rd trailhead [30.785240, -86.886772]. To continue to the start of the hike, drive uphill a half mile to the intersection. Turn right at Sandy Forest Rd onto Pleasant Home Church Rd. After almost 4 miles reach a T intersection with Indian Ford Rd. Turn left. Make a right onto Deaton Bridge Rd and continue 2 miles south, passing the main entrance to the state park on the left before the turn-in for the picnic area [30.704369, -86.883247] on the right.

Options

If your time is limited or you only have one vehicle, hike south from Red Rocks trailhead for the best scenery. It's a 2.6-mile round trip to Bluffs Campsite plus another half mile on the side trail to don't-miss Red Rock Bluffs. A trek from the north end to the Alligator Creek bridge is an 8-mile round trip and sticks close to Juniper Creek from Bluffs Campsite south. Bluffs Campsite makes a nice destination for a weekday overnighter from Blackwater River State

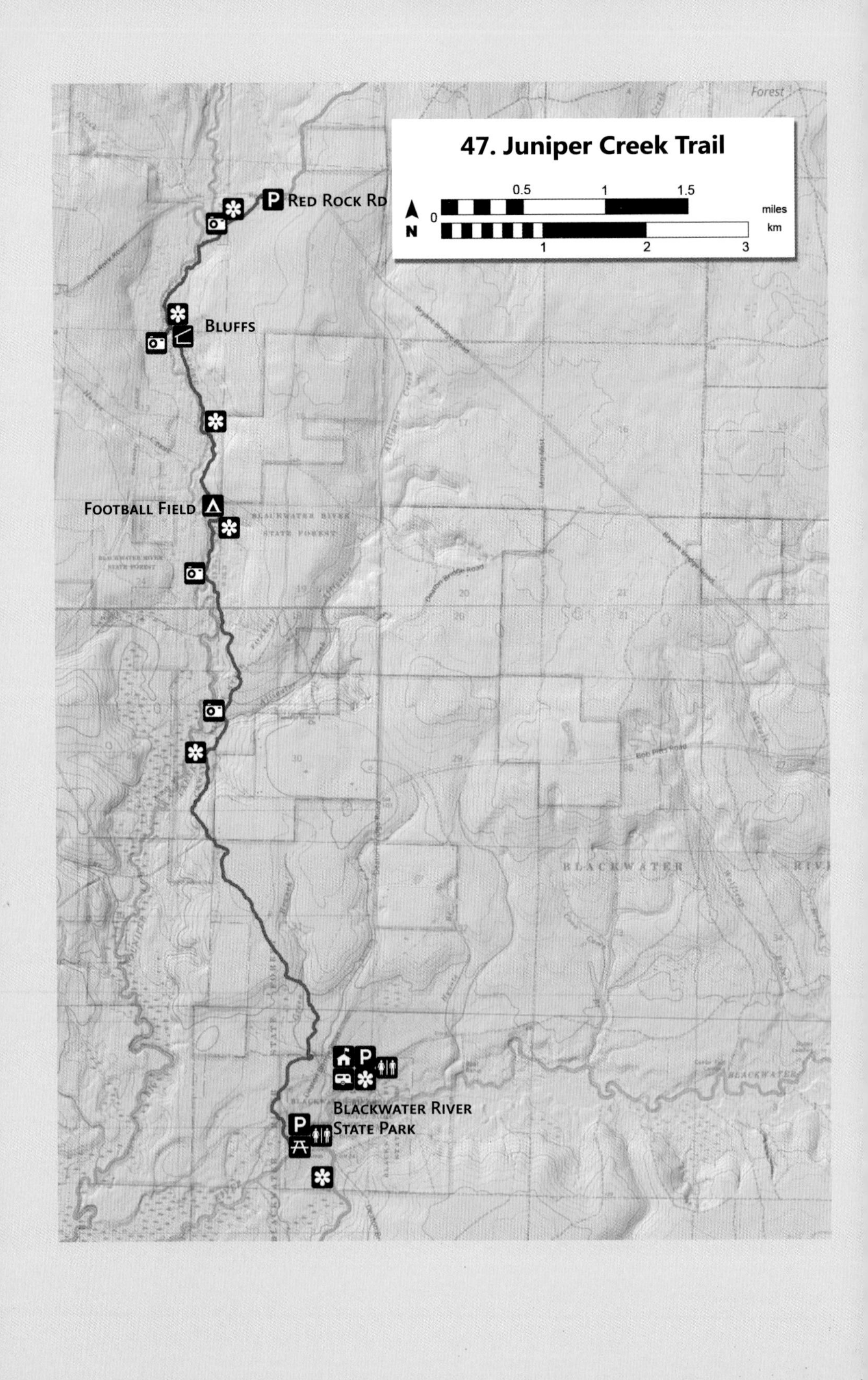

47. Juniper Creek Trail
0.5
1
1.5
0
miles
km
N
1
2
3
Red Rock Rd
Bluffs
Football Field
Blackwater River
State Park

Juniper Creek

Park, or a longer day hike. It's a 11.6-mile round trip from the park's main parking lot (where you need to park inside the gates if leaving your vehicle overnight), or 12.2 miles from the picnic area trailhead.

Hike

A path leads from the picnic area parking area to the picnic tables and adjacent restroom along bluffs above Blackwater River. Turn right to see the "Juniper Creek Trail" sign marking the start of the hike. Immediately turn away from the river to enter a floodplain swamp. Puncheons cross most of the wet and muddy spots. Reaching higher ground, squeeze through a tight gate and turn onto a forest road at a half mile. Watch for blazes reentering the woods as well as a trail junction with a connector to the main parking area inside the park gates.

Leaving the state park within the first mile, enter the state forest right before a boggy area crossed on narrow bog bridges. Ascend into an extensive longleaf pine forest and hike through it for nearly a mile and a half. Reach paved Indian Ford Road at 2.5 miles, with an old homestead within sight of the road crossing. Continue into a hardwood forest with scattered young cedars. A pitcher plant bog perches on a steep sun-drenched slope just before the Indian Ford Creek footbridge.

A sturdy bridge spans Alligator Creek at 3.3 miles, marking a shift in the character of this hike as the footpath draws close to Juniper Creek. This is a magical section, providing glimpses of the fast-moving stream and its sand beaches through the trees, the trail undulating across rugged terrain shaped by the gullies of feeder streams.

The well-beaten path at 4.4 miles ends on a sandy beach along Juniper Creek. It's one of the nicest access points at water level, providing a pleasant rest stop and sweeping views both upstream and downstream. Football Field Campsite is uphill from the trail a half mile past the beach. A lightly traveled path heads in the opposite direction to Juniper Creek for water.

For the next mile, circle around bayhead and cedar swamps, turns revealing creek views. A massive Atlantic white cedar towers over the footpath, one of many champion-sized trees in this dense stand. Leave creek level to ascend into a sandhill forest sweeping to the edge of the rising bluffs along Juniper Creek.

At 6 miles, Bluffs Campsite is a clearing with a stunning view of the creek and its beaches on the far shore. The shelter is at the end of a short trail to the right. A little past the camping area is a side trail descending to Juniper Creek Beach. In spring, riotous pink and white blossoms of mountain laurel add color and fragrance to this beauty spot.

Past the next side trail to the creek, the footpath is edged in mountain laurel and tall Atlantic white cedars, easy to recognize by their whorled bark. It's all uphill from here. Leaving the creek, rise steadily through a longleaf pine forest.

A worn path to the left at 6.9 miles leads a quarter mile to Red Rock Bluffs. This outstanding natural feature and scenic view centers around a series of clay cliffs eroding into the basin of Juniper Creek. Stay away from the edges, which are deeply undercut. More mountain laurel rims the edges of this perched basin, which drops off sharply to the creek far below.

Climb gently through the longleaf pine forest. Florida dogwood trees bloom above the trail in spring. Descend to the roadcut for Red Rock Rd. The trailhead is slightly uphill to the right along this paved road at 7.8 miles.

Mountain laurel

48. Jackson Trail South

6.9 MILES | BLACKWATER RIVER STATE FOREST, MUNSON

A high and dry hike in Blackwater River State Forest, the south end of the Jackson Red Ground Trail traverses rolling hills topped with longleaf pine savanna.

Overview

This hike follows a portion of the Jackson Trail south of SR 4, a state highway connecting the towns of Munson and Baker near the Alabama border. This is the oldest piece of the Florida Trail west of the Apalachicola River, added to the growing Florida Trail system by 1975. Spanning 21.3 miles between Red Rock Rd and a trail junction north of Karick Lake, the Jackson Red Ground Trail is the oldest footpath in this forest—it predates the state of Florida. General Andrew Jackson and 1,200 troops marched along this route toward Pensacola in 1818.

Largely through pine flatwoods and longleaf pine savanna, it's a walk in an undulating landscape dominated by towering pines with an open understory. There is little surface water, but the folds of this hilly landscape cradle streams trickling through native bamboo and pitcher plant bogs perch on seepage slopes. Spring and fall wildflowers are abundant, making this a pleasant hike in both seasons.

Trip Planning / Land Manager

See Blackwater. Leashed dogs are welcome. You will encounter hunters in this part of the forest during hunting seasons. Blackwater Shelter 2 Campsite is near the end of this hike, but we don't recommend camping there given its proximity to nearby roads. Vehicles should not be left overnight at either end of this hike.

Directions

To leave a car at the end of this hike, follow SR 191 north from downtown Milton to SR 4 in Munson, passing the forestry office just before the right turn onto SR 4. Drive east 4 miles to Old Martin Rd. Turn right. Continue a half mile to the trail crossing [30.843670, -86.805954] and park along the shoulder within sight of a farmhouse. For the starting point, backtrack west along SR 4 to Munson. Turn left and go 0.5 miles to Sandy Forest Rd. Turn left and follow this paved road for 5 miles. Make a right on Red Rock Rd and continue another half mile to the Red Rock Rd trailhead [30.785240, -86.886772] on the left.

Options

Trim the hike to 5.8 miles by parking on the shoulder of Sandy Forest Rd [30.795816, -86.873886] instead of Red Rock Rd trailhead. You'll still hit the highlights heading north. Or add to it by starting at Blackwater River State Park and hiking the Juniper Creek Trail (previous chapter) first for a 14.2-mile hike. For a pleasant 3.4-mile round trip across the rolling hills of the pine savanna, start at Old Martin Rd and hike southbound to the Boy Scout Bridge as a turnaround point.

Bear Lake Recreation Area off SR 4 is another potential starting point. The blue-blazed connector from Bear Lake to the Jackson Trail follows forest roads

Young longleaf pines

for 3.5 miles. Follow the trail east out of the campground and take the right fork away from the lake to avoid looping the lake. It's a 10.4-mile linear hike from Bear Lake to Red Rock Rd trailhead, or a 10.4-mile round trip from Bear Lake to the Boy Scout Bridge. A day-use fee applies for parking at Bear Lake, which you should use for any overnight hikes.

Hike

The Jackson Red Ground Trail begins across Red Rock Rd from the Juniper Creek Trail at a large kiosk, immediately entering a tunnel of vegetation in deep shade. Beyond the first forest road crossing, the landscape opens up into a classic longleaf pine savanna with trees of various sizes and ages. Some of the younger trees look like tufts of grass, others like bottle brushes. A curve in the trail reveals a sweeping view downhill into the Juniper Creek basin.

Climb over a gully in an abandoned forest road in longleaf pine forest. A break in the forest at 1.2 miles is Sandy Forest Rd, a paved road you drove earlier to reach the starting point. On its other side continue into a tunnel of oaks, which opens up into the greater longleaf pine forest. Cross grassy FR 47 at 1.9 miles. This is an immersive habitat, the pines increasing in size and maturity along the next mile.

A shift in habitat occurs when you enter another dense tunnel of vegetation in the forest understory at 3.4 miles. Emerge from it to cross a forest road. The understory thins slowly but the tunnel effect persists for a while before the high canopy of longleaf pine reappears. Cross a well-worn forest road at 4 miles and join another forest road briefly. Keep alert. The trail quickly leaves the road, leading into a beautiful forest of mature longleaf pines.

After walking through a stretch of younger longleaf pines, cross Pleasant Home Rd at 4.6 miles. It's a broad, unmarked, unpaved road that looks well used. A quarter mile later, traverse bog bridges across a damp swale under the pines. Climbs uphill gently, reaching a bench at a 90-degree turn in the footpath.

Cross a shallow tributary of Blue Creek on the Boy Scout Bridge at 5.2 miles. This sturdy bridge has blue signs at both ends declaring it to be a BSA Eagle Project. Turning to follow the waterway, the trail meets Charlie Foster Rd. Join this gravel road eastbound to cross Blue Creek, the only reliable water source on this hike. It flows in culverts under the road.

A deep roadcut along Charlie Foster Rd exposes a fascinating cross section of the bedrock of this forest: colorful reddish-orange layers of sandstone and clay topped with a cap of loose red rocks. Climbing out of the roadcut, the road reaches a Y intersection at the top of the hill. Keep left. Watch for where the blue blazes leave this road and enter the forest along a footpath. Cross a two-track forest road soon after.

Descend a grassy seepage slope under the tall longleaf pines. Clumps of tall white-top pitcher plants rise from perched bogs. Slip through the floodplain of Cane Creek at 5.8 miles on a series of bog bridges amid a thicket of native bamboo.

Where a shelter once stood at 6.6 miles, Blackwater Shelter 2 Camp is still a pleasant place to stop and rest under

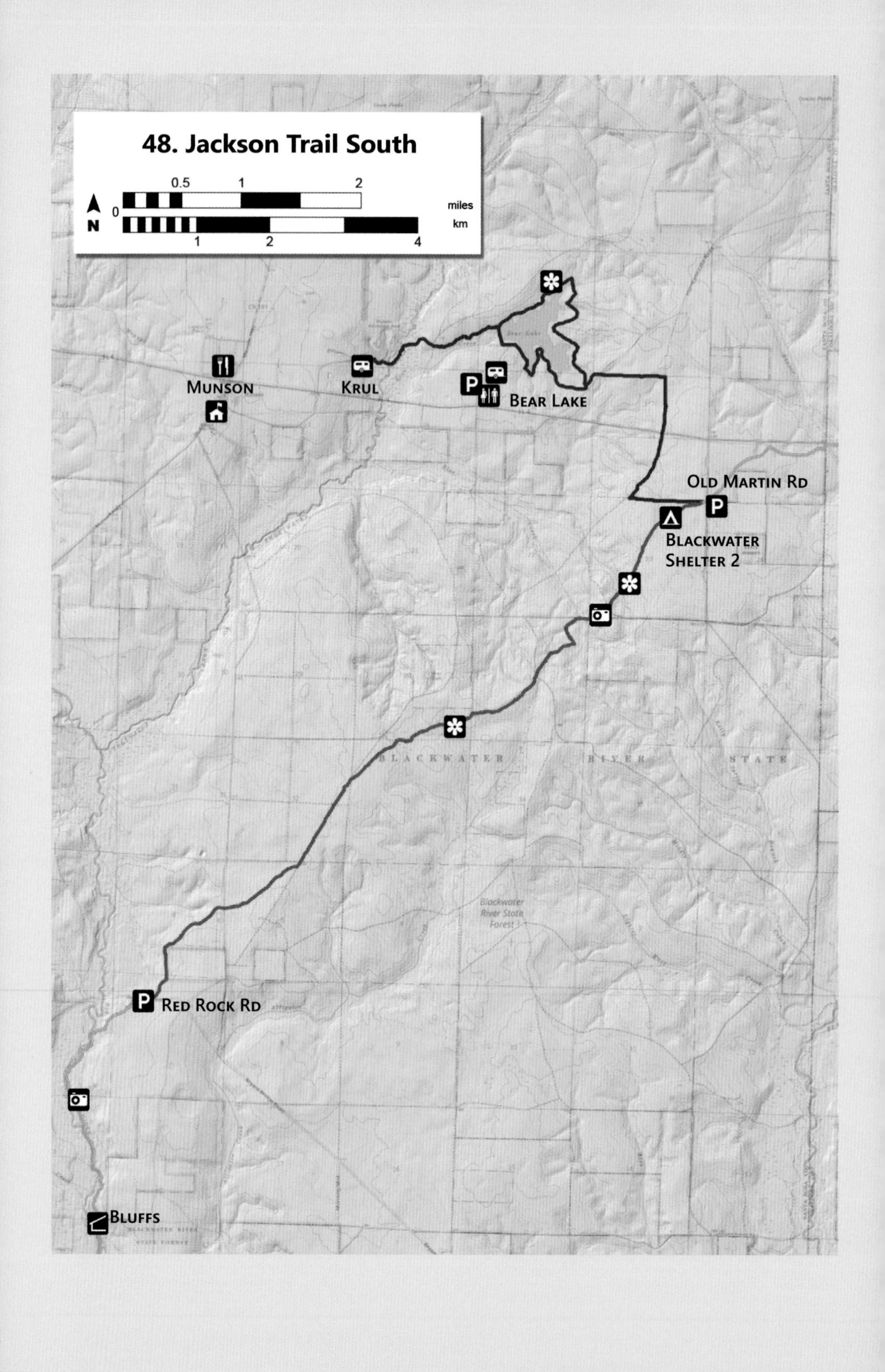
48. Jackson Trail South
0.5
1
2
0
miles
N
km
1
2
4
Munson
Krul
Bear Lake
Old Martin Rd
Blackwater
Shelter 2
BLACKWATER
RIVER
STATE
Blackwater
River State
Forest
Red Rock Rd
Bluffs

Pine flatwoods

the oaks. It has a picnic table and fire ring. The blazes you see to the north of the camping area along the edge of the pine forest are part of the Bear Lake Connector heading west to Bear Lake Recreation Area on a nearby forest road.

Stick with the blue blazes to finish this 6.9-mile hike at paved Old Martin Rd, within sight of the sign for the Bear Lake-Jackson Connector Trail junction.

Scrub-topped dune

49. UWF/SRIA Dunes Preserve

4.7 MILES | PENSACOLA BEACH

Weaving through windswept dunes between Santa Rosa Sound and the Gulf of Mexico, the Florida Trail at the east end of Pensacola Beach provides one of Florida's most unique hikes.

Overview

The Florida Trail through this bayside preserve has little actual footpath. Stiff breezes off the Gulf of Mexico perpetually shuffle the sands. While a relatively short hike, it's surprisingly rugged because of the soft footing and climbs. It's a wayfinding challenge: determine your route point-to-point as you go, looking for each orange-blazed pole or post amid ever-changing dunes and swales. Drawing close to Santa Rosa Sound, the trail tunnels into a maritime forest and plunges into a needlerush marsh.

Much of your time is spent clambering in and out of deep windblown bowls in the shifting sands. Some cradle extensive salt marshes or ephemeral salt ponds. Dune peaks afford panoramas in every direction. A coastal campsite is hidden halfway along the trek. An endangered species lives here: the Santa Rosa beach mouse. Look closely below tufts of grass for tiny burrows and tinier mouse prints.

Trip Planning

Dawn and dusk are the best times to tackle this trail. Wear sunglasses and a hat: shade is almost nonexistent and the sand reflects the sun in your face as you hike. Hiking sticks help with balance on the unbridged marsh crossings. Carry more than the usual amount of water with you: there is no fresh water along this trail or the paved recreation path paralleling it. Leashed dogs are permitted, but this isn't a great hike for them. You must clean up after them. The sand and asphalt are hot underfoot, the salt marshes mucky. All surface water is salt water.

While the trail passes the only primitive campsite available to backpackers tackling the Seashore section, there isn't much to it except a bench with a nice view and a private bayside beach. If you plan an overnight stay, haul in your water and haul out your trash.

Land Manager

Santa Rosa Island Authority
1 Via de Luna, Pensacola Beach 32561
850-932-2257
sria-fla.com

Directions

This section of the Florida Trail parallels CR 399, the sole highway along Santa Rosa Island between Navarre Beach and Pensacola Beach. The closest parking area to the starting point is Pensacola Beach Park East [30.348004, -87.054589], 1.2 miles west. It has ample parking and restrooms. The closest parking area to the end point is Via De Luna Drive beach access [30.342877, -87.080862], a small lot 0.4 miles west of the trail kiosk via the bike path.

Options

The dunes hike is 3.1 miles linear, but there is no parking at either access point. Starting at Pensacola Beach Park East and ending at Via De Luna Drive beach access, it's a 4.7-mile linear hike.

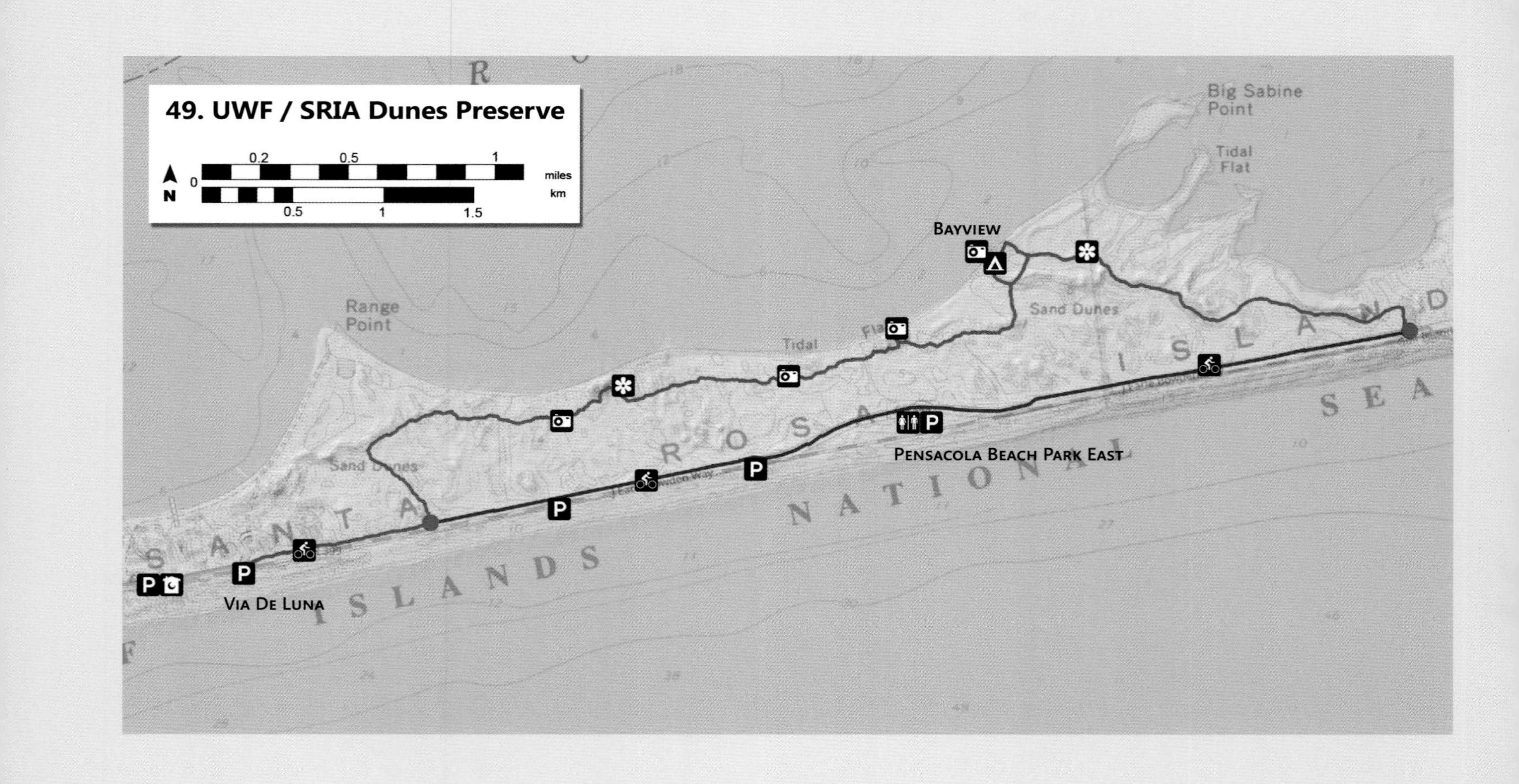
49. UWF / SRIA Dunes Preserve
0
0.2
0.5
1
miles
km
1.5
N
Big Sabine Point
Tidal Flat
Bayview
Range Point
Sand Dunes
Tidal
Sand Dunes
Pensacola Beach Park East
Via De Luna
SANTA ROSA ISLAND
GULF ISLANDS NATIONAL SEASHORE

Northbound in the dune field

Cut that distance to 3.5 miles by catching a ride to the "Welcome to Pensacola Beach" sign to walk toward a vehicle at Via De Luna. Or do a 5.3-mile loop in and out of Pensacola Beach Park East using the Pensacola Beach Bike Path as a connector. For a round trip hitting several scenic spots, start at Via De Luna and hike to Bayview Campsite. Walk the beach to the fish hatchery and rejoin the orange blazes on the ridge above the needlerush marsh northbound for a 4.8-mile round trip.

Hike

A brisk walk on pavement east from Pensacola Beach Park East along the Pensacola Beach Bike Path to the Florida Trail previews the sweep of the dunes in the preserve but provides no real clues as to the trail hidden among them. Reach the "Welcome to Pensacola Beach" sign and the crosswalk to Santa Rosa Beach at 1.2 miles.

The entry point to the dunes hike is behind the big sign. Look for the first orange-blazed pole and strike out across the sand in that direction. While there used to be many large dunes in this first quarter mile, they have been flattened by storm surges during hurricanes. The trail draws close to Santa Rosa Sound, the waterway connecting Pensacola Bay and Choctawhatchee Bay.

Walk through shorter dunes and a flattened area where small chunks of pavement from a previous washout of the highway are embedded in the sand. Pause for a look behind you as you climb, as there is a nice panorama of Santa Rosa Sound from a promontory.

A view of Santa Rosa Sound opens up a half mile into the dunes. A quarter mile later, pass cattails growing in a wetland at a base of a dune. A maritime forest tops the highest dune. Round a larger wetland at the base of a line of dunes. Enjoy a view of the Gulf of Mexico from a high sand ridge before entering a maritime forest where sand live oaks cast rare puddles of shade. Views of the sound abound. A wooden platform provides a place to take a break.

The footpath dives into a needlerush marsh, a beaten path through sharp-tipped grasses and slippery footing. Emerging from the marsh, reach a T intersection at 2.2 miles. The path to the right leads to a scenic spot, an estuary with ruins from an old fish hatchery. Turn left to follow a well-beaten path along a dune ridge.

Blue-blazed poles to the right lead through the dunes lead to Bayview Campsite along the sound at 2.3 miles. Shared with kayakers, it has minimal tent space but a nice sweep of bayfront beach and a bench with a superb view.

Beyond the trail junction for the campsite, descend the ridge. Skirt a large wetland and start into a series of sparkling white sand dunes. Natural bouquets of wildflowers blooming in yellow and purple break up an otherwise bright-white landscape. Cross a marshy area with tall, soft grasses and no obvious way to get around the swale in which the marsh sits, as it flows from an upland source toward the sound. A boardwalk crosses a swale of needlerush marsh at 3 miles.

Round a very pretty salt pond that forms after a rain and work your way around a marsh. Pass an oak hammock offering a spot of shade under the limbs of a sand live oak. Orange blazes lead to the tops of taller dunes, with another opportunity to scramble to a peak for a different perspective on Santa Rosa Sound.

The Portofino condo towers loom on the horizon where a bridge spans the final marsh crossing at 3.6 miles. Surrounding tall dunes host Florida rosemary bushes, a species found both along the coast and in scrub forests with similar ancient sands.

A deep pocket between dunes holds another ephemeral salt pond. Drawing ever closer to the condos, the trail route turns compass south toward the beach. In this last stretch of dunes, a salt pond spreads in a shallow pool across a flattened area. Traffic on CR 399 and the dune line protecting the beach are in view.

Facing the Gulf of Mexico, the Florida Trail reaches the Pensacola Beach Bike Path at a big kiosk after 4.3 miles. The orange blazes join the paved bike path toward Pensacola Beach, where the next beach parking area is 0.4 miles compass west. Complete a 4.7-mile linear hike at the Via De Luna Drive beach access, or a 5.3-mile loop by turning left at the kiosk to return to your starting point at Pensacola Beach Park East via the bike path.

50. Fort Pickens

7.2 MILES | GULF ISLANDS NATIONAL SEASHORE, PENSACOLA BEACH

After one last stroll along the shimmering sands of the Gulf of Mexico on Santa Rosa Island, the Florida Trail reaches its northern terminus in the shadow of historic Fort Pickens.

Overview

Reaching the beach at Fort Pickens, long-distance hikers can feel their goal. The northern terminus of the Florida Trail signals completion of a hike from one end of Florida to the other. But this isn't an easy wrap-up or a simple day hike, despite being at sea level. It's entirely in the open, wind-blasted and sun-drenched. It's the sense of completion and the weight of history that make this a compelling walk.

Construction of Fort Pickens began in 1829 under supervision of the Army Corps of Engineers. President Abraham Lincoln considered Fort Pickens an important coastal defense and sent Federal troops to occupy it. On November 22, 1861, these troops shot more than 5,000 cannonballs into Pensacola, damaging Confederate-held forts and the shipyard. Confederate leaders retreated and burned the city. After the Civil War, Fort Pickens served as a prison. Its most famous prisoner was the Apache chief Geronimo. During World War I, additional gun batteries were added for coastal defense. The fort remained a military operation until 1947. It became a state park until taken over by the Na-

Fort Pickens

Fort Pickens Beach

tional Park Service as part of Gulf Islands National Seashore.

In the 1980s, the north end of the Florida Trail terminated at Karick Lake in Blackwater River State Forest, where the Jackson Red Ground Trail ended. Designation of the Florida National Scenic Trail in Gulf Islands National Seashore in 1994 shifted the trail terminus to Fort Pickens.

Trip Planning

While hikers walking in on the beach do not pass the entrance station, your support vehicle will. Entrance fees for Gulf Islands National Seashore are $15 per pedestrian, $25 per vehicle, good for one week. If you have a National Public Lands pass it covers your fee. Dogs are not permitted along the beach. They may accompany you on the Fort Pickens Trail between Battery Langdon and Fort Pickens. Bicycles also use the hard-packed Fort Pickens Trail.

Hike the beach as early in the day as possible and walk west so the sun is behind you. The sun will reflect into your face off the bright sand. Sunscreen, sunglasses, and a hat are a must. Beach sand is soft except at the tide line. Hiking poles will greatly help your stride. Carry more water than you usually need for five miles in the sun. Salt air and sunshine dehydrated us quickly.

Land Manager

National Park Service
1400 Fort Pickens Rd, Pensacola Beach
850-934-2600
nps.gov/guis

Directions

Use US 98 east from Pensacola to reach Pensacola Beach. Turn right onto Fort Pickens Rd at the traffic light with CR 399. Follow Fort Pickens Rd west 2.5 miles to Park West [30.325899, -87.178787] on the beach side before the entrance to Fort Pickens. This is the starting point for the hike. The end point is the parking area at Fort Pickens [30.32865, -87.289642], another 7.1 miles along Fort Pickens Rd inside the National Seashore. Park near the fort entrance. A Florida Trail kiosk is within sight of the fort.

Options

To tackle the full hike, arrange a shuttle: taxi, Uber, and Lyft services are all available in Pensacola. Park at Fort Pickens and get dropped off at Park West outside the gate. You may have to pay the shuttle driver's entrance fee to Gulf Islands National Seashore if they don't have a pass. Ask before booking. In summer, a ferry service connects downtown Pensacola and Fort Pickens. May 24 to September 2, Pensacola Beach offers a trolley service. These can be used or combined for shuttle purposes, but summer hiking on the beach should be daybreak or dusk due to the heat.

Without a shuttle, park at Langdon Beach [30.317347, -87.261673] or Battery Langdon [30.319567, -87.26123], a central point with water and restrooms, to round trip in either direction. It's 1.8 miles to hike from Battery Langdon to loop around the Bluebird Marsh Trail and return. Another pleasant round trip is Fort Pickens to Battery Worth and back, 1.6 miles.

Hike

Walk toward the blaze posts leading to the beach as soon as you step inside the gate at Fort Pickens. Once you're on the beach, the trail is simply a walk along the Gulf of Mexico with no breaks from the shade. Hiking west means facing a natural expanse, a counterpoint to the tall buildings crowding the shoreline behind you. Dunes flank the beach to the north.

There are few distinguishing features. The first mile ticks off soon after you pass the entrance station along Fort Pickens Rd, partly hidden behind the dunes. At 1.9 miles, Parking Area 19A sits to the north, but it's not obvious unless a car is parked there. In front of you is a long, unbroken stretch of shoreline fading into sea mist.

By 2.8 miles, Fort Pickens Rd draws close enough to the edge of the beach for passing cars to draw attention. The sea has broken free several times across these narrows, washing the road into Pensacola Bay and forcing closures of the park for months at a time. Pilings and cables emerge from the sand as if docks once led into the surf. Flocks of seagulls cluster along sand spits curving into the warm shallows of the Gulf.

The sand becomes more difficult to walk in as Fort Pickens Rd pulls close to the waterfront around 3.7 miles, a narrows squeezed between waterfronts

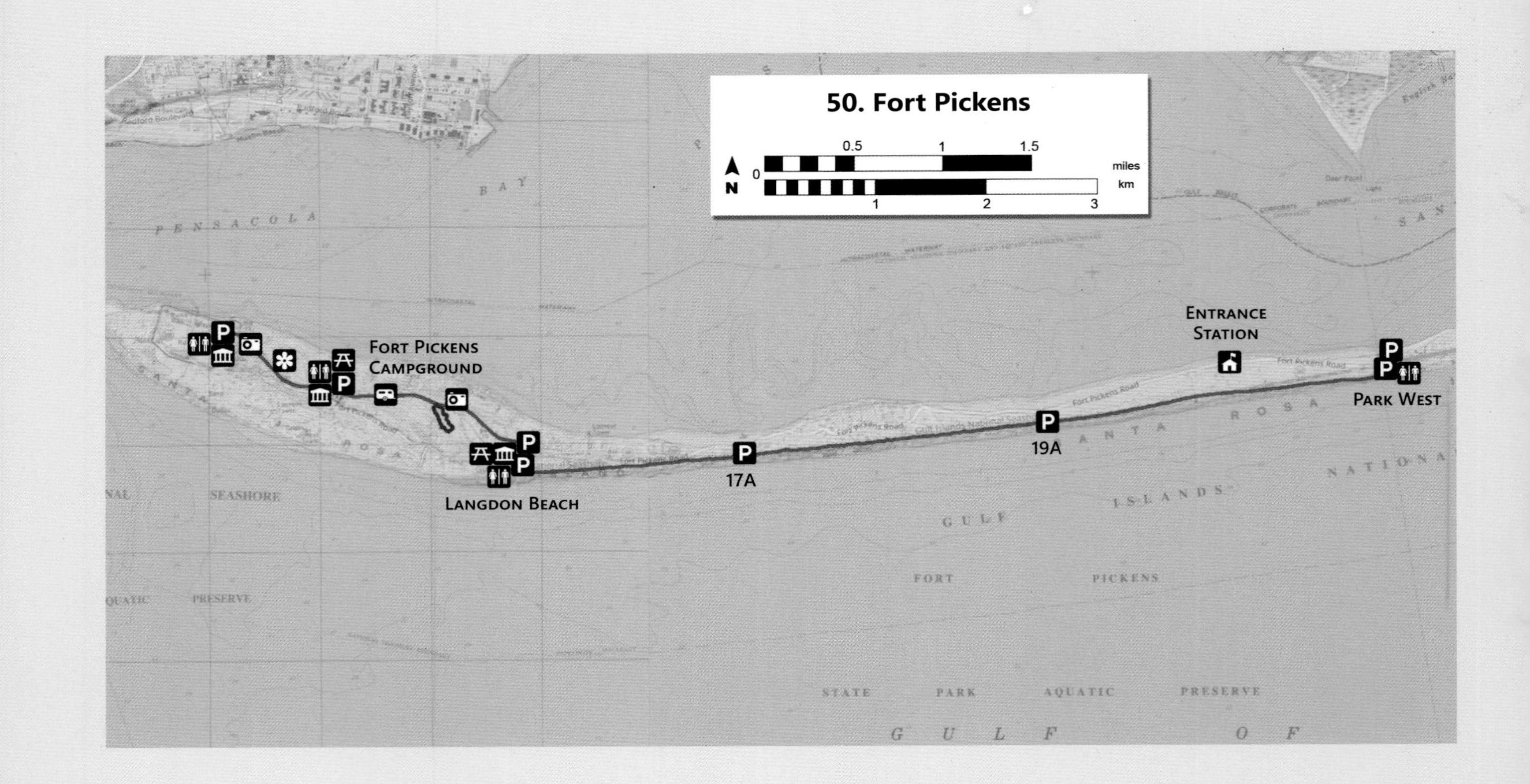
50. Fort Pickens
0
0.5
1
1.5
miles
km
1
2
3
N
Pensacola Bay
Fort Pickens
Campground
Langdon Beach
17A
19A
Entrance
Station
Park West
Santa Rosa
Gulf Islands National Seashore
Fort Pickens
State Park Aquatic Preserve
Gulf of
Fort Pickens Road

by relentless erosion. Parking Area 17A is visible a quarter mile later. Distant buildings eventually come into focus over the next half mile. Concrete structures are half-buried in the nearby dunes. A sand road and poles lead east into the dunes at 4.7 miles toward the campground check-in along Fort Pickens Rd.

Where the Florida Trail leaves the Gulf at 5 miles, Langdon Beach is a busy place. Soak up shade at the beach pavilion and top off on water if needed. After a well-earned break, cross Fort Pickens Rd to pick up the Florida Trail at the FNST sign.

The footpath circles the west side of Battery Langdon. Constructed in 1917 for coastal defense, Battery Langdon was topped with 12-inch guns that could shoot a projectile 17 miles. These guns deterred enemy ships from entering Pensacola Bay, a deep water harbor long important to United States naval operations. Built in 1826, the Pensacola Navy Yard became Naval Air Station Pensacola in 1913, the first dedicated training ground for naval aviators.

When the beaten path splits, the trail to the right leads to the top of Battery Langdon, worth the side trip for its overlooks on the Gulf of Mexico. The trail veering left is the Florida Trail. Continue along this short grassy segment to meet the Fort Pickens Trail at 5.4 miles. It's a hard-packed trail shared with bicycles. From here to Fort Pickens there are only a handful of orange blazes, but the trail is pretty obvious and excellent signage keeps you on it.

Osprey cries echo across the marshes and dunes, as there are many prominent osprey nests in tall, dead trees. The foundations of military buildings peep out of the forest and dunes on the far side of the sweep of marsh. This raised linear route is a railroad grade built by the military during World War II. It overlays a much earlier settlement, a Spanish fortress and village known as Presidio Isla Santa Rosa in 1722, the second of three locations where the Spanish settled along Pensacola Bay. In 2003, archaeological excavations by the University of West Florida uncovered artifacts on this site.

Cross a wooden bridge over a canal lined with tall grasses. Despite your distance from the ocean, the booming waves carry on the wind. Shadows of shade cast by sand live oaks alternate with stretches of sunlit sand. A canal adjoins the trail, dense with tall grasses.

At 5.8 miles, meet the junction for the Blackbird Marsh Trail, a short interpretive birding loop around a marsh. Passing it, duck into shade beneath the oaks before crossing a bridge into Fort Pickens Campground. Blazes lead straight ahead along the paved road through sections E, D, and B, passing two bathhouses. Leaving the campground, continue across the entrance road into Battery Worth. Constructed in 1899, this battery housed coastal defense mortars to protect Pensacola Bay. Climb the stairs for a birds-eye view.

Beyond Battery Worth, return to a natural setting. A healthy rosemary scrub thrives between gnarled oaks and pines. Larger trees provide more shade and benches become more plentiful. Salt marshes flank the trail. Approaching a wooden bridge, watch for the massive and ancient snapping turtles that live in

Fort Pickens Trail

the waters below, attired in swirls of colorful algae.

The official Florida Trail northern terminus marker is on the southwest side of the bridge at 7 miles. It's tucked under a frame of bricks that mimic the interior architecture of Fort Pickens. It's very low to the ground, a little tricky for taking that selfie.

The trail broadens. In this disturbed ground between marsh and moat, Confederate and Union soldiers clashed on October 8, 1861, spilling blood on these sands. The Confederates attempted to retake Fort Pickens and avenge the destruction of the Confederate ship *Judah*. They retreated with casualties. Walking up the ramp onto the outer ramparts of Fort Pickens is a reminder of Florida's long colonial history, these very sands claimed by the Spanish, French, and British long before Florida became a territory of the United States. Consider the thousands who have stood at this point and looked across Pensacola Bay as you finish this final section of the Florida Trail at 7.2 miles. Trail's end is at the kiosk just outside the entrance to the fortress.

If the fort is open, stop in and sign the trail register in the gift shop. You have to ask for it, as they keep it behind the counter. You can also get a commemorative National Parks stamp for the Florida Trail for your National Parks Passport.

Northern terminus monument

ACKNOWLEDGMENTS

It's been more than two decades since Sandra pitched the idea of this book to one of her publishers. They weren't interested. After she finished hiking the entire Florida Trail, we decided to publish this compilation of our favorite hikes ourselves. Thanks to the many friends who hiked and backpacked with us, particularly when she decided to tackle "all the rest of the miles"—not just the scenic ones—in early 2019. Nancy and Kent Wilson provided much-appreciated fellowship on the roadwalks, LuAnne Anderson joined in for sand in her shoes on Santa Rosa Island, and a whole posse plunged into Big Cypress to accompany Sandra on the last miles of her end-to-end hike: Bill Detzner, Carl Jenus, Tami Jicha, and Mary McKinley.

We're pleased to have University Press of Florida bringing the third edition of our guidebook to a far broader audience. Acquisitions editor Sian Hunter quickly laid the groundwork for a smooth transition.

For updates to this edition, we enjoyed having Mindy Elfand, Colleen Miniuk, and Chris Stevens along on research hikes. Chris and his wife Chelsey backpacked Bull Creek, Econfina Creek, and Green Swamp West to provide up-to-date details. When things got a little crazy for us at home, Chris jumped in to hike Foster's Hammock and proof Base Camp information too.

As always, our enduring thanks to the Florida Trail Association's staff and volunteers for keeping us updated on ongoing trail reroutes.

Our hats are off to Linda Patton, founding librarian of the largest library of hiking books in America, the Research Library at the Appalachian Trail Museum in Pine Grove Furnace, Pennsylvania. This book is dedicated to her efforts on and off the trail. Visit her website at bookforhikers.com.

January 2019 at Big Cypress: Tami Jicha, Bill Detzner, Mary McKinley, Sandra, and Carl Jenus.

INDEX

Page numbers in *italics* refer to illustrations.

ABOUT THE AUTHORS

Lifelong hikers Sandra Friend and John Keatley met while hiking around Lake Okeechobee during the annual Big O Hike. A few months later, they headed to the Appalachian Trail together for a thru-hike. While that effort ended earlier than planned, spending several months backpacking taught them how to work as a team. Returning to Florida, they researched and wrote *The Florida Trail Guide*. After multiple editions, it is now also an app from FarOut Guides.

As a teen, John completed a 50-mile backpacking trip on the Florida Trail across the Ocala National Forest with his Boy Scout troop. Sandra learned to backpack in Pennsylvania as an adult while writing newspaper and magazine articles on hiking. In 1999, she returned to Florida and began section hiking the Florida Trail. Joining the Florida Trail Association, she volunteered administrative skills as well as time to build and maintain the trail. Sandra served as the organization's communications director for five years. She completed the entire Florida Trail a decade later. This book is a compilation of Florida Trail hikes that she and John have enjoyed the most over the years.

Sandra and John are members of the Society of American Travel Writers and the Outdoor Writers Association of America. They are life members of the Florida Trail Association and the Appalachian Long Distance Hikers Association. Between them, they've written more than 42 books, including over a dozen covering the Florida Trail. They publish FloridaHikes.com, a popular website with in-depth information on the Florida Trail and hundreds of other trails to hike, bike, and paddle. Advocates for connecting people with the natural world through outdoor recreation, they live on Florida's Space Coast.

Photo by LuAnne Anderson